OTHER VOLUMES IN THIS SERIES

THE
BEST
AMERICAN
POETRY
2017

◇ ◇ ◇

Natasha Trethewey, Editor

David Lehman, Series Editor

SCRIBNER POETRY

NEW YORK   LONDON   TORONTO   SYDNEY   NEW DELHI

Scribner Poetry
An Imprint of Simon & Schuster, Inc.
1230 Avenue of the Americas
New York, NY 10020

First Scribner edition September 2017

SCRIBNER POETRY and design are registered trademarks of The Gale Group, Inc.,
used under license by Simon & Schuster, Inc., the publisher of this work.

For information about special discounts for bulk purchases,
please contact Simon & Schuster Special Sales at 1-866-506-1949
or business@simonandschuster.com.

The Simon & Schuster Speakers Bureau can bring authors to your live event.
For more information or to book an event, contact the Simon & Schuster Speakers
Bureau at 1-866-248-3049 or visit our website at www.simonspeakers.com.

Manufactured in the United States of America

1   3   5   7   9   10   8   6   4   2

Library of Congress Control Number: 88644281

ISBN 978-1-5011-2763-2
ISBN 978-1-5011-2775-5 (pbk)
ISBN 978-1-5011-2777-9 (ebook)

CONTENTS

David Lehman was born in New York City, the son of Holocaust survivors. Educated at Stuyvesant High School and Columbia University, he spent two years as a Kellett Fellow at Clare College, Cambridge, and worked as Lionel Trilling's research assistant upon his return from England. *Poems in the Manner Of* (2017), his most recent book, comprises poems written in imitation, appreciation, parody, or translation of poets from Catullus to Sylvia Plath. He is the author of nine earlier books of poetry, including *New and Selected Poems* (2013), *When a Woman Loves a Man* (2005), *The Daily Mirror* (2000), and *Valentine Place* (1996), all from Scribner. He is the editor of *The Oxford Book of American Poetry* and *Great American Prose Poems: From Poe to the Present*. Two prose books recently appeared: *The State of the Art: A Chronicle of American Poetry, 1988–2014* (University of Pittsburgh Press), containing the forewords he had written to date for *The Best American Poetry*, and *Sinatra's Century: One Hundred Notes on the Man and His World* (Harper-Collins). *A Fine Romance: Jewish Songwriters, American Songs* (Schocken) won the Deems Taylor Award from the American Society of Composers, Authors, and Publishers (ASCAP) in 2010. Lehman teaches in the graduate writing program of The New School and lives in New York City and in Ithaca, New York.

FOREWORD

by David Lehman

◊   ◊   ◊

If in January 2016 someone had told you that in the year ahead the Cubs will win the World Series, Bob Dylan will win the Nobel Prize in Literature, and Donald Trump will be elected president of the United States, you'd have thought that person batty. Yet all these things have come to pass, and at least one of them has a direct bearing on poetry.

No sooner was it announced that Dylan had become the first American Nobel Laureate in literature since Toni Morrison than the quarrels began. Enthusiasts cited the way Dylan has entered and modified the culture. How his phrases linger in the air: "the times they are a-changin'," "there are no truths outside the Gates of Eden," "You don't need a weatherman / To know which way the wind blows," "he not busy being born / Is busy dying."

But the cries of dismay were predictable if only because the poetry community is divided and because there is an unhealthy amount of bile and resentment out there. Any American poet—even our grand old master Richard Wilbur, now ninety-six—would get his share of Bronx cheers if he were to win the Nobel. It was said of Dylan that he didn't need the prize, that he is yet another old white guy, that he is arrogant, that he composes songs not poems or is "at best," as one disgruntled observer put it, "a pretentious high-school-notebook poet"—in other words, not a poet at all.

Purists would say that what Dylan writes are lyrics, which depend on their musical setting for coherence and are inextricably bound up with their performance. I would counter that the best of Dylan's songs work on the page, not only because of their originality but equally because they constitute the autobiography of a fascinating, shape-shifting personality that is rebellious, ornery, intense, and has proved remarkably attuned to the zeitgeist.

With the most prescient timing in recent publishing history, Bob

Dylan's *The Lyrics 1961–2012* appeared within one month of the prize announcement in October. The book contains the words of all of Dylan's songs, organized album by album from his eponymous 1962 debut to his most recent efforts. The transcendent period was the stretch between 1964 and 1967—the period of "Like a Rolling Stone," "Desolation Row," "Sad-Eyed Lady of the Lowlands," "Visions of Johanna," "Just Like a Woman," and "All Along the Watchtower." While the lyrics and their reception make the primary case for Dylan's achievement, I believe that *Chronicles* (2004), the first volume of his projected three-volume memoirs, offers a valuable window into the writer's brain. "Truth was the last thing on my mind, and even if there was such a thing, I didn't want it in my house," he wrote of trying to compose songs. "Oedipus went looking for the truth and when he found it, it ruined him. It was a cruel horror of a joke. So much for the truth. I was gonna talk out of both sides of my mouth and what you heard depended on which side you were standing. If I ever did stumble on any truth, I was gonna sit on it and keep it down."

A self-creation in the tradition of Jay Gatsby rather than that of Julius Henry Marx (i.e., Groucho), Bob discarded his birth name (Zimmerman) in favor of the moniker of the wild, word-drunk Welsh poet Dylan Thomas. A natural surrealist with bardic leanings, Dylan radiated a kind of Bohemian glamour. The lyrics reflect the stance of a put-on artist, a joker, enigmatic, elusive, and full of insolence or righteous belligerence. "Maggie's Farm" (1965) elevates "I quit" into poetry: He "hands you a nickel / He hands you a dime / He asks you with a grin / If you're havin' a good time / Then he fines you every time you slam the door / I ain't gonna work for Maggie's brother no more." Or consider the ire hurled at the false friend in "Positively 4th Street": "I wish that for just one time / You could stand inside my shoes / You'd know what a drag it is / To see you."

Usually when I discuss Bob Dylan as a poet I point to his visionary songs. "Desolation Row" (1965), which I selected for inclusion in *The Oxford Book of American Poetry*, is terrific in its phantasmagoria. The title song of *Highway 61 Revisited* (1965) begins with God and Abraham mixing it up in Genesis 22: "God said to Abraham, 'Kill me a son' / Abe says, 'Man, you must be puttin' me on.' " The allusions here and elsewhere in Dylan's lyrics—in which at any moment Genghis Khan or F. Scott Fitzgerald might put in an appearance—look random but are pointed and shrewd. Still, the case for Dylan rests as much on his powers of rhetoric as on his oracular powers. Some of his strongest lines are infused with the spirit of protest: "How many years can a mountain exist / Before it's washed to the sea?" Others verge on heartbreak ("It don't even matter to me where you're wakin' up tomorrow / But mama, you're just on my mind") or celebrate a lazy day in an easy chair ("Buy me a flute / And a gun that shoots / Tailgates and substitutes / Strap yourself / To the tree with roots / You ain't goin' nowhere"). He can bring a dream to a close with the inevitability of a rhyme: "The pump don't work / 'Cause the vandals took the handles." The rhymes in "Like a Rolling Stone" and "I Want You" show there's a lot of life left in that venerable device.

In 1880 Matthew Arnold brought to the study of poetry the concept of "touchstones" for exemplary lines that imprint themselves on the mind. It is a criterion the author of "Visions of Johanna" (1966) meets. "The ghost of 'lectricity howls in the bones of her face." With or without music, that line sings. Only a true poet could have written it.

A larger issue emerged in the Dylan debates: what qualifies as "literature"? Dylan's own response was to retreat into modesty. He didn't go to Sweden to collect the prize but sent a banquet speech. It was hard to process the news, he wrote, but then he

began to think about William Shakespeare, the great literary figure. I would reckon he thought of himself as a dramatist. The thought that he was writing literature couldn't have entered his head. His words were written for the stage. Meant to be spoken not read. When he was writing *Hamlet*, I'm sure he was thinking about a lot of different things: "Who're the right actors for these roles?" "How should this be staged?" "Do I really want to set this in Denmark?" His creative vision and ambitions were no doubt at the forefront of his mind, but there were also more mundane matters to consider and deal with. "Is the financing in place?" "Are there enough good seats for my patrons?" "Where am I going to get a human skull?" I would bet that the farthest thing from Shakespeare's mind was the question "Is this *literature*?"

These are all fair points, I reckon, though it should be noted that in making them Dylan manages to compare himself to "William Shakespeare, the great literary figure."

The choice of Dylan for the Nobel has set a precedent for widening the category of "literature" to embrace the work of other troubadours (and in future, perhaps, filmmakers and showrunners). *The New Yorker* has showcased the poetry of Leonard Cohen, who died at eighty-two just weeks after an impressive profile by David Remnick appeared in the magazine. I am happy that Natasha Trethewey chose a Leonard Cohen poem for this year's *Best American Poetry*. "California Poem," a poem by Johnny Cash that *The New Yorker* published in September, didn't make the cut, but it did reinforce the notion that the boundary between poems and lyrics is not an impossible one to cross. And when Lin-Manuel Miranda accepted the Tony Award for his colossally successful musical play *Hamilton* with a "16-line sonnet," it came as a reminder that verse continues to lend prestige to a formal occasion, be it a wedding or an award ceremony. And yet—

★   ★   ★

Ours is a great era for hate—what George Orwell called "a human barrel-organ shooting propaganda at you by the hour. The same thing over and over again. Hate, hate, hate. Let's get all together and have a good hate." These sentences are from his novel *Coming Up for Air* (1939), in the course of which our protagonist, a middle-aged man with an expanding waistline, gets frustrated trying to explain to a philosopher friend, an aesthete, why it's important to fight Hitler.

Now and then there's an odd news story demonstrating that the subject of poetry can lead to a display of high passion, even a fistfight or a duel. In January 2014 *The Independent* reported that in the town of Irbit in the Ural Mountains in Russia, a vodka-soaked advocate of poetry killed a prose partisan in a brawl over the rival merits of the literary genres each championed. (A few months earlier, in an argument over the philosophy of Immanuel Kant, one man shot another in a grocery store in southern Russia.) Reduce the amount of alcohol and raise the amount of bitterness and you arrive at the state of critical discourse at its worst. In *The Big Short*, an entertaining and instructive movie about the financial shenanigans that led to the near-collapse of Wall Street in 2008, these lines appear on the screen: "Overheard in a Washington, D.C. Bar: Truth is like poetry. And most people fucking hate poetry." That is a far cry from Keats's "Beauty is truth, truth beauty," but beauty is out of favor, and paranoia and hatred have risen in its stead. Joel Stein, *Time* magazine's humorist, wrote a cover story on "the culture of hate" and how it is taking over the Internet. The

Internet multiplies the avenues, conceals the perpetrators, loosens the restraints. There are a lot of mischief makers and propagandists out there, and the 24/7 need for news stories on cable TV keeps the hysteria level high. Keats wrote that "My imagination is a monastery, and I am its monk." Wallace Stevens exalted the imagination as superior to unredeemable actuality. That is a lot to expect of the poetic imagination. But the possibility helps to shelter you from the corrosiveness of public discourse.

Of all the arts, poetry may attract the most venomous haters and the most persistent predictors of its decay and inevitable demise. Ben Lerner argues, in *The Hatred of Poetry* (2016), that hatred itself is part and parcel of the creative impulse. "Poetry and the hatred of poetry are for me—and maybe for you—inextricable," he says. On the surface, this may seem perverse, an internalizing of the dismissive things people say (or don't say but think) about poetry. But it is possible, as Lerner suggests, that the famous opening line of Marianne Moore's "Poetry"—"I, too, dislike it"—is every poet's starting point or governing condition. Poets are control freaks with a strong streak of perfectionism and by their own standards can never be satisfied with their work. The best poem is the one that has not yet been written.

As a Platonic idealist, Lerner has some insightful things to say: "Socrates is the wisest of all people because he knows he knows nothing; Plato is a poet who stays closest to poetry because he refuses all actual poems." Lerner argues that defenses of poetry going back to Sir Philip Sidney tend to assert "an ideal of imaginative literature" rather than to exalt an individual poem. The discrepancy between the ideal and the actual poem widens. The poet as idealist finds all poetry defective. The killer, as Lerner sees it, is the demand for universality, for "the intensely subjective, personal poem" that can somehow "authentically encompass everyone." Such a poem "is an impossibility in a world characterized by difference and violence."

The question, however, is whether such idealism is common to all poets, and is it the primary standard that poets adopt while working on poems? Are poets, then, doomed to the melancholy of certain failure? The failure of poets "to be universal, to speak to and for everyone in the manner of Whitman" is neither a realistic goal nor necessarily a wise one. On the contrary, as Lerner notes, it is the logic behind foolish articles alleging the decline of poetry. There is the suspicion that *The Hatred of Poetry* is an academic exercise in the sense that it exists solely to quicken discussion. If the author were in earnest, would he continue to write poems? It might also be said that there is a difference between Lerner's title and Marianne Moore's statement. The "too" in "I, too, dislike it" slyly suggests a likeness, a secret alliance between writer and reader. We mistrust poetry, we know it is full of false sentiments and insincere rhetoric, and so we have to be won over. Less aggressive than "hate," "dislike" may be the more accurate term. It may come closer to the "perfect contempt" that poets instinctively display when addressing specimens of the art not their own. Using words from the same poem by Marianne Moore, we might argue further that poetry is in service not to an emotion or state of mind but to the quest for a certain kind of power, the power to create "imaginary gardens with real toads in them."

Not a writer of poetry himself, George Orwell was impatient with poetry for quite different reasons. Of what use could it be against a machine gun? "Ours is a civilization in which the very word 'poetry' evokes a hostile snigger or, at best, the sort of frozen disgust that most people feel when they hear the word 'God,'" Orwell wrote in 1942. "Poetry is disliked because it is associated with unintelligibility, intellectual pretentiousness and a general feeling of Sunday-on-a-weekday," he wrote a year later.[1]

Do "people fucking hate poetry," as *The Big Short* announces? Do they put up with poets as the slightly comic figures on the college faculty who do their part for the good of the community by teaching poetry in old-age homes and penitentiaries? My own view of things is that a poet can expect not hate but "unremitting indifference / broken up by patches of hostility."[2] "Barely tolerated, living on the margin / In our technological society": the opening of John Ashbery's poem "Soonest Mended" (1970) characterizes the poet's condition.[3]

And yet it sometimes seems as if everyone has a niece or nephew who writes poetry. Ben Lerner has an amusing passage about what happens when a poet is unwise enough to reveal his or her vocation to a total stranger on an airplane. Lerner writes that the embarrassment is

1. George Orwell, *My Country Right or Left* (volume two of *The Collected Essays, Journalism, and Letters*), edited by Sonia Orwell and Ian Angus, pp. 195, 334.
2. "October 1," *The Evening Sun* (Scribner, 2002).
3. Originally in *The Double Dream of Spring* (1970).

double: "There is embarrassment for the poet—couldn't you get a real job and put your childish ways behind you?—but there is also embarrassment on the part of the non-poet because having to acknowledge one's total alienation from poetry chafes against the early association of poetry and self." The problem is worse if you are identified as not only a poet but also an editor, though in my experience the "non-poet" shows no embarrassment when requesting a reading or threatening to pull out a manuscript.

W. H. Auden's solution to the problem of identifying himself to temporary companions was to say that he was a medieval historian. "It withers curiosity," he explained.[4]

★   ★   ★

In *The Best American Poetry 2017*, we have three Youngs (C. Dale, Dean, and Kevin) and an Olds. We have sonnets, several of them in rhyme; a numbered list poem; a poem in rhymed haiku stanzas; a poem in the manner of a text message; an epithalamium, and a verse epistle "To Marlon Brando in Hell." We have a master in his eighties and a Stuyvesant High School alumna who was born in 1997, when this anthology series was in its tenth year. Most unusually we have a poem, R. T. Smith's "*Maricón*," that treats the March 1962 fight between boxers Emile Griffith and Benny ("the Kid") Paret—the same bout that triggered Donald Platt's poem "The Main Event," which appeared in *The Best American Poetry 2015*.

Natasha Trethewey, the guest editor of this volume, appeared for the first time in *The Best American Poetry* in 2000. That year her first book, *Domestic Work*, assembled evidence of an ability to find the dualities of her personal history mirrored ironically but pointedly in the language that we speak. As the daughter of a white man and an African American woman in Mississippi at a time when interracial marriages were against the law, she could identify herself with the "mixed girl" in the 1959 movie *Imitation of Life*. She grew up, she writes, "light-bright, near-white, / high-yellow, red-boned / in a black place"—and was gifted at telling "white lies." In 2007, Trethewey won the Pulitzer Prize for *Native Guard*, her third book. To the poet's repertoire, the book added the challenges of poetic form. The title poem—the journal of a black soldier from a Louisiana regiment of freed slaves in the Civil War—

---

4. "The Poet & The City" in *The Dyer's Hand* (1962).

consists of ten unrhymed sonnets. The last line of each is mirrored and distorted in the first line of the next. The effect is complex: smooth continuity, elegant circularity, but also a third thing that disturbs the peace and order of the other two. The poem begins, "Truth be told, I do not want to forget." It ends with "a scaffolding of bone / we tread upon, forgetting. Truth be told." The poem exists precisely in the space between those two poles.

In 2012 Natasha was named Poet Laureate of the United States. She has held faculty appointments at Duke, Chapel Hill, Yale, Emory, and now Northwestern. Her list of favorite poems from 2016 grew slowly. "Mostly I want to be blown away when I read a poem," she told me. The poems she chose had to meet that strict criterion. Not the reputation of the poet but the poem on the page was what mattered. Numerous magazines were consulted. On the honor roll, *The Kenyon Review* and *Ploughshares* are tied at the top of the list: more poems were chosen from them, five each, than from any other single source. The subjects addressed in the poems include Aleppo, God, the life you didn't lead, "Girl from the North Country" as sung by Bob Dylan and Johnny Cash, grackles, the seventeenth century, a wristwatch, the "age of anxiety," deconstruction, and "the post-galactic abyss of sex with strangers" (Major Jackson), to limit myself to ten. The table of contents includes the work of poets who are entirely new to me as well as poets we have showcased before.

Sometimes a poem goes viral, usually to the surprise of the author. One poem that went viral in 2016 you'll find here: Maggie Smith's "Good Bones." It is probably safe to say that no poem last year had quite the effect of a piece of doggerel that a political satirist recited on a TV show in Germany about the controversial president of Turkey. The poem touched on President Recep Tayyip Erdogan's anatomy, his alleged interest in barnyard animals, and the athletically demanding sexual activities he supposedly enjoys doing with them. The effort was in the category of the crude and puerile. Nevertheless the Turkish president was not amused; the poem caused a minor diplomatic flap between Germany and Turkey, and quite a lot of snarky comment. The incident made me think of a piece of light verse that doubled as a political poem of some brilliance and bite. The writer was the late Robert Conquest, historian of Soviet Russia, author of *The Great Terror: Stalin's Purge of the Thirties*. The poem stretches the form of the limerick, disdaining crudities. In five lines Conquest sums up several decades of revolutionary Russian history: 'There was a great Marxist called Lenin / Who did two or three million men in. / That's a lot to have done in / But where he did one in / That grand Marxist Stalin did ten in."[5]

5. I have read a version of this memorable limerick in which "Bolshie" replaces "great Marxist" in line one and "grand Marxist" in line five.

Natasha Trethewey served two terms as the nineteenth Poet Laureate of the United States (2012–2014) and a term as Poet Laureate of the state of Mississippi (2012–2016). She was born in Gulfport, Mississippi, in 1966 and was educated at the University of Georgia, Hollins University, and the University of Massachusetts, Amherst. She is the author of four collections of poetry: *Domestic Work* (Graywolf Press, 2000), *Bellocq's Ophelia* (Graywolf Press, 2002), *Native Guard* (Houghton Mifflin, 2006), for which she was awarded the 2007 Pulitzer Prize, and, most recently, *Thrall* (Houghton Mifflin Harcourt, 2012). Her book of creative nonfiction, *Beyond Katrina: A Meditation on the Mississippi Gulf Coast*, was published in 2010 (University of Georgia Press). In 2015 she served as poetry editor of *The New York Times Magazine*, selecting and introducing poems for the weekly column. A fellow of the American Academy of Arts and Sciences, she has also received fellowships from the Academy of American Poets, the Guggenheim Foundation, the Rockefeller Foundation, the Radcliffe Institute for Advanced Study at Harvard University, the Beinecke Library at Yale University, and the National Endowment for the Arts. For fifteen years she taught at Emory University, where she was Robert W. Woodruff Professor of English and Creative Writing. In 2017 she joined the faculty at Northwestern University as Board of Trustees Professor of English.

INTRODUCTION

by Natasha Trethewey

◊   ◊   ◊

As early as I can remember my father recited poetry to me, not simply for the pure pleasure of it but also, I think now, to prepare for the inevitable losses to come, for the ways of the world I would inhabit, and to provide a means for making sense of it. Like Robert Frost, he believed in the necessity of a thorough and early grasp of the figurative nature of language. "What I am pointing out," Frost wrote,

> is that unless you are at home in the metaphor, unless you have had your proper poetical education in the metaphor, you are not safe anywhere. Because you are not at ease with figurative values: you don't know the metaphor in its strength and its weakness. You don't know how far you may expect to ride it and when it may break down with you. You are not safe in science; you are not safe in history.

Both my parents knew that I would need an "education by poetry" to be safe in the world I'd entered. In 1966, when I was born, their inter-racial marriage was illegal in Mississippi and as many as twenty other states in the nation, rendering me illegitimate in the eyes of the law, persona non grata. On the way to the segregated ward at the hospital my mother could not help but take in the tenor of the day, witnessing the barrage of rebel flags lining the streets: private citizens, lawmakers, and Klansmen—often one and the same—hoisting them in Gulfport and small towns all across Mississippi. The twenty-sixth of April that year marked the hundredth anniversary of Mississippi's celebration of Confederate Memorial Day—a holiday glorifying the Lost Cause, the old South, and white supremacy—and much of the fervor was also a display in opposition to recent advancements in the Civil Rights Movement: the Civil Rights and Voting Rights acts of 1964 and 1965.

My mother had come of age in Mississippi during the turbulent

1960s, turning twenty-one in the wake of Bloody Sunday, the Watts Riots, and years of racially motivated murders in the state. Unlike my father, who'd grown up a white boy in rural Nova Scotia—free-ranging, hunting and fishing in the woods—my mother had come into being a black girl in the Deep South, a world circumscribed by Jim Crow laws. If my father believed in the idea of living dangerously—the adventurer's way—the necessity of taking risks, my mother had witnessed the necessity of dissembling, the art of making of one's face an inscrutable mask before whites who expected of blacks a servile deference. In the summer of 1955, when she was eleven years old, she'd seen what could happen to a black child in Mississippi who had not behaved as expected, stepping outside the confines of racial proscription: Emmett Till's battered remains, his unrecognizable face in my grandmother's copy of *Jet* magazine. And in the years to follow she'd watched Mississippi ignite with racial violence as the Civil Rights Movement reached its zenith.

Having grown up steeped in the metaphors that comprised the mind of the South—the white South—she could not miss the paradox of my birth on Confederate Memorial Day: a child of "miscegenation," a word that entered the American lexicon during the Civil War in a pamphlet. It had been conceived as a hoax by a couple of journalists to drum up opposition to Lincoln's reelection through the threat of amalgamation and mongrelization. Sequestered on the "colored" floor, my mother knew the country was changing, but slowly.

Over the years, as my parents and I went out together, encountering people disdainful of and often hostile to their union, to our family, they grasped even more the necessity of my education in metaphor, though they began to diverge in what exactly I might need to know.

I don't recall when I first noticed that divergence, but a moment stands out to me from a trip we took to Mexico a couple of years before their marriage ended. We'd been traveling along a seemingly endless stretch of blacktop as the sun began to set, hanging low and heavy in the sky. "How'd you like to have that ball to play with?" my father asked, pointing to it. "Don't be silly," said my mother. "You know she'd burn her hands." Even then I knew something had passed between them, some difference in how they perceived the metaphors by which I would need to be guided: for my father, all was possibility; for my mother, danger from which I'd need to be protected.

Only one souvenir of that trip remains: a photograph. In it I am alone, there are mountains in the distance behind me, and I am sitting on a mule. It had been my father's idea to place me there, a linguistic joke within a visual metaphor: the sight gag of a mixed-race child riding her namesake, animal origin of the word "mulatto." In the photograph I see my father's need to show me the power of metaphor, how imagery and figurative language can make the mind leap to a new apprehension of things; that we might harness, as with the yoke of form, both delight and the conveyance of meaning; that language is a kind of play with something vital at stake. My mother knew, as another figurative level of the photograph suggests, that I would have to journey toward an understanding of myself, my place in the world, with the invisible burdens of history, borne on the back of metaphor, the language that sought to name and thus constrain me. I would be both bound to and propelled by it. She knew that if I could not parse the metaphorical thinking of the time and place into which I'd entered, I could be defeated by it. "You are not safe in science; you are not safe in history."

Growing up in the Deep South, I witnessed everywhere around me the metaphors meant to maintain a collective narrative about its people and history—defining social place and hierarchy through a matrix of selective memory, willed forgetting, and racial determinism. With the defeat of the Confederacy, wrote Robert Penn Warren, "the Solid South was born"—a "City of the Soul" rendered guiltless by the forces of history. "By the Great Alibi," he continues, "the South explains, condones, and transmutes everything . . . any common lyncher becomes a defender of the Southern tradition. . . . By the Great Alibi the Southerner makes his Big Medicine. He turns defeat into victory, defects into virtues. . . . And the most painful and costly consequences of the Great Alibi are found, of course, in connection with race."

The role of metaphor is not only to describe our experience of reality; metaphor also shapes how we perceive reality. Because the Deep South of my childhood was a society based on the myths of innate racial difference, a hierarchy based on notions of white supremacy, the language used to articulate that thinking was rooted in the unique experience of white southerners. Thus, in the century following the war, the South—in the white mind of the South—became deeply entrenched in the idea of a noble and romantic past. It was moonlight and magnolias, chivalry and paternalism. The blacks living within her borders, when they were good, were "children" to be guided, looked after, protected from their own folly, "mules of the earth," "darkies" with the "light of service" in their hearts. When they stepped out of line they were "bad niggers" from whom white women—"carriers of the pure bloodline"—needed to be protected; they were "animals" to be husbanded into a prison system modeled on the plantation system—or worse, "Strange fruit hanging from the poplar trees." On the monumental landscape, in textbooks, they were un-storied but for the stories told about them. In my twelfth-grade history book they were "singing and happy in the quarters," "better off under a master's care." According to my teacher, they were "passive recipients of white benevolence" who'd "never fought for their own freedom"—even as nearly 200,000 fought in the Civil War. And when they seemed exceptional in the mind of the South, they were magical: *You're smart for a black girl, pretty for a black girl, articulate—not like the rest of them* . . .

★   ★   ★

I recall the myriad ways poetry helped me to contend with the reality of the world I faced then, and the thinking of the people in it: how Paul Laurence Dunbar's "We Wear the Mask" gave historical context to the dissembling I saw from older black men in our neighborhood—many of them my uncles, deacons in the church—when they were confronted and harassed by police; how Langston Hughes's "I, too, sing America" imagined a future that was just, in which everyone—regardless of race—would be offered a seat at the table; how W. H. Auden's "Musée des Beaux Arts" showed me that I was not alone in feeling the seeming indifference of the whole world to my grief when I lost my mother and that loss, instead of isolating us, can make us part of a community in the world of a poem, a shared experience; and how Wordsworth's "Lines Composed a Few Miles above Tintern Abbey," from which my father often recited, prepared me not only for our geographic separation after the divorce, but also for the joy of recollection, the happy memories of familial bonds and ties to place—even in the face of sorrow:

> If solitude, or fear, or pain, or grief,
> Should be thy portion, with what healing thoughts
> Of tender joy wilt thou remember me,
> And these my exhortations!

★   ★   ★

It was in this spirit that I read and selected poems for *The Best American Poetry 2017*. It should be noted that, in many ways, any anthology could serve as an autobiography of the mind of the anthologist, and certainly this was true for me. Looking back on it now, I see clearly my preoccupations. I have been in a state of bereavement almost all of my adult life—ever since the spring I turned nineteen when my mother was killed. Over the years there have been periods of intense grief, immediately following more losses, and then other periods in which the feeling of grief was less intense but nonetheless present as an integral part of who I am. Not long ago, I felt the sharpness of it again: I lost my father, the poet Eric Trethewey, near the end of 2014. The whole year following, as I was reading poems for a weekly column in *The New York Times Magazine* and watching terrible events unfold in the news, I wanted to call him so that we might speak as we always had, that I might find comfort in his wise words, his voice on the other end of the line. I wanted to engage in the ongoing conversations we'd had my entire life about poetry and justice, and about loss—of which novelist Pat Conroy wrote, "There is no teacher more discriminating and transforming."

And then came 2016, into which the headlines of the previous two years began to bleed and overlap: images of mass shootings, scenes of refugees fleeing the devastation and violence of their homelands, videos of police using deadly force on unarmed citizens, acts of terror internationally and at home. There seemed to be no respite. Too, there were more losses of poets I'd loved and admired. It was my fiftieth year—a child of interracial marriage—and I was poised to celebrate the anniversary of advances in civil rights gained by *Loving v. Virginia* while, at the same moment, the presidential election season gave rise to increasingly visible and mainstream forms of white nationalism and separatism, uncivil discourse, and outright lies repeated and spun to look like facts. It was a hard year in which the enduring rhythms of poetry provided a singular kind of respite. In particular, I found solace in the ways in which contemporary poets were turning their piercing gazes on the many facets of our historical moment and showing us with urgency the necessity of a proper poetical education in metaphor in order to contend with the tumultuous times we now face—both individually and collectively. We need the truth of poetry, and its beauty, now more than ever.

The range of subject matter and form in these seventy-five poems is vast, moving from Albergotti to Zapruder. Albergotti's poem that opens the book employs and elevates the seemingly found language, institutional in nature, of the documents police officers must complete after using deadly force; Zapruder's poem lifts the vernacular to the uses of the sacred and ceremonious, offering a blessing for lifelong happiness at a wedding. Judson Mitcham's "White" examines racial privilege and deeply ingrained and unexamined notions of racial difference and hierarchy:

the bedrocks of ongoing and often oblivious forms of white supremacy. Kevin Young's "Money Road" is a timely intersection with a troubling history—the murder of Emmett Till—during the same year that Carolyn Bryant, the woman who accused the fourteen-year-old Till of impropriety, finally speaks the truth. She confesses that she lied about the encounter that led to his murder at the hands of her husband, Roy Bryant, and his half brother J. W. Milam. With its litany of losses, Nickole Brown's "The Dead" becomes a collective lamentation for all our dead, while Sharon Olds's "Ode to the Glans," with its singular focus, becomes a collective celebration. Like all of these poems, the late Claudia Emerson's "Spontaneous Remission" embodies the salutary achievements of poetry: the creation of a poem as an act of faith, generative in the face of death and destruction, hopeful in the face of despair, and the experience of reading a poem—at once pleasing *and* troubling *and* enlightening, a respite.

Throughout this difficult year I did not have my father to talk with, but I had the poems we'd shared, ones I'd turned to in the past, and a whole new set of poems—the ones in this anthology—to bring context and clarity and a renewed sense of joy through the pleasures and transformative powers of language. I am reminded, too, by all of the poems gathered here, of Percy Bysshe Shelley's words: "Poetry is the record of the best and happiest moments of the happiest and best minds." Though this year I was often consumed by grief and overwhelmed by the sadness of our national and international tragedies, all of these poems spoke to me as records of the best and happiest moments in American poetry. Were my father here we might spend an evening reading them out loud and, perhaps, recite to each other these lines from Czesław Miłosz's poem "Dedication," which speak to the necessary call to witness found in these pages, a charge to contend with our historical moment—the need for *truth*—through the elegant envelope of form that a poem is:

> What is poetry which does not save
> Nations or people?
> A connivance with official lies,
> A song of drunkards whose throats will be cut in a moment,
> Readings for sophomore girls.
> That I wanted good poetry without knowing it,
> That I discovered, late, its salutary aim,
> In this and only this I find salvation.

THE
BEST
AMERICAN
POETRY
2017

Weapons Discharge Report

◇   ◇   ◇

Incident involved the shooting of an animal.
—option under "Nature of Incident"
in Police Policy Studies Council's
form "Weapons Discharge Report"

. . . it looks like a demon . . .
—Officer Darren Wilson, describing
unarmed eighteen-year-old Michael
Brown in grand jury testimony

Complete this report as fully as possible to the best
of your recollection. Do not consult video evidence.

What time, what day, what week, what month, what century?

What district, what section, what subsection, what nation?

What type of incident: disturbance call,
domestic dispute, service of warrant,
homeland security activity, school disturbance,
church disturbance, disturbed individual,
disturbed family, disturbed culture,
suspicious person, suspicious color,
suspicious loyalty, suspicious love?

Select nature of incident: exchange
of gunfire between officer and offender,
perceived threats with a brandished edged object
or blunt object or unfired firearm, armed attack

was perceived by officer (but weapon never found),
another perceived threat not involving a weapon
(examples: safety of the public, involved parties
or officers threatened, officer felt threatened,
felt underappreciated, felt tired, bleary eyed,
angry, on edge, ready to pop, looked at sideways).

Pre-incident indicators of readiness:
officer arrived at the scene without
any degree of knowledge of danger,
officer totally surprised by threat,
officer knew assailant from prior police contacts,
officer was somewhat prepared for threat
due to prior knowledge of person and/or place,
officer knew exactly where he was, exactly
what he was doing, to whom, exactly why,
officer surprised by weapon's power.

Light conditions: dark, dusk, dawn, blinding white,
good artificial, poor artificial, indoor, outdoor,
pure oblivion black. Was there light?
Was it dark? Was it sufficiently dark
to mask an inner darkness? Was it dusk?

Did incident involve accidental discharge
due to handling weapon, cleaning weapon,
loading or unloading weapon, admiring weapon,
admiring oneself in mirror while holding weapon,
feeling powerful, feeling excited, shaking
with anger or fear, struggling with suspect,
struggling with respect, struggling with self,
forcing entry, falling down, falling apart?

Estimate elapsed time between officer's arrival
on scene and discharge of weapon: hours,
minutes, seconds, milliseconds.
(If nanoseconds, check "other.")

Total number of shots fired by officer
(if unsure, write "hundreds").
Total number of hits on suspect
(if unsure, write "dozens").

What weapon was used by officer:
pistol, revolver, shotgun, sniper rifle,
Taser, 37mm, Pepperball, automatic
assault rifle, tactical military device?

Estimate distance of initial shot fired by officer:
Contact, 0–3 yards, 3–7 yards, 7–15 yards,
15–25 yards, over 25 yards, over 25 miles,
from Baton Rouge to Baltimore,
from New York to Los Angeles.

Was suspect moving or stationary? Was suspect
on foot, on floor, on gravel, on sidewalk, on dirt,
on grass, on drugs, on life support, on cross?

Was officer moving or stationary? Was officer standing,
prone, running, sitting, in vehicle, kneeling, supine,
squatting/crouching, ascending/descending stairs,
only ascending, towering above like a colossus?

Were multiple officers involved?
Was officer killed or wounded by assailant action?
Was officer killed or wounded by friendly fire?
Was officer hurt by friends, reserved,
alienated, taciturn, withdrawn, despondent,
prone to prolonged periods of weeping?

Did officer make independent threat identification
before firing? Did officer attempt to disengage
before employing deadly or less-lethal force?
Did officer attempt to shake off demons?
Did officer reload his/her weapon before end
of confrontation? Did body armor influence
officer's survival? Did body armor influence
officer's decision to fire? Did officer experience

weapon stoppage or malfunction during incident?
If so, what kind? Was officer able to clear stoppage,
clear weapon, clear head, clear conscience?

Profile of offender (check here for defaults):
age, race, gender, nationality, political affiliation.
Was offender influenced by alcohol or controlled substance?
Did offender have prior history of mental illness?
Did offender display suicidal inclinations when confronted?
Did offender have prior arrest record, history
of violent felonies while armed, history of violent felonies
while unarmed, history of assault against law enforcement,
history of persistent struggle under weight of history?

Did incident involve the shooting of an animal?
Did responding officer mistake suspect
for an animal? Did officer call suspect an animal
or similar (e.g., *monkey, boy, demon, dog, child*)?
Would officer say suspect looked like a demon?
Would officer say a child? Was suspect a child?

Was suspect killed by police action?
Were bystanders killed by police action?
Were elected officials' careers ended by police action?
Was course of national history altered by police action?

Estimate the weight of history upon
officer's decision to discharge weapon.

from *storySouth*

Commotion of the Birds

◊　◊　◊

We're moving right along through the seventeenth century.
The latter part is fine, much more modern
than the earlier part. Now we have Restoration Comedy.
Webster and Shakespeare and Corneille were fine
for their time but not modern enough,
though an improvement over the sixteenth century
of Henry VIII, Lassus and Petrus Christus, who, paradoxically,
seem more modern than their immediate successors,
Tyndale, Moroni, and Luca Marenzio among them.
Often it's a question of seeming rather than being modern.
Seeming is almost as good as being, sometimes,
and occasionally just as good. Whether it can ever be better
is a question best left to philosophers
and others of their ilk, who know things
in a way others cannot, even though the things
are often almost the same as the things we know.
We know, for instance, how Carissimi influenced Charpentier,
measured propositions with a loop at the end of them
that brings things back to the beginning, only a little
higher up. The loop is Italian,
imported to the court of France and first despised,
then accepted without any acknowledgment of where
it came from, as the French are wont to do.
It may be that some recognize it
in its new guise—that can be put off
till another century, when historians
will claim it all happened normally, as a result of history.
(The baroque has a way of tumbling out at us
when we thought it had been safely stowed away.

The classical ignores it, or doesn't mind too much.
It has other things on its mind, of lesser import,
it turns out.) Still, we are right to grow with it,
looking forward impatiently to modernism, when
everything will work out for the better, somehow.
Until then it's better to indulge our tastes
in whatever feels right for them: this shoe,
that strap, will come to seem useful one day
when modernism's thoughtful presence is installed
all around, like the remnants of a construction project.
It's good to be modern if you can stand it.
It's like being left out in the rain, and coming
to understand that you were always this way: modern,
wet, abandoned, though with that special intuition
that makes you realize you weren't meant to be
somebody else, for whom the makers
of modernism will stand inspection
even as they wither and fade in today's glare.

from *Harper's*

Admission

◇   ◇   ◇

My mother was glamorous in a way I knew I never would be. Velvet belt buckle. Mascara lash. Miniature crimson lipstick alive in the pocket of a purse. Her bow mouth was forever being twinned to a tissue. I never would wear that black windowpane see-through blouse, mother-of-pearl buttons tracing the path down her spine. Every woman was her rival. You could say seriousness made me impossible, exactly the same way beauty made her. I understand men. Some like to have one woman in their arms, while a second one stands on a half-shell, both continuously shifting between being and being seen. Even as a child, I understood there were erotic fishhooks that one couldn't see. I learned to use a camera to see what I could be.

from *The Paris Review*

On a Shaker Admonition

◊   ◊   ◊

All should be so trustworthy, that locks and keys shall be needless.

Needless, useless, pointless, moot: stripped of every honest purpose,
      nothing so haplessly worthless now, so meaningless.

Needless, needless: the deadbolt, the strongbox, the padlock
      lolling from the tall spiked gate, the little metal teeth
all jingle-jangling mindlessly on their rusting ring, the all too obtuse
      fitfulness of pin and tumbler, every chain known to man.

All melted down for scrap: the whole clanking, tinkling, delirious mess
      spaded into the pitiless furnace for our trusty smiths
to put to good use, all that glorious blazing gloop walloped anew into
      buckles, skillets, windchimes, wind-up toys, more spades.

Needless, worthless, baseless, daft: the locket, the lockbox, the lockers
      slambanging in the winless locker room, the secret
hasp in the desk or the case to trip for the stash, the fireproof safe,
      the bulletproof vest, the chastity belt, the countless
stacks of patents for atomic bombproof vaults kept under lock and key,
      all gone the way of relics, ruins, fossils, flesh.

Useless, useless as useless gets: the dupe under the doormat, the blanks
      on their hooks, the plink of trinkets (church key, poker chip,
bronzed trilobite) from this or that set, the cutting kit's merciless shriek
      in the back of the shop, the brassy tang on the tongue
when wrangling hands free in a breathless rush to slip in or out, the endless
      cat and mouse of masters and skeletons laid to rest at last.

The heartless turnkey, the nerveless safecracker, the latch-key kid
        scared shitless, the relentlessly dauntless escape artist
trussed in shackles and manacles in shot after shot: who among us
        could even make up stuff so specious, so spurious?

No cutpurse to fleece us, no jackboot to roust us, no half-assed excuse
        to detain us, remand us, debase us, reform us,
no iron fist or invisible hand to quash or unleash us, no righteous
        crusade to destroy us to save us: just us, just us.

All of us no longer shiftless, feckless, careless, faithless: no losses to cut,
        no charges to press, nothing to witness, nothing to confess,
no one to cast into the wilderness, no caste to dispossess, no shamefulness,
        no shamelessness, no cease and desist, no underhandedness
under duress, nothing to peer into or peep at with a flickering eyelash,
        each cloudless passing hour lusting after less and less.

Should be, so be it: so trustworthy, so noteworthy, so rock-steady,
        so truth-hungry, so war-weary, so far from foolhardy,
so otherworldly already, no guest or ghost would guess that any of us
        were ever less than blameless, faultless, spotless, blessed.

Needless, useless, pointless, crap: the polygraph, the wiretap, the clink of cuffs,
        the accordion gate, the ankle bracelet, the honeycombed spy-cams,
the blueprints for the deluxe panopticon, all that superfluous refuse shipped off
        to the pawn shop, the swap meet, the flea mart, the boundless
county dump, the bottomless dustbin of clueless things past, all dead as
        the doornail that held fast against the hopeless crush of us.

No senseless wishfulness, no useless ruthlessness, no goods to get on us
        to bust or traduce us, no clauses to bind us, no cause
for redress, no one on the loose, on the make, on the case, nothing for us
        to jimmy or pick, nothing gone missing, not a thing amiss,
no No Tell Motel, no Big House, no Pale beyond us, no tragic chorus in a rumpus
        over the worst in us getting the best of us in spite of us,

just all of us lapsing less and less regardless how rootless, witless, gutless, pissed,
        all that thankless cussed nonsense now behind us: just us, just us.

from *The American Scholar*

Apophatic

◇   ◇   ◇

for Peter Gizzi

nothing changes nothing
grows wild nothing grows
tame nothing bends weird
the mind-space into shape
of tether and memory of
ankle gone lame the whole
hurt song called irony can-
not know how chaos aches
beneath the facts it wears
for a face the fact of a
blank page being a form
of a map that is a kind of
mask missing a mountain
or a mouth or a marble
pedestal from which the riddle
pours down and you know
a man is the answer *a man*
but nothing changes nothing
bends absence bright into a
silence called paper white
sun circle or solar sail or lonely
wind across vast despair or
blank hope bearing small repair
that this finger I point at

myself answers the question
what is not is everywhere

from *Harvard Review*

Homage to a Painter of Small Things

◇   ◇   ◇

for Matthew Cornell

Begin, not with home, but with one home
among the tiny many you will paint,
each consumed in silence, its obsessions,
its hunger for the small within the small,
the eye that pins a window to the world.

Begin with a broken cubicle of light,
the green hush that makes a cricket sing,
each brushstroke concealed in the next,
wave on wave, until the last one sinks
beneath the blue crush of all those hours.

And if you must begin, begin again
somewhere in the middle, with a boat
just beneath a radium of porch light,
leaned the way a chill leans against
the glass to press a child to the fire.

Start with a home that is not your home.
No home is. And so they all might be.
All return you to the smallness of one,
the ache a lantern casts across an alley.
So close these walls, so reticent the dark

proximities that tempt a boy to look.
The painter knows. A pupil threads needle
after needle, untouched by what it sees,
let alone what it will not. Night falls so
slowly it feels like stillness coming down.

Ask the boy he was if he must invent
the lives of the strangers to find his place.
Does he slouch like a microscope,
the scholar of a solitude that has no end.
Twilight puts its pressure to the stars.

Begin here, with the sound of dishes,
the wind-chime of the sink. Begin with hands
one never holds, a radio that plays just
one station, broken since the 1950s.
Begin with the music of that station,

with a black sedan out back that runs fine
and goes nowhere, though it is good to think
it could, any day now you could pick up,
leave, begin again. You could, echoes the song
you cannot hear. Believe me, love, you could.

from *Raritan*

13

Intrigue in the Trees

◇   ◇   ◇

Horse-collared by the high heat
of mountainous afternoons,
dogged by furious
dissatisfactions,
snakebit, buffaloed,
bird-brained. Thank you,
animals, for giving us so many
useful metaphors, and forgive
us for disappearing you,
daily and eternally.
Often I wonder:
is the earth trying to get
rid of us, shake us off,
drown us, scorch us
to nothingness?
To save itself and all other
creatures slated for destruction?
The trees around here
seem friendly enough—
stoic, philosophically inclined
toward non-judgmental
awareness and giving
in their branchings
perfect examples
of one thing becoming two
and remaining one—
but who knows
what they really feel?
Just last night I was walking

to my favorite café,
The Laughing Goat,
when I saw a murder of crows
circling raincloudy sky,
arguing, speaking strangely,
suddenly alight on
a maple tree, dozens of them
closing down their wings
like arrogant, ill-tempered
magistrates. Everybody
was looking up and
watching. Some kind of
consultation was happening there
(animals think we're crazy
for thinking they can't think),
and I said to a woman
passing in the crosswalk:
I wonder what they're
planning. She laughed and
kept right on going,
happy as a lark.

from *The Sun*

Bullet Points

◇ ◇ ◇

I will not shoot myself
In the head, and I will not shoot myself
In the back, and I will not hang myself
With a trashbag, and if I do,
I promise you, I will not do it
In a police car while handcuffed
Or in the jail cell of a town
I only know the name of
Because I have to drive through it
To get home. Yes, I may be at risk,
But I promise you, I trust the maggots
And the ants and the roaches
Who live beneath the floorboards
Of my house to do what they must
To any carcass more than I trust
An officer of the law of the land
To shut my eyes like a man
Of God might, or to cover me with a sheet
So clean my mother could have used it
To tuck me in. When I kill me, I will kill me
The same way most Americans do,
I promise you: cigarette smoke
Or a piece of meat on which I choke
Or so broke I freeze
In one of these winters we keep
Calling worst. I promise that if you hear
Of me dead anywhere near
A cop, then that cop killed me. He took
Me from us and left my body, which is,

No matter what we've been taught,
Greater than the settlement a city can
Pay to a mother to stop crying, and more
Beautiful than the brand new shiny bullet
Fished from the folds of my brain.

from *BuzzFeed*

The Dead

◇   ◇   ◇

> *It was the ones no one remembered who pulled at me.*
> —Dorothy Allison

So tell me, who remembers Topa, her daddy, his face marked with smallpox
or his two sisters, *one that died one day, the otheren the next?*

Who remembers quarantined houses marked with a red card, the brain
fevers and blood fluxes, or the uncle who found a rafter in the tobacco barn

for his neck? And wasn't there a second cousin
who phoned his brother before making a confetti

of his own brains? Or that other young uncle—*a good-looking
son of a bitch*—who, face down in the river, took mud

into his handsome lungs? Or the babies—Jesus, always the babies—
drowned in washtubs or bit by brown recluse, or Claire, a girl born

four months early, small enough to crib in a shoebox
and thrived, but her brother—*full-term, healthy as a horse*—

who was sleeping sound on his second day when he
just died?

And who remembers Yael but me, that girl with the name so pretty
I could taste the syllables—*Yah Elle*—

and called her again and again? She was only
seven, her blood a sandstorm of cells, at war with itself.

Or my soft-spoken cousin, that kid
surfer who thought he could crush time-

release painkillers with his teeth and
live? Does anyone remember how impossible

death seemed in Florida, how like a sun-scorched
fern his hands curled, two black fiddleheads, the foam at his mouth

when all his chickenshit friends left him
for dead? On the way to his funeral, Fanny got after us for wearing black:

All you young girls always wearing dark, dark, dark, she said. *You need to put on a bright
and purdy color, something that don't make you look so depressed all the fucking time.*

We laughed, reminded her where we were going, but who can say
her fussing was a joke—her amnesia seemed

fender-struck, a switch flipped
off inside a woman *who couldn't take no more.*

Later that day we walked to church under mangroves swarmed
with the bright green fluster of wild parakeets.

I can't say I remember much more than my aunt, how she looked
up into the trees, said, *Oh, little birds, don't you know?*

And the birds, briskly chittering back, answered her:
No.

from *Cave Wall*

Elegy with a Gold Cradle

◊　◊　◊

Now that you're forever
ministering wind and turquoise, ashes

eclipsed by the sea's thrust
and the farthest tor

(I know you were always
more than my mother)—

giveaway flecks tipped and scattered
from an island palisade;

now that you're a restless synonym
for the whistling fisherman's

surfacing mesh,
the alluring moon's path and progress

through a vast chaos
of unrelenting waves,

let me reveal:
in the at-a-loss days

following your scattering,
in my panoramic hotel, I found

a sun-flooded cradle—
so pristine, so spot-lit, and sacramental

beside my harbor-facing bed,
I couldn't bear to rock

or even touch it, Mother:
I marveled at the gold-leafed bars

and contours—the indomitable,
antique wood beneath, an emblem

of unbeatable hope
and prevailing tenderness—

then, for a crest-like, hallowing hour,
listen, my mourning was suffused

with the specter of your lake-calm
cascade of hair, inkwell-dark

in the accruing shadows,
your rescuing, soothing contralto,

and oh yes, Isabel,
the longed-for fluttering

of my nap-time lids:
entrancing gold

of the first revealing dawns,
the first indispensable lullabies—

from *AGNI*

Fidelity and the Dead Singer

◊　◊　◊

for Michael Donaghy

If I set a new stylus on an old record—
my mother's teenage single of Roy Head and the Traits,
a second-hand Howlin' Wolf, the B-side of *Hey Jude*
I played until I couldn't hear it—it's the same catch,
same scratch, same scratch again, same clouds
of static subsiding into soft focus. The first beat
brings it all back home, the dead singer's voice
alive like a recurring dream, or like a ritual
as a ritual wishes it could be, unreeling perfectly
over rhythms cherished to the point of sanctity.

Not so for poems. The blank before the words
has no voice of its own, and when the verbs
unfurl they change a little every time
—not in errors of transcription but in changes
of the throat the poem courses through:
grown lazy, gruff, impatient through the years,
or passing from your mouth to mine like a flu
then passing limply through a stranger's lips
incognito, stumbling, in strange accents.

If only you were in the words, or between them.
I want to hear them again the way you said them:
the pauses, in accordance with your wishes;
the full stops, rough with markings for your breath.

from *The American Scholar*

I Forgive You

◇   ◇   ◇

I forgive you fingers. I forgive you wrists and palms. I forgive you web of veins, the nameless knuckles, twenty-seven bones, the nails and moons below. I forgive you feet, the toes and toenails, metatarsals arching up, cuneiform, the cuboids, and navicular. I forgive you sole of foot, fibrofatty pressure chambers, dense packed nerve and tissue, the spring ligament. I forgive you ankle, lovely with twin bone swells. I forgive you calf abundant, knee cap, knee joint extra complex and temperamental. I forgive you bone and sinew, blood vessel and braid of muscle. I forgive you tidal lymph. I forgive you skin, the coast on which all washes up. I forgive you thigh and buttock, anus, vagina, clitoris, urethra, mons a rounded mass of fatty tissue, inner and outer lips, the smooth stretch of perineum. I forgive you sacroiliac, the bone wings laced with tendon, the pelvic inlet and the brim. I forgive you coiled intestines lined in tissue soft as velvet, the uterus and eggs inside of ovaries, the fluting tubes Fallopian, the docile stomach sack. I forgive you my esophagus, moist mucosa, heart and lung lobes, liver, kidneys, pancreas and gall bladder, the spleen—all the inner organs curled together in the dark and muttering like clocks, like memories of clocks. I forgive you. I forgive you breasts, your lobes and lobules, ducts and alveoli rising to the darkened areola and the nipple passage outward. I forgive you golden seams of fat in semi-liquid state, encasing in your oily cells the poisons of the world. I forgive you mouth, the teeth and budded tongue, the epiglottis, pharynx and the tough-ringed trachea, the larynx with its cords for making sound. I forgive you nasal cavity and sinuses, the ear canal and clear-walled eyeballs—all the head holes opened to the rain of light, the floating atoms of the air, the jacked together molecules of the stupid human world. I forgive you ropey muscles of the neck and face, so overstrained from constantly composing mirrors. I forgive you brain, three pounds of convoluted meat plastered with grey nerve cells, wrapped in blood-rich tissue, floating in your own sweet bath of fluid. I forgive you spinal column sprouting from the brain stem, flaring wires to spark electric charges through dumb tissue. I forgive you glands, both tubular and alveolar, releasing streams of chemicals and mucus, sweat and milk and oil. I forgive you every hair bulb, constantly dividing, pressing hardened protein shafts up toward the light. I forgive you cells, all one hundred trillion, the inner ocean that has ebbed and flowed across three million years. I forgive you every part performing all the intricate and simple tasks that make this mass alive. I forgive you all for already having died.

from *Denver Quarterly*

Steer Your Way

◇   ◇   ◇

Steer your way through the ruins of the Altar and the Mall
Steer your way through the fables of Creation and the Fall
Steer your way past the Palaces that rise above the rot
Year by year
Month by month
Day by day
Thought by thought

Steer your heart past the Truth you believed in yesterday
Such as Fundamental Goodness and the Wisdom of the Way
Steer your heart, precious heart, past the women whom you bought
Year by year
Month by month
Day by day
Thought by thought

Steer your path through the pain that is far more real than you
That has smashed the Cosmic Model, that has blinded every View
And please don't make me go there, though there be a God or not
Year by year
Month by month
Day by day
Thought by thought

They whisper still, the injured stones, the blunted mountains weep
As he died to make men holy, let us die to make things cheap
And say the Mea Culpa, which you've gradually forgot
Year by year
Month by month

Day by day
Thought by thought

Steer your way, O my heart, though I have no right to ask
To the one who was never never equal to the task
Who knows he's been convicted, who knows he will be shot
Year by year
Month by month
Day by day
Thought by thought

from *The New Yorker*

MICHAEL COLLIER

A Wild Tom Turkey

◇   ◇   ◇

When he's in the yard he's hard to find,
not like when he stands in the stubble
across the road brewing his voice

with deeper and deeper percolations
of what sounds like, "I'll fuck anything
in feathers," stopping now and then

to display his fan and perform a wobbly
polka, chest heavy as he breasts forward
but never closing on the hens who stay

in wary steps ahead conversing only
with themselves, their spindly heads foraging,
measuring the distance that frustrates

his occasional flustering leaps so that
when they reach the street, their scurry
provokes him to fly, as if he's both

bull and matador, charging and turning
in the air but landing in a bounding
rolling heap as the whole rafter

of them disappears into the grass—
where after much silence, after the sun
rises and sets and rises, after commandments

come down from mountains, after armistices
and treaties are written, what happens
unseen in the grass still sounds like murder.

from *Ploughshares*

The Present

◊ ◊ ◊

Much has been said about being in the present.
It's the place to be, according to the gurus,
like the latest club on the downtown scene,
but no one, it seems, is able to give you directions.

It doesn't seem desirable or even possible
to wake up every morning and begin
leaping from one second into the next
until you fall exhausted back into bed.

Plus, there'd be no past,
so many scenes to savor and regret,
and no future, the place you will die
but not before flying around with a jet-pack.

The trouble with the present is
that it's always in a state of vanishing.
Take the second it takes to end
this sentence with a period—already gone.

What about the moment that exists
between banging your thumb
with a hammer and realizing
you are in a whole lot of pain?

What about the one that occurs
after you hear the punch line
but before you get the joke?
Is that where the wise men want us to live

in that intervening tick, the tiny slot
that occurs after you have spent hours
searching downtown for that new club
and just before you give up and head back home?

from *New Ohio Review*

Two Lives

◇ ◇ ◇

In my other life the B-17 my father is piloting
Is shot down over Normandy
And my mother raises her sons alone
On her widow's pension and on what she earns
As a nurse at the local hospital, a sum
That pays for a third-floor walk-up
In a neighborhood that's seen better days.
I play stick ball after school in the lot
Behind the laundry. I come home bruised
From fist fights and snowball fights
With boys who live in the tenement on the corner.
Not once do I play with the boy I am
In this life, whose father, too old for the draft,
Starts a paint company in a rented basement
Which almost goes under after a year
And then is saved, as the war continues,
By a steady flow of government contracts
That allows my mother to retire from nursing
And devote herself to work with the poor.
I find our quiet neighborhood of handsome houses
And shady streets crushingly uneventful.
No surprise I spend hours each day turning the pages
Of stories about trolls, wizards, giants,
Wandering knights, and captive princesses.
In my other life, I have to leave high school
To bolster the family income as lab boy
In the building attached to the factory that in this life
My father owns. I clean test tubes and beakers,

With a break for stacking cans on the loading dock
Or driving the truck to make deliveries.
In this life it takes only one summer
Of work at the office, addressing announcements
Of a coating tougher than any made by competitors,
To decide that the real world, so called,
Is overrated, compared to the world of novels,
Where every incident is freighted with implications
For distinguishing apparent success from actual.
No wonder I'm leaning toward a profession
Where people can earn a living by talking
In class about books they love. Meanwhile,
In my other life, after helping to bring the union
To a non-union shop, I rise in the ranks
To become shop steward, and then,
Helped by a union scholarship,
I earn a degree in labor law.
I bring home casebooks on weekends
To the very block where I happen to live
Ensconced in this life, here in a gray-green house
With dark-brown trim. If I don't answer the bell
On weekends in summer, I'm in the garden,
Strolling the shady path beneath the maples,
Musing on the difference between a life
Deficient in incident and a life uncluttered.
Seated at my patio table, I write a letter
Asking a friend what book has he read
In the last few months that has opened his eyes
On a subject that's likely to interest me.
Meanwhile, across the street, in the garden
Of my other life, I can often be found
Hoeing the rutabaga and beans and cabbage
I plan to share with neighbors in the hope they're moved
To consider planting a garden where many
May do the weeding together, and the watering.
It won't be long till I knock at the door of the house
Where in this life I'm at my desk preparing a class
On solitude in the novels of the Romantics.
Do I say to myself it's one more stranger

Eager to sell me something or make a convert,
Or do I go down to see who's there?

from *The New Yorker*

Spontaneous Remission

◊   ◊   ◊

In the rare example, it disappears
   in the aftermath—
      or in the midst—

who can tell,
   of a fever, extreme,
      unrelated to the cancer:

a girl's leukemia gone
   when she awakes
      from smallpox, a woman's

tumor dissolved
   in her breast after
      heat consumes her for

two full days. Perhaps
   such remission is the result
      of the rude surprise

of the archaic, derelict
   malady, most fevers made,
      now, obsolete—polio,

rubella, influenza,
   things of the past,
      of vial and syringe.

And so, why not,
        I consider how
                I might engender it,

immunized
        as I have been against
                all but what has

taken this hold
        in me. Idiopathic
                it must be, then,

something fiendishly
        mine, inwrought,
                unknown to it.

I could bury
        myself in a pit
                I will make of coals

and ash the way
        my father banked a fire;
                I could enshroud

myself in a scald
        of steam; I could inject
                myself with malaria,

an unnamed jungle's
        hot restlessness—
                somehow make

the velocity of heat
        so intense and decided
                that I become clear

and radiant, my scalp,
        my skull a nimbus,
                like a dandelion's filling out

with its crazed halo
   of seed, what I
      was taught when small

to blow out
   like a flame, the remaining
      seed slim pins

my mother told me
   to tell as time.
      And when I wake

as from the childhood
   bed, it will have
      broken, all of it,

the veil of seeded
   water on my brow
      a sign there: something

atomized, cast
   out, now, blown away,
      by the arson that has

become the God in me.

from *The Southern Review*

Kaddish

◇   ◇   ◇

Strapped into black

there is only one theme song

on earth tonight.

Giant death machine,

play it for me.

Of all the silent killers

none is weaker than my smile

after a tasteless joke,

something I would never have said

in your company. According to my people

there is no heaven or hell

only earth and memory,

the normal hunger

that hits this time of night

trying to picture you

walking back to us

across the strip mall parking lot of this century.

My brother and I, still buckled in,

slurping grape soda

as the same war crawls across the radio.

There are bodies and to see them

is to know they are yours

to forget, to know there's nothing
that won't be forgotten.
On the dark windshield
I use my finger to write your name,
I watch the world move through it.

from *jubilat*

The Boatman

◊　◊　◊

We were thirty-one souls all, he said, on the gray-sick of sea

in a cold rubber boat, rising and falling in our filth.

By morning this didn't matter, no land was in sight,

all were soaked to the bone, living and dead.

We could still float, we said, from war to war.

What lay behind us but ruins of stone piled on ruins of stone?

City called "mother of the poor" surrounded by fields

of cotton and millet, city of jewelers and cloak-makers,

with the oldest church in Christendom and the Sword of Allah.

If anyone remains there now, he assures, they would be utterly alone.

There is a hotel named for it in Rome two hundred meters

from the Piazza di Spagna, where you can have breakfast under

the portraits of film stars. There the staff cannot do enough for you.

But I am talking nonsense again, as I have since that night

we fetched a child, not ours, from the sea, drifting face-

down in a life vest, its eyes taken by fish or the birds above us.

After that, Aleppo went up in smoke, and Raqqa came under a rain

of leaflets warning everyone to go. Leave, yes, but go where?

We lived through the Americans and Russians, through Americans again, many nights of death from the clouds, mornings surprised

to be waking from the sleep of death, still unburied and alive

but with no safe place. Leave, yes, we obey the leaflets, but go where?

To the sea to be eaten, to the shores of Europe to be caged?

To *camp misery* and *camp remain* here. I ask you then, where?

You tell me you are a poet. If so, our destination is the same.

I find myself now the boatman, driving a taxi at the end of the world.

I will see that you arrive safely, my friend, I will get you there.

from *Poetry*

Given to These Proclivities, By God

◇   ◇   ◇

> *. . . bound by sin's galling fetters*
> —hymn

And like every sinner, I prayed,
"Take this sin from me" but
the sin was mine, and how to take it
and not call it stealing? And why
place my sin upon another? So

I ate my sin. Like any good sinner
I have an appetite. I could eat as much
as I drink. And you know how much
I like a neat Mark. I don't think twice.
    I swallow it down.
    Two fingers, no water.
Once, then once more. So it burns?
    What won't?
Like any dirty girl, I went down
to the river to wash it all away.
To be made clean. But
    the river threw me up,
    water wouldn't have me,
back onto the trail left to my trials.
And sin reigned down upon me

like those hot rays of sun that penetrate
the leaf. Like the feathers of a blackbird

come down like rage. "O God," I cried,
       "Lay me down in a cool bed
       of rhododendrons"

and "Let them cover my naked ambition"
but like all sinners I don't get what I want, so
I want it all the more, the petals' sweet droop
like lips, their generous spill over the verge,
the shade below where I might be safe

from the light that did not love me enough,
       not really.
All sinners know that. We stumble
enough to know: not everyone rises again.

from *Cherry Tree*

Dead Butterfly

◇   ◇   ◇

dead empress of winged things
weightless flake of flight
you rest in state on my desk
more delicate and flatter than
this scrap of foolscap you lie on
flatter even than my dad's voice
when he was mad   like death
anger drained him of color
but his temper was gentle
flare-ups were rare
and of course nonexistent now
since he was found
lifeless in bed   a cut on his head
how did he make it down the hall
after he fell do you think? homing instinct?
the undersides of your wings
have elongated spots
silver iridescences whose shapes
vary like globs of oil floating on water
your three visible legs
are tiny whiskers slightly curved
your head a majestic black seed
I fetch my magnifying glass
to view your life form
so difficult to glimpse
except fleetingly while in motion
for twelve days I have selfishly kept you
for private study on a corner of my desk
you seem a saint

remaining uncorrupt   obligingly intact
perhaps your oranges yellows and blacks
are imperceptibly dimming
but I can't see it yet   you look fresh
I long to pet you but know
you would crumble to dust
like pollen on my fingertips
dead monarch will you ferry
my dead father a missive in which I admit
he was right about everything:
my cousin's sham marriage
and 9/11   about how one should never eat
a loveless meal   about craving more time
alive   about the eternity of our ends?

   from *Fifth Wednesday*

Canasta

◊   ◊   ◊

Houston, 1953

Masses of one un-housed
household added to another, all abandoned and made
to abandon their names. A non-colonnade
of gray clods. An un-quadrangle
of neo-rational obliteration. An arcade
of ashes. Ditch-buried
hordes of kin left akimbo, a strangled
necropolis on the verge of the farthest acres of the settled
precincts of our planet—or maybe at the corner angle
of the poisoned field
of remembrance, only one little creaking shed.
And in the low gray corner inside, a weak tangle
of the last echoes of a last word
that ever was uttered to a beloved child,
or of that child's reply. "I know how to play," I said

to my grandmother, I lied—
so wanting to be included, and interrupting her card
game in America—the card table, the discard,
the talk in their languages, the tea—no more than a decade
after all that hate-whipped
grief without a shroud.
Her three card-playing women friends, as displaced
as she, did not (I remember this) like to be interrupted.
It might be too much for me to say I understand
that what they did,
their canasta and bridge, their mahjong, they did

so as, even then, not to be destroyed.
And they went out together, too—converged
with fellow Theosophists and singers and even tramped
off in pants to a mossy, snakey wood
to see a migrating bird.

If, as I stood near the card game, my grandmother reached
and touched my head—
I'm saying: if she did, I don't remember that she did.

Her own youngest son had gone all the way back there to be killed
in that war. If touch me she did,
it might have been because I, her blood-
descendant but knowing nothing—could
not have restored
to her for one second—
even if unwittingly I could have touched
her with the grace of a small child—
I could not have restored
"one iota," as she used to say, of the world
that had been obliterated, world
she never once mentioned.

from *Ploughshares*

Passage

◊   ◊   ◊

Once in sunlight I pinned to the clothesline a cotton sheet, a plane of light
sheer as the mind of God,

before we imagined that mind creased by a single word.
With my hand I smoothed any rivel, any shirr, any suggestion of pleat or furrow.

Whatever it was I wanted from that moment, I can't say. It failed to edify.
Nor did I bow.

And yet the memory holds, and there is a joy that recurs in me much as the scent
of summer abides in air dried sheets I unfold long after,

lying down in them as one might in a meadow,
as one might with a lover, as one might court the Infinite, however long it takes.

from *The Southern Review*

from The Black Maria

◊　◊　◊

after Neil deGrasse Tyson, black astrophysicist &
director of the Hayden Planetarium, born in 1958,
New York City. In his youth, deGrasse Tyson was
confronted by police on more than one occasion when
he was on his way to study stars.

"I've known that I've wanted to do astrophysics since I was nine years
old, a first visit to the Hayden Planetarium. . . . So I got to see how
the world around me reacted to my expression of these ambitions. And
all I can say is, the fact that I wanted to be a scientist, an astrophysicist,
was, hands down, the path of most resistance. . . . Anytime I expressed
this interest teachers would say, Don't you want to be an athlete? Or,
Don't you wanna . . . I wanted to become something that was outside
of the paradigms of expectation of the people in power. . . . And I look
behind me and say, Well, where are the others who might have been
this? And they're not there. And I wonder, What is [the thing] on the
tracks that I happened to survive and others did not? Simply because
of the forces that prevented it. At every turn. At every turn."
                              —NdT, The Center for Inquiry, 2007

Body of space. Body of dark.
Body of light.

　　The Skyview apartments
　　　　circa 1973, a boy is
　　kneeling on the rooftop, a boy who
　　　　　(it is important
　　to mention here his skin

is brown) prepares his telescope,
the weights & rods,
        to better see the moon. His neighbor
(it is important to mention here
        that she is white) calls the police
because she suspects the brown boy
        of something, she does not know
what at first, then turns,
        with her white looking,
his telescope into a gun,
        his duffel into a bag of objects
thieved from the neighbors' houses
        (maybe even hers) & the police
(it is important to mention
        that statistically they
are also white) arrive to find
        the boy who has been turned, by now,
into "the suspect," on the roof
        with a long, black lens, which is,
in the neighbor's mind, a weapon &
        depending on who you are, reading this,
you know that the boy is in grave danger,
        & you might have known
somewhere quiet in your gut,
        you might have worried for him
in the white space between lines 5 & 6,
        or maybe even earlier, & you might be holding
your breath for him right now
        because you know this story,
it's a true story, though,
        miraculously, in this version
of the story anyway,
        the boy on the roof of the Skyview lives
to tell the police that he is studying
        the night & moon & lives
long enough to offer them (the cops) a view
        through his telescope's long, black eye, which,
if I am spelling it out anyway,
        is the instrument he borrowed
& the beautiful "trouble" he went through

                    lugging it up to the roof
to better see the leopard body of
              space speckled with stars & the moon far off,
much farther than (since I am spelling *The Thing*
              out) the distance between
the white neighbor who cannot see the boy
              who is her neighbor, who,
in fact, is much nearer
              to her than to the moon, the boy who
wants to understand the large
              & gloriously un-human mysteries of
the galaxy, the boy who, despite "America,"
              has not been killed by the murderous jury of
his neighbor's imagination & wound. This poem
              wants only the moon in its hair & the boy on the roof.
This boy on the roof of this poem
              with a moon in his heart. Inside my own body
as I write this poem my body
              is making a boy even as the radio
calls out the Missouri coroner's news,
              the Ohio coroner's news.
2015. My boy will nod
              for his milk & close his mouth around
the black eye of my nipple.
              We will survive. How did it happen?
The boy. The cops. My body in this poem.
              My milk pulling down into droplets of light
as the baby drinks & drinks them down
              into the body that is his own, see it,
splayed & sighing as a star in my arms.
              Maybe he will be the boy who studies stars.
Maybe he will be (say it)
              the boy on the coroner's table
splayed & spangled
              by an officer's lead as if he, too, weren't made
of a trillion glorious cells & sentences. Trying to last.

Leadless, remember? The body's beginning,
splendored with breaths, turned,
by time, into, at least, this song.

This moment-made & the mackerel-"soul"
caught flashing inside the brief moment of the body's net,
then, whoosh, back into the sea of space.

The poem dreams of bodies always leadless, bearing
only things ordinary
as water & light.

from *Harvard Review*

Higher Education

◊　◊　◊

Antioch, Berkeley, and Columbia
were the ABC's of colleges
my father said he wouldn't pay for—
breeding grounds for radicalism
he called them, as if their campuses
were giant Petri dishes spawning
toxic cultures. Our own pathology
was pretty toxic at the time, both of us
stubbornly refusing to learn
anything about each other, or
about ourselves for that matter, stuck
in a rudimentary pattern of
defining ourselves as opposites.
I wouldn't even look at Kenyon,
his beloved alma mater, despite
its long tradition as a school for
future poets. I hadn't read a word
of Robert Lowell or James Wright yet,
but I'd read Ginsberg, and the first stop
on my college tour was Columbia,
and that's where I ended up going.
And my father, to his credit, must
have seen it was the right place for me
or at least was unavoidable,
so he let me go, and he paid for it.
And the only price I had to pay
was, when I was home on holidays,
to suffer his barbed commentary
about the very education he

was financing, which ironically
had to do with the core values of
Western Civilization. I can't
remember—is forgiveness one of them?
We both got a C in Forgiveness
but later bumped it up to a B minus
when, in a surprising twist, my son
ended up at Kenyon. My father
took real pleasure in that, though he
was already dying by then. I thought
of him at graduation, how proud
he would have been for his grandson
who, he might have joked, was a better
student than he had ever been—all
our ignorance put aside at least
for that one day of celebration.

from *The Yale Review*

Ars Poetica with Bacon

◊　◊　◊

Fortunately, the family, anxious about its diminishing
food supply, encountered a small, possibly hostile pig
along the way. The daughter happened upon it first
pushing its scuffed snout against something hidden
at the base of a thorn bush: a blood covered egg, maybe,
or small rubber ball exactly like the sort that snapped
from the paddle my mother used to beat me with
when I let her down. At the time the father and mother
were tangled in some immemorial dispute about cause
and effect: who'd harmed whom first, how jealousy
did not, in fact, begin as jealousy, but as desperation.
When the daughter called out to them, they turned
to see her lift the pig, it was no heavier than an orphan,
from the bushes and then set it down in their path.
They waited to see whether the pig might idle forward
with them until they made camp or wander back toward
the home they'd abandoned to war. Night, enclosed
in small drops of rain, began to fall upon them.
"Consequence" is the word that splintered my mind.
Walking a path in the dark is about something
the way a family is about something. Like the pig,
I too wanted to reach through the thorns for the egg
or ball, believing it was a symbol of things to come.
I wanted to roll it in my palm like the head
of a small redbird until it sang to me. I wanted
to know how my mother passed her days having
never touched her husband's asshole, for example.
Which parts of your body have never been touched,
I wanted to ask. I'd been hired to lead the family

from danger to a territory full of more seeds than bullets,
but truth was, in the darkness there was no telling
what was rooting in the soil. Plots of complete silence,
romantics posing in a field bludgeoned by shame.
The heart, biologically speaking, is ugly as it pumps
its passion and fear down the veins. Which is to say,
starting out we have no wounds to speak of
beyond the ways our parents expressed their love.
· We were never sure what the pig was after or whether
it was, in fact, not a pig, but some single-minded soul
despair had turned into a pig, some devil worthy of mercy.
Without giving away the enigmatic ending, I will say
when we swallowed the flesh, our eyes were closed.

from *The New Yorker*

W . J . H E R B E R T

Mounting the Dove Box

◊　◊　◊

I ordered it for him online and then
I nailed it under eaves where he could see
a pair fly in and out with twigs, and when
chicks fledged, they'd wobble, testing wings, and he
would be distracted, maybe feel less pain,
but no doves seemed to nest, though one flew in
and we both held our breath. Then heavy rain.
More chemo. He withdrew, black terrapin
that settled in the mud and disappeared
while I sat there and thought about the box.
That fall as days seemed slow and cold, I cleared
out ivy, watched the "v" of passing flocks
while under eaves, a twig cup, half-hewn boat
its hold, like his, unraveling, remote.

from *Southwest Review*

Cause of Death: Fox News

◇   ◇   ◇

Towards the end he sat on the back porch,
sweeping his binoculars back and forth
over the dry scrub-brush and arroyos,

certain he saw Mexicans
moving through the creosote and sage
while the TV commentators in the living room

turned up loud enough
for a deaf person to hear
kept pouring gasoline on his anxiety and rage.

In the end he preferred to think about illegal aliens,
about welfare moms and health care socialists
than the uncomfortable sensation of the disease

sneaking through his tunnels in the night,
crossing the river between his liver and his spleen.
It was just his typical bad luck

to be born in the historical period
that would eventually be known
as the twilight of the white male dinosaur,

feeling weaker and more swollen every day
with the earth gradually looking more like hell
and a strange smell rising from the kitchen sink.

In the background those big male voices
went on and on, turning the old crank
about hard work and god, waving the flag

and whipping the dread into a froth.
Then one day the old man had finally finished
his surveillance, or it had finished him,

and the cable TV guy
showed up at the house apologetically,
to take back the company equipment:

the black, complicated box with the dangling cord
and the gray rectangular remote control,
like a little coffin.

from *The Sun*

Hamlet Texts Guildenstern about Playing upon the Pipe

◊　◊　◊

True that. Rue that.
That whch wld cause us 2 mscnstrue
that whch we alwys hve knwn 2 be true,
that we r a part of an unholy crew
that drms we cn do whtvr we do.
2 be honest eschw that. Chw that
fr a while. Msticate. Xpctorate.
Engnder only that whch will elevate. Do that.
Elminate that whch invites u 2 spculate,
pooh pooh that. Untrue that. Undo that.
At least try. Set ur azmuth 2 aim at what-
evr sky will allow u 2 prsue that.
And avoid at all csts the truths ur uncouth at,
squndring ur youth at, growng long in the tooth at,
7 a.m. drinkng vermouth at, 9 a.m. flyng to Duluth at.
Fnd that hue in the sky. Thn cry. Boohoo that. Hew 2 that.
True blue that sky course, that heart settng. Few do that. Sail 2 that.
And 2 anything that wld skew that, u know what to say. Screw that.

from *The Antioch Review*

Certain Things

◊ ◊ ◊

For the sake of my father, certain things
must be done in a certain way:
tightening of bolts, of nuts around threads;
coiling of hoses; firm, instant replacement of lids;
spreading of seed from the hand held just so,
in furrows dug to the joint or the knuckle, depending;
wash it when you use it, never put it up wet;
don't be opening and closing the screen door
as if you were a cat.
Be grateful for a job, a meal, a leg up.
All that.
In the seasons set aside for such emotions,
of course I hated him.
All things, even hatred, wear away.
In the season set aside I became him,
doing what he did in the way he did it,
hiding the injured heart the way he hid it.
Waking so many hours before full day
from the dream
that something certain's gone astray.

from *New Ohio Review*

MAJOR JACKSON

The Flâneur Tends a Well-Liked Summer Cocktail

◇   ◇   ◇

curbside on an Arp-like table. He's alone
of course, in the arts district as it were, legs folded,
swaying a foot so that his body seems to summon
some deep immensity from all that surrounds:
dusk shadows inching near a late-thirtyish couple debating
the post-galactic abyss of sex with strangers,
tourists ambling by only to disappear into the street's gloomy mouth,
a young Italian woman bending to retrieve
a dropped MetroCard, its black magnetic strip facing up,
a lone speckled brown pigeon breaking from a flock of rock
doves, then landing near a crushed fast-food wrapper
newly tossed by a bike messenger, the man chortling
after a sip of flaxen-colored beer, remembering
that, in the Gospel of John the body and glory converge
linked to incarnation and so, perhaps, we manifest each other,
a tiny shower of sparks erupting from the knife sharpener's
truck who daily leans a blade into stone, a cloudscape reflected
in the rear windshield of a halted taxi where inside
a trans woman applies auburn lipstick, the warlike
insignia on the lapel jacket of a white-gloved
doorman who opening a glass door gets a whiff
of a dowager's thick perfume and recalls baling timothy
hay as a boy in Albania, the woman distractedly watching
a mother discuss Robert Colescott's lurid appropriations
of modernist art over niçoise salad, suddenly frees her left breast
from its cup where awaits the blossoming mouth of an infant
wildly reaching for a galaxy of milk behind her dark areola,

the sharp coughs of a student carrying a yoga mat,
the day's last light edging high-rises on the West Side
so that they seem rimmed by fire just when the man says, *And yet,*
immense the wages we pay boarding the great carousel of flesh.

from *Virginia Quarterly Review*

History (n.)

◇   ◇   ◇

*"I didn't make these verses because I wanted to rival that
fellow, or his poems, in artistry—I knew that wouldn't
be easy—but to test what certain dreams of mine might be
saying and to acquit myself of any impiety, just in case they
might be repeatedly commanding me to make this music."*
—*Plato*, Phaedo

Viewed from space, the Chilean volcano blooms.
I cannot see it. It's a problem of scale. *History*—the branch
of knowledge dealing with past events; a continuous,
systematic narrative of; aggregate deeds; acts, ideas, events
that will shape the course of the future; immediate
but significant happenings; finished, done with—"he's history."

—

Calbuco: men shoveling ash from the street.
Third time in a week. And counting.
Infinite antithesis. Eleven
miles of ash in the air. What to call it—
just "ash." They flee to Ensenada.

—

*The power of motives does not proceed directly from the will—
a changed form of knowledge.* Wind pushing
clouds toward Argentina. *Knowledge is merely involved.*
Ash falls, it is falling, it has fallen. *Will fall.* Already flights
cancelled in Buenos Aires. I want to call it snow—

what settles on the luma trees, their fruit black, purplish black,
soot-speckled, hermaphroditic—*if this book is unintelligible
and hard on the ears*—the oblong ovals of its leaves.
Amos, fragrant. Family name *Myrtus*. The wood is extremely hard.

—

Ash falling on the concrete, falling on cars, ash
on the windshields, windows, yards. *They have lost
all sense of direction. They might as well be deep
in a forest or down in a well. They do not comprehend
the fundamental principles. They have nothing in their heads.*

—

*The dream kept
       urging me on to do
what I was doing—
       to make music—
since philosophy,
       in my view, is
              the greatest music.*

—

History—from the Greek *historía*, learning
or knowing by inquiry. *Historein* (v.) to ask.
The asking is not idle. From the French *histoire*,
story. *Hístor* (Gk.) one who sees. *It is just a
matter of what we are looking for.*

from *The Kenyon Review*

Homecoming

◇   ◇   ◇

One place is as good as another to be born
and return after years, like Odysseus to Ithaca or mildew to a rotting plank.

How Sunday it all looks now, paved and pastured, fieldless and storeless.

Burglar music. Late morning. No one home.

And the past, still and under: its sawdust ice, its milk jugs screwed tight and
suspended in spring water.

County life, pre-telephone, without verbs.

Small houses, a quarter of a mile apart, of whitewashed or unpainted clapboard,
each with a well and outhouse.

Larger houses with barns, chicken coops, toolsheds, and smokehouses. Hounds
of some significance. Men. Women. Children.

Nary and tarnation. A singing from the fields. A geeing and hawing.

A voice here and there with a smidgeon of Euclid and a soupcon of Cicero to
hifalute what twanged from across the fence and the other side of the bucksaw.

Each day of 1953 like a pupa in a chrysalis.

Phenomenology buzzing like wasps in the stripped timbers of the gristmill.

The road out busting from trace and logging ruts. Now and then a backfiring
Studebaker with its doggy entourage and roostertails of dust.

But less and less in 1954, a mare and wagon, orbited by a yearling colt.

The evolution of the cabin to dogtrot, the boarding up of the hall between the west side's living room, kitchen, and pantry, and the east side's two bedrooms.

Stone chimneys at each end, and on the porch across it, the kitty-holed door to the attic's must, mud daubers, and déjà vu.

A spinning wheel with spavined and missing spokes, a warped sidesaddle, boxes of wooden tools, gaiters, spectacles, dried gloves, shoe lasts, letters from dead to dead.

The cellar beneath it all. Wooden casks, wine bottles dusky and obsolesced by the hardshell feminism of the great Protestant reawakening

that quarried legions of infidels from saloons and brothels and restored them to their families. Portis's own.

Tom Portis's vineyard east of the house, his vines of small sour grapes still strung with rusted baling wire to rotting posts.

His continuance bolstered and intensified should a client void a decade and show up early morning, stumble-drunk, moaning, "Virgie, Virgie."

Prose fragments.

The smokehouse. Hams, shoulders, and side meat interred in separate salt bins.

The hog lot.

The well into which, it has been told, Portis once dropped a Persian cat.

And what is the name of the cat? And what word now from the after?

~

Here are some verbs: woke, saw, stretched, heard, washed, smelled, sat, blessed, ate, listened, rose, waited, walked, felt, shat, dug, meditated, buried, gone

though somewhere, perhaps by some odd fractal of the principle of the conservation of matter, a remnant of the original template holds.

Home odor, unreconstructed, peasant, third world—
"Nostalgia of the infinite," the nearly forgotten Bob Watson called it.

Maybe it's just like that. Maybe it's exactly what they say
after years to the old when they were children.

from *The Kenyon Review*

Progress Notes

◊ ◊ ◊

The age of portrait is drugged. Beauty
is symmetry so rare it's a mystery.
My left eye is smaller than my right,
my big mouth shows my nice teeth perfectly
aligned like Muslims in prayer.
My lips are an accordion. Each sneeze
a facial thumbprint. One corner
of my mouth hangs downward when I want
to hold a guffaw hostage. Bell's Palsy perhaps
or what Mark Twain said about steamboat piloting,
that a doctor's unable to look upon the blush
in a young beauty's face without thinking
it could be a fever, a malar rash,
a butterfly announcing a wolf. Can I lie
face down now as cadavers posed
on first anatomy lesson? I didn't know mine
was a woman until three weeks later
we turned her over. Out of reverence
there was to be no untimely exposure of donors,
our patrons who were covered in patches
of scrubs-green dish towels,
and by semester's end we were sick of all that,
tossed mega livers and mammoth hearts
into lab air and caught them. My body
was Margaret. That's what the death certificate said
when it was released before finals. The cause
of her death? Nothing memorable,
frail old age. But the colonel on table nineteen
with an accessory spleen had put a bullet through

his temple, a final prayer. Not in entry or exit
were there skull cracks to condemn the house
of death, no shattered glass in the brain,
only a smooth tunnel of deep violet that bloomed
in concentric circles. The weekends were lonely.
He had the most beautiful muscles
of all 32 bodies that were neatly arranged,
zipped up as if a mass grave had been disinterred.
Or when unzipped and facing the ceiling
had cloth over their eyes as if they'd just been executed.
Gray silver hair, chiseled countenance,
he was sixty-seven, a veteran of more than one war.
I had come across that which will end me, ex-
tend me, at least once, without knowing it.

from *The Kenyon Review*

Grackle

◊ ◊ ◊

What a grackle is doing perched on the rail
of her baby's crib, noiselessly twitching its
tail, she doesn't wonder. The way this baby
gleams he's bound to catch a grackle's
eye. Besides, birds have flit in and out
of these baby dreams forever. Sapsucker,
blue jay. Sparrow, kingfisher, titmouse.
She just likes to *say* grackle, a crack-your-
knuckles, hard-candy word. In the dream,
her baby's black as a grackle, meaning
when she holds him to the light he shines
purple and blue, a glittery bronze. Silent
and nameless. Sometimes he is a she but
always the dream-baby is hers. That is
the miracle. Her nights of nursery rhymes
and sorrow. Of yellow quilts and song
birds. Enough to break a bow. Enough
to fell a cradle.

from *The Massachusetts Review*

JOHN KOETHE

The Age of Anxiety

◇ ◇ ◇

isn't an historical age,
But an individual one, an age to be repeated
Constantly through history. It could be any age
When the self-absorbing practicalities of life
Are overwhelmed by a sense of its contingency,
A feeling that the solid body of this world
Might suddenly dissolve and leave the simple soul
That's not a soul detached from tense and circumstance,
From anything it might recognize as home.
I like to think that it's behind me now, that at my age
Life assumes a settled tone as it explains itself
To no one in particular, to everyone. I like to think
That of those "gifts reserved for age," the least
Is understanding and the last a premonition of the
Limits of the poem that's never done, the poem
Everyone writes in the end. I see myself on a stage,
Declaiming, as the golden hour wanes, my long apology
For all the wasted time I'm pleased to call my life—
A complacent, measured speech that suddenly turns
Fretful as the lights come up to show an empty theater
Where I stand halting and alone. I rehearse these things
Because I want to and I can. I know they're quaint,
And that they've all been heard before. I write them
Down against the day when the words in my mouth
Turn empty, and the trap door opens on the page.

from *Raritan*

YUSEF KOMUNYAKAA

from The Last Bohemian
of Avenue A

◊　◊　◊

It makes me sad to look up
at the crest of a building
& see washed-out names,
decals, numbers, lettering
half-gone, muted tinges
of the past, edges of lives
discolored & flaking off
signs, the bold signatures
now silenced & mildewed
a hundred times in gray.

I see them come & go, new
faces with question marks
& dollar signs in their eyes,
believing they can still birth
the Immaculate. But I know
when the heart's only a big
mouth & the pumping is not
a cutting contest at Slug's.
A paint job has taken away
patinas of years, romance,
& chance. I have stumbled
upon a thing that stuns me
beneath a busted light globe.

Even if loneliness arrives
around 3 a.m., it isn't easy

to touch myself because
it's a sin. But now & then
I must hold on to something
to keep me here on Earth,
in the middle of an old tune
& a new one—I touch myself
as a face blooms in my head
& somehow worlds collide
gently. What set did she step
from, or was it on my last gig
at Smoke? Or, maybe she was
wearing a garden of orchids
when we passed, or the face
of a waitress among changes
in a Trane solo as I almost
walked in front of a taxicab.
When I touch myself I am
reaching for some blue note
on the other side of an abyss.
Mary Travers stands before me
in Washington Square Park
in a silvery dress, whispering
"Where Have All the Flowers Gone?"
as I lean against Garibaldi
reaching for his sword,
& blow riffs of luster,
ready to die & go to hell.

Do you know the Egyptians
had temples filled with dog bones
stacked in rows along stone walls?
I can understand mummified
crocodiles predicting rainfall,
& even the sacred Nile ibis.
They're speaking about time.
The gutted loot is long gone,
but the bones confess.

I still see Seneca ghosts
because under my feet

are talismans, blanched seeds
& bones of extinct species,
& paved-over shortcuts
around these glass vaults,
& you can forget the tab
I dropped with Burroughs
in '79. They still believe
I'm a torchbearer for one
or the other, a tangle of thorns
for the breastplate. My brain
maybe lashed to the helm
but I am still my own man.
No one accuses me
of tying silver bells
on my hands & feet,
& I don't need eyes
deliberately on me
to breathe or talk
with the crows
at dusk. That lost river
under a fallen bridge.

How many votes do you think
George Wallace received here
on our enlightened East Coast
stage? Not to ignore the South
or the Midwest. Here I am
talking history with you,
but I should just stand here
& gaze out this basement
window, counting the shoes
lamenting along the sidewalk.
Yeah, there's a basic rhythm
in everything we do & think,
whether it's buying & selling
magic, or talking a brother
or sister down from a roof.
Seldom a demigod wishes
for John Cage's silence,
whether Germany or Alabama.

That's why the avant-garde
blows against a void & nudges
gods awake, to give body
to soul as the highs & lows
come together. I'm tired
of questions accosting me
in the streets, because Wallace
still scares me in suburban light.
He'd strut upon a puckish set
of *A Midsummer Night's Dream*
as Brutus, & leave as Hamlet
with a boy's grin on his face.
He knew the rhythm of a day
could bring a crowd to its feet.

Sometimes people get tangled up
inside themselves over a single word—
noble or ennoble, whatever—a great
difference when it comes to life
or death. That pretty cashier
Camille at the corner bodega
she didn't know a muskmelon
from a cantaloupe, & kept saying,
What do you call this so
I can put it into the computer
& it can tell us the price,
& I said, This is a muskmelon
darling, & she said, Well,
I never heard it called that
before, & don't call me darling,
& that's when I said, Okay,
to save your soul you can call
this a cantaloupe & let me
get outta here. You see
I know a muskmelon
by its rough skin, because
that's what my daddy called it,
& I loved rubbing my fingers
over it before my mama
cut into it with a knife

pulling the sun into our window,
& she'd place the biggest slice
on my blue rooster plate.

from *The American Poetry Review*

The Watch

◇   ◇   ◇

At night, my husband takes it off
puts it on the dresser beside his wallet and keys
laying down, for a moment, the accoutrements of manhood.
Sometimes, when he's not looking, I pick it up
savor the weight, the dark face, ticked with silver
the brown ostrich leather band with its little goosebumps
raised as the flesh is raised in pleasure.
He had wanted a watch and was pleased when I gave it to him.
And since we've been together ten years
it seemed like the occasion for the gift of a watch
a recognition of the intricate achievements
of marriage, its many negotiations and nameless triumphs.
But tonight, when I saw it lying there among
his crumpled receipts and scattered pennies
I thought of my brother's wife coming home
from the coroner, carrying his rings, his watch
in a clear, ziplock bag, and how we sat at the table
and emptied them into our palms
their slight pressure all that remained of him.
How odd the way a watch keeps going
even after the heart has stopped. My grandfather
was a watchmaker and spent his life in Holland
leaning over a clean, well-lit table, a surgeon of time
attending to the inner workings: spring,
escapement, balance wheel. I can't take it back,
the way the man I love is already disappearing
into this mechanism of metal and hide,

this accountant of hours
that holds, with such precise indifference,
all the minutes of his life.

from *The American Poetry Review*

Lapse

◊　◊　◊

Poem beginning with a line from Gwendolyn Brooks

I am not deceived, I do not think it is still summer. I
see the leaves turning on their stems. I am
not oblivious to the sun as it lowers on its stem, not
fooled by the clock holding off, not deceived
by the weight of its tired hands holding forth. I
do not think my dead will return. They will not do
what I ask of them. Even if I plead on my knees. Not
even if I kiss their photographs or think
of them as I touch the things they left me. It
isn't possible to raise them from their beds, is
it? Even if I push the dirt away with my bare hands? Still-
ness, unearth their faces. Bring me the last dahlias of summer.

from *Plume*

Rain in Winter

◊   ◊   ◊

Outside the window drops caught
on the branches of the quince, the sky
distant and quiet, a few patches of light
breaking through. The day is fresh, barely
begun yet feeling used. Soon the phone
will ring for someone, and no one
will pick it up, and the ringing will go on
until the icebox answers with a groan.

The lost dog who sleeps on a bed of rags
behind the garage won't appear
to beg for anything. Nothing will explain
where the birds have gone, why a wind rages
through the ash trees, why the world
goes on accepting more and more rain.

from *The Threepenny Review*

Kill List

◇   ◇   ◇

1. At a certain distance, it looks like a poem.
2. Transliterated, maybe, from the Arabic.
3. Short lined.
4. Short lived.
5. At a certain distance, it reads beautifully.
6. What its authors cultivate is anesthetic distance.
7. Don't think wreckage, think Brecht.
8. Warfare is the theater of detachments.
9. At a certain distance, an angry emperor becomes a god.
10. Distances are more certain now, thanks to satellites.
11. From the desert here to the desert there: 7252.86 miles.
12. At a certain distance, wing lights look like stars.
13. Cars look like Hot Wheels.
14. A human body looks like the stick figure in a game of Hangman.
15. We guess and fill in the blank of each letter.
16. When we make mistakes, line by line we construct the hanged man.
17. The hanged man represents the guesser.
18. The word in question may remain unknown at the end of the game.
19. The word can be a thing or a place.
20. Or a name.
21. At a certain distance, a kill list could be any kind of list.
22. Grocery.
23. Things to Do.
24. Top Ten.
25. Bucket.
26. When hanging a man, any distance between his body and the earth will suffice.
27. Just so long as he cannot touch the ground by extending his feet.
28. Like a thief on tiptoe stealing into airspace.

29. The list is a poetic device much favored by the American poet Whitman.
30. Whitman was the first to establish that a body can be sung electric.
31. American prisons promptly switched to the electric chair.
32. This gave way in some states to the lethal injection.
33. Apparently, physicians wanted a piece of the execution business.
34. At a certain distance, it looked like vaccination.
35. In the same way two thousand volts looks like an orgasm.
36. Or a seizure.
37. Seizures, too, are of various kinds.
38. Drugs can be seized at the border.
39. Fugitives can be seized in motel rooms.
40. By the collar, or failing that, the throat.
41. Moments, too, can be seized.
42. I seized this one, for example, to prepare a kill list in the form of a poem.
43. A kill list, like a poem, bears the signature of its compiler at the bottom.
44. After its lines are revised away, that one name will remain.
45. Your eye, scanning from above, will focus on it.
46. You will make certain assumptions about my ethnicity, my religion, my politics.
47. At a certain distance, I admit, I do look like an Arab.
48. Your pupils will constrict, like a Predator's faced with a flashlight.
49. I have been waiting here for you, on the floor of this room.
50. *As-salamu alaykum.*

from *The Nation*

Things That Break

◇ ◇ ◇

Skin of a plum. Rotting tooth.

Switches cut down by a child
to lash a child's legs.

A siege does something like this
against sturdy walls. The wrong rules.

A dozen angel figurines flying
from a balcony.

Flailing fist. Splint.
Forefinger and index,

dislocated (not broken). One points
to the left of a man

and the rubbery thing inside quivers

familiar. Raise your hand
if you know how to do this.

If enough hair fails to escape
the pull of a drain and the drain

sputters and fails to swallow water
we will likely say it's broken.

Waves. Traffic lights.

The craven infantry
of roaches at the flick of a switch.

Will—A child in a shrinking living room
sitting more still than the father.

from *Ploughshares*

White

◇   ◇   ◇

1.

Two years before I was born and less than five miles
from my grandfather's farm,
                        somebody killed two women and two men,
filled them with so many rounds
the dead were hard to recognize—
                        young black men, one a veteran
just returned from the war,
and two young black women, shot to death
                        by a gathering of men
as white as the Georgia senate,
all persons unknown, or so testified
                        the single witness, also a white man.
Truman made a statement,
the FBI came down. After seventy years,
                        the case is still nowhere,
and surely the killers are dead.
But this is not about those who did it.
                        This is not about justice.
There will be no justice.
It's about us, me and my friends,
                        the first generation raised white
in that town after the massacre,
allowed to cakewalk into adulthood,
                        self-assured, but as unaware
as cattle of what had happened. I didn't know,
somehow, until I was forty-five years old,
                        and this is a poem

of dumb, sputtering astonishment
at the ignorance of our lives—we who went
                              to our churches and our homes
and our history classes, where no one said a word,
we who lived each day like blank pages,
                    mistake after mistake after mistake
in the history book.

2.

You think you so smooth, even blackface
is okay for you. Go on then, fool.
                          Look here: God is not mocked.
Ticket or not, you will be on that train, and soon.
And when you take that ride,
                    you better put on your face right,
wipe off the tarbaby
that came too easy. And how about the way
                    you talking right this minute?
You better let that go, but you won't.
So keep it up, strut and hambone,
                    buck and wing, pick a bale of cotton.
You think you in the big house
for a reason, but son, sometimes
                    what looks like the sun coming up
is the sun going down,
the world has spun the other way.
                    There is nothing else to do then
but to turn your sorry ass around. You been going ahead
backwards.

3.

So now you have something to say?
You know who I mean.
                    Now, when there's a street in every town,
often a back street that runs past

pawn shops and liquor stores—
                    named Martin Luther King, Jr. Boulevard?
Now you have something to say? That is mighty white,
now that nothing is required,
                    nothing at all, to have coffee at the old place
on the corner with the woman from Cameroon
who runs your office. No refusal of service,
                    no greasy crew crowded at the window
to beat you both bloody when you leave, no
proprietor with a pick handle
                    telling you to get out, no sham law
to look the other way, no church to preach
the curse of Ham, no slurs in the air
                    to keep you, too, in your place.
You know who I mean. Back then, you might have been
a frightened little white boy like me,
                    or you might have been as cool
as a ducktail—slow-riding by the café
to spit out the window, rolling past
                    in your glass-packed Chevrolet,
playing that race music loud on the radio.

4.

On the notes showing the provenance, you'll notice,
only first names. That was the etiquette,
                    and we hold to the old ways
at the underground auction. This is the nose
of a Carlton, this is the eyetooth of a Lucille,
                    now a charm
for a girl's bracelet.
What we have here, in the original jars,
                    are the knuckles and the genitals
of a William. This is the big-toe watch fob of an Odell.
Here is the polished kneecap
                    of a Randolph, a family keepsake
engraved with the date. Let me be clear, though:
To consider what any of this, or all of it,

might bring at auction
is evidence of a bad misunderstanding. When has anyone
paid a thing?

from *Cave Wall*

Upon Reading That Eric Dolphy Transcribed Even the Calls of Certain Species of Birds,

◊   ◊   ◊

I think first of two sparrows I met when walking home,
late night years ago, in another city, not unlike this—the one

bird frantic, attacking I thought, the way she swooped
down, circled my head, and flailed her wings in my face;

how she seemed to scream each time I swung; how she
dashed back and forth between me and a blood-red Corolla

parked near the opposite curb; how, finally, I understood:
I spied another bird, also calling, his foot inexplicably

caught in the car's closed door, beating his whole bird
body against it. Trying, it appeared, to bang himself free.

And who knows how long he'd been there, flailing. Who
knows—he and the other I mistook, at first, for a bat.

They called to me—something between squawk and chirp,
something between song and prayer—to do something,

anything. And, like any good god, I disappeared. Not
indifferent, exactly. But with things to do. And, most likely,

on my way home from another heartbreak. Call it 1997,
and say I'm several thousand miles from home. By which

I mean those were the days I made of everyone a love song.
By which I mean I was lonely and unrequited. But that's

not quite it either. Truth is, I did manage to find a few
to love me, but couldn't always love them back. The Rasta

law professor. The firefighter's wife. The burlesque dancer
whose daughter blackened drawings with m's to mean

the sky was full of birds the day her daddy died. I think
his widow said he drowned one morning on a fishing trip.

Anyway, I'm digressing. But if you asked that night—
did I mention it was night?—why I didn't even try

to jimmy the lock to spring the sparrow, I couldn't say,
truthfully, that it had anything to do with envy, with wanting

a woman to plead as deeply for me as these sparrows did,
one for the other. No. I'd have said something, instead,

about the neighborhood itself, the car thief shot a block
and a half east the week before. Or about the men

I came across nights prior, sweat-slicked and shirtless,
grappling in the middle of the street, the larger one's chest

pressed to the back of the smaller, bruised and bleeding
both. I know you thought this was about birds,

but stay with me. I left them both in the street—
the same street where I'd leave the sparrows—the men

embracing and, for all one knows (especially one not
from around there), they could have been lovers—

the one whispering an old, old tune into the ear
of the other—*Baby, baby, don't leave me this way.* I left

the men where I'd leave the sparrows and their song.
And as I walked away, I heard one of the men call to me,

please or *help* or *brother* or some such. And I didn't break
stride, not one bit. It's how I've learned to save myself.

Let me try this another way. Call it 1977. And say
I'm back west, south central Los Angeles. My mother

and father at it again. But this time in the street,
broad daylight, and all the neighbors watching. One,

I think his name was Sonny, runs out from his duplex
to pull my father off. You see where I'm going with this.

My mother crying out, fragile as a sparrow. Sonny
fighting my father, fragile as a sparrow. And me,

years later, trying to get it all down. As much for you—
I'm saying—as for me. Sonny catches a left, lies flat

on his back, blood starting to pool and his own
wife wailing. My mother wailing, and traffic backed,

now, half a block. Horns, whistles, and soon sirens.
1977. Summer. And all the trees full of birds. Hundreds,

I swear. And since I'm the one writing it, I'll tell you
they were crying. Which brings me back to Dolphy

and his transcribing. The jazzman, I think, wanted only
to get it down pure. To get it down exact—the animal

wracking itself against a car's steel door, the animals
in the trees reporting, the animals we make of ourselves

and one another. Flailing, failing. Stay with me now.
Days after the dustup, my parents took me to the park.

And in this park was a pond, and in this pond were birds.
Not sparrows, but swans. And my father spread a blanket

and brought from a basket some apples and a paring knife.
Summertime. My mother wore sunglasses. And long sleeves.

My father, now sober, cursed himself for leaving the radio.
But my mother forgave him, and said, as she caressed

the back of his hand, that we could just listen to the swans.
And we listened. And I watched. Two birds coupling,

one beating its wings as it mounted the other. Summer,
1977. I listened. And watched. When my parents made love

late into that night, I covered my ears in the next room,
scanning the encyclopedia for swans. It meant nothing to me—

then, at least—but did you know the collective noun
for swans is a *lamentation*? And is a lamentation not

its own species of song? What a woman wails, punch drunk
in the street? Or what a widow might sing, learning her man

was drowned by swans? A lamentation of them? Imagine
the capsized boat, the panicked man, struck about the eyes,

nose, and mouth each time he comes up for air. Imagine
the birds coasting away and the waters suddenly calm.

Either trumpet swans or mutes. The dead man's wife
running for help, crying to any who'd listen. A lamentation.

And a city busy saving itself. I'm digressing, sure. But
did you know that to digress means to stray from the flock?

When I left my parents' house, I never looked back. By which
I mean I made like a god and disappeared. As when I left

the sparrows. And the copulating swans. As when someday
I'll leave this city. Its every flailing, its every animal song.

from *Poetry*

To Marlon Brando in Hell

◊   ◊   ◊

Because you suffocated your beauty in fat.
Because you made of our adoration, mockery.
Because you were the predator male, without remorse.

Because you were the greatest of our actors, and you threw away greatness like trash.
Because you could not take seriously what others took as their lives.
Because in this you made mockery of our lives.

Because you died encased in fat
And even then, you'd lived too long.

Because you loathed yourself, and made of yourself a loathsome person.
Because the wheelchair paraplegic of *The Men* was made to suffocate in the fat of the bloated Kurtz.
Because your love was carelessly sown, debris tossed from a speeding vehicle.
And because you loved both men and women, except not enough.

Because the slow suicide of self-disgust is horrible to us, and fascinating
as the collapse of tragedy into farce is fascinating
and the monstrousness of festered beauty.

Because you lured a girl of fifteen to deceive her parents on a wintry-dark December school day, 1953.
Because you lured this girl to lie about where she was going, what she was doing, in the most reckless act of her young life.

Because you lured this girl to take a Greyhound bus from Williamsville, New York to downtown Buffalo, New York, alone in the wintry dusk, as she had not ever been *alone* in her previous life.

Because you lured this girl shivering, daring to step onto the bus in front of Williamsville High School at 4:55 PM to be taken twelve miles to the small shabby second-run Main Street Cinema for a 6 PM showing of *The Wild One*—a place that would've been forbidden, if the girl's parents had known. *What might have happened!*—by chance, did not happen.

Because inside the Main Street Cinema were rows of seats near-empty in the dark, commingled smells of stale popcorn and cigarette smoke—(for this was an era when there was "smoking in the loge"), and on the screen the astonishing magnified figure of "Johnny" in black leather jacket, opaque dark sunglasses, on his motorcycle exuding the sulky authority of the young predator-male.

Because when asked what you were rebelling against you said with wonderful disdain, *Whaddya got?*

Because that was our answer too, that we had not such words to utter.

Because as Johnny you took us on the outlaw motorcycle, we clung to your waist like the sleep of children.

Because as Johnny you were the face of danger, and you were unrepentant.

Because as Johnny you could not say *Thank you.*

Because as Johnny you abandoned us in the end.

Because on that motorcycle you grew smaller and smaller on the road out of the small town, and vanishing.

Because you have vanished. Because in plain sight you vanished.

Because the recklessness of adolescence is such elation, the heart is filled to bursting.

Because recklessness is the happy quotient of desperation, and contiguous with shame, and yet it is neither of these, and greater than the sum of these.

Because the girl will recall through her life how you entered her life like sunlight illuminating a landscape wrongly believed to be denuded of beauty.

Because there is a savage delight in loss, and in the finality of loss.

Because at age twenty-three on Broadway you derailed *A Streetcar Named Desire*, and made the tragedy of Blanche DuBois the first of your triumphs.

So defiantly Stanley Kowalski, there has been none since.

Because after Brando, all who follow are failed impersonators.

Bawling and bestial and funny, crude laughter of the polack-male, the humiliation of the Southern female whose rape is but another joke.

Because you were the consummate rapist, with the swagger of the rapist enacting the worst brute will of the audience.

Because you were Terry Malloy, the screen filled with your battered boy's face.
Because sweetness and hurt were conjoined in that face.
Because you took up the glove dropped by Eva Marie Saint, and put it on your hand, appropriating the blond Catholic girl and wearing her like a glove.

Because you exposed your soul in yearning—*I coulda been a contender!*—knowing how defeat, failure, ignominy would be your fate.

Because in 1955 at the age of thirty-one, after having won an Academy Award for *On the Waterfront*, you were interviewed by Edward R. Murrow wreathed in cigarette smoke like a shroud and in your rented stucco house in the hills above Los Angeles already you were speaking of trying to be "normal." Because you endured the interviewer's lame questions—"Have you discovered that success can have its own problems?"—"Are you planning a long career as an actor?" Because you conceded, "I can't do anything else well."
Because you said you wanted to sing and dance on screen, you wanted to be "superficial"—you wanted to "entertain."
Because on the mantel of the rented house was a portrait of your mother at forty, your alcoholic mother who'd failed to love you enough.

Because your discomfort with the interview was evident.
Because you spoke of the fear of losing "anonymity" when already "anonymity" was lost.
Because the awkwardly staged interview ended with you playing bongo drums with another drummer, in the bizarrely decorated basement of the rented house.
Because quickly then your hands slapped the drums with a kind of manic precision, your eyes half-shut, a goofy happiness
softened your face.

Because at this moment it was not (yet) too late.

Because you grew into the predator male careless in fatherhood fathering eleven children whom you would scarcely know and of whom three were with your Guatemalan housekeeper.

Because you were the absent father of a drug-addled son most like yourself except lacking your talent ("Christian") who shot to death the fiancé of his younger sister ("Cheyenne") in your house in Los Angeles, was incarcerated for manslaughter, and died young; and the absent father of the "Cheyenne" who hanged herself soon after the murder, aged twenty-five.

Because your beauty seduced you, and made of you a prankster.
Because the prankster always goes too far, that is the essence of *prank*.
Because you were a prankster, sowing death like semen.
Because all you had, you had to squander.

Because you tried, like Paul Muni, to disappear into film.
Because you were Mark Antony, Sky Masterson, Zapata, Fletcher Christian, Napoleon! You were the clownish cross-dresser-outlaw of *One-Eyed Jacks*—a film debacle you'd directed yourself. You were Vito Corelone and you were the garrulous bald fat Kurtz of *Apocalypse Now*, mumbling and staggering in the dark, bloated American madness.

Because as the widower Paul of *Last Tango in Paris* you stripped your sick soul bare, in the radiance of disintegration. Because you were stunned in terror of annihilation yet played the clown, baring your buttocks on a Parisian dance floor.

Because confounded by the corpse of the dead beautiful wife framed ludicrously in flowers you could hardly speak, and then you spoke too much. Because you were stupid in grief. Because you could not forgive.
Wipe off the cosmetic mask! You hadn't known the dead woman, and you would not know the dead woman, who had not been faithful to you. All you can know is the compliant body of your lover far too young for you, and only as a body.

The futility of male sexuality, as a bulwark against death.
The farce of male sexuality, as a bulwark against death.

Because nonetheless you danced with astonishing drunken grace, with the girl young as a daughter. On the tango dance floor you spun, you fell to your knees, you shrugged off your coat, you were wearing a proper shirt and a tie to belie drunkenness and despair, fell flat on your back on the dance floor amid oblivious dancers and yet at once in rebuke of all expectation you were on your feet again and—dancing . . .

And in a drunken parody of tango you were unexpectedly light on your feet, radiant in playfulness, clowning, in mockery of the heightened emotions and sexual drama of tango—as in your youth you'd wanted to be "superficial" and to "entertain"—

And then, lowering your trousers and baring your buttocks in the exhilaration of contempt.

Because the actor does not exist, if he is not the center of attention. Because the actor's heart is an emptiness no amount of adulation can fill.

Because after the slapstick-tango you lay curled in the exhaustion of grief and in the muteness of grief, a fetal corpse on a balcony in greylit Paris.

In Hell, there is *tango*. The other dancers dance on.

Because you made of self-loathing a caprice of art.

Because what was good in you, your social conscience, your generosity to liberal causes, was swallowed up in the *other*.

Because you squandered yourself in a sequence of stupid films as if in defiance of your talent and of our expectations of that talent.

Because by late middle-age you'd lived too long.

Where there has been such love,
there can be no forgiveness.

Because at eighty you'd endured successive stages of yourself, like a great tree suffocated in its own rings, beginning to rot from within.

Because when you died, we understood that you had died long before.

Because we could not forgive you, who had thrown greatness away.

Because you have left us. And we are lonely.
And we would join you in Hell, if you would have us.

from *Salmagundi*

SHARON OLDS

Ode to the Glans

◊   ◊   ◊

I know—why did I wait until now,
the last moment, almost the moment
after the last moment, to sing
to you, outermost, tender, heart.
Respect held me back, and shyness.
Before I first saw you, I had not
seen even a picture of you, and you were
fearsome—when it would come down to it,
between you and my maidenhead,
I knew I could trust you to push until I was
torn from my virginity—
and you were adorable, you and the penis
like the dearest most basic doll, you were like
a brain without a skull, you were like
a soul. When I was eye to eye,
for the first time, with you, and I saw you
weep, the gleaming tear emerge
from the top of your mind, from your fontanelle,
I saw how it was going to be—
it was going to be what the movie, in the dark
school auditorium, had
promised, the blossoming flower, the rich
spongy corolla, the firm male
softness, it was going to be
mercy, and ecstasy—and, in there,
there were real babies, tiny, brand-new,
with tinier babies inside them, enough
to last a lifetime, and beyond a lifetime and a lifetime.

from *Ploughshares*

Letter Beginning with Two Lines by Czesław Miłosz

◊ ◊ ◊

You whom I could not save,
Listen to me.

Can we agree Kevlar
backpacks shouldn't be needed

for children walking to school?
Those same children

also shouldn't require a suit
of armor when standing

on their front lawns, or snipers
to watch their backs

as they eat at McDonald's.
They shouldn't have to stop

to consider the speed
of a bullet or how it might

reshape their bodies. But
one winter, back in Detroit,

I had one student
who opened a door and died.

It was the front
door to his house, but

it could have been any door,
and the bullet could have written

any name. The shooter
was thirteen years old

and was aiming
at someone else. But

a bullet doesn't care
about "aim," it doesn't

distinguish between
the innocent and the innocent,

and how was the bullet
supposed to know this

child would open the door
at the exact wrong moment

because his friend
was outside and screaming

for help. Did I say
I had "one" student who

opened a door and died?
That's wrong.

There were many.
The classroom of grief

had far more seats
than the classroom for math

though every student
in the classroom for math

could count the names
of the dead.

A kid opens a door. The bullet
couldn't possibly know,

nor could the gun, because
"guns don't kill people," they don't

have minds to decide
such things, they don't choose

or have a conscience,
and when a man doesn't

have a conscience, we call him
a psychopath. This is how

we know what type of assault rifle
a man can be,

and how we discover
the hell that thrums inside

each of them. Today,
there's another

shooting with dead
kids everywhere. It was a school,

a movie theater, a parking lot.
The world

is full of doors.
And you, whom I cannot save,

you may open a door
and enter

a meadow or a eulogy.
And if the latter, you will be

mourned, then buried
in rhetoric.

There will be
monuments of legislation,

little flowers made
from red tape.

What should we do? we'll ask
again. The earth will close

like a door above you.
What should we do?

And that click you hear?
That's just our voices,

the deadbolt of discourse
sliding into place.

from Poem-a-Day

Three Dark Proverb Sonnets

◇   ◇   ◇

1.

None have done wrong who still
Have a tongue: even Cain
Can explain.
                    Yet every atrocity
Breeds its reciprocity:
No murder
That doesn't lead to further.

If I was in charge, those who
Praise rage would be made
To visit more graves.
                    Skulls
Annul. All knives should be dull.

And yet, once we'd built the coffin
We had no choice: we had to find a corpse.

2.

Watch the leopard, not its spots.

It's the tiger that strikes,
Not the stripes.

The smart hide their claws
In their paws, then add
Fur for allure.

Combining smiles and wiles
And calling it "style."

A sword has a point,
But a needle
Is sharper and cleaner—
Less mess, less evidence.

It was never just the arrow
We bowed to; it was also the bow.

3.

Remember: every fist
Began as an open hand.

Even a bridge is a ledge
If you stray to its edge.

You can lead a horse
To water, but
You can't make it drink.

You can guide a fool
To wisdom,
But you can't make him think.

You can close one eye to evil,
But you'd better not blink.

In the dark, adjust your eyes.
In the darker, your heart.

from *Mississippi Review*

CARL PHILLIPS

Rockabye

◊   ◊   ◊

Weeping, he seemed more naked
than when he'd been naked—more, even, than when
we'd both been. Time to pitch your sorrifying
someplace else, I keep meaning to say to him, and then
keep not saying it. Lightning bugs, fireflies—hasn't what
we called them made every difference. As when history
sometimes, given chance enough, in equal proportion
at once delivers
                    and shrouds meaning . . . About love: a kind
of scaffolding, I used to say. Illumination seemed
a trick meant to make us think we'd seen a thing more
clearly, before it all went black. Why not let what's broken
stay broken, sings the darkness, I
                    make the darkness
sing it . . . Across the field birds fly like the storm-shook shadows
of themselves, and not like birds. Never mind. They're flying.

from *Callaloo*

Halo

◊   ◊   ◊

We wander round ring after ring of life,
One after another, blossoms of light
To which we're but a mere flotsam of bees.

And although this isn't true, the poem says
This is true; life, light, flowers and bee: truths.
So stop and hold this poem above your head.

Hold it up to whatever light you find.
Then let it go: forget it if you can.
If it is meant to remain it will remain.

And if it is meant to light, it will light.
Your hands will have moved on to something else
But your head will have, say it, its halo.

from *The American Scholar*

Names

◊   ◊   ◊

Arbitrary but also essential.

Before you can remember you will have found
You are Parvati or Adam, Anne or Laquan, all

With one same meaning: the meaning of the past,
A thunder cloud. Byron de la Beckwith, Primo Levi.
Medgar, Edgar, Hrothgar. Ishbaal.

Not just an allusion, but also an example:
Each with its meaning but also
An instance of the meaning of naming.

Lightning. Tamir. Abdi. Ikey Moe.
"What kind of name is that?"

Your own: the one word you can't ever
Hear clearly, but as in a carnival mirror.

Found and to find. Sandra Bland.
Tereke, Ehud. Jason. Duy. Quan.
Lost and to find.

Stammering Moses of Egypt, found
Afloat among bulrushes. Royal.

Aaron of Goshen, the articulate.

from *Salmagundi*

Poliomyelitis

◇   ◇   ◇

Magical numbers! Roosevelt the most famous infantile paralysis
adult to ever live with it, thrive with it, die with it, at sixty-three,
contracted at thirty-nine, the same integral number as my birth year
and the year, 1939, when the world war that changes everything starts—
the President treading water with his hands and arms, standing
at poolside in Warm Springs, the life in his legs different from any feeling.
Polio the proof that the child in us never disappears but turns against us
just when we think we've outgrown its memory and become who we are
and were meant to be, a whole other human body with a mind like a city,
more beautiful at night, while the still heart is a pastoral, with a piper.
A man said Roosevelt, at the end, looked like the most dead man alive
he'd ever seen: the girl in the iron lung, too, resembling what children
imagine death in the satin of its coffin looks like, her face roughed up
with rouge, her soft brown hair straightened, the rest of her forgotten.

from *Ploughshares*

PAISLEY REKDAL

Assemblage of Ruined Plane Parts, Vietnam Military Museum, Hanoi

◇ ◇ ◇

My eye climbs a row of spoilers soldered
into ailerons, cracked bay doors haphazarded
into windows where every rivet bleeds
contrails of rust. An hour ago, the doctor's wand
waved across my chest and I watched blood
on a small screen get back-sucked
into my weakened heart. It's grown a hole
I have to monitor: one torn flap
shuddering an infinite ellipses of gray stars
back and forth. *You're the writer*, the doctor said
in French. *Tell me what you see*. Easier to stand
in a courtyard full of tourists scrying shapes
from this titanic Rorschach. Here's a pump stub
shaped like a hand; something celled,
cavernously fluted as a lobster's
abdomen. How much work
it must have taken to drag these bits
out of pits of flame, from lake beds
and rice paddies, and stack them in layers:
the French planes heaped beneath
the American ones, while the Englishwoman
beside me peers into this mess
of metals, trying to isolate one image
from the rest. Ski boot buckle

or tire pump, she muses at me, fossilized
shark's jaw, clothespin, wasp nest?
According to the camera, it's just a picture
changing with each angle, relic
turned to ribcage, chrome flesh
to animal: all the mortal details
enumerated, neutered. I watch her trace
an aluminum sheet torched across a thrust
as if wind had tossed a silk scarf
over a face. If she pulled it back, would I find
a body foreign as my own entombed
in here, a thousand dog tags
jangling in the dark? I tilt my head: the vision slides
once more past me, each plane reassembling
then breaking apart. Spikes of grief—
or is it fury?—throb across the surface.
Everything has a rip in it, a hole, a tear, the dim sounds
of something struggling to pry open
death's cracked fuselage. White sparks,
iron trails. My heart rustles
in its manila folder. How the doctor smiled
at the images I fed him: *A row of trees*, I said,
pointing at my chart. *Stone towers,*
a flock of backlit swallows—

                Now I kneel beside a cross
of blades on which the Englishwoman
tries to focus. *Do you think I'll get it*
all in the shot? She calls as she steps back.
Steps back and back. Something like a knife sheath.
Something like a saint's skull. The sky
floats past, horizon sucked into it. She won't.

from *The Kenyon Review*

The Mercy Home

◊   ◊   ◊

Your mother died in fear.
No one was with her.
You didn't want to be with her.
The last time you saw her, two months before,
while you were saying goodbye to her,
her turkey-claw hand shot up like a viper
from under her wheelchair lap-cover
to clasp your hand and keep you with her,
to bind you to her,
to not let you leave her ever.
I CAN'T STAY HERE
she screamed like a toddler, over and over,
insane with fear, lost in fear,
without a mind to guide her,
her brain saying horrific truths to her.
You were on the Mercy Home basement floor,
by the nurses station, where she slept in her wheelchair,
because she couldn't be alone ever,
because the moment another human being left her
she was left with her fear, which instantly seized her,
so she couldn't sleep in her room or ever go there
except when a nurse took her for a sitting shower
and stripped her and undid her diaper
and propped her weeping under the water
and soaped her and rinsed her and dried her and dressed her
and lifted her back into her wheelchair.

Did she know the man standing over her
was her son, saying goodbye to her?

Your hand was any hand, a human tether.
She wanted you to take her home in a car
but the Mercy Home was her home—she had no other—
she meant home with her husband and children fifty years before.

What does it matter who you were to her?
Or whether she had ever been your mother?
She was a shrunken old woman, ninety-four,
plundered by years of medical torture,
installed in a wheelchair with a backpack oxygen canister
that fed tubes up her nose so she wouldn't drown in air.

You felt all her fear-strength clamping your fingers
as if she had slipped from a cliff and you were holding her,
only it wasn't gravity pulling your hand from her—
it was you, pulling a trigger:
your hand snapped free, recoiling like a revolver
as if you had shot her,
and you watched her fall into terror,
into her nightmare future,
and she couldn't stop screaming over and over
I CAN'T STAY HERE
which is where you left her.

★

She was right: she couldn't stay there.
She suffered her life only two months more—
if every hour to her were not a year,
if her death in fact meant her suffering was over.
For all you know, she endured centuries there.
(For all you know about what others suffer.)

★

How did she fall out of her wheelchair?
That was a question no one could answer.
She gouged her leg so they stopped the blood thinner
that kept her alive despite congestive heart failure
so she died in the night three nights later

in her bed in her room on the basement floor,
alone with her fear, her tormenter, her familiar.

*

The Mercy Home for aged and infirm Mercy Sisters
and your mother, a devout believer,
not a Sister but a faithful Catholic school teacher
so they made an exception and accepted her.
Those who need minimal care live on the second floor.
Those who need assisted care live on the first floor.
Those who need nursing care live on the basement floor,
and one by one all of them die there.
How do they bear moving lower
when the last move left is to the basement floor?
Their "personal items" and family pictures
are gathered into cardboard boxes by the nurses helper
because they don't own luggage anymore,
because they will never go anywhere.
Hospital rooms off the basement floor corridor
border the common rooms in the center:
TV room, game room, lunch room, beauty parlor
where a volunteer does the ladies' hair.
When someone dies in the night like your mother,
the next morning the telling Lysol smell is everywhere
while the room is aired, door propped open, bed stripped bare,
and in the corner her former wheelchair
empty except for its backpack oxygen canister.
At breakfast there's an extra prayer,
and a prayer too by those in wheelchairs and walkers
when they pass her room and try to remember her.

*

How do the old nuns remember her?
Tubes up her nose, dozing in her wheelchair?
With you, the Cheerful Son when you visited her?
This will be your attempt to remember her—
not how she failed you so you failed her,
not how confused she was by your anger,

not how she needed your kindness as you had needed her
when you couldn't walk either and also wore a diaper
and she carried you with her and pushed you in your stroller
to parks and playgrounds to show you to neighbors.
That last moment you were together,
after you pulled your hand free and were about to leave her,
you leaned over to kiss her, for what good it did her.
At least you did that, helpless to help her.

★

Now you may take her out of there.
Now you'll never fail each other.
No drunk father, no molester neighbor,
no sadist coaches, no nasty teachers,
no nuns, no priests, no Pope, no hellfire,
no need for her to be your protector,
no need for her to suffer her failure
or watch you grow absorbed by anger
and wilder and wilder teenage behavior
that scared the bejesus out of her
(you loved scaring the bejesus out of her)—
you who thought you invented despair,
you who drank despair with your father.

mother fear father despair molester neighbor

shame fouling the air

shame everywhere

★

Now you may take her out of there.
No need anymore to fear her fear.
Now you can be kind to her.
Wasn't there a time when she was happier?
Before you were alive to make everything harder?
When all that hurt her had not yet touched her?
Take her back now to being engaged to your father,

twenty-three in nineteen thirty-four,
on a country picnic in an open roadster,
when she could breathe easily the purest air,
when she had just found love that filled her and fulfilled her,
when she believed everything life has to offer
was opening before her.
                And leave her there.

from *The Kenyon Review*

DAVID ST. JOHN

Emanations

◊　◊　◊

—Jeffers Country

As the trees conspired toward evening I walked below the tor
    its long grass edged & interrupted by rock

& low bracken in an air sifted by the sea's scent powdered
    by kelp & foam   Jeffers said

Of Weston as he might have said exactly of himself it takes great
    strength to believe truly

In solitude trusting its sinews & silence holding yourself against
    waves of your own darkness

★

I was taking Evangeline to rehab in Pacific Grove twenty years ago
    a place near Point Pinos Lighthouse

Lance had just moved to a new manse in Carmel at Scenic & Stewart
    & he'd said to come by because

He was right by Tor House & he was pretty sure I could find my way

& when I arrived I saw Jimi the Lion there & Cissie too & I yelled into
    the kitchen where Lance was swirling

Pasta in a pan & finally as I made my way to greet him I saw just
    past the kitchen patio not

Thirty feet beyond his window those huge looming eggs of stone
        the granite boulders Jeffers

Hauled & rolled from the shore beyond the tor every afternoon
        its medieval & majestic power

One whole side of Hawk Tower stolidly ascending in front of me
        & sometimes

The land can seem as harsh or even harsher than a skeptical man
        who walks mornings not speaking

The world's raw sea edge awaiting him—he who slowly made
        stone love stone

★

There's a photo of my namesake son at eight beside me as we follow
        the trail to Pinnacle Rock

& Cypress Grove on his first visit to Point Lobos exactly the age I was
        when first there with my aunt

& I remember feeling like the father I wasn't until that day my son
        & I stood together above those lethal rocks

Smashed by purposeful waves & those skyrocket cathedrals of spray

★

Above Castro Creek a redwood circle illumined—its lichen lit
        by sunlight

An early silence & the day is released along the whole length
        of Castro Canyon   Anna's waking

Beneath the skylight of our cabin as outside the birds unchain
        again the many swaying promises of limbs

Within those nearby pines & naturally in this room beyond

★

Last night feeling as random as the rain . . . I read in *Daybooks*
    Weston praising Jeffers & that fierce pulse

Weston called the resurgent will of the natural world & I thought
    of Anna yesterday

Approached by a doe & curious fawns walking the circumference
    of Whaler's Cove

& last week returning along the high cliffside trail from China Cove
    we'd stopped so I could shoot all

Point Lobos fanned out & ragged—its exquisite prospects rising up
    & just below us a discrete pebble beach

& familiar tide pools where Ansel Adams told anyone who'd listen
    must one day be named Weston Beach

& so it was   & so it is

★

The summer I turned sixteen visiting my aunt in the skylit studio
    she'd built onto the cottage

In my grandmother's landscaped garden among rose beds & curved
    lawns & tall candles of iris—& as

We talked across the rising perfume of turpentine & fresh oils my aunt
    turned from the canvas

She'd been painting of the Santa Lucia Range & paused a moment
    handing me

A birthday gift a fresh hardcover of *Not Man Apart* with Jeffers's poems
    & images of Big Sur's coast

& she opened the book to a photograph by Weston of the familiar cove
        its surly rocks & twisted kelp & pebbles

& asked *Do you remember the day I took you here? That man who called*
        out hello with the tripod & box camera was

Weston's son—my gorgeous old Graflex I always use & love was his once

★

A few years after Lance moved from his place down along
        Yankee Point up to the Highlands

We rendezvoused in Carmel & I followed him past the turnoff
        leading to Weston's house on Wildcat Hill

Until we looped up Mal Paso onto San Remo & then we all just
        sat watching

That scarlet sunset fan-dance over the Pacific's darkening jade

★

For years I'd kept a notebook of obscure trails between Point Lobos
        & Gorda all those glories

Of both Big & Little Sur but that morning we decided let's be obvious
        & drove down toward McWay Falls

Stopping on the roadside to spend time along Partington Cove Trail

—I broke stride a moment as above the meadow in the dense pines
        a shadow cross

Hung overhead barely clearing the pines' tips a silent condor just
        arcing away

The span of its wings ten feet one fan-feathered tip to the other

★

I grew up in a house of redwood glass & stone the house my mother
      built from Cliff May's blueprints

A lesson in organic mid-century modern aspiration huge exposed
      beams of solid redwood its ceiling planks too

The fireplace a mosaic of flagstones & multicolored volcanic rocks
      & living room walls pale Australian gum

A house that could comfortably have fit in Mill Valley or Carmel
      yet somehow also in the arid San Joaquin

The Fresno of my childhood where it stood as testament to possibility
      —my California of the '50s

  *

Today we walked down to Henry Miller's library to steal Wi-Fi
      & sit with an espresso

—as news of the world came a hawk overhead dipped one wing

So I turned off my phone & opened *The Air-Conditioned Nightmare*
      & that's all the irony anyone should share

  *

In 1936 a hundred miles south of these rock crags sloping low & falling
      abruptly off into the Pacific

Charis drove Weston to Oceano & its miles of dunes so he could plant
      his 8 x 10 Century Universal camera on its skinny tripod

Into the sands & one day Charis sunbathing nude decided simply to roll
      down the face of one dune & another

& so posing for Edward the Spy those hours & days while they stayed
      in Gavin Arthur's (see *The Circle of Sex*)

Old beach shack & this morning I awoke thinking of Charis driving back
      up Highway 1 along the coast

Past Morro Rock & Moonstone Beach past Piedras Blancas & Lucia
      & up over Bixby Creek then to the Highlands

All the way to Wildcat Hill & the swarm of felines tame & feral & then
      Edward making coffee

As she began slicing the apples she'd left on the wood counter to ripen
      & now emanations

Of naked Edenic fruits were scenting the whole length of the room

Its bare redwood planks & ripening apple flesh held in late dusk
      & the wood stove

Heated up as Charis knelt to feed more limbs to its belly & she knew
      these next days in the darkroom

They would bring to paper this sequence of nudes her body white on
      white against Oceano's dunes

Her final acquiescence & reverence for skin married to a future light

★

One day last fall I went to Tor House early to be alone a few hours
      before the tours began

& climb the stairs of Hawk Tower in solitude & later stand in silence
      by the bed *by the sea-window*

Jeffers chose as *a good death-bed* thirty years before the fact to see

The pulse of waves licking raw the shore stones as pines & cypress
      chimed in the sea wind

★

It hardly matters to anyone but me how sometimes as I walk this coast
     Point Pinos Point Lobos Point Sur   I'm singing

South Coast the wild coast is lonely . . . the lion still rules the barranca
     & a man there is always alone

              from *The Southern Review*

SHEROD SANTOS

I Went for
a Walk in Winter

◊   ◊   ◊

The snow didn't fall so much as blow past
horizontally. People heading east leaned into it,
people heading west leaned back, then one after another
they disappeared, as in the fade-out of a movie screen.
As if the world were reduced to the simplest natural law—
that of erasure—a hotel doorman struggled to clear
a sidewalk path that quickly filled in behind him.
So, too, the hollow left behind on a bus stop bench.
Above the entry to a corridor, a blue and yellow
neon sign lit my side of the street; I felt my body
pass through it, and I felt the colors pass
through me, as though a mood had suddenly
come and gone leaving only a tremor behind.

After I returned to my apartment, I found it difficult
to focus on anything; and when I switched on
the television it took me a moment to realize
that a movie in a foreign language was on,
though what language that was I couldn't say.
The uniforms of the soldiers locked in battle
were likewise unfamiliar, and the frozen landscape
provided no clue. Muskets were fired, swords
were drawn, orders were shouted and, I assumed,
carried out, for bodies continued to drop in numbers
carnage alone explained. Somewhere off-screen,
wagons were already being readied to haul away

the dead, and this too I took in, less to imagine
the event than foresee the end: the battlefield cleared,
the blood covered over by ever-amassing drifts of snow.

from *Harvard Review*

Where to Put It

◇   ◇   ◇

The room in which I start sobbing again and wonder
if my sobs will hurt the baby inside me, and the room
in which I hope so, a room made entirely of a window.
                    The room of my husband's goodnight,
which is a room in a large municipal building with Styrofoam ceilings
where lines must be formed so forms can be signed, a room
surrounded by parking lots, and he knocks opening its door
and says, *You can't be this sad for the next five months—it's not tenable.*
                    The room overlooking the perfectly circular hole
in our street that's at least ten feet deep and no neighbor
knows when it appeared or if there's a reason.
                    The room in which instead of eating dinner
I drive for hours past porches where women with voices
like hammered fenders call out baseball scores
into the peeled blue air that will not link itself to a season.
                    The room in which a man the color of sand
stands on a median toward the end of dusk with a sign saying
he has children and will do anything
and the room of the cars before lights turn green.
                    The room in which we are filled with longing
like a wave too large. *Do you see me* is what we can't
find words to ask.
                    The room in which a new student shows up
for my poetry class for formerly homeless people who are mentally ill
and she has my mother's smile.
                    The room in which so many women
have my mother's smile: women entering restaurants, women
standing at counters with handfuls of change.
                    The room of the dream in which the baby

is my mother and I am the vent between steam and the street.
              The room in which I tell my father,
I miss Mom so much I can't think about her and the room in which
he answers back, *Me too*, lit as it is by the end of dusk and the cars
passing through when the stoplights turn; now the man's sign drops, I'll
do anything.
              The room in which my father is living
with a woman younger than I am and the room in which he is my father
and the corridor between them down which no one walks, and *Do you see me*,
Yes I see you, and *Do you see me, No I'm lonely*,
              and the room of my seventy-year-old father
and his seventy-year-old friends pretending to trip each other and laughing,
and the room in which they're invisible, age like the white ceiling
and white walls, the window dissolved to a water-shaped memory of touch.
              The room in which I ask the no-longer-homeless woman
what the poem about kindness is about and she says it's about anger,
says this with my mother's smile, the smile of my mother's illness
that could have decimated grown men in agreement with each other, and did.
              The room in which the woman's smile
becomes an ordinary moth that lifts off the table and slips through a hole
in the star-cracked slats of the ceiling's foam—Are we sharing a space,
do you see me.
              The room of the water-shaped tenable.
The room in the house, the lit room upstairs, books on the shelves
by the window, the room we drive by in the nighttime, someone inside.

from *The Georgia Review*

Seeing Things

◇ ◇ ◇

I came here in my youth,
A wind toy on a string.
Saw a street in hell and one in paradise.
Saw a room with a light in it so ailing
It could've been leaning on a cane.
Saw an old man in a tailor shop
Kneel before a bride with pins between his lips.
Saw the President swear on the Bible
While snow fell around him.
Saw a pair of lovers kiss in an empty church
And a naked man run out of a building
Waving a gun and sobbing.
Saw kids wearing Halloween masks
Jump from one roof to another at sunset.
Saw a van full of stray dogs look back at me.
Saw a homeless woman berating God
And a blind man with a guitar singing:
"Oh Lord remember me,
When these chains are broken set my body free."

from *The Threepenny Review*

last summer of innocence

◇ ◇ ◇

there was Noella who knew i was sweet
but cared enough to bother with me

that summer when nobody died
except for boys from other schools

but not us, for which our mothers
lifted his holy name & even let us skip

some Sundays to go to the park
or be where we had no business being

talking to girls who had no interest
in us, who flocked to their new hips

dumb birds we were, nectar high
& singing all around them, preening

waves all day, white beater & our best
basketball shorts, the flyest shoes

our mamas could buy hot, line-up fresh
from someone's porch, someone's uncle

cutting heads round the corner cutting
eyes at the mothers of girls i pretended

to praise. i showed off for girls
but stared at my stupid, boney crew.

i knew the word for what i was
but couldn't think it. i played football

& believed its salvation, its antidote.
when Noella n 'nem didn't come out

& instead we turned our attention
to our wild legs, narrow arms & pigskin

i spent all day in my brothers' arms
& wanted that to be forever—

boy after boy after boy after boy
pulling me down into the dirt.

from *Prairie Schooner*

MAGGIE SMITH

Good Bones

◇   ◇   ◇

Life is short, though I keep this from my children.
Life is short, and I've shortened mine
in a thousand delicious, ill-advised ways,
a thousand deliciously ill-advised ways
I'll keep from my children. The world is at least
fifty percent terrible, and that's a conservative
estimate, though I keep this from my children.
For every bird there is a stone thrown at a bird.
For every loved child, a child broken, bagged,
sunk in a lake. Life is short and the world
is at least half terrible, and for every kind
stranger, there is one who would break you,
though I keep this from my children. I am trying
to sell them the world. Any decent realtor,
walking you through a real shithole, chirps on
about good bones: This place could be beautiful,
right? You could make this place beautiful.

from *Waxwing*

Maricón

◊ ◊ ◊

i.m. Emile Griffith (1938–2013),
Benny "Kid" Peret (1937–1962)

And a man who has found prowess in boxing,
grant him favor and joy. . . .
— Pindar

1.

"Whoever controls the breathing in the ring
controls the fight," my father says. Smell of sweat,
Vaseline and bleach, sting of ammonia. "The art

of self-defense is crucial." The gym is damp
and the speed bag singing his beliefs. Elsewhere,
a husky boy from the Virgin Islands quietly

designs hats in a Bronx shop, his chest bare
as he hefts storeroom cartons. His boss says,
"Boy's got a boxer's body," and that begins it.

Emile is bewildered, with no desire for the sweet
science of footwork and fist, no assassin's
eye. When a backyard bully named Jeffrey

lures me to his ring of jeering rednecks,
I clear a path with my ball bat, rush home
to mother, because I'm skinny, afraid. Later,

seeing me teary on the mat at a Scout outing
and pawing feebly at Jimmy Kizner, my father
resolves to plunge me into the discipline.

"To win, you control the breathing," he insists.
Morning roadwork, shadowboxing, mitts.
On his bike, the old man swears as I sweat,

"Your target's never where his goddamn head
is, but where it's going next." Willowy, skittish,
without finesse, I never overcome my fear.

Griffith is a better fit—welterweight, bobcat
quick, graceful as ballet. Coach Gil Clancy
taunts him: "Don't you get that matador strut."

Deft and canny through the fifties, his gold tooth
gleaming and bombshell blondes clenching
his biceps at ringside, the shutterbug's flash

catching the velvet dandy in action,
pearls on his cuffs, satin cravat. Dark mouse
on my brow, I bus back across town

from the gym to mother's tears,
tonic and gin, a dead cigarette. "My other
half ought to know better," she spits.

He travels, sleuthing out insurance fraud,
arson while slick-dealing firehouse
poker. She twists her opal ring, exhales

blue breath. I don't want to be prissy,
hope to show I've got moxie, like a pro,
like that March night when ring pundits

all agree: Peret opened inspired.

2.

Whoever controls the breathing. . . .
Jab and tuck, shoot the right high, hook
to the ribs, drive him to the turnbuckle,

the ropes, the canvas. Griffith has to be
schooled in fury: "It's red sport, boy,"
and rumor has it the insiders suspect

he's keeping a secret, the private life
of linen suits, the pink Lincoln crucial
to his macho disguise. Still, no one

will say "pansy." Control the breathing,
control a rival's will and snuff his soul.
"Wind and feet win it. You have to show

an iron intent": in the garage my father
pops me. "Love taps," he says. "You've
got to learn to shrug it off. Forget thinking.

Make me miss, slugger. Everybody
has a plan, but it's gone to smoke soon
as you get hit. Duck now. Control your

breath, counterpunch, get mad. Murder
me, creampuff. Make me suffer." Years
later, his career over, Emile jokes,

"I like girls and men pretty much equal.
You reckon that make me bilingual?"
He'd known Peret since boyhood, but never

heard those venomed syllables: *maricón.*
I hammered into the heavy bag mummied
in duct tape, pounded that son of a bitch.

"Punish the sap. Maul him up. Make
him miss." Still, my father's snarl. . . .
I skip the rope as it hums, side step,

hop and cross-over, wrists whipping,
weaving, sparring my shadow—left, left
right uppercut. At the weigh-in Peret

keeps whispering what Griffith can't
bear to catch. He guesses the word's
out and starts lurching and whirling,

breathless, shamed. Kid has crossed
the line. *Maricón, maricón*, slur worse
than *tu mamá*—"You faggot!" Mild Emile

bides his time. It's sixty-two, my bouts all
history, scuffed gloves and lace-up boots
in a footlocker . . . one local trophy—runner-up.

3.

March 24, Saturday night: Gillette's parrot
cawks about razors—"Feel sharp, be sharp."
The male world seethes: Muriel cigars,

Edie Adams's racy ringside purr: "Why
don't you pick one up and smoke it
sometime?" Her sexy sigh and vixen eyes.

The Garden's a riot of hazed bloodlust,
our Philco's volume high. Mother
flips *Life* in the kitchen with her

sisters, filter tips, a gray kitten. Ruby
Goldstein scolds: "No head butts, boys,
no low blows or rabbits. Protect

yourself, break clean." The pair already
glisten, sponged wet for combat,
breathing easy, both believing, mouth

guards pouting their lips, as if to kiss
and make nice. All a question of mettle
and skill. No one present thinks, "Death."

Bell after bell, circling, sizing up, an even
match for the gaudy belt, the world
sport-smitten, trance-tense, breathless.

A clinic: dole-it-out and roll-with-punches,
clenches, weave, dance, until Emile
finds his moment: no one later can say

how the energy shifts. Rationed breath,
second wind, willpower, a dark gift.
Revived, Emile goes ballistic in the twelfth.

Benny is rubber-kneed, reeling, Emile a man
on fire, windmilling such fury the analysts
go quiet. Some will later say it was only

chance; a few, that a word kept him angry
and whipping in frenzy, making history—
sixteen blows in eight seconds. Others

count it different, but Benny the Kid was
Cuban: "Them Castro boys would possum,"
is the common wisdom, while Griffith's

one rumored weakness is "can't finish."

4.

Sugar Ray claimed Emile was frantic to lay
the rumor in its grave, sew every smirk
shut. I never skipped or bobbed fast enough,

but could hit quick for a white boy—gut
punch, cross, straight shot to the kisser,
a southpaw. I got whipped over and over.

Why did nobody throw in the towel?
Crowd-crazed, Griffith was a tornado,
a blur, oblivious. "I just kept hitting,"

he'd tell a ringside guru still sporting
his blood-spattered tux. "Kid, he didn't
gone down. I kept hitting." Even after,

the specialists said, "a fighter, a soldier,
he'll recover." My father hit the OFF
knob, declaring, "That boy won't fight

again. Neither of them. Animals." For ten
days, Emile paced and prayed. The hacks
wrote, "Benny is a warrior." The coma

ended in a wake and blame—referee,
Emile, even the corner crew who never
lofted the rolled towel into the melee

to ask for mercy. Was it two full years
afterwards with no prizefights on TV?
For decades I never heard the story

behind that word. Years later, leaving
a dance bar called Hombre, Griffith was
ambushed by a dozen and barely breathing

when the siren arrived. A bystander said
they taunted him with: "*Maricón.*
Rise up, boy, show us how it's done

back there in the nigger islands."

5.

Emile had a silk voice, shy eyes, a smile
to lure songbirds from their perches.
He danced with every step he took.

Kid's weeping mother slapped him
in the hospital lobby, spat the word
in his eyes—*maricón*. In his sleep

he saw Benny *perdito*, bleeding from
every mirror and never unleashed again
that stormy combination. History

has nearly erased his name like cheroot
smoke and Edie, Gene Fulmer, Dick Tiger,
Hurricane and Archer. It surely lurks for

everyone, a burning word, forbidden, worse
than split eyelids, bruised kidneys. Is it
yearning for mercy that drives us to misery?

In a world of desperate skirmish and work,
the teardrop bag still hangs in my attic,
and I will not whip it. Does that win me

a measure of grace? My old man was
nearly right: to beat fear I have to feed anger,
I pray there's some better purpose for fury

than knocking another man into the dark.

from *Prairie Schooner*

Shattered

◇   ◇   ◇

Another smashed glass,
wrong end of a gauche gesture
towards a cliff—compass-

rose of mis-direc-
tions, scattered to the twelve winds,
the wine-dark sea wreck.

Wholeness won't stay put.
Why these sweeping conclusions?
Always you're barefoot,

nude-soled in a room
fanged with recriminations,
leaning on a broom.

How can you know what's
missing, unless you puzzle
all the shards? What cuts

is what's overlooked,
the sliver of the unseen,
faceted, edged, hooked,

unremarked atom
of remorse broadcast across
lame linoleum.

Archaeologist
of the just-made mistake, sift
smithereens of schist

for the unhidden
right-in-plain-sight needling
mote in the midden.

Fragments, say your feet,
make the shivered, shimmering
brokenness complete.

from *Harvard Review*

Afraid to Pray

◊   ◊   ◊

Dear God I'm afraid if I pray for my daughter's safety you'll blithely
allow her to get raped or abducted or crash on a highway
on a perfect summer day. Forget I mentioned my daughter. What daughter?

I remember how Anne Frank believed in the goodness of mankind.
I wonder how she felt the moment her diary was knocked from her hands
because that's how I'm feeling these days: like Job with post-traumatic

stress disorder. Don't worry, God, I know you exist; but I'm having some
serious trust issues. Maybe it began with that nightmare about my
mother shoving my grandmother into a swift-running river.

I jumped in to save her, and I saved her all right, but O the branches
and Kentucky mud stuck in our hair and mouths—the disbelief
in her eyes—and me having to tell her the truth.

Dear God if you made us in your likeness because you were
lonely then uh-oh. I'm so tired of Nazis marching to the rhythm of my
        prayers.
I prayed that the love of my life would survive his cancer then he died on my
        birthday.

And for thirty years I prayed my ex-husband would survive his insanity, but
        he
finally blew his brains out. I know there's a heaven because
I walked along a tightrope of Atlantic foam after Joel died and

a rainbow lassoed the sun. The sky was timorous and thin
as an eardrum and I knew if I pushed with all of my rage
that the sky would burst and we would touch hands one last time.

I'm so tired of praying and getting punched in the gut. I prayed that
my parents would not sell my sister's black Morgan horse with the star
on its forehead, but they sold it all right and now she's afraid to love her own
    children.

I prayed that my parents would not sell the hand-built log cabin on the
Indian reservation, but when they knew they could die without selling it,
    they sold
it all right and the new owners bulldozed it down along with everything in it

including a Bible my mother had placed just so. And they chopped down the
    forest
and threw my canoe in a dumpster. Now all I do is scour real estate ads for
    log cabins
on the Indian reservation. I've found a few places but they're just not the
    same. Still,

I'd like to move back to the northwoods and live in a cabin and pray to the
    lake
and the woods and the wolves. Like God the wolves would not answer my
    prayers,
but unlike God, by God they would listen for once and look me straight in
    the eye.

from *Prairie Schooner*

Sad Song

◇   ◇   ◇

It's ridiculous, at my age,
to have to pull the car onto the shoulder

because Bob Dylan and Johnny Cash
are singing "Girl from the North Country,"

taking turns remembering not one girl,
but each of their girls, one and then the other,

a duet that forces tears from my eyes
so that I have to pull off the road and weep.

Ridiculous! My sadness is fifty years old!

It travels into sorrow and gets lost there.

Not because it calls up first love, though it does,
or first loss of love, though both
are shawls it wears to hide its wound,

a wound to the girl of which
all men sing, the girl split open,

the sluice through which all of childhood pours,

carrying her out of one country
into another, in which she grows up
wearing a necklace of stones,

one for each girl not her,

though they all live together here
in the North Country, where the winds

hit heavy on the borderline.

from *Salmagundi*

Something

◇   ◇   ◇

The minute the doctor says colon cancer
you hardly hear anything else.
He says other things, something
about something. Tests need to be done,
but with the symptoms and family something,
excess weight, something about smoking,
all of that together means something something
something something, his voice a dumb hum
like the sound of surf you know must be pounding,
but the glass window that has dropped down
between you allows only a muffled hiss
like something something. He writes a prescription
for something, which might be needed, he admits.
He hands you something, says something, says goodbye,
and you say something. In the car your wife says
something something and something about dinner,
about needing to eat, and the doctor wanting tests
doesn't mean anything, nothing, and something
something something about not borrowing trouble
or something. You pull into a restaurant
where you do not eat but sit watching her
eat something, two plates of something,
blurry in an afternoon sun thick as ketchup,
as you drink a glass of something-cola
and try to recall what the doctor said
about something he said was important,
a grave matter of something or something else.

from *The Sun*

Dear Skull

◊   ◊   ◊

beloved braincase, body's bleeding heart
helmet law

dear ribs thick with implied meat, disused central
railroad, reverse spec house unplumbed
to propitious frame

dear double-strung forearm, dear violin bow,

dear pachyderm-eared pelvis,

dear barnacle spine—

tolerate this animate interlude, nervous tic of cell & swoosh,
elasticity & vein

& you'll emerge, democratically beautiful,

armature to nothing

you'll make the case for stasis, grow
each year more ravishingly still

yes, the flesh is weak,
but you are forged of patience,

ill inclined to cheer or mourn
the extraneous

—respiration, cartilage—as it trundles away

from *The Georgia Review*

Deconstruction

◇   ◇   ◇

The chickadee is all about truth.
The finch is a token. The albatross
is always an omen. The kestrel is mental,
the lark is luck, the grouse is dance,
the goose is quest. The need for speed
is given the peregrine, and the dove's
been blessed with the feminine.

The quail is word and culpability.
The crane is the dean of poetry.
The swift is keen agility,
the waxwing mere civility,
the sparrow a nod to working class

nobility. The puffin's the brother
of humor and prayer, the starling the student
of Baudelaire. The mockingbird
is the sound of redress, the grackle the father
of excess. The flicker is rhythm,

the ostrich is earth, the bluebird a simple
symbol of mirth. The oriole
is the fresh start. The magpie is prince
of the dark arts. The swallow is warmth,
home, protection—the vulture the priest

of purification, the heron a font
of self-reflection. The swisher belongs
to the faery realm. Resourcefulness

is the cactus wren. The pheasant is sex,
the chicken is egg, the eagle is free,

the canary the bringer of ecstasy.
The martin is peace. The stork is release.
The swan is the patron of grace and discretion.
The loon is the watery voice of the moon.
The owl's the keeper of secrets, grief,
and fresh fallen snow, and the crow

has the bones of the ancestral soul.

from *The Hopkins Review*

LUCY WAINGER

Scheherazade.

◇   ◇   ◇

after Richard Siken

comes wave after wave after wave the derivative & harvest, the myrtle
tops of sandstorms & milk glasses, apple, horse & song, list, listen, light
leaks from the spaces between the bubbles—call it foam—tender pocket
of *yes yes yes* call it flesh—eat tonight & you'll still have to eat tomorrow,
eat tonight & it still won't be over—eat tonight: peaches bloom even
in the dark, as wet as a girl—hands & feet, horse & song, the same
hole bandaged over & over, not a wound but its absence—a sum of
histories—the nights colliding like marbles, & if there is an end then
it's too dark to see, if there is an end then it's too bright to see, hands
folding, unfolding, & you, Scheherazade!, milky goddess of recursion,
best DJ in the city, you spin records, spin heads, cross legs & cross
deserts, & always pause just moments before he

from *Poetry*

Double Helix

◊ ◊ ◊

~for Joseph J. Freeman and Richard P. Williams

~after Jacob Lawrence's Migration Series &
Isabel Wilkerson's *The Warmth of Other Suns*

~*I have walked through many lives,*
some of them my own,
   Stanley Kunitz, from "The Layers"

I.

At night, my father played piano & sang, his voice our raft on a quiet
lake, an island of gentleness & because gentleness is a choice, I know
something—, I have told you something essential about my father & the
history of black people in America. & because he looked at my mother
& me as if we were divine, brilliant, bright children of god & because
if gesture & spirit have weight, my father's equaled two thousand
blooming peonies, I have told you something about faith & the history
of black people in America.

**

Scientists are full of news these days: We are rotting fruit lain to
ground. In each breath we inhale thousands of humans collected on
the tongues of leaves, in the pink eyes of peonies, on the powdery backs
of pollen. Exhaled. With each draw, a millennium of history enters us

& we cannot control, can only harness whom or what we host. Our traumas, the bright blue mysticisms & burnt orange murmurs, our joys & muddled currencies are archived in genetic code.

★★

I am not of my father's blood but am of my father, which is also the history of black people in America.

★★

At my 6th birthday party, the parents drank martinis & sangria in white linen & silk as we played on the Slip-n-Slide while the desolate beast next door snarled & snapped through the fence, our jubilation magnifying his rage. He leapt & whipped into an ever-reddening frenzy. & because pain will out, & because hatred will out, & because my father sensed a shift in the air because he deeply believed my mother & me divine & the faithful have second sight, & because some Alabama-born malice had taught him a lesson to do with mercilessness, the way danger wets the wind, my father tore into the house emerging with a finger on a gun's trigger. He stood sentinel the rest of the day, gun slack on his thigh, squinting at the feverishness at the fence—as we leapt & shrieked & ate cake.

★★

This is what I was trying to explain to Avi when I sent him that book about the black migration from the American south. I was trying to say: we have cause to care for & track our wounds. To be anything other than enraged or dead is to be a success if black in America. To become a refuge, a safe harbor is to be a miracle if black in America.

★★

His ailing father listened quietly as Avi read aloud passages about the vicious hand of the south & burnings & bodies & swinging, cold chicken & packed trains, escapees casting towards a northern brink they could not fully understand, away from an ending they did. & because hatred will out & because we cannot control whom or what we host. &

because his father is a holocaust survivor, in a moment of lucidity, he asked sadly: "Son, why do you insist on reading me my story?"

★★

So we, the Jewish son and African daughter, mouths bursting & soured with flowers & fauna, rotting leaves & peonies & men banging at the midnight door, stood as an ecosystem of gas & fire, double helixes & light, the story of-, the choices of-, our fathers knotted between us. & because I wanted to touch his face as my own, & because I felt his skin shudder as my own, understood his father's stubble as my own & because what are we if not our brothers? & because there has always been binding & burning & escaping & enduring & because I know no better way to understand the history of humans than to tell you the story of my father's choice to be a raft on a lake, which, no matter what more you might be told, is the true story of black thought, black life, black people in America.

II.

At night my father sang & because in each breath we inhale thousands of humans on the powdery backs of pollen I have told you something essential & because he looked at my mother & me as if we were divine & because we are really only rotting fruit lain to ground & because if gesture & spirit have weight my father's equaled two thousand blooming peonies & at my 6th birthday party the beast next door snarled & snapped through the fence & because our mysticisms & currencies are archived genetic code & because hatred outs & because some malice had taught him mercilessness my father emerged from the house a gun's trigger & for the rest of the day stood as a safe harbor glaring feverishness down as we leapt & shrieked & then Avi read passages from the book & because we cannot control whom or what we host & because Avi's father is a holocaust survivor he asked "Son, why?" we stood as an ecosystem of double helixes Alabama & Holocaust knotted between us & because I wanted to touch his face as my own as if we were divine & because I felt his skin shudder as my own as if we were brilliant bright gods understood his father's stubble as my own & because what are we? & because there has always been binding &

escaping & enduring & because I am not of my father's blood but am of Avi's father I know no better way to explain the history of humans than to tell you at night my father played piano & sang his voice our raft on a quiet lake an island of gentleness & gentleness is a choice is a miracle in America.

from *The American Poetry Review*

Prelude

◊ ◊ ◊

Church or sermon, prayer or poem:
the failure of religious feeling is a form.

★

The failure of religious feeling is a form
of love that, though it could not survive

the cataclysmic joy of its inception,
nevertheless preserves its own sane something,

a space in which the grievers gather,
inviolate ice that the believers weather:

church or sermon, prayer or poem.

★

Finer and finer the meaningless distinctions:
theodicies, idiolects, books, books, books.

I need a space for unbelief to breathe.
I need a form for failure, since it is what I have.

from *The Sewanee Review*

Greenacre

◇   ◇   ◇

Gold flecked, dark-rimmed, opaque—

    like a toad's
        stolid unsurprise—

    the lake never blinks
        its hazel eye.

Man-made, five feet deep,
the exact square footage of a city block.

    Lakewater murk
        precipitates

    a glinting silt of algae,
        specks of soil,

minnows wheeling in meticulous formation,
the occasional water snake, angry, lost.

★   ★   ★

    Two pale figures in the lake,
        half-

submerged, viewed
    at an oblique angle.

At thirteen, I spent summer afternoons
reading in my treehouse, a simple platform

    without walls,
               like a hunting blind,

    a white painted birdhouse,
                  without walls

so no bird ever visited it.
Leaf-light dissolving in still water.

★   ★   ★

    Two pale figures in the lake,
                  half-

    seen, chest-deep
            in the mirroring

lakewater so they seemed all bare
shoulders, all lake-slick hair.

    Standing face to face—
               not embracing,

    but his upper arm
              entering the water,

half-concealed, at an angle that must have meant
he was touching her, beneath the surface.

    Unblinking, the lake
               giving nothing away,

    caring nothing
            for whatever shape

displaced it, unremembering,
uncurious. Did his arm bend,

and, if so,
　　　　　to what exact degree?

At what point
　　　　　did his hidden hand

intersect her half-submerged body?
The mirrored horizontal of the lake is where

　　　　　memory presses itself
　　　　　　　　　　against its limit,

　　　　　where hypothesis,
　　　　　　　　　　overeager,

rushes to fill the void, to extrapolate
from what is known. Because I knew them both:

　　　　　Ann Towson,
　　　　　　　　　　a year ahead of me,

　　　　　scrawny, skilled
　　　　　　　　　　at gymnastics, gold

badges emblazoning the sleeve of her green
leotard, her chest as flat as mine.

　　　　　And John Hollis—
　　　　　　　　　　the most popular boy

　　　　　in our class,
　　　　　　　　　　his tan forearms emerged

gold-dusted from rolled-up shirtsleeves.
He fronted a band called White Minority,

　　　　　which played at weekend parties
　　　　　　　　　　across the lake.

We shared a bus stop,
                a subdivision.

Once he spoke to me, the day I swapped
my glasses for contact lenses. *Something's different,*

       he said, eyes narrowing,
                  Yeah, no kidding!

       I snapped back,
                turning away. Later,

my best friend scolded me for rudeness.
Every day, boarding the school bus,

       John Hollis
             faced the bus driver

       with a bland smirk—
               What's up, black bitch?—

as if shoving her face down into a puddle
scummed with humiliation, which was always

       dripping from her,
              dripping down on her—

       she hunched her shoulders
               against it, narrow-eyed.

Every day, some kids smirked,
some kids hunched down, stolid, unblinking.

★   ★   ★

       Two pale figures in a lake,
              half-

witnessed, half-conjectured,
              a gold arm

like sunlight slanting down through lakewater.
But now a clinging, sedimentary skin

   outlines every contour:
                         what is known.

   No longer faceless shapes
                       displacing water,

the voids they once inhabited can't be lifted
dripping from the lake, rinsed clean

   enough for use.
                   What drips from them

   coats the lake
                   with a spreading greenness—

an opaque glaze lidding the open eye.

   from *New England Review*

Precatio simplex

◇   ◇   ◇

in memoriam Mavis Clarke (1936–2016)

Father, Holy Father, Prime Mover, God Almighty—
I have forgotten what to call you. Standing here
before the Pacific, I am tempted to call you

Poseidon, Green Neptune, someone I understand
more clearly than I have ever understood You.
The sea's slow tide, its almost-hidden riptide dragging

handfuls of foam under the surface, has no answers
for me. Sitting here on the crest of the sand dunes,
there is no one by my side. I have come here

alone because I remember what the nuns
taught me, that You do not appreciate a show
of these things. Not success with words, not

the lottery prize now worth millions, not the
usual things I am sure others request: I come now
to ask for something unthinkable for one like me.

Almost 3,000 miles away, near the brighter coast
of this godless country, my aunt's pain is
outpacing the cancer tearing her abdomen apart.

No amount of morphine can break it. I do not
come to ask You for miracles. I know better
than to ask for miracles. I know the world

is filled with miracles. No, no, not miracles.
Take her right now, Father. Here stands the cancer doctor
asking you to take his aunt because he cannot stomach

the idea of her in so much pain. Send me a small sign:
wheeling gulls, a sudden gust of wind, anything. Anything.
Just this once, Holy Father, don't let me down.

from *The Collagist*

DEAN YOUNG

Infinitives

◇   ◇   ◇

To pick up where Tomaž left off.
To pick off another oniony layer
down to the eye. To chomp.
To walk around all day buttoned wrong.
Light is coming from rocks, the little froggie
jumps even though he hasn't been wound up.
Here's where the wolves before us drank.
Too long, we have cock-blocked
day from mating with night.
The world is bluer than I thought.
To be stopped at security
for sobbing.
For something wrapped in foil.
For the soul finding its face.
For liquid.
I don't know if I forget
my dreams or life more.
To smudge out the features.
To endure blasted.
To drown in a raindrop.
To nestle in a dark place
inside the floodlight.
To contain multitudes.
To calm the hurt animal.
To be inside another.
To have been there all along.

from *The American Poetry Review*

Money Road

◊ ◊ ◊

On the way to Money,
  Mississippi, we see little
ghosts of snow, falling faint

  as words while we try to find
Robert Johnson's muddy
  maybe grave. Beside Little Zion,

along the highwayside, this stone
  keeps its offerings—Bud & Louisiana
Hot Sauce—the ground giving

  way beneath our feet.
The blues always dance
  cheek to cheek with a church—

Booker's Place back
  in Greenwood still standing,
its long green bar

  beautiful, Friendship Church just
a holler away. Shotgun,
  shotgun, shotgun—

★

rows of colored
  houses, as if the same can
of bright stain might cover the sins

of rotting wood, now
mostly tarpaper & graffiti
   holding McLaurin Street together—

RIP Boochie—the undead walk
   these streets seeking something
we take pictures of

   & soon flee. The hood
of a car yawns open
   in awe, men's heads

peer in its lion's mouth
   seeking their share. FOR SALE:
Squash & Snap Beans. The midden

   of oyster shells behind Lusco's—
the tiny O of a bullethole
   in Booker's plate-glass window.

★

Even the Salvation
   Army Thrift Store
closed, bars over

   every door.
We're on our way again,
   away, along the Money

Road, past grand houses
   & porte cochères set back
from the lane, over the bridge

   to find markers of what's
no more there—even the underpass
   bears a name. It's all

too grave—the fake
  sharecropper homes
of Tallahatchie Flats rented out

  along the road, staged bottle trees
chasing away nothing, the new outhouse
  whose crescent door foreign tourists

                    ★

pay extra for. Cotton planted
  in strict rows
for show. A quiet

  snow globe of pain
I want to shake.
  While the flakes fall

like ash we race
  the train to reach the place
Emmett Till last

  whistled or smiled
or did nothing.
  Money more

a crossroads
  than the crossroads be—
its gnarled tree—the Bryant Store

  facing the tracks, now turnt
the color of earth, tumbling down
  slow as the snow, white

                    ★

& insistent as the woman
  who sent word
of the uppity boy, her men

who yanked you out
your uncle's home
  into the yard, into oblivion—

into this store abutting
  the MONEY GIN CO.
whose sign, worn away,

  now reads UN
or SIN, I swear—
  whose giant gin fans,

like those lashed & anchored
  to your beaten body,
still turn. Shot, dumped,

  dredged, your face not even
a mask—a marred,
  unspared, sightless stump—

★

all your mother insists
  we must see to know
What they did

  to my baby. The true
Tallahatchie twisting
  south, the Delta

Death's second cousin
  once removed. You down
for only the summer, to leave

  the stifling city where later
you will be waked,
  displayed, defiant,

a dark glass.
  There are things
that cannot be seen

  but must be. Buried
barely, this place
  no one can keep—

                    ★

Yet how to kill
  a ghost? The fog
of our outdoor talk—

  we breathe,
we grieve, we drink
  our tidy drinks. I think

now winter will out—
  the snow bless
& kiss

  this cursed earth.
Or is it cussed? I don't
  yet know. Let the cold keep

still your bones.

        from *The New Yorker*

Poem for Vows

◊   ◊   ◊

(for E. and G.)

Hello beautiful talented
dark semi-optimists of June,
from far off I send my hopes
Brooklyn is sunny, and the ghost
of Whitman who loved everyone
is there to see you say what
can never be said, something like
partly I promise my whole life
to try to figure out what it means
to stand facing you under a tree,
and partly no matter how angry
I get I will always remember
we met before we were born,
it was in a village, someone
had just cast a spell, it was
in the park, snow everywhere,
we were slipping and laughing,
at last we knew the green secret,
we were sea turtles swimming
a long time together without
needing to breathe, we were
two hungry owls silently
hunting night, our terrible claws,
I don't want to sound like I know,
I'm just one who worries all night
about people in a lab watching
a storm in a glass terrarium

perform lethal ubiquity,
tiny black clouds make the final
ideogram above miniature lands
exactly resembling ours, what is
happening happens again,
they cannot stop it, they take off
their white coats, go outside,
look up and wonder, only we
who promise everything despite
everything can tell them
the solution, only we know.

from Poem-a-Day

CONTRIBUTORS' NOTES AND COMMENTS

DAN ALBERGOTTI was born in Orangeburg, South Carolina, in 1964. He is the author of *The Boatloads* (BOA Editions, 2008) and *Millennial Teeth* (Southern Illinois University Press, 2014), as well as a limited-edition chapbook, *The Use of the World* (Unicorn Press, 2013). He holds an MFA in poetry from UNC Greensboro and is a professor of English at Coastal Carolina University.

Albergotti writes: "The Police Policy Studies Council's form 'Weapons Discharge Report' can be found online. When I began to read it, I imagined the killers of Michael Brown, of Tamir Rice, of Walter Scott (and of many others) sitting at precinct desks, checking boxes. I felt ill. Most of my poem of the same title is made up of language adopted, or adapted, from the PPSC form.

"I am writing this comment on the day of Donald J. Trump's inauguration as President of the United States: January 20, 2017. Within hours of his swearing in, the WhiteHouse.gov page on civil rights has been removed, and one titled 'Standing Up for Our Law Enforcement Community' has been added."

JOHN ASHBERY was born in Rochester, New York, in 1927. His most recent collection of poems is *Commotion of the Birds* (Ecco/HarperCollins, 2016). A two-volume set of his collected translations from the French (prose and poetry) was published in 2014 by Farrar, Straus and Giroux. Active in various areas of the arts throughout his career, he has served as executive editor of *Art News* and as art critic for *New York* magazine and *Newsweek*; he exhibits his collages at Tibor de Nagy Gallery (New York). He has received a Pulitzer Prize, two Guggenheim Fellowships, a MacArthur Fellowship, and recently the Medal for Distinguished Contribution to American Letters from the National Book Foundation (2011) and a National Humanities Medal, presented by

President Obama at the White House (2012). He was the guest editor of *The Best American Poetry 1988*, the first volume in this series.

MARY JO BANG was born in 1946 in Waynesville, Missouri, and grew up in Ferguson, Missouri. She is the author of seven books of poems: *Apology for Want* (UPNE, 1997), winner of the Bakeless Prize; *Louise in Love* (Grove Press Poetry, 2001); *The Downstream Extremity of the Isle of Swans* (University of Georgia Press, 2001); *The Eye Like a Strange Balloon* (Grove, 2004); *Elegy* (Graywolf Press, 2007), winner of the National Book Critics Circle Award; *The Bride of E* (Graywolf, 2009), and *The Last Two Seconds* (Graywolf, 2015). Her translation of Dante's *Inferno*, with illustrations by Henrik Drescher, was published by Graywolf in 2012. She teaches English and creative writing at Washington University in St. Louis.

Of "Admission," Bang writes: "The title of the poem gestures to Walter Gropius's 'Bauhaus Manifesto and Program' (1919), which states, under the section 'Admission,' that: 'Any person of good repute, without regard to age or sex, whose previous education is deemed adequate by the Council of Masters, will be admitted [to the program], as far as space permits.' It equally gestures to the fact that because Gropius believed women could think only in two dimensions, unlike men, whom he believed could think in three, women were initially admitted only to the weaving workshop. The poem also has in mind a 1926 black-and-white photograph, *Walter and Ilse Gropius's Dressing Room*, taken by Lucia Moholy. Moholy took most of the iconic photographs of the Bauhaus buildings in Dessau and of the products produced in the workshops. The story of Gropius's later use of her images in books without attributing them to her, and her legal efforts to have the negatives returned to her, is the subject of an article she published in 1983 in *The British Journal of Photography*, 130 (7.1), pp. 6–8, 18. For three months in the spring of 2015, during a fellowship at the American Academy in Berlin, I spent many hours at the Bauhaus-Archiv, reading Moholy's letters and journals and looking at her photographs.

"The poem contains an echo of two Botticelli paintings: *Birth of Venus* (where a nude Venus stands on a half shell) and *Primavera* (also known as *Allegory of Spring*). In *Primavera*, a fully dressed Madonna-like Venus stands slightly off center, framed by an arch, beneath a blindfolded cupid; stage right, Mars pokes at a raincloud with a staff and the Three Graces, each wrapped in diaphanous fabric, meet in the middle of a shared dance step and interlace fingers; stage left, Chloris matures before our eyes into a full-grown Flora, despite a blue-green Zephyrus's best efforts to hold her back."

DAVID BARBER is the author of two collections of poems published by Northwestern University Press: *Wonder Cabinet* (2006) and *The Spirit Level* (1995), which received the Terrence Des Prez Prize from Tri-Quarterly Books. "On a Shaker Admonition" is included in his recently completed collection, *Secret History*. Born in Los Angeles and raised in Pasadena, he was educated at the University of California, Santa Cruz and Stanford University before putting down roots in the environs of Boston. He is the poetry editor of *The Atlantic* and currently teaches in the Harvard Writing Program.

Of "On a Shaker Admonition," Barber writes: "I've long had a penchant for winkling poems out of all manner of marginalia and ephemera, oftentimes in an effort to breathe a flicker of new life into long-gone or far-flung lexicons and vernaculars. I've been known to say, only half in jest at best, that this one or that one was 'ripped from the footnotes.' This is certainly the way 'On a Shaker Admonition' came about. In the Dover revised edition of Edward Deming Andrews's landmark 1953 book, *The People Called Shakers*, the main appendix contains the complete text of Millennial Laws of 1821 drawn up by the Shaker settlement in New Lebanon, New York. As Andrews explains, 'The socalled Millennial Laws of the Shakers, never printed nor even widely circulated in written form, implemented the doctrines of the order, and thus, in effect, greatly illuminate not only its government but the intimate habits and customs of the people.' To which I might add, they make for yeasty reading for anyone with more than a passing interest in erstwhile utopias and other lost worlds. The 'admonition' that gave rise to the poem is found in Part III: Concerning Temporal Economy, Section V: Orders concerning Locks & Keys (Andrews, p. 283, Dover ed. 1963)."

DAN BEACHY-QUICK was born in Chicago in 1973, and currently directs the MFA Program in Creative Writing at Colorado State University in Fort Collins, Colorado, where he lives with his wife and two daughters. He is a poet and essayist, whose most recent books include *gentlessness* (Tupelo Press, 2015), a chapbook of poetry, *Shields & Shards & Stitches & Songs* (Omnidawn, 2015), and a study of John Keats, *A Brighter Word Than Bright: Keats at Work* (Iowa University Press, Muse Series, 2013). His work has been supported by the Lannan Foundation, the Monfort Professorship at CSU, and the Guggenheim Foundation.

Beachy-Quick writes: "For the past few years, I've been writing poems that take their initial impulse to fill a page by thinking toward a poet whose work has been important to me—a set of dedications that are also expressions of gratitude. 'Apophatic' hopes to think of and feel toward Peter Gizzi, whose selected poems, *In Defense of Nothing*, opens up that strange ground (in its title alone, and then poem by poem) in which what exists must recognize itself first by positing what doesn't—*something* depends so much on *nothing*. This sense of knowledge obtained through negation, or realization gained only through absence, feels to me one of the cruxes of poetic experience. In the poem, the hidden figure of that work is Oedipus, foot made lame as a baby by the ankle being pierced with a tether, who, before the horror of his deeds was revealed to him, was renowned for that abundant intelligence that answered the Sphinx's riddle with the answer he himself embodied: 'a man.' But Oedipus is also that figure who comes to see that knowing the answer answers very little. And when he sees that awful fact fully, he blinds himself. I've come to think of his blindness as the manifestation of the nothingness that weaves and wends its way through the world entire, some fundamental requirement stitched through existence that keeps life uncertain, unstable, troubled by source, doubtful of its own nature. Dreary things to say, I know. But the apophatic also points always toward its opposite, and so that *nothing* also whispers to us of realization, illumination, understanding, and love, and maybe even points us the way there."

BRUCE BOND was born in 1954 in Pasadena, California. He is the author of sixteen books, including *Immanent Distance: Poetry and the Metaphysics of the Near at Hand* (University of Michigan Press, 2015), *For the Lost Cathedral* (LSU Press, 2015), *The Other Sky* (Etruscan Press, 2015), *Black Anthem* (Tampa Review Prize, University of Tampa Press, 2016), and *Gold Bee* (Crab Orchard Series in Poetry, Southern Illinois University Press, 2016). Three of his books are forthcoming: *Blackout Starlight: New and Selected Poems 1997–2015* (E. Phillabaum Award, LSU Press), *Sacrum* (Four Way Books), and *Dear Reader* (Free Verse Editions, Parlor Press). He is regents professor at University of North Texas.

Bond writes: " 'Homage to a Painter of Small Things' explores the work of the painter Matthew Cornell, how, beyond the virtuosity, he brings to his precision a sense of yearning and warmth, of worlds in transition, on the verge of a connection to something we do not understand. Sure, there is the solitude of a Hopper there, but with greater sublimity, as reflected in the quality of emerging light, the tender proximity of private spaces, and the ache of small things seen precisely, made transcendent less by romantic distortion than by an honoring of the given mystery of things. Matthew once said that he, in his painting, is ever looking for the home he never had. He the kid who lived in a different town each year or two. And yes, there is something so singular about being that boy, and something broadly human in Matthew's search for him in the child he never was. Long ago, the future was enormous. Still is."

JOHN BREHM was born in Lincoln, Nebraska, in 1955 and educated at the University of Nebraska and Cornell University. He is the author of two books of poems from University of Wisconsin Press, *Sea of Faith* (2004) and *Help Is on the Way* (2012); the editor of *The Poetry of Impermanence, Mindfulness, and Joy*; and the associate editor of *The Oxford Book of American Poetry*. Brehm lives in Portland, Oregon, where he teaches for the Literary Arts and Mountain Writers Series. He also teaches for the Lighthouse Writers Workshop in Denver, Colorado.

Brehm writes: "I began 'Intrigue in the Trees' not long after the Four-Mile Canyon fire just outside of Boulder, Colorado. Severe drought conditions coupled with high winds, high heat, and low humidity whipped the fire right to the edge of the neighborhood where I was living at the time. The fire was my second experience of an extreme weather event—I'd been caught in a flash flood in Guadalajara several years before—and it occurred to me that perhaps we had worn out our welcome on the planet, that the earth, in increasingly violent acts of self-protection, was trying to get rid of us. I'd also been reading about animal intelligence, particularly in crows, and thinking about the arrogance of assuming that only we possess consciousness—an instance of just the sort of human exceptionalism that has helped create our current crisis. (Even trees, we now know, are capable of communicating with each other—to warn of insect attacks, for instance.) And I was feeling our indebtedness to animals for all the ways they help us understand ourselves—the many creaturely metaphors that serve as mirrors for our behavior and inner states. Such were my preoccupations at the time. Seeing crows gathering ominously in a tree while walking to the Laughing Goat Coffee House catalyzed these concerns into a poem."

JERICHO BROWN has received a Whiting Writers' Award and fellowships from the John Simon Guggenheim Foundation, the Radcliffe Institute for Advanced Study at Harvard University, and the National Endowment for the Arts. His first book, *Please* (New Issues Poetry & Prose, 2008), won the American Book Award, and his second book, *The New Testament* (Copper Canyon Press, 2014), won the Anisfield-Wolf Book Award and was named one of the best of the year by *Library Journal*, *Coldfront*, and the Academy of American Poets. He is an associate professor of English and creative writing at Emory University. He was born in Shreveport, Louisiana.

Of "Bullet Points," Brown writes: "Fear of unwarranted and unexplainable murder by police is as individual and personal as it is political. Please Google: Sandra Bland of Texas, Jesus Huerta of North Carolina, and Victor White III of Louisiana."

As a poet with an MFA in fiction, NICKOLE BROWN has a strong leaning toward hybrid work, an interest reflected in her two books. *Fanny Says*, published by BOA Editions in 2015, is a biography-in-poems about her bawdy, tough-as-new-rope grandmother, and *Sister*, her debut collection published by Red Hen Press in 2007, is a novel-in-poems. Though much of her childhood was spent in Deerfield Beach, Florida, Nickole was born in Louisville and considers herself a Kentucky native. She studied at Oxford University as an English Speaking Union Scholar, was an editorial assistant for the late Hunter S. Thompson, and received her MFA from Vermont College of Fine Arts. For ten years, Nickole worked at the independent literary press Sarabande Books, and she was a publicity consultant for Arktoi Books and the Palm Beach Poetry Festival. She has received grants from the National Endowment for the Arts, the Kentucky Foundation for Women, and the Kentucky Arts Council. She has taught creative writing at the University of Louisville, Bellarmine University, and for four years was an assistant professor at University of Arkansas at Little Rock. She has also been on the faculty of the low-residency MFA program at Murray State, the Sewanee Young Writers Conference, the Writing Workshops in Greece, and the Sewanee School of Letters MFA program. She is the editor for the Marie Alexander Poetry Series at White Pine Press and lives with her wife, poet Jessica Jacobs, in Asheville, North Carolina.

Of "The Dead," Brown writes: "As early as second grade, I wanted to know my family's ancestry. I came home with the word 'ancestor' rolling around in my mouth after hearing friends bragging about all the green and exotic lands from which their families came. I was excited, I had to know, so I came home to my grandmother and begged, *Fanny*, *please, can't you tell me where we're from?* Right quick, she squinted her right eye like she was sighting a rifle and said, *Child, don't you worry your pretty little head 'bout that. We weren't nothing but a bunch of chicken thieves.* What I thought she meant by this was *trash,* as in *white.* Because always, she'd joke: *Girl, you was born trash, and you'll die trash.* We'd laugh, and so she'd say it again: *Yep, you trash alright. That's how you were born, that's how you'll die.* But now that I'm grown and have heard the old stories, I realize behind her jokes was a long line of people she'd just as soon we forget altogether, and along with them, their deep history of poverty, ignorance, and ache. No one ever spoke of the dead in her house, and she certainly didn't keep old photos. We dealt with tragedy in my family by putting it behind us—*Blow up, blow out, blow over,* Fanny would say, by which she meant, *Get over it, forget the past.* So when my beloved cousin died tragically and too young, I saw the depths of her willed amnesia—as always, she was fussing at me for wearing black clothing, and when I told her why I was dressed the way I was—that I was on my way to his funeral—she genuinely seemed to have forgotten. This perhaps is why I have the opposite problem—like a lot of writers, I don't want to forget one single scrap. My wife calls me 'a real nostalgia machine' . . . ridiculously, I try to keep time still by stitching even small moments to the page, and more than once, I dare the dead to come, to sit up beside me and speak again, whispering their names."

CYRUS CASSELLS was born in 1957 in Delaware. He is a professor of English at Texas State University; this year marks the thirtieth anniversary of his teaching career, which began in Boston. He has published four books with Copper Canyon Press: *Soul Make a Path through Shouting* (1994), *Beautiful Signor* (1997), *More Than Peace and Cypresses* (2004), and *The Crossed-Out Swastika* (2012). His first book, *The Mud Actor,* was a 1982 National Poetry Series winner, published by Henry Holt and then reprinted in Carnegie Mellon's Classic Contemporary Series. His sixth volume, *The Gospel According to Wild Indigo,* is forthcoming in the spring of 2018 from Southern Illinois University Press. Cassells has won a Lannan Literary Award, a Lambda Literary Award, the Poetry Society of America's William Carlos Williams Award, and two National Endowment for the Arts grants.

Of "Elegy with a Gold Cradle," Cassells writes: "For my part, crafting an elegy often entails a delayed revelation, an attempt to convey what was unexpressed or even unsayable while the lost one was alive. It took nearly a decade for me to write this poem describing what it felt like to scatter my mother's ashes on Maui, a place she'd never been but dreamt of going all of her life: One phenomenon I recall, in the days following my mother's death from leukemia, was the powerful sense of our earliest bond: finding the antique cradle seemed a profound emblem of a sudden, inspiriting return to my origins as her son."

ISAAC CATES was born to Texan parents in Würzburg, Germany, in 1971. He teaches in the English department at the University of Vermont. Some of his comics appeared online last year in *Okey-Panky*. He writes scholarly criticism about both comics and poetry. He also edits and publishes an all-ages comics anthology called *Cartozia Tales*.

Of "Fidelity and the Dead Singer," Cates writes: "I was never very close friends with the poet Michael Donaghy—we were friendly acquaintances—but I heard him read his amazing poems enough times that when I reopen his books now, if I strain, I can almost hear some of them in his voice. He died unexpectedly of a sudden brain hemorrhage, aged only fifty, leaving a silent void where a poet should still have been. It hit me surprisingly hard, as have the losses of other poets I was closer to, like Rachel Wetzsteon, Craig Arnold, and Brett Foster. I wish I could hear them, like ghostly voices, instead of only reading their words. But the words are something.

"And about that catalog of records: they're a little bit of fiction. My mother's collection of 45s didn't actually include any Roy Head and the Traits, though it could have. And I never owned any Howlin' Wolf on vinyl. I did have a copy of the Beatles' compilation LP *Hey Jude* (which has now vanished into *Past Masters*), though in my callow vinyl youth I overplayed *Reel Music* even more. It's funny to think what a narrow demographic played their parents' Beatles LPs and heard that needle hiss. Now the silence around the songs doesn't have that personal quality."

ALLISON COBB is the author of *Born Two* (Chax Press, 2004), *Green-Wood* (Factory School, 2010), *Plastic: an autobiography* (Essay Press EP series, 2015), and *After We All Died* (Ahsahta Press, 2016), which was a finalist for the National Poetry Series. She was born in 1971 in Los Alamos, New Mexico, where the first atomic bombs were made. She performs her poems as part of a collaboration called *Suspended Moment* with visual artist Yukiyo Kawano, a third-generation atomic bomb survivor from Hiroshima. Cobb works for the Environmental Defense Fund and lives in Portland, Oregon, where she co-curates The Switch reading, art, and performance series.

Cobb writes: " 'I Forgive You' is the opening poem of my book *After We All Died*. I wrote the book because I kept hearing friends and colleagues talk about the Anthropocene—how the current extinction and climate crises foreshadow coming catastrophes, and the potential end of the human species. I thought, what if the end has *already happened*, as many climate scientists suggest? What would it be like to write from the point of view of living after the end? The book, and this poem, were the result."

LEONARD COHEN, the Jewish-Canadian singer, songwriter, poet, novelist, and painter, died in 2016. Born in the Westmount area of Montreal in 1934, brought up as an orthodox Jew, Cohen was educated at McGill University, where he studied with Irving Layton and Louis Dudek. A member of the "Montreal School of Poets," he published his first book of poems, *Let Us Compare Mythologies*, at the age of twenty-two. In the mid-1960s, Cohen moved to the United States to pursue a recording career and was discovered by renowned producer and scout John Hammond. Over a nearly fifty-year solo career, Cohen recorded fourteen albums, writing some of the most revered songs in popular music, including "Hallelujah," "Suzanne," "Chelsea Hotel," "Bird on the Wire," and "I'm Your Man." Judy Collins's cover of "Suzanne" was a huge hit. Cohen continued to observe the Sabbath even when on tour and performed for Israeli troops during the Yom Kippur War.

Cohen's music was marked by his distinctive baritone voice and a melancholy tempered by wit, candor, and invention. In a 2016 interview with *The New Yorker*, Bob Dylan said that Cohen's "gift of genius is his connection to the music of the spheres," while Australian songwriter Nick Cave wrote that Cohen was "the greatest songwriter of them all. Utterly unique and impossible to imitate." Cohen's thirteen books of poems include *Flowers for Hitler*, *Book of Mercy*, and *Book of Longing*. He wrote two novels, *The Favorite Game* and *Beautiful Losers*. He was a Companion of the Order of Canada, the nation's highest civilian honor, and was inducted into both the Canadian Music Hall of Fame and the Canadian Songwriters Hall of Fame, as well as the Rock and Roll Hall of Fame. With humor and lyricism, his work explored the uncertainties of faith, religion, sexuality, and politics, and has had a profound influence on generations of musicians and writers. "People are doing their courting, people are finding their wives, people are making babies, people are washing their dishes, people are getting through the day, with songs that we may find insignificant," he observed. "But their significance is affirmed by others. There's always someone affirming the significance of a song by taking a woman into his arms or by getting through the night. That's what dignifies the song. Songs don't dignify human activity. Human activity dignifies the song."

David Remnick concludes his 2016 profile of Cohen by quoting the writer. "I know there's a spiritual aspect to everybody's life, whether they want to cop to it or not," Cohen said. "It's there, you can feel it in people—there's some recognition that there is a reality that they cannot penetrate but which influences their mood and activity. So that's operating. That activity at certain points of your day or night insists on a certain kind of response. Sometimes it's just like: 'You are losing too much weight, Leonard. You're dying, but you don't have to coöperate enthusiastically with the process.' Force yourself to have a sandwich.

"What I mean to say is that you hear the *Bat Kol*." The divine voice. "You hear this other deep reality singing to you all the time, and much of the time you can't decipher it. Even when I was healthy, I was sensitive to the process. At this stage of the game, I hear it saying, 'Leonard, just get on with the things you have to do.' It's very compassionate at this stage. More than at any time of my life, I no longer have that voice that says, 'You're fucking up.' That's a tremendous blessing, really."

MICHAEL COLLIER was born in Phoenix, Arizona, in 1953. His two most recent collections of poetry are *An Individual History* (W. W. Norton, 2012) and *My Bishop and Other Poems*. He teaches at the University of Maryland and is the director of the Bread Loaf Writers' Conferences.

Of "A Wild Tom Turkey," Collier writes: "Part of the year I live in the country on a three-mile-long paved town road that connects two much longer state roads. Other than the manure spreaders, silage and hay trucks, livestock trailers, tractors, harvesters, pickups of all sizes and makes, a neighbor loading his flatbed with his backhoe and Bobcat, and the back-and-forth traffic of what passes for morning and evening rush hour, it's a mostly quiet place, agriculturally bucolic. When it's quiet, and sometimes when it's not, I can hear creatures that live in the woods and fields around me. Most of the time when I hear them they seem to be in distress of one kind or another. Mating is a very common distress, so is being hunted and killed or trapped. A hummingbird once got caught behind plastic sheeting I had stapled over a partially broken garage window. The high pitch of its panicking voice, combined with an even more rapid than usual oscillation of its wings as well as the creepy distortion of its form behind the plastic, frightened me into an initial paralysis, until I freed the bird by ripping away the sheeting. A fox one evening last summer after the sun had gone down stood in the grass between our vegetable garden and the house and at consistent intervals cried and screamed with the heat of a wheel bearing burning up. I saw it from an upstairs window and wondered not only why it was making that sound but also what it was watching because its head was turned in a backward-looking, fixed glance. There are, of course, coyotes, near and far, that sound like cowards trying to scare each other. In an example of interspecies cooperation, an opossum sleeps on a crate in the garage next to where our adopted cat sleeps on a padded box. The sound the opossum makes is the drag of its hairless tail, like a heavy cable, over the floor as it slinks away when I appear. What else? On one occasion a cow, escaped from a neighbor's dairy farm, stood in the driveway, swinging its head back and forth in acknowledgment of its predicament, or maybe like the swishing of its tail, just trying to swoosh away the flies on its ears. Now and then, it lifted its head and let out a mournful bellow that echoed across the valley. Birds, lots of birds screeching, singing, hammering, but not so many in distress, except when a robin chick fell out of its nest, tucked in a house eave, and was immediately surrounded by a mob of squawking adults. I had no idea there were so many robins living so close that would respond to such an emergency. And then there are the wild turkeys but that's what 'A Wild Tom Turkey' is about, so I'll leave it there."

BILLY COLLINS was born in the French Hospital in New York City in 1941. He was an undergraduate at Holy Cross College and received his PhD from the University of California, Riverside. His books of poetry include *The Rain in Portugal* (Random House, 2016), *Aimless Love: New and Selected Poems* (Random House, 2013), *Horoscopes for the Dead* (Random House, 2011), *Ballistics* (Random House, 2008), *The Trouble with Poetry and Other Poems* (Random House, 2005), a collection of haiku titled *She Was Just Seventeen* (Modern Haiku Press, 2006), *Nine Horses* (Random House, 2002), *Sailing Alone Around the Room: New and Selected Poems* (Random House, 2001), *Picnic, Lightning* (University of Pittsburgh Press, 1998), *The Art of Drowning* (University of Pittsburgh Press, 1995), and *Questions About Angels* (William Morrow, 1991), which was selected for the National Poetry Series by Edward Hirsch and reprinted by the University of Pittsburgh Press in 1999. He is the editor of *Poetry 180: A Turning Back to Poetry* (Random House, 2003) and *180 More: Extraordinary Poems for Every Day* (Random House, 2005). He is a former distinguished professor of English at Lehman College (City University of New York) and a distinguished fellow of the Winter Park Institute of Rollins College. A frequent contributor and former guest editor of *The Best American Poetry* series (2006), he was appointed United States Poet Laureate 2001–2003 and served as New York State Poet 2004–2006. He also edited *Bright Wings: An Illustrated Anthology of Poems About Birds* illustrated by David Sibley (Columbia University Press, 2010). He was recently inducted into the American Academy of Arts and Letters.

Of "The Present," Collins writes: "As is the case with time itself, we choose to picture the present in many ways. How do you pin down something that is both apparent (we are always in it) and elusive (where did it go?). We may think of it as a relentless series of nanoseconds, which are zipping by far too rapidly to be grasped. But that's not the way we actually experience the existence of the present. Experiments in human attention show that we *feel* the present as a moment lasting about 2.5 seconds, which is—come to think of it—about as long as it takes to read a line in a poem. And that's not a bad way to think of a poem: as a series of 'presents,' one after another tumbling down the page. My poem, which is simply a meditation on its title, pokes a little fun at the common advice to 'live in the present' as if it were a room where you could pull up a chair and have a look around. What the poem suggests is that there's no here here."

CARL DENNIS was born in St. Louis in 1939. He lives in Buffalo, where for many years he taught in the English department of the State University of New York. Among his most recent books, all published by Penguin, are *New and Selected Poems 1974–2004* (2004), *Callings* (2010), and *Another Reason* (2014). "Two Lives" is scheduled to appear in a new book, *Night School*, that Penguin will be publishing in spring 2018.

Dennis writes: "In 'Two Lives' I wanted to give flesh to the notion that the life we live is only one of many we might have lived had any single fact of our history been altered. It seemed to me that the best way to make this notion worth considering seriously was to imagine the ghostly alternative abutting on the actual, so that the two seem like part of a single story, one in which the unlived life has a chance to enlarge the lived one. The poem is based on the faith that the more fully we can imagine other lives for ourselves the more fully we can inhabit the life we have."

CLAUDIA EMERSON (1957–2014) was born and raised in Chatham, Virginia. She received a BA in English from the University of Virginia and an MFA in creative writing from the University of North Carolina, Greensboro. She received fellowships from the Library of Congress, the Virginia Commission for the Arts, and the National Endowment for the Arts. Her third collection of poems, *Late Wife*, was awarded the Pulitzer Prize in 2006, and in 2008 she was appointed poet laureate of Virginia. Emerson was poetry editor for *The Greensboro Review* and a contributing editor for *Shenandoah*. She taught at Washington and Lee University, Randolph-Macon Women's College, the University of Mary Washington, and Virginia Commonwealth University. Emerson published six poetry collections with LSU Press, including *Late Wife*, *Secure the Shadow*, *The Opposite House*, and *Impossible Bottle*.

DAVID FEINSTEIN was born in Chapel Hill, North Carolina, in 1982. He is the author of the chapbooks *Woods Porn: The Adventures of Little Walter* (No Dear/Small Anchor Press, 2014) and *Tarantula* (Factory Hollow Press, 2016). He lives in Amherst, Massachusetts, where he teaches writing and is a member of the Connecticut River Valley Poets Theatre.

Of "Kaddish," Feinstein writes: "The Mourner's Kaddish is a hymn of praise and remembrance recited near the end of the Jewish prayer service. I have a weird relationship with the Hebrew language; because I only learned it in order to recite certain prayers (including the Kaddish) I can pronounce most words without having any idea what they mean. Mumbling in synagogue as a kid was probably one of my earliest encounters with the mysteries of language—of sensing that words were objects originating from beyond to temporarily inhabit the body. I think poems are in search of a similarly strange and elusive purity of sound; they are forever 'en route,' in the words of Paul Celan, 'heading towards something open, inhabitable, an approachable you, perhaps an approachable reality.'

"The poem 'Kaddish' is dedicated to all people of the book, for whom the book is holy and never complete, and who have prayed their names be inscribed in the book of life. It is to my grandparents Ida Feinstein, Sabina and Sam Kowlowitz, and to all the beloved both named and unnamed, who I want to live and die with and who will never die, in that constant song that is not a song at all but is solely our singing."

CAROLYN FORCHÉ is the author of four books of poetry, most recently *Blue Hour*, and has edited two volumes of poetry: *Against Forgetting: Twentieth Century Poetry of Witness* and, with Duncan Wu, *Poetry of Wit-*

ness: The Tradition in English, 1500–2001. She has translated the poetry of Claribel Alegría, Mahmoud Darwish, and Robert Desnos, and her own work has been translated into more than twenty languages. She has received many fellowships and awards, including the Edita and Ira Morris Hiroshima Foundation Award for Peace and Culture (Stockholm) and, recently, the Windham Campbell Prize in Literature from Yale University. She is university professor at Georgetown University, where she serves as director of the Lannan Center for Poetics and Social Practice. Her forthcoming works include a book of poetry, *In the Lateness of the World*, and a memoir, *What You Have Heard Is True.*

Forché writes: "For the past seven summers, I have lived on two islands in the Aegean: Serifos in the Cyclades and Thasos, near the island of Lesvos, the landing place for many refugees attempting to reach Europe. 'The Boatman' is a poem written in the aftermath of those summers, but it is a record of conversations with one particular refugee from Homs, Syria, who is now driving a taxi in a city in the upper Midwest of the United States. This is his story, which he asked me to tell, and somehow it came to the page intact."

VIEVEE FRANCIS was born in San Angelo, Texas, in 1963. She is the author of *Forest Primeval* (Northwestern University Press, 2016), which won the Kingsley Tufts Poetry Award, *Horse in the Dark* (Northwestern University Press, 2012), and *Blue-Tail Fly* (Wayne State University Press, 2006). Her work has appeared or will soon appear in *Smartish Pace, The Common, Waxwing, The Best American Poetry* (2010 and 2014), and *Angles of Ascent: A Norton Anthology of African American Poetry.* She recently received the 2016 Hurston/Wright Legacy Award. An associate editor for *Callaloo*, she is on the faculty of the Pacific University low-residency MFA program and is an associate professor of English (creative writing) at Dartmouth College.

Of "Given to These Proclivities, By God," Francis writes: "In an oh so conventional world, a world insistent upon its rightness, where *goodness* becomes a skinny stretch of blinding road that few may walk without falling or failing, what is a poet with no inclination toward toeing the straight and narrow to do? So fine. If a sinner is what I'm called, then a sinner I'll be. Now what? Whatever it is I am I got there honestly. I'm here honestly. This is a facetious ditty meant to push back against uninterrogated ideas of personal 'uplift' and 'ascension.' Mad woman. Bad woman. Woman refusing to follow patriarchal orders or cultural constraints. I've been given my walking papers and I still trip up. Poor puss. I don't write poems that assume the hero wins, hope, or even survival. Instead, I am asking why can't we admit failure or the loss of hope or the inevitability of death, and by considering it perhaps we will indeed find a way to handle such realities. Further, who's to say what 'failure' is? I resent the positivism that passes for insight, the fear of anything that upsets the convenience and comfort of the social order. While on a trail in western North Carolina I saw a wall of early rhododendrons and my first thought was how lovely it would be to feel that cascade against my naked skin. I am given to the sensual world. To its delights as much as the world would have me meet its damage. I've fallen, to put it in pedestrian terms. I trip. I skip and attempt a quicker pace then down I go. The stairwell. Any given slope. My ankles are weak. My ability to resist stretching my limits, forcing my weight against a closed door, moving past the boundaries, even weaker. So I will fall again, God help me. And perhaps at some point I'll stop frustrating those giving me the side-eye (or a push) and stay down. Let the ancient roots of some mountain grapevine wrap round me like a blanket or rest upon me like an incubus."

AMY GERSTLER was born in 1956 in San Diego, California. She teaches at the University of California, Irvine. Her most recent books of poems are *Scattered at Sea* (Penguin, 2015) and *Dearest Creature* (Penguin, 2009). She was the guest editor of *The Best American Poetry 2010*.

Of "Dead Butterfly," Gerstler writes: "When I found an intact but lifeless orange and black butterfly lying on the floor of my office, I wondered whether this was a 'good sign' or a 'bad' one. That's a pretty selfish and reductive reaction, I admit. Surely, being dead was far from an excellent development for the poor butterfly. And periodically I have to remind myself that not everything is a portent, and that many events are neither entirely good nor entirely bad. I tried to do some research, but as there are several kinds of similar-looking butterflies, and I'm a terrible lepidopterist, I couldn't figure out whether this one was a true monarch or not. I started thinking about the butterfly as royalty, anyway, due to the word 'monarch.' Hoping to try to write about it, I kept the butterfly for almost a month, until I began to feel a bit morbid, and guilty, for not taking its leaflike body outside to rejoin nature. And I feared by that point that it was going to turn to dust any minute, anyway. I hadn't planned for my dead father to enter the poem, but he did, after a few drafts. Maybe that happened when I remembered that according to Japanese tradition, butterflies may 'carry the souls of the dead or represent the souls of the dead. . . .' Or so I read long ago in a book, and more recently, on the Internet. The poem was also inspired by my deep admiration for Henri Cole's poem 'Dead Wren.' "

REGINALD GIBBONS was born in Houston in 1947, attended public schools, then Princeton University (BA in Spanish and Portuguese) and Stanford University (MA in English and creative writing; PhD in comparative literature). He was the editor of *TriQuarterly* magazine from 1981 to 1997, and is now Frances Hooper Professor of Arts and Humanities at Northwestern University. His many works include ten books of poems, most recently *Last Lake* (University of Chicago Press, 2016); a critical book, *How Poems Think* (Chicago, 2015); the novel *Sweetbitter* (Broken Man Press, 1994); translations (Sophocles, *Selected Poems: Odes and Fragments* [Princeton University Press, 2008]; Sophocles, *Antigone* [with Charles Segal, Oxford University Press, 2003]; Euripides, *Bakkhai* [with Charles Segal, Oxford, 2001]; *Selected Poems of Luis Cernuda* [Sheep Meadow, 1999]; and other volumes); a collection of short fiction, *An Orchard in the Street* (BOA Editions, 2017), and other books. With Ilya Kutik, he is completing a volume of translations of poems by Boris Pasternak. His book *Creatures of a Day* was a finalist for the National Book Award in poetry, and he has fellowships from the Guggenheim Foundation, the NEA, and the Center for Hellenic Studies. He is a longtime volunteer for the Guild Literary Complex and the American Writers Museum (both in Chicago).

Gibbons writes: " 'Canasta' came out of my growing understanding of emotional losses over time—in this poem, not my own losses, but those of Sophie, my maternal grandmother. She was a young woman when she emigrated to the United States in 1900 with her husband and the first of her eight children, who had been born earlier that year. By the time I, a small boy, began to know her, her losses had already accumulated devastatingly: the murdered world of her extended family and her cultural sphere in Poland; her lost opportunities in America to be the person she must have thought she would become, when during her gold-medal student days in her gymnasium in Lodz she had imagined her future; the five years of absence from four of her children when their father took them away with him to the Far East and Australia to tour as child musicians with him; later, the deaths of three of her children in their twenties (two of illness, the third in World War II); and more.

"Yet in her minor way, she made a life buoyed at least somewhat by her intellect, her knowledge of languages, the pleasures of music, and evidently by her pursuit of religious novelty. I don't know how many religions she tried or joined; she and her husband (to me a fascinating but forbidding grandfather whom I was not allowed to know very well) seemed to have completely disavowed Judaism, and I don't think I heard them or any of their children, certainly not my mother, ever even say the word 'Jewish.'

"From my childhood and youth I have images that bring Sophie to mind, yet without my knowing very fully what they might stand for or why these particular images are still with me. In the context of Sophie's catastrophes—historical, cultural, spiritual, and familial—I want to think of her independence, too, through all the years (I was not yet born) when she and her husband lived separately in nearby small frame houses in the old Houston neighborhood called The Heights. Writing this poem, I felt the impulse to put among my words a repeated sound like a slow beating of a small drum, which seemed to help me create what is simply an acknowledgment, however imperfect, of Sophie—helped me suggest her efforts to live with some lightness despite the heaviness of a past that was experienced by so many as an eradication not only of what was, but also of what could then never come to be."

MARGARET GIBSON was born in Philadelphia, Pennsylvania, in 1944. She is the author of eleven books of poems, all from LSU Press, most recently *Broken Cup* (2014), whose title poem won a Pushcart Prize for 2016. *Broken Cup* was a finalist for the 2016 Poets' Prize. Awards include the Lamont Selection for *Long Walks in the Afternoon* (1982), the Melville Kane Award for *Memories of the Future* (1986), and the Connecticut Book Award in Poetry for *One Body* (2007). *The Vigil* was a finalist for the National Book Award in Poetry in 1993. LSU will publish a new volume of poems, *Not Hearing the Wood Thrush*, in 2018. She has written a memoir, *The Prodigal Daughter* (University of Missouri Press, 2008). Gibson is professor emerita, University of Connecticut, and lives in Preston, Connecticut. For more information, visit her website and Facebook page: www.margaretgibsonpoetry.com and www.facebook .com/MargaretGibsonPoetry.

Gibson writes: "As I was writing poems for what has become *Not Hearing the Wood Thrush*, a series of individual poems, each entitled 'Passage,' began to emerge, each poem finding its place at intervals throughout the longer work. In the first of these, the speaker is standing in a dark room, sensing an open door, and beyond that door also darkness. Generally speaking, the series of poems moves toward or into the light. All short, most with long lines, the poems seem to put the speaker at a threshold one might easily miss, the length of passage often being as short as a single breath or the flicker of an image. But all are transformational or hold that possibility. The 'Passage' selected for *The Best American Poetry 2017* is the final passage of that series and also the last poem in the book. I have no idea why it surfaced and declared itself. While I love hanging laundry in summer on a line outside, I haven't done that for some years, as the line has seized up and won't move and has turned green. Well, we're all getting on out here in the woods. But once I had the opening image of pinning the cotton sheet, I remembered smoothing the sheet, and from that came the swift passage toward . . . what might have happened, but didn't. Whatever did happen, however, is remembered as a recurring joy that embraces everything. And so it continues."

ARACELIS GIRMAY was born in Santa Ana, California, in 1977. She is the author of the collage-based picture book *changing, changing* (George Braziller, 2005), as well as the poetry collections *Teeth* (Curbstone Books, 2007), *Kingdom Animalia* (BOA Editions, 2011), and *The Black Maria* (BOA Editions, 2016). Girmay is on the faculty of Hampshire College's School for Interdisciplinary Arts and Drew University's low-residency MFA program.

JEFFREY HARRISON was born in Cincinnati, Ohio, in 1957. He has published five books of poetry: *The Singing Underneath* (E. P. Dutton, 1988), selected by James Merrill for The National Poetry Series; *Signs of Arrival* (Copper Beech Press, 1996); *Feeding the Fire* (Sarabande Books, 2001); *Incomplete Knowledge* (Four Way Books, 2006); and *Into Daylight* (Tupelo Press, 2014), the winner of the Dorset Prize. A volume of selected poems, *The Names of Things: New and Selected Poems*, was published in 2006 by the Waywiser Press in the United Kingdom. A recipient of fellowships from the Guggenheim Foundation and the National Endowment for the Arts, he lives in eastern Massachusetts.

Of "Higher Education," Harrison writes: "Since the poem is straightforwardly autobiographical, there's not much to explain. My father really did list those three colleges as off-limits, and I really did go to Columbia anyway, where I was lucky to be able to study with Kenneth Koch and David Shapiro while also taking the courses that comprise the college's core curriculum, which the poem obliquely mentions.

"As is often the case with me, I wrote the first few lines without knowing where they were going to lead, and the poem went through many versions before it found its shape and current ending. It became clear fairly early that the poem was not so much about college education as about the learning that goes on, or does not go on, between fathers and sons. But facts still underpin the poem, and one of them was sitting in plain sight but came into the poem surprisingly late in the game: that my own son had recently graduated from my father's alma mater, Kenyon. Getting that in led to the imagined, temporary reconciliation at the end of the poem."

TERRANCE HAYES was born in Columbia, South Carolina, in 1971. He is the author of *How to Be Drawn* (Penguin Books, 2015). His other books are *Lighthead* (Penguin, 2010), *Wind in a Box* (Penguin, 2006), *Hip Logic* (Penguin, 2002), and *Muscular Music* (Tia Chucha Press, 1999). He received a 2010 National Book Award and a 2014 MacArthur Fellowship. He was the guest editor of *The Best American Poetry 2014*.

Hayes writes: "If 'Ars Poetica with Bacon' was a painting, its focal point might stir somewhere in the vicinity of 'we have no wounds to speak of / beyond the ways our parents expressed their love.' "

W. J. HERBERT was awarded the Anna Davidson Rosenberg Prize, second prize in the 2015 Morton Marr Poetry Competition. Born in Cleveland, Ohio, she was raised in Southern California, where she earned a bachelor's degree in studio art and a master's in flute performance. She lives in Brooklyn, New York.

Of "Mounting the Dove Box," Herbert writes: "The poem conflates two longings. The first, that fledglings born in our arbor would come back to build a nest. Our older daughter had left for college and the younger would soon follow and, for several years, I chose a new spot each spring for the unused box. The last was high up under the eaves and I couldn't see inside, but sometimes I'd watch, hoping a dove would fly in with a twig in her beak. All this was long ago. We sold our house. But before leaving, I climbed a ladder to take down the box and found a bundle of half-stitched twigs, dry weeds, and pine needles deep inside. The second longing is to go back to the last days of my father's life and act with more compassion."

TONY HOAGLAND's sixth book of poems, *Priest Turned Therapist Treats Fear of God*, will be issued by Graywolf Press in 2018. He teaches at the

University of Houston, and is working on a craft book about poetry, called *Five Powers, Forty Lessons*. He has also published two collections of essays about poetry, both from Graywolf, *Real Sofistakashun* and *Twenty Poems That Could Save America and Other Essays*.

Hoagland writes: " 'Cause of Death: Fox News' originated in a 'joke' I spontaneously made at a dinner one night soon after my father had died. I claimed that when I went to the morgue, the autopsy report on my dad's body said, 'Cause of Death, Fox News.' As jokes often are, it was truer than the literal facts. In his last decade, my father had become increasingly more conservative, paranoid, and vitriolic. Whenever I visited him and his third wife in their ranch house, at the end of a six-mile-long dirt road in rural Colorado, the voices of Fox News commentators raged from the living room TV, spewing their choleric version of the world.

"At first this seemed like a kind of sport or entertainment for them. My father and his wife relished the wild stories of welfare mothers and urban crime; the dire predictions about impending economic collapse; the contemptible intellectual follies of Ivy League apologists. They also delighted in giving offense to visiting liberals. Gradually, though, they seemed to believe their own paranoid, furious narratives about the decline of the country. Their garage filled up with bales of bottled water, canned beans, and toilet paper; a survivalist's checklist.

"Most striking to me was the way in which my father's vision of an embattled nation seemed like a metaphor for his personal decline, his own diminished male power; his body itself with its increasingly weakened borders, a body being invaded and taken advantage of by 'opportunistic' outsiders, immigrant viruses, and alien life-forms.

"The psyche is surely a mad genius in its ability to generate the story it needs. Commentators like Bill O'Reilly, authoritarian and bullying, are the id-monsters of the inner patriarchy, the unconscious costumed as superego, spreading fear like a transmittable disease, one that is readily transmuted into a contagion of rage.

"For much of his life, I wish to say for the record, my father was a hardworking doctor in a poor part of southern Louisiana; his skilled hands and medical expertise did a great deal of good, and, as far as I know, he never turned a patient away for lack of payment. Our family freezer was often full of shrimp and wild game dropped off by grateful patients.

"But sometimes things go wrong; the story, as they say, 'goes south.' In his retirement, my father drastically mismanaged his savings by gambling on the stock market, and he died broke, his credit cards cut to pieces by his wife; his computer access to the stock market blocked. He was a man dismayed and baffled by his misfortunes.

" 'Cause of Death: Fox News' is, I suppose, a polemical poem, and probably guilty of the oversimplifications that accompany certainty. When we tell a story, consciously or unconsciously, we usually tell it to our own advantage. I hope that in this poem, the speaker's certainties are redeemed, at least in part, by tones of human sympathy, and also perhaps by inflections of dark humor. Trustworthy or not, such a poem is a sort of time capsule, the snapshot of a moment in our social (and personal) history, which will do for the time being, until the story needs to be reopened, unpacked, and freshly scrutinized, from a different angle in the ever-changing light."

JOHN HODGEN lives in Shrewsbury, Massachusetts. He is a visiting assistant professor of English at Assumption College in Worcester, Massachusetts. He is the author of *Heaven & Earth Holding Company* (University of Pittsburgh Press, 2010), *Grace* (winner of the 2005 AWP Donald Hall Prize in Poetry, University of Pittsburgh Press, 2006), *In My Father's House* (winner of the 1993 Bluestem Award from Emporia State University Bluestem Press, 1993), and *Bread Without Sorrow* (winner of the 2002 Balcones Poetry Prize, Lynx House Press/Eastern Washington University Press, 2001). He has won the Grolier Prize for Poetry, an Arvon Foundation Award, the *Yankee Magazine* Award for poetry, and a Massachusetts Cultural Council Finalist Award in poetry. He has also received the Ruth Stone Poetry Prize, the Foley Prize from *America Magazine*, and the Chad Walsh Poetry Prize for the best poems published in *Beloit Poetry Journal*.

Of "Hamlet Texts Guildenstern about Playing upon the Pipe," Hodgen writes: "Hard sometimes seeing students shuffling soundlessly across the quad, out of the cradle endlessly texting, passing each other like lost friendships in the night. Easy, however, seeing them holding their phones like bouquets of glow worms or handfuls of fireflies up to their faces, how they are transformed, blazed with delight, someone's lighted little words having languaged them, religioned them, with (what else?) love, something shining, wholly theirs, at the tips of their fingers, shimmering, gleaming, true.

"Easy as well within the nutshell of the classroom amidst those hefty tomes, those other texts, analyzing, contextualizing, for those selfsame students to raise their temporarily empty hands to say that Romeo and Juliet would've lived if they had had cell phones back in the day. And Hamlet would've run off with Ophelia, met her in Room 2B, or not, Snapchatting, Instagramming, Tumblring, MadThumbs, Finger Swiping, Tinder Is the Night, Tweeting like nightingales or larks. And they'd be right, Hamlet, that fuzzy gray cloud over his head, his typing awareness indicator, his TIA, wiggling, telling Gldnstrn/Rsncrntz, *we nd 2 tlk, jst tll the truth, SAD, SAD, SAD."*

DAVID BRENDAN HOPES was born in 1950 in Akron, Ohio. He practices poetry, fiction writing, playwriting, and painting in Asheville, North Carolina, where he has been professor of English at UNCA for thirty-four years. He has had books published by Dodd Mead (back in the day), Scribner's, Milkweed Editions, and Pecan Grove Press.

Hopes writes: " 'Certain Things' arose from one of those moments when you realize you are doing EXACTLY the thing that used to irritate you about your father. Not only is it a moment of realization, but a moment of compassion, when you forgive your parent much, guessing for the first time why he did what he did in the way he did it."

MAJOR JACKSON was born in Philadelphia, Pennsylvania, in 1968. His latest book is *Roll Deep* (W. W. Norton, 2015). He is the editor of Library of America's *Countee Cullen: Collected Poems*. He has been included in multiple volumes of *The Best American Poetry*. The recipient of a Cave Canem Poetry Prize, a Whiting Writers' Award, a Pushcart Prize, and a Pew Fellowship in the Arts, he has also received awards and fellowships from the Fine Arts Work Center in Provincetown, the Guggenheim Foundation, the National Endowment for the Arts, the Radcliffe Institute for Advanced Study at Harvard University, and the Witter Bynner Foundation in conjunction with the Library of Congress. Major Jackson lives with his wife, the poet Didi Jackson, and their children in South Burlington, Vermont, where he is the Richard Dennis University Distinguished Professor at the University of Vermont. He serves as the poetry editor of the *Harvard Review*.

Of "The Flâneur Tends a Well-Liked Summer Cocktail," Jackson writes: "Having lived primarily for the past two decades in regions of the United States best described as either rural, pastoral, or mountainous, I treasure my trips to large cities (mostly New York City) for what they remind me of my youth, the aliveness and excitement of humanity choreographed together in some concert not of our design, and for the palpable sense of simultaneity, that everything is happening all at once. Thanks to Walter Benjamin, much has been written about the flâneur as an emblematic figure of modernity. Because of the crush and immediacy of life around us, the challenge of living in cities is learning to discern what is truly remarkable about existence, is learning to stay awake, and thus, to remain human. This poem is composed of some observations and bits of conversations I have transcribed and recorded in journals over the past five years, chiefly as a means of slowing down and savoring the pleasures of life in a metropolis."

JOHN JAMES was born in Los Angeles, California, in 1987 and grew up in Louisville, Kentucky. He is the author of *Chthonic* (CutBank, 2015), winner of the 2014 CutBank Chapbook Contest. He holds an MFA in poetry from Columbia University, where he held multiple fellowships and received an Academy of American Poets Prize. He is completing an MA in English at Georgetown University, where he serves as graduate associate to the Lannan Center for Poetics and Social Practice and directs the summer school's creative writing institute. Also a scholar, he researches William Blake and ecological Romanticism. He lives in Washington, DC, with his partner and daughter.

James writes: "I wrote 'History (n.)' in about an hour. My daughter was maybe one and a half and my mother was downstairs keeping an eye on her. I was working under a serious time constraint, and because of that, I had to write quickly, putting my inhibitions aside and giving myself over to associative leaps I wouldn't normally make. I composed the poem on my computer, as a single prose block consisting of sixteen lines in Perpetua font, a numeric limitation I placed on myself in order to fill a space with language, without much regard for what the language itself actually said. (I decided to worry about that later.) Strictures are good for me; I often need something to write against in order to write at all. It's in part a fidelity to the numeric nature of metrical form, even though I—and practically all of my contemporaries—write primarily in free verse. I see myself within that poetic lineage. I grabbed a few books I knew to be relevant to the ideas on which I was meditating—tomes by Hegel, Haruki Murakami, Anne Carson, and others—and started excerpting text that for various reasons seemed interesting to me, using it to fill out the prose block when I got stumped. That's what the italicization is about. It's all excerpted text. Once I was finished—and this might have been the next day—I cut what felt like excess language from the poem and began to put it into lines. I was experimenting at the time with spacing and alignment, as well as with the short, fragmented sections that comprise the poem. Actually, I wrote a series of similar poems, which comprise the final section of my book manuscript, *The Milk Hours*. Once I was finished with that process, the poem was done. I cut one line—the last one—when *The Kenyon Review* took the poem, but that was all. The line just seemed a little too heavy handed. My partner, who is usually my best critic, actually made fun of it. And then it ended up here. Somehow I think it was the time constraint that allowed me to write the poem. Being forced to make those associative leaps opened me up to a mode of perception that I don't always inhabit. All of the pieces, from the Plato epigram to the Calbuco volcano, somehow melded together, and I had a decent poem on my hands. Surprisingly, even alarmingly, it didn't take much effort at all."

RODNEY JONES was born in Hartselle, Alabama, in 1950. His new volume, *Village Prodigies* (Mariner Books, 2017), doubles as a poetry book and an experimental novel. His other books include *Salvation Blues: One Hundred Poems 1985–2005* (Houghton Mifflin Harcourt, 2006), winner of the Kingsley Tufts Prize, *Elegy for the Southern Drawl* (Houghton Mifflin, 1989), and *Transparent Gestures* (Houghton Mifflin, 1989), which received the National Book Critics Circle Award. He lives in New Orleans and teaches in the MFA low-residency program at Warren Wilson College.

Of "Homecoming," Jones writes: "I was thinking in 2006, when I first wrote several drafts of this piece, that I would shape them into a poem later, so I noted what mattered and put them down mostly in fragments. Mostly nouns. When I came back to it seven years later, I wrote 'Here are some verbs.' Then I took the point of view, which had been autobiographical, and gave it to an imaginary character who had lived there as a boy, made a few alterations, and it became the last section, CX of *Village Prodigies*."

FADY JOUDAH was born in Austin, Texas, to Palestinian parents. He has three poetry collections and four volumes of poetry in translation from the Arabic, and has received a Yale Series award, a Guggenheim Fellowship, and the Griffin Poetry Prize, among other honors for his work. He is a practicing physician of internal medicine in Houston.

Of "Progress Notes," Joudah writes: "This poem is one of a handful that took me years to complete. I think in terms of the body, the corporeal journey in life as we, partners of the body (and partly owned by it), historicize its corpus. This poem is one formulation of that haunting."

MEG KEARNEY's newest collection of poems for adults, *Home by Now* (Four Way Books, 2009), won the 2010 PEN New England Laurence L. & Thomas Winship Award. The title poem of *Home by Now* appears in Garrison Keillor's *Good Poems: American Places* anthology (Viking, 2011). Meg's first collection of poetry, *An Unkindness of Ravens*, was published by BOA Editions in 2001 and is still in print. She has written three interconnected novels-in-verse for teens, all from Persea Books: *The Secret of Me* (2005), *The Girl in the Mirror* (2012), and *When You Never Said Goodbye* (2017). Her short story "Chalk" appears in *Sudden Flash Youth: 65 Short-Short Stories* (Persea, 2011). Meg's picture book, *Trouper* (Scholastic, 2013), illustrated by E. B. Lewis, was awarded the Kentucky Bluegrass Award and the State of Missouri's Show Me Readers Award. Meg is the founding director of the Solstice low-residency MFA in creative writing program of Pine Manor College in Massachusetts. For more than eleven years, she was the associate director of the National Book Foundation, sponsor of the National Book Awards. A native New Yorker, she now lives in New Hampshire. For more information: www.megkearney.com.

Of "Grackle," Kearney writes: "I am working on a manuscript of poems inspired by *100 Birds and How They Got Their Names* by Diana Wells. Using the description and story of each bird as a prompt, I've written well over one hundred poems so far, and have thrown out more than half. One of these days, I hope to have enough 'keepers' to form a book."

JOHN KOETHE was born in San Diego in 1945. He received an AB from Princeton and a PhD in philosophy from Harvard. He has published ten books of poetry (as well as books on Wittgenstein and philosophical skepticism) and has received the Lenore Marshall, Kingsley Tufts, and Frank O'Hara awards. His most recent book is *The Swimmer* (Farrar, Straus and Giroux, 2016). FSG will publish a volume of new and selected poems, *Walking Backwards: Poems 1966–2016*, in 2018. He is distinguished professor of philosophy at the University of Wisconsin–Milwaukee and lives in Milwaukee.

Of "The Age of Anxiety," Koethe writes: "I don't remember what made me think of the title of Auden's longest poem, but when I did I thought of construing it to refer not to a public social or historical epoch but rather to a time in one's own personal life. The poem is simply an elaboration of that thought and so writing it was pretty straightforward. I usually take a long time—often weeks—to finish a poem, but since this one was so straightforward I finished it in a few days."

YUSEF KOMUNYAKAA's books of poetry include *Taboo*, *Dien Cai Dau*, *Neon Vernacular* (for which he received the Pulitzer Prize), *The Chameleon Couch*, *The Emperor of Water Clocks*, and *Testimony: A Tribute to Charlie Parker*. He has received the William Faulkner Prize (Université de Rennes, France), the Kingsley Tufts Poetry Award, the Ruth Lilly Poetry Prize, and the 2011 Wallace Stevens Award. His plays, performance art, and libretti have been performed internationally. They include *Slipknot*, *Wakonda's Dream*, *Nine Bridges Back*, *Saturnalia*, *Testimony*, *The Mercy Suite*, and *Gilgamesh: A Verse Play* (with Chad Garcia). In 2016 he was announced as New York's eleventh state poet. He teaches at New York University. He was guest editor of *The Best American Poetry 2003*.

DANUSHA LAMÉRIS was born in Cambridge, Massachusetts, in 1971, but has spent most of her life in the Bohemian enclaves of California: Mill Valley, Berkeley, and, for the past twenty-seven years, Santa Cruz. Her first book, *The Moons of August* (2014), was chosen by Naomi Shihab Nye as the winner of the Autumn House Press poetry prize. She lives in Santa Cruz, California, and teaches private writing workshops.

Laméris writes: "Every poem, in its making, opens a world, and I have learned many things since writing 'The Watch.' For example, in some cultures, you never give someone a watch. Why remind them they are going to die? The same way, at least in my personal cosmology, you never give a person you love a knife, because of the severance it implies. Perhaps every gift has a psychic cost.

"In the process of writing the poem, I realized the similarities between the work of the poet and the watchmaker. Both occupy arenas of smallness, detail, and well-defined constraints. Marriage is like this, too. My husband still wears this watch most days, and so now I am reminded of his mortality both by the actual watch, and its semblable on the page.

"Recently, after a reading, the guy sitting next to me asked if I knew that there's a name for an extra feature on the face of the watch—say it shows the phases of the moon, or tells the date. Apparently, it's called a 'complication.' "

DORIANNE LAUX was born in Augusta, Maine, in 1952. Her most recent books of poems are *The Book of Men*, winner of the Paterson Poetry Prize, and *Facts about the Moon*, recipient of the Oregon Book Award, both from W. W. Norton. Laux is also the author of *Awake*, *What We*

Carry, and *Smoke*. In 2014 the singer/songwriter Joan Osborne adapted her poem "The Shipfitter's Wife" and set it to music on her newest release, *Love and Hate*. Laux teaches poetry at the MFA program at North Carolina State University and is a founding faculty member at Pacific University's low-residency MFA program.

Laux writes: " 'Lapse' is a 'Golden Shovel,' a form Terrance Hayes invented in which one takes a line from a poem by Gwendolyn Brooks and uses each word in the line, in order, as the new poem's end words. The poem originally appeared in *Plume* and was later reprinted in *The Golden Shovel Anthology: New Poems Honoring Gwendolyn Brooks*, edited by Peter Kahn, Ravi Shankar, and Patricia Smith, published in 2017 with the University of Arkansas Press."

PHILIP LEVINE (1928–2015) was born into a family of Russian-Jewish immigrants and worked in Detroit auto factories from the age of fourteen. Described by Edward Hirsch as "a large, ironic Whitman of the industrial heartland," Levine was the celebrated author of more than twenty poetry collections and a legendary teacher who influenced countless young poets from California State University, Fresno, on the West Coast to NYU and Columbia on the East. He was the recipient of two National Book Awards and the Pulitzer Prize. In 2011 he was appointed Poet Laureate of the United States. In *The Bread of Time: Toward an Autobiography*, he wrote about his experiences as a factory worker and about such of his mentors as Berryman and Yvor Winters. About Berryman he commented, "He was a guy who didn't want you writing like him. He considered himself, and rightly so, as a rather eccentric poet, and he urged me away from that kind of eccentricity." Levine told his *Paris Review* interviewer that he used to memorize poems "when I worked in factories and recited them to myself. The noise was so stupendous. Some people singing, some people talking to themselves, a lot of communication going on with nothing, no one to hear." Levine's final two books, *The Last Shift*, a collection of poems, and *My Lost Poets*, a prose book, were published posthumously in 2016.

AMIT MAJMUDAR (b. 1979) is a diagnostic nuclear radiologist who lives in Columbus, Ohio, with his wife, twin sons, and daughter. His poetry has appeared in previous editions of this anthology (2007, 2012) as well as *The Best of the Best American Poetry 1988–2012*. His first poetry collection, *0°, 0°*, was published by Northwestern in 2009. His second poetry collection, *Heaven and Earth*, won the 2011 Donald Justice Prize. His third collection, *Dothead*, was published by Alfred A. Knopf in 2016. Ohio's first poet laureate, he blogs for *The Kenyon Review* and has written two novels, *Partitions* in 2009 and *The Abundance* in 2011, both published by Holt/Metropolitan in the United States and Oneworld in the United Kingdom. His forthcoming book is a verse translation from Sanskrit of the *Bhagavad Gita* entitled *Godsong* (Knopf, 2018).

Of "Kill List," Majmudar writes: "The earliest Sumerian cuneiform tablets were thought to be scripture or poetry when they were first discovered. Deciphered, they proved to be a merchant's ledger.

"If I take off my glasses and look at a poem, the blurred vision releases those lines into pure potential. Any list can blur into a potential poem.

"The epic poem of the twentieth century may well be those lists of names that totalitarian regimes consigned to the Gulag or to the death camps—poems whose every line was a life. You can recite the names of those dead by candlelight and make a litany.

"In our era of large-scale data collection, hacked consumer databases, and government watchlists, Anonymous (American, circa AD 2000) is producing many Gilgameshes' worth of list poems. These comprise our own national epic. Every line of it is a life.

"A kill list, by contrast, is often shorter and more concentrated. It is a lyric poem. Every line of it is a death."

JAMAAL MAY was born and raised in Detroit, Michigan. He now lives in Hamtramck, a 2.2-square-mile city inside of Detroit's borders. His two books of poetry, *Hum* (Alice James Books, 2013) and *The Big Book of Exit Strategies* (Alice James Books, 2016), received awards from the Lannan Foundation and the American Academy of Arts and Letters, respectively. He codirects OW! Arts with Tarfia Faizullah and teaches at the University of Michigan–Ann Arbor.

May writes: " 'Things That Break' is an example of the space between things I tend to reach for. Like Sei Shōnagon's *The Pillow Book*, the listing lends a participatory aspect to the poem, as the mind instinctively tries to tie everything back to breaking (hopefully). In doing so, the reader becomes a coconspirator in the experience. Rather than stay with the list poem mode, the syntax shifts to trouble the comparisons and add more shades of meaning. By the end, I use what's been built already to create a moment where the child holds a steady form, paradoxically indicating a break."

JUDSON MITCHAM was born in June of 1948 in Monroe, Georgia. His books of poetry include *Somewhere in Ecclesiastes* (University of Missouri Press, 1991), *This April Day* (Anhinga Press, 2003), and *A Little Salvation* (University of Georgia Press, 2007). His novels are *The Sweet Everlasting* (Georgia, 1996) and *Sabbath Creek* (Georgia, 2004), both winners of the Townsend Prize for fiction. He holds a PhD in psychology from the University of Georgia and taught psychology for thirty years at Fort Valley State University. He has also taught creative writing at Mercer University, Emory University, and Georgia College & State University. In 2013 Mitcham was inducted into the Georgia Writers Hall of Fame. He is the current poet laureate of Georgia.

Of "White," Mitcham writes: "The massacre described in the poem's first section is the Moore's Ford lynching, which occurred on July 25, 1946, just outside Monroe, Georgia, my hometown. The names of the murdered are Roger Malcolm, Dorothy Malcolm, George W. Dorsey, and Mae Murray Dorsey. The story made headlines in *The New York Times* and resulted in what was the largest FBI investigation in history at that time. Laura Wexler's book, *Fire in a Canebrake*, is a detailed examination of the case. As the poem says, I grew up in that town but never heard a word about what had happened until I was middle-aged. I have yet to find anyone of my generation who knew about it while young, a fact that leaves me in 'dumb sputtering astonishment at the ignorance of our lives.' "

JOHN MURILLO was born 1971 in Upland, California. He is an assistant professor of creative writing and African American literary arts at Hampshire College. His first collection of poems, *Up Jump the Boogie*, was published by Cypher Books in 2010.

JOYCE CAROL OATES is currently Visiting Writer in the Graduate Writing Program at New York University. She is the author most recently of the novel *A Book of American Martyrs* and the essay collection *Soul at the White Heat: Inspiration, Obsession, and the Writing Life*. "To Marlon Brando in Hell" will be included in her next book of poems, *The Gathering Storm*.

Oates writes: " 'To Marlon Brando in Hell' grew out of a fascination with the cinematic images of my long-ago childhood and girlhood. Marlon Brando, but also Elvis Presley and Marilyn Monroe, each iconic figures of twentieth-century America whom we can perceive, at a distance of decades, as unique, fated, doomed. How the ardor of youth is transformed by degrees to something like torpor—the suffocation of the spirit. How, in Brando's case in particular, an unfathomable talent (for acting) was transformed into self-loathing and self-destruction. The admiring observer—(the poet)—is stunned to realize how contemptuous the bearer of great talent might be for his own talent—how careless of his talent, as of his life.

"Yes, the stanza about the fifteen-year-old girl is autobiographical. Of course! This is the springboard for the poem."

SHARON OLDS was born in San Francisco, California, in 1942. Her most recent collection of poems, *Odes*, was published by Knopf in 2016; other books include *The Dead and the Living*, which received the National Book Critics Circle Award, and *Stag's Leap*, which won both the T. S. Eliot Prize and the Pulitzer Prize. She teaches in the graduate creative writing program at New York University, and was a founder, in 1986, of the Goldwater Hospital Writing Workshops. She was New York state poet from 1998 to 2000.

Of "Ode to the Glans," Olds writes: "Once Neruda's *Odes to Common Things* had fallen into my hands, in December 2008 (I remember it falling literally, from a high shelf, in the back of a dark, dusty old bookstore, far off my beaten path), I read it with passionate admiration, dazzled by the concepts, the plainness of speech, and the unfettered, animizing imagination—everything so *alive*. I did not think of trying my hand at it. Its originality seemed absolute. (The Spanish facing the English [in Ferris Cook's translation] was part of the richness of the experience.) And a few weeks later, it came to me that there were everyday objects, common things, which I had never thanked or sung.

"Well, that's not true. It wasn't an idea. The beginning of a description of an ordinary object just came into my mind—or rather my mind thought of some things a familiar object was like—my mind started playing with simile. A tampon was like 'Inside-out clothing; / queen's robe; / white-jacketed worker who clears the table / prepared for the feast which goes uneaten.' The poem began to carry some of the pride of a girl becoming a woman, with a woman's reproductive powers, and some of the gratitude for the helpfulness of the tampon like a friend comforting and protecting one.

"As I was writing the first draft, I did not notice, much, that the poem was coming out not in my usual 4/4 time of the church-hymn line, but each image had its own space. I liked that. Later I thought that was part of the praise, and part of the plainness, the commonness. And when I see the poem now, I see it did not address its subject, the object of its attention, until fifteen of the twenty-five lines had been written—I think the poem suddenly turned itself from a description into a direct address.

"That was 'Ode to the Tampon,' the first in what turned out to be a series. Once I began to see the outline of a series, I thought I might eventually put what I thought were the best of the odes in a book as one section of a book—not a whole book, lest I reveal my obsessionalness.

" 'Ode to the Glans' was one of the last poems I wrote which ended up in *Odes*. Looking at it today, I noticed for the first time the familiar friendly tone of its opening, the speaker surprised she had forgotten this character (the glans), this *dramatis persona*. By then I was deep in the premise of serenading not one beloved's body, or its attributes, but some kind of aggregate or representative of some common things, and common parts of people. Somehow it felt to me liberating, affectionate, comfortable, and body-politic in a humorous and respectful enough way.

"I failed, in many other poems (not included in the book), with the tone—not my strong point, to know how close one can go to the body, to the matter, and still honor the spirit."

MATTHEW OLZMANN was born in Detroit, Michigan, in 1976. He is the author of two books of poetry, *Mezzanines* (2013) and *Contradictions in the Design* (2016), both from Alice James Books. He has received fellowships from Kundiman, the Kresge Arts Foundation, and the Bread Loaf Writers' Conference. He is a lecturer at Dartmouth College and teaches in the MFA Program for Writers at Warren Wilson College.

Of "Letter Beginning with Two Lines by Czesław Miłosz," Olzmann writes: "This poem is from a book-length series of epistolary poems. It was originally published on January 5th, and on that day, the president gave a speech on gun violence. A month or so earlier, on the day I sent the poem out for publication, the place where I was working at that time went on lockdown because a man with a rifle was spotted on campus. Is there ever a time when this isn't an issue? A time when we're not either reflecting upon a previous tragedy or bracing for a new one? Is this supposed to be normal? Despite the polemics of the subject matter, I think of this less as an 'anti-gun' poem, and more of an 'anti-ridiculous-debates-where-nothing-gets-done-about-guns' poem. In early drafts, I thought of it exclusively as an elegy. Later, I started thinking of it as being more about a certain refusal to act in the face of an obvious catastrophe."

GREGORY ORR was born in Albany, New York, in 1947. Since 1975, he has taught at the University of Virginia, where he founded its MFA program in writing in 1982. He has published ten collections of poetry, the most recent of which is *River Inside the River* (W. W. Norton, 2013). He is also the author of *A Primer for Poets and Readers of Poetry*, which W. W. Norton will publish in 2017. These poems are from a recently completed collection, *What Cup?* His current project is a stage adaptation of his memoir, *The Blessing*. He lives with his wife, the painter Trisha Orr, in Charlottesville, Virginia.

Of "Three Dark Proverb Sonnets," Orr writes: "The aphoristic has always appealed to me. And it's occurred to me (and others) that a proverb could be thought of as a one-line folk lyric, or at least as an ultimately compressed lyric of anonymous origin. The form of the proverb also gave me permission to heighten the sound-play, to indulge in rhyme and off-rhyme and even puns. Making them up became a kind of game that went on in my head/on the page for about two or three months, the fall of 2013. By the time my fascination with the proverb form subsided I had a good number of them. Having celebrated the dense autonomy of the aphoristic, I came up against a wish to have them gain some scope as well. Obviously, given the nugget-nature of the form, I wasn't going to be able to construct much in the way of narrative unity, but I wanted more than just individual proverbs—I felt they could gather force if I clustered them either by tone or theme or both. I think that's when I decided some of them (these three for example) could be 'sonnets.' My definition of sonnet is quite loose I suppose; possibly even tongue-in-cheek.

"As for the content. I felt somewhat that I had been emphatically affirmative in some recent work and got to thinking about that. One of my favorite texts is Blake's *The Marriage of Heaven and Hell*—and part of the pleasure in it is the way the 'Proverbs of Hell' are a bracing antidote to the one-sided, 'angelic' view of the world. I thought also of William James's put-down of Whitman—that he was almost 'pathologically healthy-minded' and essentially lacked a 'vision of evil' to reality-check his insistent celebrations. I've never lacked a dark or sardonic side and so I decided to let it loose in this form: 'dark proverbs.' "

CARL PHILLIPS was born in Everett, Washington, in 1959. His new book of poems, *Wild Is the Wind*, will come out from Farrar, Straus and Giroux in 2018. Previous books include *Reconnaissance* (FSG, 2015), *Silverchest* (FSG, 2013), and a book of essays, *The Art of Daring: Risk,*

Restlessness, Imagination (Graywolf, 2014). Phillips is professor of English at Washington University in St. Louis.

Of "Rockabye," Phillips writes: "Sometimes one of the hardest things to admit to in a relationship is vulnerability—in my own experience this has seemed especially so between men. Also brokenness, be it physical or psychological. But what if we not only admit to, but embrace the fact of brokenness? And if we end up arriving together at a place we set out for, does it matter that our road was a broken one, that our minds and bodies that we used, to get there, were likewise broken? For me, there's hope in thinking of vulnerability as its own kind of strength, in embracing the so-called flaws we all travel with, and in not thinking of the distance between two people as an uncrossable divide. I suppose the poem came out of all that."

ROWAN RICARDO PHILLIPS was born in New York City in 1974. He received a bachelor of arts in English from Swarthmore College and a doctorate in English from Brown University. His first book of poems, *The Ground* (Farrar, Straus and Giroux, 2012), won the PEN/Joyce Osterweil Award and the GLCA New Writers Award. His next book, *Heaven* (FSG, 2015), won the Anisfield-Wolf Book Award. He has received a Whiting Writers' Award and a Guggenheim Fellowship and divides his time between New York City and Barcelona.

Of "Halo," Phillips writes: "The peculiar power of poetry, its particular panache, rises out of its inherent ability to blur the boundaries between the sacred and the divine, absence and presence, indeed between a thing and nothing at all. 'Halo' is a poem that thrives in the space of that divide. As someone who does much writing in my head, I'm fascinated by how a poem is a material object and a diaphanous idea simultaneously; that its beauty is one that flickers between these states. A bit of Baudelaire's 'Perte d'auréole' swims somewhere in the seams of it but 'Halo' is its own strange thing: a light on the mind's horizon."

ROBERT PINSKY was born in Long Branch, New Jersey, in 1940. His recent book of poems is *At the Foundling Hospital* (Farrar, Straus and Giroux, 2016). His awards include the Italian Premio Capri, the Harold Washington Award from the city of Chicago, the Korean Manhae award, and the Los Angeles Times Book Prize in Poetry for his translation *The Inferno of Dante* (FSG, 1994). The videos from his Favorite Poem Project can be viewed at www.favoritepoem.org. He was guest editor of *The Best of the Best American Poetry: 25th Anniversary Edition* (2013).

Of "Names," Pinsky writes: "The nominal token of my name confronts me with the past, for good or ill and plenty of both. The delusory, often pathological, occasionally beautiful associations of culture, the chimerical, crucial, often enough murderous baloney of 'race' and 'ethnicity.' They are there in how you designate me and how I designate you.

"We come into the world, for a moment or two, innocent of all that, but soon enough it begins determining us. For example: if you call that certain moment 'christening' you associate yourself with an American majority, thereby making yourself at that moment more secure than Mohamed, Vijay, or Menachem.

"Anyone's name: an essential, minimal particle of culture. A meaning. Some readers will not recognize the aggressive history and meaning of the question 'What kind of name is that?' Some readers will not recognize 'Byron De La Beckwith' or 'Ikey Moe.' That possible darkness, too—the unknowing itself—is part of my meaning."

STANLEY PLUMLY is a distinguished university professor at the University of Maryland. His most recent book is *The Immortal Evening: A Legendary Dinner with Keats, Wordsworth, and Lamb* (W. W. Norton, 2014). He is finishing a book on Constable and Turner and the sublime landscape. "Poliomyelitis" appeared in *Against Sunset* (W. W. Norton, 2016).

Of "Poliomyelitis," Plumly writes: "Polio was a part of the childhoods of anyone born right around or after the Second World War. I had many classmates who suffered various stages of the disease. My poem 'The Iron Lung'—from the late nineteen seventies—is my first attempt to identify with the consequences of polio, which, in those days, normally amounted to paralysis or death. Infantile paralysis was (is) its common name."

PAISLEY REKDAL is the author of a book of essays, *The Night My Mother Met Bruce Lee* (Pantheon, 2000, and Vintage Books, 2002); a hybrid-genre memoir entitled *Intimate* (Tupelo Press, 2012*)*; and several books of poetry: *A Crash of Rhinos* (University of Georgia Press, 2000), *Six Girls Without Pants* (Eastern Washington University Press, 2002), *The Invention of the Kaleidoscope* (University of Pittsburgh Press, 2007), and *Animal Eye* (University of Pittsburgh Press, 2012), which won the UNT Rilke Prize. Her newest book of poems, *Imaginary Vessels*, is out from Copper Canyon Press, and her latest book of nonfiction, *The Broken Country: On Trauma, a Crime, and the Continuing Legacy of the*

Vietnam War, won the AWP Nonfiction Prize (University of Georgia Press, 2017). Her work has received the Amy Lowell Poetry Traveling Fellowship, a Guggenheim Fellowship, and an NEA Fellowship. She is the editor and founder of the web history archive project, Mapping Salt Lake City (www.mappingslc.org).

Of "Assemblage of Ruined Plane Parts, Vietnam Military Museum, Hanoi," Rekdal writes: "For a period of six months I lived in Hanoi, next door to the Vietnam Military History Museum, which is where I came across this sculpture. I wrote this poem in dozens of wildly different versions over the course of three years but nothing, for me, could ever formally approach the *monumentality* of this monument. The sculpture is an artwork of both propaganda and history, as all war monuments are, and yet something about these reassembled planes felt, the more I observed them, restless, enlarging. These planes are not representational figures made of stone and marble, as they might be in a more sanitized monument that line a capital's landscaped mall. They are *planes*. They are the real planes real men died in, from which real men killed other people. For me, the artwork is a sliver of war's terrible sublime, and perhaps it is the enormity of sensations that this piece arouses in me that first made me suspect the sculptor had been duped by his creation or, better yet, had helped it slip the control of the politicians who commissioned it, who wanted to tell only one story about the war, rather than the story the artist seemed to recognize. This was a sculpture that, accidentally or not, elegizes the deaths of Vietnam's enemies as much as it celebrates Hanoi's victors. During my time in Hanoi, I visited this sculpture frequently, taking notes, thinking that someday I would write a poem that could encapsulate what I felt while looking at it, or that perhaps I would come to this courtyard one day and sit by it and look at it and simply feel *less*. For a time, I even visited the museum daily, believing that repeated exposure would numb these sensations that arose in the planes' presence, assure me that I had at last pinpointed the final sentiment behind the monument; that, by articulating it for myself, I might encapsulate some idea central to understanding the war. But I never did. I never wrote a satisfactory poem about that sculpture. I just stopped."

MICHAEL RYAN has published five books of poems, an autobiography, a memoir, a novel, and a collection of essays about poetry and writing. Four of the books were *New York Times* Notable Books of the year. The autobiography was reviewed on the front page of *The New York*

Times Book Review and the memoir was excerpted in *The New Yorker*. His poetry has won the Lenore Marshall Prize and the Kingsley Tufts Poetry Award. He is director of the MFA program in poetry at the University of California, Irvine.

Of "The Mercy Home," Ryan writes: "As Joseph Williams wrote in *Style: Ten Lessons in Clarity and Grace*, 'The writer knows least about his work because he knows most about it.' This is particularly true when the writer is writing autobiographically.

"The writer's material is essential, but what really matters to me is what he or she makes of it. The writing I love most is finally about the reader, not just the writer. This makes autobiographical writing even more challenging. It's where the art comes in.

"I try to do something different in every poem. I try even harder when drawn to habitual subjects like how people bear the unbearable.

" 'The Mercy Home,' all 132 lines of it, rhymes—or half-rhymes—on a terminal '-r' sound. What rhyme does in verse (and doesn't do) is still very poorly understood. In this poem I hope it creates an incantation that underlies and overrides the narrative and exposition, and helps the poem's rendering of the unbearable and providing it a shape in language.

"Writing and reading are both ways people bear the unbearable.

"The self-address as 'you' can be an effective self-critical, self-punishing voice in writing. Everyone I know has that voice inside them.

"I hope that, for all its insistence on the brutal facts, 'The Mercy Home' resolves in an act of peace through the imagination that does not underestimate the magnitude of human grief."

DAVID ST. JOHN was born in Fresno, California, in 1949. His collections of poetry include, most recently, *The Auroras* (HarperCollins, 2012), *The Window* (Arctos Press, 2014), and *The Last Troubadour: New and Selected Poems* (Ecco, 2017). He is the editor of two posthumous collections of poetry by Larry Levis: *The Selected Levis* (University of Pittsburgh Press, 2000), and *The Darkening Trapeze: Last Poems* (Graywolf, 2016). A member of the American Academy of Arts and Sciences and a Chancellor of the Academy of American Poets, he is university professor and chair of English at the University of Southern California.

Of "Emanations," St. John writes: "This poem is an homage to the Big Sur coast of California and to two of its presiding artistic spirits, Robinson Jeffers and Edward Weston, as well as to two other remarkable figures of that landscape, Charis Wilson and the painter Pat St.

John Moran, my aunt. The threads of narrative moving through the poem are meant to string historical and personal vignettes into a precarious mobile, each piece reflecting a restless light upon the other."

SHEROD SANTOS's most recent book of poems is *The Intricated Soul: New and Selected Poems* (W. W. Norton, 2010). A new collection of prose/poetry pieces, *The Square Inch Hours*, was published in 2017. In 2006, he was presented with the Umhoefer Prize for Achievement in the Humanities for his book of translations, *Greek Lyric Poetry*. He has also received an Award in Literature from the American Academy of Arts and Letters. He lives in Chicago, where he works in an outreach program for the homeless.

Of "I Went for a Walk in Winter," Santos writes: " 'Time is an accident.' That statement, by Maimonides, seems like an apt summary of my poem. I ran across it years ago, and while it interested me then, it interests me far more now, for if age has taught me anything, it's that time is less a succession of moments than an accumulation of perceptions that present themselves largely by happenstance; in the case of this poem, during a late-night walk through the streets of Chicago in the middle of a snowstorm. How and what we think about our perceptions is, of course, another matter, another 'time,' so to speak, though that wasn't my primary concern. My concern was simply to record my random observations as fully and accurately as possible as they appeared and disappeared in the ever-amassing drifts of snow."

TAIJE SILVERMAN was born in San Francisco, California, in 1974. She teaches poetry and translation at the University of Pennsylvania. Her book *Houses Are Fields* was published by Louisiana State University Press in 2009 and her poem "Grief" appeared in *The Best American Poetry 2016*.

Of "Where to Put It," Silverman writes: "I don't know how to explain where this poem came from—whether to preempt an explanation with reassurance that I hope nothing and least of all my sobs will hurt the baby inside me who is now five and likes to say, 'Mamma, pretend I'm in your belly,' and then burrow into my sweater while he looks up at me and meows. Or whether to state the obvious and belligerent truth that we can feel and live both the thing and its opposite, and that there must in some interior and immaterial castle be room for such contradiction. I hated being pregnant. I felt my body had been hijacked by an indifferent alien tribe and that my self had, against all previous suspicion, proved to be inseparable from my body. At the insistence of doctors, friends, and strangers, I quit taking the antidepressant that has long kept me buoyant (and has since shown to have no negative impact on pregnancy) until my brain without it unraveled into versions of self-loathing that now seem about as real as the X-Men. All the spaces in this poem existed and were contemporaneous, but still they needed imagining. And each one, once imagined, engendered the next. Like the self that is terribly loyal to the body but only moves toward it asymptotically, all the spaces did—do—lead toward but not into each other through hallways where we live. I felt, as I wrote the poem, a longing to experience witness differently. I kept picturing its last line, even as I wrote the first one."

CHARLES SIMIC is a poet, essayist, and translator. He is the recipient of many awards, including the Pulitzer Prize, the Griffin Prize, and a MacArthur Fellowship. In 2007 Simic was appointed the fifteenth Poet Laureate of the United States. *The Lunatic*, his new volume of poetry, and *The Life of Images*, a book of his selected prose, were published in 2015 by Ecco Press. He was the guest editor of *The Best American Poetry 1992*.

DANEZ SMITH (Their Mother, 1989) is a Black, queer, poz writer & performer from St. Paul, Minnesota. Danez is the author of *[insert] boy* (YesYes Books, 2014), winner of the Kate Tufts Discovery Award and the Lambda Literary Award for Gay Poetry, and *Don't Call Us Dead* (Graywolf Press, 2017). Danez is also the author of two chapbooks, *hands on your knees* (Penmanship Books, 2013) and *black movie* (Button Poetry, 2015), winner of the Button Poetry Prize. They are the recipient of fellowships from the Poetry Foundation, the McKnight Foundation, and the National Endowment for the Arts. Danez's work has been featured widely including on *BuzzFeed*, Blavity, *PBS NewsHour*, and on *The Late Show with Stephen Colbert*. They are a two-time Individual World Poetry Slam finalist, three-time Rustbelt Poetry Slam Champion, and a founding member of the Dark Noise Collective.

MAGGIE SMITH was born in Columbus, Ohio, in 1977. She is the author of *Weep Up* (Tupelo Press, forthcoming); *The Well Speaks of Its Own Poison* (Tupelo Press, 2015), winner of the Dorset Prize and the IPPY Gold Medal in Poetry; *Lamp of the Body* (Red Hen Press, 2005), winner of the Benjamin Saltman Award; and three prizewinning chapbooks. In

2016 her poem "Good Bones," originally published in *Waxwing*, went viral internationally and has been translated into nearly a dozen languages. PRI (Public Radio International) called it "the official poem of 2016." The recipient of fellowships from the National Endowment for the Arts, the Ohio Arts Council, and the Sustainable Arts Foundation, Smith works as a freelance writer and editor.

Smith writes: "I wrote 'Good Bones' about raising my children in a world that's as full of injustice and violence as it is beauty and wonder. I'm still in awe of how far the poem has traveled, and how it's resonated with people around the world."

R. T. SMITH was born in Washington, DC, in 1947 and was raised and educated in Georgia and North Carolina. For many years he served as alumni writer-in-residence at Auburn University. He is the author of six books of stories and fourteen collections of poetry, including Library of Virginia Poetry Book Award winners *Messenger* (Louisiana State University Press, 2001) and *Outlaw Style* (University of Arkansas Press, 2007), as well as *Brightwood* (LSU, 2003), *The Hollow Log Lounge* (University of Illinois Press, 2003), and *The Red Wolf* (Louisiana Literature Press, 2013). He received the Virginia Governor's Award for Achievement in the Arts in 2008 and the Carole Weinstein Poetry Prize in 2013. Smith edits *Shenandoah* for Washington and Lee University, where he is writer-in-residence. He lives on Timber Ridge in Rockbridge County, Virginia.

Of *"Maricón,"* Smith writes: "Because it has haunted me for half a century, I wanted to tell the story of that tragic title fight in 1962 between Emile Griffith and Benny 'Kid' Peret, followed by the death of the latter, which underscored the dark irony of calling pugilism 'the sweet science.' When it occurred, only a few fans but most boxing insiders knew that the handsome Casanova Griffith was bisexual. Only many years after the bout did I learn that Peret had taunted Griffith with the term *maricón* at the weigh-in and during the fight. I made notes and talked to people for years but was completely stifled in my attempts to begin the poem. I found some traction only after Griffith died and I understood that his story was, for me, spliced together with the story of my own intense interest in and ambivalence about boxing. I started watching boxing on TV for the first time in decades, and watched the YouTube video of the fight. Then the literary tinder began to kindle. It seemed a self-brutalizing process I may have needed to endure, but I'm not watching boxing matches now."

Born in 1968, A. E. STALLINGS grew up in Decatur, Georgia; studied classics in Athens, Georgia, and Oxford, England; and has lived since 1999 in Athens, Greece. Her most recent collection is *Olives* (TriQuarterly/Northwestern University Press, 2012). Her new translation of Hesiod's *Works and Days* is recently out from Penguin Classics.

Of "Shattered," Stallings writes: "This isn't the first poem I've written about breaking a glass or sweeping. So I suppose that attests first of all to an innate clumsiness. Also, when you have kids, the fact that you have suddenly strewn the kitchen with cutting edges and children are running around barefoot fills you with that glamour-jagged horror of hypervigilance that seems to be a kind of attention to the moment shared by parents and poets. I have long been fascinated by the moment of the mistake, the action or word that changes what comes after (and thus what comes before) and cannot be undone or unsaid. Disasters on the domestic scale have always put me in a more cosmic philosophical mood.

"My lines are usually metrical, but I enjoy experimenting with syllabics (and particularly haiku-shaped syllabic stanzas) while including rhymes, the way the count pushes extreme enjambments and line breaks that ignore word-boundaries, and how the arithmetic turns up end rhymes in spots unanticipated by the ear. Maybe there is something apotropaic too in the writing of such a poem, an effort to ward off injury from the wounding sharpness of the world. At least in a poem, I can make a clean sweep."

PAMELA SUTTON was born in Ypsilanti, Michigan, in 1960. She holds an MS in journalism from Northwestern University and an MFA in creative writing from Boston University. She taught creative writing and critical writing at the University of Pennsylvania from 1993 to 2008, where she was nominated by her students for the Charles Ludwig Teacher-of-the-Year Award. She worked as associate editor for *The American Poetry Review* from 1989 to 1993 and was a consulting editor until the death of *APR*'s editor-in-chief, Stephen Berg. Sutton currently lives on Marco Island, Florida, where she is finishing a novel, writing a third book of poetry, and looking for a university teaching position. Her first book of poems, *Pocket Gospel*, was published by Sheep Meadow Press in 2012. Her second, *Burning My Birth Certificate*, won the Ashland Poetry Press Richard Snyder Memorial Publication Prize, and is forthcoming from Ashland Press.

Of "Afraid to Pray," Sutton writes: "This poem attacked me like a pack of wolves. The Novel version is better."

CHASE TWICHELL was born in New Haven, Connecticut, in 1950. She has published seven books of poetry, the most recent of which is *Horses Where the Answers Should Have Been: New and Selected Poems* (Copper Canyon Press, 2010), which won the Kingsley Tufts Poetry Award from Claremont Graduate University and the Balcones Poetry Prize. A new book, *Things as It Is*, is forthcoming in 2018. After teaching for many years, she left academia in 1999 to start Ausable Press, a not-for-profit publisher of poetry. Ausable was acquired by Copper Canyon in 2009. From 2014 to 2016 she served as chair of the Kate and Kingsley Tufts Awards at Claremont Graduate University. She is currently on the faculty of the Warren Wilson MFA Program for Writers. She lives with her husband, the novelist Russell Banks, in the Adirondack Mountains of northern New York.

Of "Sad Song," Twichell writes: "A couple of years ago, my first boyfriend found me on Facebook, and we've been back in touch ever since. I was in love—we'd been friends since childhood—but we were far too young, and he soon left to go adventuring in Thailand, and I to college. I waited for him for an absurdly long time, but he never came back, which froze my emotion in the glacier of time. Fifty years later, here it is again, poking out, half-thawed, a baby mastodon!"

JAMES VALVIS was born in Jersey City, New Jersey, in 1969. After some college and a stint of homelessness, he enlisted in the United States Army and served during Desert Storm, though he did not see combat. He began writing poetry for publication while in the army and has since published hundreds of poems and scores of short stories in such journals as *Ploughshares*, *Rattle*, *Tampa Review*, *The Louisville Review*, and *The Sun*. He won the Chiron Review Poetry Contest. His poetry books are *How to Say Goodbye* (Aortic Books, 2011) and *What Exactly Is a Valvis?* (NightBallet Press, 2013). He lives in Issaquah, Washington, with his wife and daughter.

Valvis writes: "Let me first thank Poet Laureate Natasha Trethewey for including 'Something' in this year's anthology, and the editors at *The Sun* for originally publishing the poem. I maintain great editors are more rare and less appreciated than great writers, and so I thank them and all who have supported my work.

"The events depicted in 'Something' happened six months before I wrote the poem. As a young man, I used to suffer from severe panic disorder, symptoms of which included sweating, shortness of breath, a sense of unreality, and rapid heartbeat. Often, for seemingly no reason, while riding on a train, while reading in the library, while waiting in a grocery store line, the symptoms arrived and I thought I was dying. I've largely beaten back this awful condition, but there remain times when the stress is severe enough I psychologically shut down. I knew guys in the army who claimed during firefights they would inexplicably sit on the battlefield and start weeping. Or they'd start daydreaming and looking up at the stars as tracer rounds flew overhead. Each recorded a buzzing, a punch-drunk sensation where the blow is emotional rather than physical. Something like this happened to me in that doctor's office, and I wanted to record the feeling as accurately as possible and to bring the reader into this moment.

"A flat narrative wouldn't do. It wouldn't illustrate the humming, droning sound one hears, which shuts off linguistic clarity and understanding—at a time when understanding is most needed. The repetition of 'something' is meant to be that 'dumb hum.' The word 'some' even rhymes with hum, and the word 'thing' rhymes with ping, like a heart monitor ping.

"If you pushed me I might credit Raymond Carver with some influence and perhaps give a nod to Poe's 'The Bells,' but here I start to question too much hindsight analysis. For me, a poem happens mostly in the moment of composition and, in this regard, this poem was no different than any of my others. I will say that after I finished drafting 'Something' I knew I'd written a good poem. If there's any better feeling than that, I surely don't know what it is.

"One final note. Because people have asked, I should say the health concerns turned out to be, as my wife said, borrowed trouble. I'm fine; I had and have no cancer. I'm very lucky. May God provide His mercy and compassion to those not as fortunate."

EMILY VAN KLEY's book, *The Cold & The Rust Smell*, won the 2017 Lexi Rudnitsky First Book Prize and is forthcoming from Persea Books. Raised in Michigan's Upper Peninsula, she now lives in Olympia, Washington, where she also teaches and performs aerial acrobatics.

Van Kley writes: " 'Dear Skull' was written in response to images of decorated skeletons kept as holy relics in the early Catholic world, as shared with me by the poet Jessica Walsh. My life had been recently shaken by the sudden loss of a dear friend, and I was intrigued by the relative permanence of these human remains, their continued significance—even participation—in the world of meaning, despite having been separated from selfhood, that quality so perplexingly erased (?) transformed (?) interrupted (?) by death."

WENDY VIDELOCK lives in a small agricultural town on the Western Slope of the Colorado Rockies. This is her second appearance in *The Best American Poetry*. Her books include *Nevertheless* (Able Muse Press, 2011), *The Dark Gnu* (Able Muse, 2013), *Slingshots and Love Plums* (Able Muse, 2015), and *What's That Supposed to Mean* (EXOT Books, 2009).

Of "Deconstruction," Videlock writes: "We have made our home on the edge of the Rockies, on the fringe of an arroyo in the high deserts of western Colorado. From here, nestled against the mesa, we are given an endless parade of wildlife and dramatically changing skies and weather. This is no country for unstudied birds, or ignorant ones. The poem in question arrived, as it were, in one fell swoop, and is told from the point of view, it seems, of a loquacious old crow."

LUCY WAINGER was born in New York City in 1997. She attended Stuyvesant High School and studies creative writing at Emory University.

Wainger writes: "The first draft of 'Scheherazade.' was a found haiku, culled from my third-period English class notes at the end of sophomore year. I rewrote it as a prose poem during third-period English my junior year, and again during third-period Acrylic Painting my senior year. After that it no longer felt like 'my' poem, which is how I knew it was finished."

CRYSTAL WILLIAMS was born in 1970 in Detroit, Michigan. She is the author of four books of poems, most recently *Detroit as Barn* (Lost Horse Press, 2014). Her third book, *Troubled Tongues*, was chosen by Marilyn Nelson for the 2009 Naomi Long Madgett Poetry Prize. A graduate of New York University (BA) and Cornell University (MFA), she is professor of English and associate vice president for strategic initiatives at Bates College. She has been on the faculty at Reed College and Columbia College Chicago. In 2012 she was appointed an Oregon Arts Commissioner, and currently serves on the boards of the Maine Humanities Council and the Barbara Deming/Money for Women Fund.

Of "Double Helix," Williams writes: "I've become interested in the ways in which what we do to each other and how we are with each other are repeated and reflected across time and distance. After I read Isabel Wilkerson's *The Warmth of Other Suns*, I shared the book with a colleague and it became clear to me that his father's experience as a Holocaust survivor and my father's experience as a black man born in 1907 in Alabama were similar in seminal and instructive ways. I wanted to explore the personal choices both of these men made in their lives that made it possible for their children to feel deep affinity toward one another. I was also interested in finding a way—through form—to reflect the transmutation of meaning, what I imagine a double helix structure might look like in words, and to ultimately suggest that no matter those complications and differences, we humans are a single thing, of a single experience, complicated though it may be. This poem was one of two commissioned by the Museum of Modern Art for the Jacob Lawrence Migration Series exhibit. My enduring gratitude to Leah Dickerman, the Marlene Hess Curator of Painting and Sculpture at MoMA, for her vision and leadership, and to Elizabeth Alexander for inviting me to participate in the project."

CHRISTIAN WIMAN was born in West Texas in 1966. He is the author of five books of poetry, most recently a selected poems, *Hammer Is the Prayer* (Farrar, Straus and Giroux, 2016), and two books of prose, *Ambition and Survival* (Copper Canyon Press, 2007) and *My Bright Abyss* (FSG, 2013). From 2003 to 2013 he was the editor of *Poetry*. He now lives in New Haven and teaches at the Yale Institute of Sacred Music.

Wiman writes: " 'Prelude' no longer has that title, though it remains a prelude to what follows, which is the book of poems I'm working on, which is propelled by, and punctuated with, other untitled fragments, all of which seem to be facets of some ultimate form that will, any day now, I feel quite sure, bring me everlasting peace."

MONICA YOUN is the author of *Blackacre* (Graywolf Press, 2016), *Ignatz* (Four Way Books, 2010), and *Barter* (Graywolf Press, 2003). The daughter of Korean immigrants, she was born in 1971 and raised in Houston, Texas. A former lawyer, she teaches poetry at Princeton University and in the Columbia University and Sarah Lawrence College MFA programs.

Youn writes: "In 'Greenacre,' I wanted the reader to occupy the estranged perspective of growing up Asian American in the South, where racial dynamics historically have functioned along a black/white binary. So the positionality of the speaker in the poem—both as not-black and as not-white—is crucial, racial identity as the coincidence of two competing negations, each coming into play at a different point. The central image—the two pale figures in the lake—acts as a fulcrum point for desire and revulsion, rejection and complicity, witness and culpability. And stylistically, this poem was quite a departure for me, veering close to narrative autobiography as I tried to trace the boundary between memory and the transformative imagination."

C. DALE YOUNG was born in 1969 and grew up in the Caribbean and South Florida. He was educated at Boston College (BS 1991) and the University of Florida (MFA 1993, MD 1997). He is the author of the poetry collections *The Day Underneath the Day* (Northwestern University Press, 2001), *The Second Person*, *Torn*, and *The Halo* (Four Way Books, 2007, 2011, 2016) and a collection of linked short stories, *The Affliction*, forthcoming from Four Way Books in 2018. He practices medicine full-time and teaches in the Warren Wilson MFA Program for Writers. A recipient of fellowships from the NEA, the Guggenheim Foundation, and the Rockefeller Foundation, he lives in San Francisco with his spouse, biologist and classical music composer Jacob Bertrand.

Of "*Precatio simplex*," Young writes: "I spend the vast majority of my time working as a radiation oncologist, a physician who treats cancer patients with radiation therapy. Early in 2016, my aunt, for whom this poem is written, began the very rapid decline seen with many who have pancreatic cancer. Her pain was intense and severe. Despite caring for patients with cancer every day, I was not prepared for the feelings of helplessness I felt when faced with my aunt in this way. I found myself walking along the beach near my home one day talking to myself, verbalizing my awful desire that she pass because it seemed better than the pain she could not manage. And then I felt immediate guilt. I'm a doctor, a cancer doctor, who works every day to help people survive and live, and here I was asking God to take my aunt. A few days later, she died. Roughly one month after her funeral, I discovered a voice-mail message my aunt left on my phone. I don't know how I missed it, but I had. When I heard her voice on my phone, I burst into tears. All of it came back to me: her decline; her pain; the awfulness of it. The poem came within hours of my outburst."

DEAN YOUNG was born in Columbia, Pennsylvania, in 1955. He has published eleven books of poetry and a book of prose about poetry, *The Art of Recklessness* (Graywolf Press, 2010).

Of "Infinitives," Young writes: "Me and a million other poets will feel the loss of Tomaž Šalamun for the rest of our lives. There is for me an indisputable truth to his work, a truth that can only be accessed through the sort of volatile, unsubjugated imagination that seems in very short supply in our myopic contemporary picture. That's the work I want to try to do."

KEVIN YOUNG is the director of the Schomburg Center for Research in Black Culture, newly named a National Historic Landmark. Inducted into the American Academy of Arts and Sciences in 2016, Young is the author of eleven books of poetry and prose, most recently *Blue Laws: Selected & Uncollected Poems 1995–2015* (Alfred A. Knopf, 2016), longlisted for the National Book Award; *Book of Hours* (Knopf, 2014), a finalist for the Kingsley Tufts Poetry Award and winner of the Lenore Marshall Prize for Poetry from the Academy of American Poets; *Ardency: A Chronicle of the Amistad Rebels* (Knopf, 2011); and *Dear Darkness* (Knopf, 2008). His collection *Jelly Roll: A Blues* (Knopf, 2003) was a finalist for both the National Book Award and the *Los Angeles Times* Book Prize. His first nonfiction book, *The Grey Album: On the Blackness of Blackness* (Graywolf, 2012), won the Graywolf Press Nonfiction Prize and the PEN Open Book Award; it was also a *New York Times* Notable Book for 2012 and a finalist for the 2013 National Book Critics Circle Award for criticism. Young's next nonfiction book, *Bunk: The Rise of Hoaxes, Humbug, Plagiarists, Phonies, Post-Facts, and Fake News*, will be out from Graywolf in November 2017.

Young writes: " 'Money Road' traces my driving the Delta with friend and Southern Foodways Alliance leader John T. Edge—we started out visiting Booker's Place in Greenwood, Mississippi, for an oratorio the SFA had commissioned from me on Booker Wright, barkeep, activist, waiter, and local legend. Turns out Greenwood is where the term Black Power was popularized at a rally by Stokely Carmichael in 1966, just a few blocks from Booker's. Nearly fifty years later one could still see why—not least of which because Emmett Till was lynched a few miles away in Money, with its cotton gins and train tracks, in 1955. Driving to Money that day, it was bitter cold, snow accompanying what became the pilgrimage recorded in the poem. The site of Till's lynching feels both holy and haunted.

"I am writing this just days after the news revealed—at least to those who had bought the story—that the white woman at the center of the case, who had claimed Till whistled at her or called her *baby*, confessed that Till had in fact not done a thing. I am heartened that the poem had already said he 'whistled or smiled / or did nothing,' though I still wonder why had even well-meaning southern and American accounts decried the lynching but somehow believed the lynchers? Till's murderers—who lied in court, got acquitted in no time by an all-white jury, then promptly sold their story without fear of reprisal—should not be believed. I think in some small way it's because we cannot believe the whole of the truth—that evil does discriminate—much like, in more recent cases from Trayvon Martin to Michael Brown, some cling to some sense of black culpability in their own killings. The poem calls out to us to remember but also to revisit and revise what we think of the past—not in the ways of bluesman Robert Johnson's unlikely gravesite along the Money Road, or the fake plantation there that proves almost as haunting—but in the reality of the now-crumbling storefront where Till was brought and then killed in the night for no earthly, or only earthly, reasons."

Matthew Zapruder was born in Washington, DC, in 1967. He is the author of four collections of poetry: *Sun Bear* (Copper Canyon Press, 2014), *Come On All You Ghosts* (Copper Canyon, 2010), *The Pajamaist* (Copper Canyon, 2006), and *American Linden* (Tupelo Press, 2002). He is cotranslator, with historian Radu Ioanid, of the Romanian poet Eugen Jebeleanu's last collection, *Secret Weapon: Selected Late Poems* (Coffee House Press, 2008). Zapruder's most recent book is *Why Poetry* (Ecco/HarperCollins, 2017). An associate professor in the MFA program in creative writing at Saint Mary's College of California, he is also editor-at-large at Wave Books, and from 2016 to 2017 served in the annually rotating position of editor of the poetry column for *The New York Times Magazine*. He lives in Oakland, California, with his wife and son.

Zapruder writes: "I wrote 'Poem for Vows' on the occasion of the wedding of two friends, the composer Gabriel Kahane and Emma Tepfer. I was unable to attend so wanted to send along something that naturally conveyed my genuine feelings of happiness for them, along with my equally genuine (and, from personal experience, ever-growing) sense of the mysteries of marriage. It's such a strange and ancient thing to say, at a certain point in time, that 'I bring to you my entire past: not just my own, but whatever came before that made me. And also, I bring to you my future, everything that cannot yet be known.' As I worked on the poem, I was surprised that I started writing about my imagined version of climate scientists trying to figure out how to save our planet. I saw them looking at miniature storms. And then as I wrote the last lines, I discovered I believe that the deep act of faith two people bring to a union might, in some elusive yet essential way, be related to what we will need in order to rescue our species from its path toward destruction."

MAGAZINES WHERE THE POEMS
WERE FIRST PUBLISHED

Academy of American Poets, Poem-a-Day, ed. Alex Dimitrov. www
.poets.org

AGNI, poetry eds. Sumita Chakraborty and Lynne Potts. www.bu.edu
/agni

The American Poetry Review, eds. David Bonanno and Elizabeth Scanlon.
320 S. Broad St., Hamilton #313, Philadelphia, PA 19102. www
.aprweb.org

The American Scholar, poetry ed. Langdon Hammer. www.theamerican
scholar.org

The Antioch Review, poetry ed. Judith Hall. P.O. Box 148, Yellow
Springs, OH 45387. review.antiochcollege.org/antioch-review
-home-page

BuzzFeed, executive ed., culture Saeed Jones. www.buzzfeed.com
/reader

Callaloo, ed. Charles Henry Rowell. www.callaloo.tamu.edu

Cave Wall, eds. Rhett Iseman Trull and Jeff Trull. www.cavewallpress
.com

Cherry Tree, ed. Jehanne Dubrow. www.washcoll.edu/centers/lithouse
/cherry-tree

The Collagist, poetry ed. Marielle Prince. www.thecollagist.com

Denver Quarterly, poetry ed. Bin Ramke. www.du.edu/denverquarterly

Fifth Wednesday, eds. James Ballowe, Nina Corwin, and Susan Azar
Porterfield. www.fifthwednesdayjournal.com

The Georgia Review, ed. Stephen Corey. Main Library, Room 706A, 320
S. Jackson St., University of Georgia, Athens, GA 30602-9009. www
.thegeorgiareview.com

Harper's, ed. James Marcus. www.harpers.org

Harvard Review, poetry ed. Major Jackson. Lamont Library, Harvard
University, Cambridge, MA 02138. www.harvardreview.fas.harvard
.edu

The Hopkins Review, ed. David Yezzi. www.hopkinsreview.jhu.edu

jubilat, eds. Kevin González and Caryl Pagel; executive ed. Emily Pettit.
www.jubilat.org/jubilat/

The Kenyon Review, poetry ed. David Baker. www.kenyonreview.org

The Massachusetts Review, poetry eds. Ellen Doré Watson and Deborah Gorlin. Photo Lab 309, 211 Hicks Way, University of Massachusetts, Amherst, MA 01003. www.massreview.org/

Mississippi Review, editor-in-chief Steve Barthelme. www.mississippireview.com

The Nation. www.thenation.com

New England Review, poetry ed. Rick Barot. www.nereview.com

New Ohio Review, poetry ed. Jill Rosser. English Dept. 360 Ellis Hall, Ohio University, Athens, OH 45701. www.ohio.edu/nor

The New Yorker, poetry ed. Paul Muldoon. www.newyorker.com

The Paris Review, poetry ed. Robyn Creswell. 544 W. 27th St., New York, NY 10001. www.theparisreview.org

Ploughshares, poetry ed. John Skoyles. www.pshares.org

Plume, editor-in-chief Daniel Lawless. www.plumepoetry.com

Poetry, ed. Don Share. www.poetryfoundation.org

Prairie Schooner, editor-in-chief Kwame Dawes; poetry eds. Arden Eli Hill and Rebecca Macijeski. 123 Andrews Hall, Lincoln, NE 68588-0334. www.prairieschooner.unl.edu

Raritan, editor-in-chief Jackson Lears. 31 Mine St., New Brunswick, NJ 08901. www.raritanquarterly.rutgers.edu

Salmagundi, eds. Robert Boyers and Peg Boyers. Skidmore College, 815 N. Broadway, Saratoga Springs, NY 12866. www.skidmore.edu/salmagundi

The Sewanee Review, poetry ed. Robert Walker. www.thesewaneereview.com

The Southern Review, poetry ed. Jessica Faust. 338 Johnston Hall, Baton Rouge, LA 70803. www.thesouthernreview.org

Southwest Review, editor-in-chief Greg Brownderville. www.smu.edu/SouthwestReview

storySouth, poetry ed. Luke Johnson. www.storysouth.com

The Sun, ed. Sy Safransky. 107 North Roberson St., Chapel Hill, NC 27516. www.thesunmagazine.org

The Threepenny Review, ed. Wendy Lesser. www.threepennyreview.com

Virginia Quarterly Review. www.vqronline.org

Waxwing, poetry eds. Justin Bigos and W. Todd Kaneko. www.waxwingmag.org

The Yale Review, ed. J. D. McClatchy. Yale University, P.O. Box 208243, New Haven, CT 06520-8243. www.yalereview.yale.edu

ACKNOWLEDGMENTS

The series editor thanks Mark Bibbins for his invaluable assistance. Warm thanks go also to Ron Horning, Stacey Harwood, Thomas Moody, and Keri Smith; to Glen Hartley and Lynn Chu of Writers' Representatives; and to Ashley Gilliam, David Stanford Burr, Daniel Cuddy, Erich Hobbing, and Jessica Yu at Scribner.

Grateful acknowledgment is made of the magazines in which these poems first appeared and the magazine editors who selected them. A sincere attempt has been made to locate all copyright holders. Unless otherwise noted, copyright to the poems is held by the individual poets.

Dan Albergotti, "Weapons Discharge Report" from *storySouth*. Reprinted by permission of the poet.

John Ashbery, "Commotion of the Birds" from *Commotion of the Birds*. © 2016 by John Ashbery. Reprinted by permission of Ecco/Harper-Collins. Also appeared in *Harper's*.

Mary Jo Bang, "Admission" from *The Paris Review*. Reprinted by permission of the poet.

David Barber, "On a Shaker Admonition" from *The American Scholar*. Reprinted by permission of the poet.

Dan Beachy-Quick, "Apophatic" from *Harvard Review*. Reprinted by permission of the poet.

Bruce Bond, "Homage to a Painter of Small Things" from *Raritan*. Reprinted by permission of the poet.

John Brehm, "Intrigue in the Trees" from *The Sun*. Reprinted by permission of the poet.

Jericho Brown, "Bullet Points" from *BuzzFeed*. Reprinted by permission of the poet.

Nickole Brown, "The Dead" from *Cave Wall*. Reprinted by permission of the poet.

Cyrus Cassells, "Elegy with a Gold Cradle" from *AGNI*. Reprinted by permission of the poet.

Isaac Cates, "Fidelity and the Dead Singer" from *The American Scholar*. Reprinted by permission of the poet.

See pages 20–47

PRATO

FLORENCE

FLORENCE,
AREZZO
AND
CASENTINO

CHIANTI
AND SIENA

AREZZO

SIENA

MONTALCINO
AND THE SIENESE
CRETE

MAREMMA
AND MONTE
AMIATA

GROSSETO

FLORENCE,
AREZZO
AND
CASENTINO

CHIANTI
AND
SIENA

See pages 96–123

MONTALCINO
AND THE
SIENESE CRETE

See pages 124–151

0 kilometers   400

0 miles   400

EYEWITNESS *TRAVEL GUIDES*

A Taste of
Tuscany

A TASTE OF
TUSCANY

edited by
GUIDO STECCHI

DK

DORLING KINDERSLEY PUBLISHING, INC
LONDON • NEW YORK • MUNICH
MELBOURNE • DELHI
www.dk.com

◁ A Tuscan farmhouse in the countryside near Pienza

DORLING KINDERSLEY PUBLISHING, INC.

www.dk.com

Produced by Fabio Ratti
Editoria Libraria e Multimediale, Milan, Italy

TEXT Guido Stecchi, Maria Cristina Beretta, Marco Scapagnini
EDITORS Diana Georgiacodis, Laura Recordati,
Federica Romagnoli

DESIGNERS Massimo Costa, Carlotta Maderna

MAPS AND ILLUSTRATIONS Massimo Costa, Carlotta Maderna,
Alberto Ipsilanti, Daniela Veluti, Oriana Bianchetti,
Roberto Capra

Dorling Kindersley Ltd.
EDITORS Felicity Jackson, Fiona Wild PROOFREADER Stewart Wild
ENGLISH TRANSLATION Richard Sadleir
DTP DESIGNER Jason Little PRODUCTION Marie Ingledew
SENIOR PUBLISHING MANAGER Louise Bostock Lang

Reproduced by Colourscan, Singapore

Printed and bound in Italy by Graphicom

First published in Italy in 2000 by Arnoldo Mondadori Editore
S.p.A., Milan and Fabio Ratti Editoria S.r.l., Milan as Guida
Gourmet Toscana

First American Edition, 2001
01 02 03 04 05 10 9 8 7 6 5 4 3 2 1

Published in the United States by
Dorling Kindersley Publishing, Inc.,
95 Madison Avenue, New York, NY 10016

ISBN 0-7894-8068-9

The photographs and information in this book are intended to
help the reader select produce, particularly mushrooms, in a
market, and are not intended as a guide to picking wild produce.
If you are in any doubt about the edibility of any species,
do not cook or eat it.

**The information in every
DK Eyewitness Guide is checked annually**.
Every effort has been made to ensure that this book is as
up-to-date as possible at the time of going to press. Some
details, however, such as telephone numbers, opening hours,
prices, and travel information are liable to change. The
publishers cannot accept responsibility for any consequences
arising from the use of this book, nor for any material on third
party websites, and cannot guarantee that any website address in
this book will be a suitable source of travel information.
We value the views and suggestions of our readers very highly.
Please write to: Senior Publishing Manager, DK Travel Guides,
Dorling Kindersley, 80 Strand, London WC2R 0RL.

CONTENTS

How to Use this Guide

This guide uncovers the best of Tuscany's food and wine for visitors to the region. Tuscany has been divided into six areas or zones (see the map inside the front cover). There is a brief description of places of gastronomic interest: shops, wineries, vineyards, and estates, and restaurants with local character. To make it easy for travelers to find them, there is a map and a *Places of Interest* section for each of the areas. There is practical information about the most important *Traditional*

Produce, such as wine, cheese, and *salumi* (cured meats), all clearly illustrated. *Wild Produce* with its descriptions of truffles and mushrooms, herbs and wild fruits will encourage excursions into meadows and woods to search for them (or at least to keep an eye open for them in the markets). The delights of the local cuisine are highlighted in a selection of traditional dishes from each area, and the region's restaurants are assessed for quality, atmosphere, traditional dishes, good service, and value for money.

A TASTE OF TUSCANY AREA BY AREA

The guide has divided Tuscany into six areas, each of which covers a geographical area based on the local produce and the gastronomic traditions.

The title page *for each area illustrates one of the most important local products.*

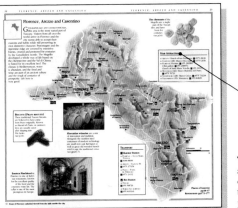

Star Attractions *indicates important artistic and cultural sights no visitor should miss.*

The map illustrates the area dealt with in the chapter and illustrates the region's most important produce and places.

*In the traditional **recipes**, quantities are for six people unless otherwise stated.*

*There are descriptions of **traditional produce**, such as wine, salumi, olive oil, and cheese.*

Wild produce traditionally picked by local people in Tuscany includes truffles, mushrooms, herbs, and various wild fruits.

Each entry *for a place of interest gives the address, phone number, opening and closing days. It is advisable to telephone before stopping by a farm, vineyard, or agriturismo.*

Places of interest are marked with a symbol (see inside back cover for key to symbols) to indicate the kind of produce available, and they are listed in alphabetical order by place.

Each restaurant entry *gives the address, telephone number, and weekly closing day.*

Price categories for a three-course meal including a bottle of wine:
€ under 25 euros
€€ 25–36 euros
€€€ 36– 46 euros
€€€€ 46– 60 euros
€€€€€ over 60 euros

The restaurant entries assess quality, comfort, traditional food, service, and value for money.

Tuscany Throughout the Year

SPRING

Tuscan spring can come as early as March, especially along the coast. In the hedgerows and thickets, you can find the young, tender wild shoots known locally as "asparagus," such as butcher's broom or even the sweet young tips of wild hops. Waste ground is studded with borage flowers – one of the most valuable of wild herbs – looking like little blue stars. Coastal pine woods and the inland woods on hills and mountains conceal magnificent morel mushrooms, while richly scented St. George's mushrooms form circles around sloe trees which are sprinkled with white blossom. Specially trained hounds nose out white truffles under the pine woods that stretch along the coast from Cecina to Argentario.

Spring is when Tuscan extra-virgin olive oil reaches peak quality, shedding the bitter, pungent taste it has when newly pressed. This is the ideal time to visit the olive groves and presses to buy oil. Northwest Tuscany has some of the finest chocolate confectioners in Italy – Europe even – and spring is the perfect time to sample their wares in the form of chocolate eggs, the traditional Easter gift. Another Tuscan springtime tradition is the Easter lamb or kid: those raised in the Garfagnana or the Casentino are particularly famous. This is also a good time to sample some of the seafood specialities: local mullet and swordfish cooked Livorno-style, cuttlefish in sauce, and grilled eels from Orbetello are tasty in April.

SUMMER

Summer is the time for wandering through Tuscany's mountain woods or exploring the coast, but this time of year is a mixed blessing for gourmets. In June the coast offers a wealth of wonderful fish, but July and August bring hordes of vacationers from the towns, and there is not enough fish caught in the local seas to go around. Then there is the breeding period when fishing is banned and only a fortunate few are able to buy from the small boats exempt from the ban. Shellfish are at their finest in the summer, but make sure you buy from reputable sources.

For those who prefer not to risk the seafood, the hinterland compensates with an abundance of flavorful vegetables: taste the *bruschetta* (bread rubbed with garlic, toasted and topped with ripe tomato) or *panzanella* (moist bread seasoned with oil, vinegar, and herbs). In June and early July the small artichokes on sale are perfect for preserving in oil. Peaches, yellow in Tuscany, white on Elba, are especially good if bought at orchards where they are allowed to ripen on the tree. Summer brings thyme, oregano, and other herbs that color and scent the dry meadows, while the woods on the Apennine ridges provide juicy bilberries, raspberries, and wild strawberries. In the mountains there are mushrooms, but the season is short. Generally, high summer is too dry for them, and you have to wait until late September, when they are plentiful.

FALL

For gourmets, this is Tuscany's prime season. At San Miniato, Volterra, the Sienese Crete, around Arezzo and many other small villages, the white truffles are ripening. In the Garfagnana and the Casentino there are very fine porcini (cèpe mushrooms), while other parts of Tuscany have an abundance of different mushrooms, which sometimes linger until after Christmas. They include numerous varieties that are essential to the peasant dishes of the region – sauces with fresh pasta and thick seasonal soups like *acquacotta* (tomatoes, mushrooms, vegetables, eggs, and bread). This is the season for sweet chestnuts, a staple of the cuisine of areas like the Lunigiana, Amiata, and the Mugello, and for the renowned wild boar of Maremma, which adorns tables in both homes and restaurants. Game birds are traditional throughout the region, with wood pigeons a particular favorite.

At Chiusi, and above all Torre del Lago, this is the season for the famed local dish of coot cooked *alla Puccini* and wild duck. Game dishes go well with Brunello and the region's other fine red wines. In the fall the ban on fishing is lifted, and this is the time to eat the young squid and mullet, skillfully prepared by the chefs of Viareggio or San Vincenzo, plus the larger fish passing through local waters at this time, especially the amberjack *(ricciola)*.

WINTER

In mediterranean regions like Tuscany, outdoor life continues through the mild winter months, and both the local cuisine and the natural setting are tempting for the gourmet tourist. Nature is still active: there are lots of evergreen herbs, all kinds of

tasty mushrooms and fruits there for the picking in the woods, hedgerows, and meadows. The typical Tuscan meal, with a choice of meats roasted on a spit over the fire, and the rustic cooking found in farmhouses and simple *trattorie* all over the region, serving up traditional thick soups and full-bodied red wines, seem designed to warm up the diners gathered convivially around a large table.

The first mild days are traditionally enjoyed among the crowds at the famous carnival of Viareggio in February. This is the chance to sample the excellent local shellfish, especially scampi and mantis shrimp. Nature is particularly generous in certain localities dotted across Tuscany where the valuable black truffle is found. Not far from the sea there are market gardens producing early artichokes and black cabbage, an important ingredient in *ribollita* (vegetable soup). This is the time when the pig is killed, after a fall spent grazing in the woods on the chestnuts and acorns, giving its flesh a rich flavor. Now, homemade *salumi* (preserved meats) begin their long slow curing, lasting up to two years for a *prosciutto crudo*.

Wines

Tuscany is one of Italy's prime wine regions, producing great red wines. The rather folksy image of Chianti in its straw-lined flask has given way in recent years to designer bottles of fine wine that rival the best French reds. This is not the result of some invention of modern marketing but the rightful success of a deep-rooted local tradition, as illustrated by the ancient farmhouses that stand amid the vines. The changeover from a patrician, but antiquated, management of the estates to a bold modern business approach is recent.

Despite the miracles worked by technology, Tuscany will never become a region of great white wines because the French vines planted here produce wines lacking in local character, and the traditional Trebbiano and Malvasia vines are limited by the soil. There are three exceptions: Vernaccia di San Gimignano, Montecarlo, and the whites of the islands, all of which show great potential. Dessert wines also show great promise – if the Vin Santo (Tuscany's traditional "holy wine") lacks the noble flavor of the great French dessert wines, here too the Tuscans are learning to exploit the potential of their yeasts to obtain outstanding wines made from grapes that have been semidried on racks.

A Choice Selection of Tuscan Wines

To accompany the full range of the typical cuisine of the region you need a choice selection of Tuscan wines, which should include the following:
- ♦ Vermentino from the Luni hills, Apuan Alps, or hills of Lucca (a light summer aperitif).
- ♦ Vernaccia di San Gimignano, aged (as a general table wine and as an accompaniment to white meats).
- ♦ Montecarlo Bianco (good with seafood).
- ♦ Young Vernaccia di San Gimignano (with fish, summery first courses, savory toast).
- ♦ Young Chianti (with *cacciucco* – Livornese fish soup; for dining al fresco; with *salumi* – cured meats; and with *crostini* and *bruschetta* – savory toasts).
- ♦ Chianti, medium-aged reds of Montalcino and Montepulciano, Morellino of Sansano (traditional first courses, main courses with white meat).
- ♦ Chianti Classico or Rufina, Brunello di Montalcino, Vino Nobile di Montepulciano, (roasted or stewed red meat).
- ♦ Brunello di Montalcino cru, fully aged, Sassicaia (well-aged *pecorino* cheese).
- ♦ Vin Santo (*cantucci* cookies).
- ♦ Ansedonia Passito or Moscadello (various desserts)
- ♦ Aleatico (for desserts and social drinking).

THE RIGHT GLASS

The shape of a wine glass is designed to reduce contact between the hand holding the glass and the wine itself. Its form reduces possible interference from any odors or the heat of the hand. The glass should be held by the stem, between the goblet that holds the wine and the foot of the glass. Modern designers produce wine glasses that are both beautiful and practical. Wine glasses should be perfectly transparent so you can appreciate the wine's color and also check its state of health (for example, too few bubbles or too large bubbles in a spumante *metodo classico*, or an orangey color in a young red wine, which is a symptom of early aging). The best glasses are made of crystal.

BALLOON
This glass is perfect for fine wines of a great age such as Brunello, as its distinctive rounded form slowly releases the complex subtle elements of the bouquet. (Serve at 60–68°F/16–20°C.)

FLUTE
The elongated shape of the flute holds the subtle aromas of spumanti *metodo classico* or charmat, dry, very dry, or semidry. (Serve at 43–46°F/6–8°C.)

RED WINE GOBLET
Serve medium-aged wines such as Chianti Classico in this glass, which is wider than an ordinary wine glass, to gather the bouquet more fully. (Serve at 57–60°F/14–16°C.)

WHITE WINE GOBLET
This glass is much shorter, though larger and more rounded, than a flute. Use for Montecarlo. (Serve at 45–50°F/8-10°C.) Fine white wines such as certain varieties of Vernaccia or San Gimignano, or a rosé or young red – a Novello or Chianti, are better served cooled rather than chilled. (Serve at 50–57°F/10–14°C.)

DESSERT WINE GOBLET
For Vin Santo and similar dessert wines, this small, narrow-mouthed glass concentrates the bouquet. (Serve at 57–60°F/14–16°C.)

SPARKLING WINE GOBLET
The flared mouth of this glass allows the intense bouquet of sweet and aromatic spumanti (sparkling wine) to disperse without overwhelming the nose. (Serve at 43–46°F/6–8°C.)

DECANTER
The purpose of a decanter, usually used for an aged red wine, is to awaken the dormant bouquet of the wine. Pouring it into a decanter oxygenates the wine and also allows any sediment to be left in the bottom of the wine bottle. In ceremonial decanting, the color of the wine is viewed against a lighted candle and the wine is then poured straight from the decanter.

Olive Growing in Tuscany

TUSCANY IS A FAMOUS olive-growing region and the olive groves on the wooded hillsides are a characteristic feature of the Tuscan landscape, though some areas are more favorable than others. Olive groves are usually small, so the local crop is not large but produces very fine olive oil. The traditional business skills of the region and the expertise of olive growers have played an important role in the success of Italian olive oil worldwide, providing a model for other olive oil producers.

Olive growing in Italy goes all the way back to the Etruscans of the 6th century BC, and it was further developed by the Romans. With the fall of the Roman empire the vast organization for growing and marketing olives fell into disarray. Monasteries were the first to tend the great olive groves again before the medieval city states started to foster olive growing once more. The trade in olive oil grew in economic importance until it became a formidable instrument of political power in the 14th century. Today, olive oil remains an essential ingredient of Tuscan cuisine, a vital flavoring in cooked dishes and salads.

THE ORIGINS OF OLIVE GROWING

The Medici (a powerful political family in the 15th, 16th, and 17th centuries) fostered the growing of olives. They gave wooded hillsides to the municipalities on the condition that they were leased cheaply for planting olive groves and vineyards. Growing olives became one of the main economic resources of the region, resulting in the distinctive Tuscan landscape of today.

THE FLAVOR OF TUSCAN OLIVE OIL

Tuscany produces some of the finest olive oils in Italy and, although they vary in much the same way that wines do, generally they have a strong aromatic scent. Tuscan olives are harvested well before they ripen, to produce oils richer in antioxidants and other nutritious substances. The early harvesting, combined with the soil, climate, and the local olive varieties, results in peppery, slightly bitter oils with a rich color.

OLIVE OIL

The quality of Italy's olive oil is guaranteed by strict legislation. Olives are picked, mostly by hand, and crushed to produce oil and a watery liquid, which are then separated. This oil is the first cold-pressed virgin olive oil – "virgin" because it is pure, not having been heated or processed. Virgin olive oil varies in flavor and quality and is graded according to the level of acidity; lower is better. The best quality is extra-virgin olive oil which has an acidity of less than 1 percent. Olive oils are usually blended so the flavor is constant.

OLIVE VARIETIES

With its long olive-producing history and the diversity of soil and climate within the region, Tuscany has developed numerous cultivated varieties (cultivars) of the olive tree, including 106 that have been classified, some of which are of great importance. In addition to the varieties described below, other important ones include **Pendolino**, a type which is widespread, hardy, and produces abundant oil of reasonable quality; **Maurino**, a variety typical of the area between Monte Albano and Lucchesia, with a medium-sized tree bearing fruits that ripen early and produce fine oil; **Santa Caterina**, a large vigorous tree that produces bright green olives that are usually harvested in September for immediate eating. Other common varieties are **Corniolo, Craputea, Lavagnino, Leucarpa, Manzanilla, Nebbio, Ogliarola, Passola, Piangente, Ravece, San Francesco,** and **Taggiasca**.

MORAIOLO

This variety originated in Tuscany but is widely grown in other parts of Italy, especially Umbria, and in other Mediterranean countries. It has a good resistance to wind but not to intense, prolonged cold. It produces an abundance of olives, which ripen over a medium-to-long period of time, and have a good oil yield. The oil is very fine, without marked aromatic notes but with excellent texture and a distinctly bitter and pungent flavor.

CORREGGIOLO

A self-pollinator similar to Frantoio, this variety's fruit ripens late and over a long period. The trees are fairly vigorous, with drooping branches and the fruits borne on thin, supple canes. The olive yield is high and consistent, producing an oil that is particularly aromatic, full-bodied, and flavorsome.

MAREMMANA

A vigorous plant with large, intensely green, spear-shaped leaves. It produces a good oil with somewhat muted bitter notes.

LECCINO

Grown in nearly all olive-producing regions both in Italy and worldwide, this variety is well-known for its resistance to inclement weather, cold, and disease. A consistent high-yielding variety, the olives ripen early and uniformly. Its oil is not particularly aromatic.

FRANTOIO

A Tuscan original, this variety has spread throughout Italy and nearly all olive-growing areas of the world, a testimony to its consistently high yields and the notable quality of its oil, which is fine, aromatic, and flavorsome. The variety is not resistant to bad weather and is very sensitive to cold.

Fish and Seafood

UNLIKE THE LIGURIAN COAST, the Tuscan coastline is not studded with little fishing harbors, but its larger ports, notably Viareggio and Livorno, provide fine fish. The waters of Gorgona and other islands, the shallows of Vada, and the Formiche of Grosseto offer an excellent range of fish, including scampi and crayfish, delivered live to the counters of the fish shops. The lagoon of Orbetello, with its modern fish farms, is particularly productive, but this is not always reflected in the restaurants. Inland there are not that many restaurants specializing in fish cuisine, although fish is commonly eaten on a Friday throughout Tuscany. The best fish restaurants are found mainly along the coast.

RICCIOLA SERIOLA DUMERILI (AMBERJACK)
Amberjack, which grow to a large size, are found in schools in deep water around rocky headlands and steep cliffs. They abound in the Tuscan archipelago and are prized for their firm, flavorsome white flesh. They are usually eaten as fish steaks or grilled whole.

PESCE SPADA (SWORDFISH)
The white close-grained flesh of this fish is delicious provided it is not overcooked and it remains moist. Swordfish is found particularly in the port of Livorno, usually sold as steaks.

CALAMARETTI (YOUNG SQUID)
The fry of squid are one of the delicacies of Tuscan cuisine. They need to be cooked only a few seconds by steaming or tossing in a pan with vegetables. Their delicate flavor provides great scope for many delicious dishes.

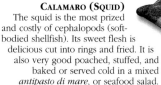

CALAMARO (SQUID)
The squid is the most prized and costly of cephalopods (soft-bodied shellfish). Its sweet flesh is delicious cut into rings and fried. It is also very good poached, stuffed, and baked or served cold in a mixed *antipasto di mare*, or seafood salad.

VONGOLA VERACE OR ARSELLA NERO (CLAMS)

This very common shellfish is usually cooked but may be served raw like oysters. Though somewhat expensive, clams are found in numerous modern Tuscan seafood dishes as well as the traditional *cacciucco* (fish soup). Called *vongole veraci* or *arselle* in Italian, in Viareggio they are known as *nicchi*.

MISTO DI SCOGLIO (MIXED SEA FISH)

The fish referred to as *misto di scoglio* include small bream, wrasse, young scorpion fish and rainbow wrasse, gurnard, sea perch, and hake. Delicious but too small to grill or fry on their own, they are essential for an authentic *cacciucco* and a variety of other fish soups.

PAGRO (PORGY)

This is a white fish typical of the Tyrrhenian coast and is highly prized in Tuscany, especially when it is baked. Sea bream (called *pagelli* in Italian, *paraghi* in the Tuscan dialect) is similar but has a flatter snout and pinkish markings. Larger specimens are called *occhialone* or *fragolino*.

SARDINA

A common and very economical fish, the sardine is tasty and very nourishing. It is ideal fried, grilled, made into fish cakes, or preserved in oil.

SPARNOCCHIA OR MAZZANCOLLA (MANTIS SHRIMP)

The mantis shrimp is common in Tuscan waters, especially around the island of Gorgona. It is popular for grilling and steaming and is also an ingredient in more expensive versions of *cacciucco* (fish soup). Mantis shrimp are sold live at the market at Viareggio – always avoid those sold headless.

Porcini Mushrooms

TUSCAN CUISINE REGULARLY FEATURES *porcini* mushrooms, which are also known as cèpes, from the French. *Porcini* are distinguished from other *Boletus* mushrooms – a family which has tiny tubes under the cap instead of gills – by four features: strong smell, sweet taste, a netlike pattern covering the stalk, and by the white flesh, which does not discolor when cut. They are found all over the region, fresh, dried, or preserved in oil, in homes and all types of restaurant, from the humblest *trattoria* to the grandest *ristorante.* Dishes featuring *porcini* do not vary greatly, and the mushrooms are eaten in quite simple ways, in *risotto,* or in *ravioli,* for example. In certain areas of Tuscany, including Lunigiana, Garfagnana, and Casentino, you can find the world's finest examples of *porcini,* judged on aroma, flavor, and texture. In other areas, such as Monte Amiata, the Maremma Grossetana, Colline Metallifere, the hinterland of Livorno, the Mediterranean scrublands, and the woods of Siena and Arezzo, the quality is not as high but they are more abundant.

PORCINI D'AUTUNNO
(*Boletus edulis*)
The fall *porcini* shuns the heat, so in summer it is found only in the mountains and in the depths of woods; in fall it appears on hillsides, but prefers cool areas. The mushroom's stalk is usually white and the cap appears in various shades of brown, sometimes almost white, under beech trees, and is slimy in wet weather. The most flavorsome examples are found growing under chestnut trees, the firmest examples among fir and beech trees; those in oak woods are much less prized.

PORCINO DEL FREDDO
(*Boletus pinicola*)
This species grows between May and November but rarely during the hottest months. It is found under chestnut, beech, pine, or fir trees, especially with bilberries or heather. It has unusual red coloring and is the largest of all the *porcini.* It is best suited to preserving in oil because it is generally very hardy, not particularly aromatic, and the color is very striking.

FIORONE OR PORCINO D'ESTATE
(*Boletus reticulatus*)
This summer *porcini* starts growing in May and is rarely found after September. It grows throughout the region at all altitudes but only in grassy glades and in sunny areas. This is the most richly scented and flavorsome of the *porcini* but it is vulnerable to parasites. The cap is velvety and slightly cracked, the stalk is beige with a raised netlike pattern, and the flesh has a very light texture.

MORECCIO OR PORCINO NERO
(Boletus aereus)
This black *porcini* mushroom is most common along the coast and on warm hillsides. It grows almost exclusively in the fall, usually under holm oaks, deciduous oaks, and chestnut trees. It has a dark brown cap marbled with ocher and an ocher-colored stalk. It is full-flavored and aromatic when picked but the scent and taste soon fade. The flesh remains snowy white when dried, making it ideal for keeping in this way.

PORCINI IN OIL
Jars of *porcini* preserved in oil are a feature of the region's farmhouses and traditional *trattorie*. In keeping with tradition, the oil is usually extra-virgin olive oil. Jars should be stored in a cool dark place and kept no later than the spring after the season of picking.

DRIED PORCINI
Porcini secchi, or dried *porcini*, are even more common throughout Tuscany than fresh ones. The local varieties are prized over those from other regions, although the latter have flooded the market. If possible, buy unpackaged dried mushrooms directly from the pickers or at small shops in areas where they are found locally. Store them either in the freezer or at least place them there from time to time to kill the eggs of potential parasites.

Truffles

Tuscany is one huge truffle patch with many areas producing black truffles and even the prized white variety. Numerous fairs and festivals celebrate this wonderful gift of nature, especially in the areas that are lucky enough to produce white truffles, such as the Sienese Crete and San Miniato. Truffles are seasonal but, fortunately, Tuscany has a truffle for every month of the year, so there are always fresh ones available. Always buy truffles in season when they are very fresh and clearly identifiable. Be wary of various speciality foods described as "truffle flavored" *(al tartufo)*: in reality, they may be perfumed with a synthetic aroma. The high prices these truffles command and the strong international demand for them have led to some cases of fraud. The most common type of swindle is to import flavorless truffles from abroad, bought cheaply (sometimes less than 50 cents for two pounds), and then artificially perfume them with a synthetic aroma. Tasteless unripe truffles are sometimes gathered – seriously damaging the truffle patches – and these are likewise flavored artificially.

TARTUFO BIANCO PREGIATO
(Tuber magnatum)
The white truffle is actually a light hazel color if found growing under oak, almost whitish if under poplar or willow, or with reddish tones if under linden (lime) trees. It is identifiable by its strong and distinctive aroma and fine, densely veined flesh – marked veining is the first sign of proper ripeness. It ripens from October to December and by law it can only be gathered in these three months. Its flavor is best appreciated when added raw to hot dishes. Areas where it is found are San Miniato, the Sienese Crete, Volterra, and there are some small patches near Arezzo.

BIANCHETTO OR MARZOLO
(Tuber borchii)
The perfume of this March truffle is strong and very garlicky but it lasts only a few hours after picking and then begins to fade. It adds an excellent flavor to soups. Picking is permitted from January 15 to April 20. It is found in many parts of Tuscany, and is abundant in the coastal pine woods.

The March truffle differs from the prized white truffle by the coarse loose veining and domed shape.

The wrinkled gray surface of this truffle has dark reddish tints.

TUBER MACROSPORUM
This truffle occasionally turns up among batches of summer black truffles. It is often mistakenly sold at the same price even though it is far more highly prized because its perfume is almost identical to that of the white truffle. Sadly, it is very rare. Harvesting is permitted from September to December.

The flesh is gray with fine reddish veins, which are often not evident because they darken on contact with the air.

Hazel-colored flesh has white veining.

SCORZONE
(Tuber aestivum)

The summer black truffle is the most common truffle in Tuscany, found all over the region. It is excellent when fresh, though not as good as the black truffle *(see below)*, but it usually costs about one-tenth of the price of the white truffle. Its flavor is heightened in stuffings and in baked dishes. Harvesting is allowed from May to December.

Black surface is knobbly.

Surface is rough but not knobbly.

TARTUFO NERO PREGIATO
(Tuber melanosporum)

The prized black truffle is usually found in oak woods where the sun can penetrate. This is the *diamant noir* (black diamond) of the French; in Italy it also called *nero di Norcia* (black truffle of Norcia). It has a delicious scent of ripening fruit with a whiff of garlic. It has an extraordinary capacity to blend with other foods, and it will enhance the flavor of hot sauces and stuffings, terrines, and pâtés. It is at its best from November 15 to March 15 and costs about half as much as the white truffle. It grows in scattered patches across the region.

Grayish flesh with sparse, thick veins.

Flesh is black with fine white, translucent veining.

TARTUFO D'INVERNO
(Tuber brumale)

Hazel trees rather than oak are preferred by the winter black truffle, though it is sometimes found together with the prized black truffle. At the market (and in the kitchen) it is somewhat less valuable than the summer black and the prized black (its perfume is less delicate and persistent), but its gastronomic uses are the same. Harvesting is permitted from November 15 to March 15.

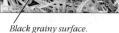

Black grainy surface.

OTHER TRUFFLES

There are various small truffles that are very similar to the March truffle. These can be distinguished only with a microscope but they ripen at different times from the March truffle. These include the *Tuber puberulum, Tuber dryophilum,* and *Tuber maculatum.* While the law does not allow their sale, the law is not enforced. A black truffle called *Tuber mesentericum* is sometimes found in the Tuscany region. Unfortunately, it has an unpleasant smell of carbolic acid and is not worth buying.

Florence, Arezzo, AND Casentino

Florence, Arezzo, and Casentino

GEOGRAPHICALLY AND GASTRONOMICALLY, this area is the most varied part of Tuscany. Visitors from all over the world arrive in Florence and the city seems able to accept their customs and habits while still preserving its own distinctive character. Pratomagno and the Apennine ridge are covered by extensive forests, created and protected for centuries by the Camaldolesi monks. The Mugello developed a whole way of life based on the chestnut tree, and the Val di Chiana is famed for its excellent beef. The climate is Mediterranean, water is abundant, and the food and wine are part of an ancient culture and the result of centuries of prosperity. Life here is very good.

Firenzuola
Scarperia
San Pietro a Sieve
Borgo San Loren
Montemurlo
Bivigliano
PRATO
Calenzano
Carmignano
Sesto Fiorentino
Fiesole
Lastra a Signa
FLORENCE
Arno
Capraia a Limite
Scandicci
Pontassie\
Fucecchio
Montelupo Fiorentino
EMPOLI

BISCOTTI (PRATO COOKIES)

These traditional Tuscan cookies are believed to have come from Prato originally. Known as *biscotti di Prato*, or *cantucci*, they are usually eaten after dipping into Vin Santo *(see p34)*.

Florentine wineries are a mix of innovation and tradition. The stainless steel containers of modern technology exist alongside small new oak *barriques* as well as great old wooden barrels used to age the traditional wines *(see pp24–7)*.

Enoteca Pinchiorri in Florence is one of Italy's top restaurants, known for the excellent quality of the food and the extensive wine list. The cellar is one of the most prestigious in Europe.

◁   **Dome of Florence cathedral viewed from the hills outside the city**

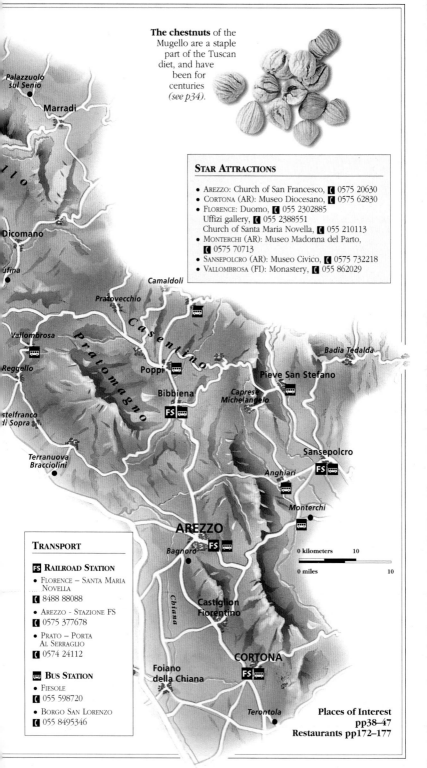

The chestnuts of the Mugello are a staple part of the Tuscan diet, and have been for centuries *(see p34).*

STAR ATTRACTIONS

- Arezzo: Church of San Francesco, ☎ 0575 20630
- Cortona (AR): Museo Diocesano, ☎ 0575 62830
- Florence: Duomo, ☎ 055 2302885
  Uffizi gallery, ☎ 055 2388551
  Church of Santa Maria Novella, ☎ 055 210113
- Monterchi (AR): Museo Madonna del Parto, ☎ 0575 70713
- Sansepolcro (AR): Museo Civico, ☎ 0575 732218
- Vallombrosa (FI): Monastery, ☎ 055 862029

TRANSPORT

FS RAILROAD STATION

- Florence – Santa Maria Novella
  ☎ 8488 88088
- Arezzo - Stazione FS
  ☎ 0575 377678
- Prato – Porta Al Serraglio
  ☎ 0574 24112

BUS STATION

- Fiesole
  ☎ 055 598720
- Borgo San Lorenzo
  ☎ 055 8495346

Palazzuolo sul Senio

Marradi

Dicomano

úfina

Camaldoli

Pratovecchio

Vallombrosa

Reggello

stelfranco di Sopra

Poppi

Bibbiena

Terranuova Braccolini

Caprese Michelangelo

Pieve San Stefano

Badia Tedalda

Sansepolcro

Anghiari

Monterchi

AREZZO

Bagnoro

Chiana

Castiglion Fiorentino

Foiano della Chiana

CORTONA

Terontola

0 kilometers 10

0 miles 10

Places of Interest
pp38–47
Restaurants pp172–177

Wines

FLORENTINE WINES WERE FAMOUS as long ago as the early Middle Ages. At the start of the 18th century the Grand Duke of Florence identified a number of localities that were famed for their vineyards, including Carmignano, Pomino and Valdarno di Sopra. (The Chianti area was not included because at that time it was limited to the territory of Siena and only later extended to the hills around Florence.)

In the Florence area, which lends itself to producing fine reds, the prince of the vines is the Sangiovese, which has gained a good reputation following recent modifications in Chianti-making. Sangiovese provides 75–100 percent of the grapes, Canaiolo Nero up to 10 percent, Trebbiano Toscano, Malvasia del Chianti, and other red grapes up to 10 percent). Its potential is still being studied, but Sangiovese is producing wines of great character. Other vines producing red grapes in this area are Canaiolo Nero, Cabernet Franc, Cabernet Sauvignon, and Merlot. Among white grape vines, the traditional Malvasia del Chianti and Trebbiano Toscano are now second-string grapes, while Pinot Bianco and Chardonnay are increasingly used blended or as single varieties.

CHIANTI COLLI FIORENTINI

This is the Chianti of the subzone south of Florence as far as Impruneta; to the east and west the zone stretches south along the banks of the Arno and between the Pesa and Elsa valleys to Barberino. The terrain to the east, with a warm, dry climate and sandier soils, yields wines of less body and greater saltiness. The soils to the east, on wooded hillsides, have a damper, cooler climate that yields finer perfumes and a longer life.

Chianti Colli Fiorentini is well suited to flavorsome dishes like cacciucco *(fish soup) and first courses of pulses and cereals such as* zuppa di farro *(grain soup). The Superiore, which is stronger, and the Riserva, which is aged longer, are more suited to robust first courses with meat sauces, meat grilled or cooked on the spit, and game.*

CHIANTI RÙFINA

This is considered the most refined of the various types of Chianti. The territory stretches northeast from Florence. The wine is born fairly rich in tannins, ensuring it ages well – it will keep for up to 40 years or more – but it is also slightly tingling to the palate. For this reason the wine needs to be allowed to mellow slowly.

A well-balanced wine with good body, particularly suited to dishes with a strong flavour, such as trippa alla fiorentina *(Florentine-style tripe), red meat, and mature cheeses.*

MAIALE UBRIACO

6 pork chops • 2 cloves garlic, chopped • 1 teaspoon fennel seeds • 2 glasses Chianti • salt • pepper

Heat a nonstick pan over a medium heat. Season the pork chops with plenty of salt and pepper and place them in the hot pan. Add the chopped garlic and the fennel seeds and cook over a high heat until the chops are golden on both sides. Pour in the red wine and continue cooking until most of the wine has evaporated.

CHIANTI MONTALBANO

This Chianti area covers some of the provinces of Florence to the west of the city and also Pistoia to the northwest. The wines produced around Vinci and Lamporecchio were already renowned in the 18th century, as was noted by the Grand Duke Cosimo III. At that time it was a robust wine with a high alcohol content. The current trend is for a red wine with a more elegant structure and less alcohol.

Generally Chianti Montalbano is light and fresh and makes pleasant drinking. It is very versatile, complementing both red and white meat.

CARMIGNANO

Production of this wine is restricted to hillsides in the municipal areas of Carmignano and Poggio a Caiano. It differs from other local reds because of the use of Cabernet Franc and Cabernet Sauvignon grapes, which give it a quite distinctive character. These grapes were already in use in the 18th century, when they were known as *uva francesca*. The DOCG label is reserved for Rosso and Rosso Riserva.

The rosé labelled Carmignano followed by the letters DOC is often called Vin Ruspo.

BARCO REALE DI CARMIGNANO

This wine is the young version of Carmignano, made from the same grapes but aged for a shorter period. Fresh and mellow, it is ideal as an all-purpose table wine. The name comes from a wall, called the Barco Reale, 31 miles (50 km) long. It was erected for Cosimo I, the Grand Duke of Tuscany in the 1570s, to separate his farmland from his game reserve.

Carmignano DOC also appears on the label of various kinds of Vin Santo: dry, semi-sweet (also Reserve) and Occhio di Pernice (ordinary or Reserva).

A Reserve red is also produced and the Pomino line is completed with a white and a red Vin Santo, both especially good wines.

POMINO

The zone of production for Pomino wine is very small and forms part of the municipal territory of Rùfina. A feature is the presence of French vines, introduced in the early 19th century, which found a suitable microclimate in the high altitudes (1600–2400 feet/500–800 m) above sea level. White wine is produced from Pinot Bianco and Chardonnay grapes and red from Sangiovese, Canaiolo, Cabernet Franc, and Cabernet Sauvignon grapes.

CHIANTI COLLI ARETINI

Chianti from the Colli Aretini is lighter-bodied and has a lower alcohol content than other Tuscan Chianti. Chianti Colli Aretini is ideal for general use as a table wine and is also well suited to first courses with meat sauces and also to pork and veal dishes, even those with well-seasoned sauces.

BIANCO VERGINE VALDICHIANA

This white wine is produced either still, lightly sparkling, or fully sparkling in eight communes of the province of Arezzo and roughly half the province of Siena. It goes well with delicate *antipasti*, soups, vegetable dishes, and unsalted fish.

The basic grape is Trebbiano Toscano, comprising at least 60 percent, blended with other white grapes, especially Malvasia.

WINE TYPE	GOOD VINTAGES	GOOD PRODUCERS	WINE TYPE	GOOD VINTAGES	GOOD PRODUCERS
Red Wine			**Red Wine**		
Chianti Rùfina	97, 95, 90	Frescobaldi di Firenze, Fattoria di Basciano a Rùfina	Carmignano	97, 95, 90	Tenuta Capezzana di Carmignano
Super Tuscans *(see p130)*	98, 97, 95, 90	Antinori di Firenze, D'Alessandro di Cortona, Frescobaldi di Firenze, Ruffino di Pontassieve	Chianti	97, 90	Antinori di Firenze

Salumi

Tuscany has a quite different approach to *salumi* (cured meats) from the rest of Italy, preferring a dry, highly seasoned product with plenty of pepper (often whole black peppercorns), made for eating with the unsalted local bread. These preserved meat products reflect a taste developed over many centuries. In Tuscany, pigs were not fed on swill, scraps, and cereals but were raised wild, free to graze and root about in the woods where they ate acorns, sweet chestnuts, truffles, and other tubers, which in turn made their flesh firm and flavorsome and naturally produced hams and salami with these tasty qualities. Because of the warm Tuscan climate, the meat products were then salted abundantly to ensure they kept well.

TUSCAN SALAMI

This salami (cured sausage) is eaten uncooked. It is made of ground lean pork and lardons of hard fat chopped with a knife. It has a firm texture and is extremely tasty, with a marked flavor of black pepper.

Natural casing.

Pure pork filling.

Filling is a mixture of beef and pork.

SPALLA (SHOULDER)

Shoulder of pork is often cured to produce ham, but not on all estates since it may also be used for salami. This is "poor man's *prosciutto* (cured ham)," the fare of people who work on the land. Compared with the leg, the shoulder tastes more salty, peppery, and fatty. It must be stored in cool, dry conditions.

RIGATINO

In Tuscany this *pancetta* (cured pork belly) is always rather dry and well seasoned. Sometimes chilli is added to give it a spicy flavor.

PIEDUCCI (PIG'S FEET)

Pig's feet are seasoned with salt, vinegar, garlic, and rosemary, then dried. They are used to flavor soups.

ZUPPA DI FAGIOLI CON I PIEDUCCI

1 pig's foot • 1 lb (450 g) dried zolfini *beans*

Soak the pig's foot in cold water for 48 hours to remove the salt. After 24 hours, add the beans to soak with the pig's foot. The next day, drain the meat and beans and put them in an earthenware pot or large saucepan. Cover with water, bring to the boil, then cover and simmer over a low heat for 2 hours. Remove some of the beans with a slotted spoon and mash them. Break up the meat and return it to the pot with the mashed beans. Reheat. Serve the soup with *bruschetta* rubbed with garlic and drizzled with olive oil, or use it as stock for soups made with grains or cabbage.

Traditionally, Florentine salami with fennel (finocchiona) *is a fairly large size.*

Meat is finely ground for a soft texture.

This medium-sized type of salami is usually less garlicky. It is often found at small traditional delicatessens.

SBRICIOLONA OR FINOCCHIONA

These salamis are flavored with fennel seed and, frequently, with plenty of garlic as well.

Thick layers of fat are streaked with lean meat.

GUANCIALE (PIG'S CHEEK)

The cheek of the pig is salted, seasoned with pepper, and matured. *Guanciale* is very tasty but is usually used as a flavoring ingredient in other dishes rather than eaten on its own.

SALSICCIA

This classic sausage is made from different cuts of pork, finely ground, seasoned with salt, pepper, and a little garlic, and stuffed into a thin natural casing. Sausages are best eaten straight from the grill. Cured sausage, which may contain spices, liver, fennel, or red wine, can be sliced and eaten on *crostini* (toasted Tuscan bread).

SOPPRESSATA OR COPPA (PIG'S HEAD SAUSAGE)

This sausage is prepared using all parts of the pig's head. The head is boiled with herbs and spices, chopped coarsely, and flavored with garlic and pepper. Parsley and chilli may also be added.

This sausage has a firm, gelatinous, spongy texture.

Tuscan prosciutto crudo should be sliced very thinly.

TUSCAN PROSCIUTTO CRUDO (CURED HAM)

Cheaper hams are saltier and smell mainly of pepper. A fine *prosciutto crudo* has a delicate aroma, and, while it is more salty than classic Parma ham and San Daniele from the Veneto, it is not excessively so. The texture is firm and it has a definite, lingering meaty flavor, spiced with pepper. The quality depends on the ingredients and the skill of the producer, and no two hams taste exactly the same.

OTHER PORK SPECIALITIES WORTH TRYING

Sanguignaccio or **buristo** (blood sausage) is made of pork blood and cartilage and may come in a sausage shape such as *buristo di Cinta (see p104)* or in a large piece such as the *buristo* of Montalcino *(see p137)*. Other cured meats made from lean cuts of pork – fillet, loin, or the collar – are common. **Capocollo** (cured neck of pork) is similar to the *coppa* from Lombardy and Emilia-Romagna, but is much drier and more peppery. Some producers flavor small spicy salamis by adding chilli to them. **Lardo** (lard), flavored mainly with rosemary, is another very popular delicacy in Tuscany.

Extra-Virgin Olive Oil

FLORENCE IS RINGED with olive groves, and all the lower ridges of the Valdarno and its tributaries are dotted with olive trees. The types of oil produced in the area differ greatly, not so much through tradition – because nearly everywhere the tendency is to harvest early and produce fruity oils – but because of differences in soil and the choice of different varieties of olive tree. Most olive-growing estates in the region are small or medium-sized and the majority aim for high quality. Nearly all the estates combine olive oil production with wine-making or, in areas unsuited to growing vines, with other types of agriculture such as growing grain or vegetables.

RÙFINA OLIVE OIL
This oil is produced in an area north of Florence comprising the communes of Rùfina, Dicomano, and Londa. The oil is fruity with a marked scent of herbs, strong, very full-bodied and flavorsome. Selvapiana olive oil is one of the best in the area.

OIL FROM THE COLLI FIORENTINI
Inland south of Florence is the area that produces this oil. The territory covers Bagno a Ripoli, Fiesole, Scandicci, Impruneta, Incisa, and San Casciano, stretching as far as Poggibonsi and San Gimignano. The oil is medium-bodied with a full, smooth, fruity flavor which has a vegetable aftertaste and some slightly bitter, pungent notes.

OIL FROM PRATOMAGNO
This oil is produced in the territory east of Florence in the bend of the upper Valdarno lying between the provinces of Florence and Arezzo. The territory includes the communes of Reggello (FI), Castelfranco di Sopra, and Loro Ciuffenna (AR). The oil is very similar to that of the Colli Fiorentini, but generally less intense.

OIL FROM MONTE ALBANO

East of Lucca, between the province of Pistoia and the northern part of the province of Florence, is the area producing this olive oil, especially at Vinci, Carmignano, Artimino, and Montelupo Fiorentino. The oil is generally medium-light and fruity with herbal scents and a balanced flavor. This flavor varies in intensity from season to season.

OIL FROM THE COLLI ARETINI

Produced in the territory south of Arezzo, covering various communes including Castiglione Fiorentino and Cortona, this is a medium-bodied fruity oil, fresh and aromatic. Body and fluidity is average. It has a harmonious taste with slightly bitter and pungent notes and a hint of artichoke.

PUTTANAIO

3–4 tablespoons virgin olive oil • 3 onions, sliced • 2 sprigs rosemary, chopped • 3 cloves garlic, crushed • 2 stalks celery, sliced • 3 potatoes, diced • about 2 lb (800 g) green peppers, seeded and diced • 3 eggplants, diced • 2 carrots, diced • 2 zucchinis, diced • 18 lb (8 kg) ripe tomatoes, chopped • 3 tablespoons chopped fresh basil, thyme, and parsley • salt

Heat the oil in a large pan, add the onions, rosemary, and garlic; fry until soft. Add the diced vegetables and tomatoes. Season and simmer until the vegetables are cooked. Garnish with the chopped herbs before serving the soup.

The olive tree breaks the monotony of great fields of grain.

LAUDEMIO OLIVE OIL

This was originally the finest oil – the one that the sharecropper was required to reserve for the landowner – it was referred to as "the master's oil." Today, Laudemio is a brand name given to the produce of a consortium of estates, all of which use the same bottle design. The denomination does not represent a traditional area or specific properties or quality, and the regulations are vague about some essential factors. They cover a very broad area of membership (central Tuscany), best-by dates, harvesting by December 15 (normal for Tuscany, weather permitting), and rather vaguely defined production techniques. In other words, the quality from different estates may vary.

Chianina Beef

THE CELEBRATED DISH *Bistecca alla Fiorentina* (Florentine T-bone steak), traditionally cooked over hot wood embers, is best when made with beef from pedigree Chianina cattle, which is generally rated as of superior quality. Chianina cattle are traditionally reared in the Val di Chiana, particularly around Cortona. The distinctive, white-coated breed – one of the oldest breeds in existence – only produces high quality meat if it has been raised in exactly the right conditions, however. While other breeds of cattle are rarely temperamental, Chianina cattle are unusually sensitive and their state of well-being influences the quality of the meat – if the animal is high-strung, the meat is tough. The Chianina cow flourishes when looked after by the same person. It objects to sharing its stall with other cattle, and the calf has to be raised alongside its mother. There is debate as to whether the quality of beef is better when the cattle graze freely outdoors or when they are kept in a stall and fed on a mixture of fresh grass and hay.

For Chianina beef to be first-rate, the animal should be mature – this means over 16–18 months old – and it should have grown to over 1,760 lb (800 kilos), yielding 1,100 lb (500 kilos) of meat.

BISTECCA ALLA FIORENTINA
This is a T-bone steak (rib steak with the fillet steak still attached). Its total weight varies from 1 lb 2 oz–2 lb 4 oz (500 g–1 kg) and it is usually sliced thickly, up to about 2 inches (5 cm).

An essential feature of Chianina beef is the very firm flesh which is tender but never dry, despite the small amount of surface fat and marbling. The flavor is quite distinctive.

BISTECCA ALLA FIORENTINA

1 T-bone steak, about 2 lb 4 oz (1 kg) in weight and including the fillet steak, rib, and under-rib • extra-virgin olive oil • salt • pepper

Heat the grill or light the barbecue. Sprinkle both sides of the steak with pepper and lay it on the grill, keeping it some distance from the embers, if cooking on a barbecue. Cook for 5 minutes, then turn over and season the cooked side with salt. Cook the second side for 5 minutes (or longer, if preferred) and season with salt. Remove from the grill and brush with olive oil (season the oil with garlic and herbs, if preferred).

BISTECCA (CHOP)
This is the ordinary rib steak without the fillet. It is often used as part of a plate of assorted roast meats for a typical Tuscan meal.

For the thickness to be just right for perfect cooking, there has to be both the rib and the under-rib.

POLZO
This is the cut under the shoulder, good for *stracotto* (braising), boiling, and, above all, *scottiglia* (stew).

This small fat-free joint is suitable for machine slicing for carpaccio *(steak sliced very thin and eaten raw).*

GIRELLO (TOPSIDE)
This lean cut is good for roasting and for cutlets.

The layers of lean beef alternating with fat and bone make a tasty broth when boiled.

SPICCHIO DI PETTO (MIDDLE BRISKET)
This is called *biancostato* in the rest of Italy and is typically used for making boiled beef. It is also used for *scottiglia* (stew) after part of the fat has been removed.

This lean cut is very popular because it is easy to cook.

NOCE (RUMP)
This lean part of the leg is used for scallops, breaded cutlets, and small steaks.

OTHER CHIANINA CUTS
Because the Chianina breed is mainly associated with the T-bone steak, other cuts tend to be neglected. However, the superiority of Chianina beef is obvious in all cuts, from forequarter to rump. In Tuscany it is particularly important to use Chianina beef for traditional dishes, recipes devised for that type of very tender beef. For *stracotto alla fiorentina* (Florentine braised beef), for example, the best cuts, in addition to **polzo**, are **scannello** (sirloin) and **cappello del prete**; for *scottiglia* ask for **reale**.

Traditional Produce

A DEEP-SEATED LOVE of tradition ensures the continuing popularity of all kinds of local produce. A traditional meal in this region will never stray far from a long-standing pattern: *crostini (see p36)*, *prosciutto (see p29)*, *pappardelle* (a type of ribbon pasta) with hare, and mixed roast meats. The mild Tuscan climate and the exacting demands of producers and consumers mean that you can still find free-range chickens, *salumi (see p27)* made with local ingredients, local varieties of vegetables, traditional cakes, and freshly baked breads.

CHESTNUTS
The quality of a chestnut is determined by the size and the number of nuts in a single husk. Chestnut trees may produce fruit with a single large nut in each husk or several small ones. The larger varieties with a single nut are much prized by confectioners for their fine flavor and also for their appearance because the inside shell does not press into the kernel. Larger nuts are also easier to work with.

CHESTNUT FLOUR
A staple in mountain areas since ancient times, chestnut flour *(farina di castagne)* is the basic ingredient of *castagnaccio* (chestnut cake). The flour becomes stale very quickly so it should not be stored for too long.

ZOLFINI BEANS FROM PRATOMAGNO
These small, pale yellowish beans, which are now very rare, are exclusive to Pratomagno. The thin-skinned beans have a dense texture and a good flavor. They are easily digested and particularly rich in iron and fiber.

Small zolfini beans are a pale yellow color.

These sweet almond cookies are traditionally eaten after dinner, dipped in sweet Vin Santo.

ZUCCOTTO
This cream and sponge-cake dessert is a Florentine speciality, now seen all over Italy. A mold of sponge is filled with whipped cream, confectioner's custard, and chocolate. The chilled *zuccotto* is turned out to serve.

BISCOTTINI DI PRATO
These almond cookies, which come from Prato, are also called *cantuccini*. They are made from flour, eggs, sugar, almonds, and pine nuts. The dough is shaped into a long loaf and baked, then it is sliced and baked again until the slices are crunchy.

MUTTON

Pecora (mutton), which is meat from the adult sheep, is widely eaten in the Campi Bisenzio area. Shepherds used to move their flocks seasonally and customarily paid their way in kind. They handed over the weaker sheep exhausted by traveling the Passo dei Pecorai before they made their descent to marshy plains that were difficult for sheep to cross.

SUGO DI PECORA

2 lb 4 oz (1 kg) boned shoulder or leg of mutton, trimmed of excess fat and cubed • olive oil for frying • 2 onions, chopped • 3 cloves garlic, finely chopped • 1–2 sprigs of rosemary • 1 sprig of sage • 8 oz (200 g) ground lean mutton • 4 oz (100 g) chopped prosciutto crudo • the zest of ¹/₂ a lemon • pinch of freshly grated nutmeg • 1 tablespoon tomato paste diluted in a little warm water • 1 lb 2 oz (500 g) tomatoes, peeled • salt • pepper

Heat a frying pan, add the cubed mutton, and fry for 1–2 minutes to seal the meat. Heat a little oil in a saucepan, add the onions, garlic, rosemary, and sage and fry until softened. Add the ground mutton and ham, stirring well. Add the cubed mutton, nutmeg, lemon zest, and diluted tomato paste. Cook over a moderate heat until the water has evaporated. Add the tomatoes and season. Cook over a low heat for about 1 hour, until the meat is tender, adding extra hot water, if necessary. Serve the mutton sauce with pasta.

PANE SCIOCCO (UNSALTED BREAD)

When it comes to bread, Tuscans are great traditionalists. The large loaves, elongated or rounded, above all unsalted, have a fairly heavy texture well suited for making the popular *crostoni* (toasted bread), for mopping up sauces, or as a base for soups.

GEMMA D'ABETO

The monks of Monte Senario produce this aromatic liqueur from herbs and fir cone seeds.

VALDARNO CAPONS

These free-range capons with yellow legs and a bright red crest are typical of certain villages in the Valdarno. They have firm, flavorsome flesh and are especially delicious in casseroles.

WHAT TO SAMPLE

Cantucci all'anice are sweet crunchy cookies flavored with aniseed. They are usually dunked in red wine before eating. They are made in Prato by the same firm that makes *cantuccini (see p34)*. Various **herbal liqueurs** are produced by the monks of Monte Senario and Camaldoli, who also sell **honey, candies,** and **chocolate.** The Sieve and other rivers yield very fine **trout.** In the Casentino in particular, many shepherds make cheese, and some of their **pecorino** and **ricotta** is as good as that produced in the Crete region, a popular cheese-making region to the south of Siena. **Schiaccioni** are a local large white bean worth trying. The Mugello, the pretty area to the north and east of Florence, has black truffles, and the Valdarno region has white as well. The Empoli area produces fine vegetables, including **white asparagus.**

Wild Produce

PINAROLO
(Boletus luteus)
Winter *porcini* has a distinctive cap covered with a skin that comes away easily (the skin has to be removed before eating). Its skin is very slimy and brownish in color, while the stalk has a broad ring. Found only in pine woods, it is one of the best *porcini* for preserving in oil as well as being excellent deviled fresh.

PORTENTOSO
(Tricholoma portentosum)
This silky gray mushroom is very common in the late fall and can be found in the stands of fir or pine trees mostly in Vallombrosa and Lunigiana. It is excellent preserved in oil or deviled, and is ideal in stews.

CROSTINI CON I CIMBALLI

1¼ lb (600 g) caps of cimballi (funnel-cap mushrooms), chopped coarsely • 3 cloves garlic, chopped • pinch of chilli pepper • extra-virgin olive oil • 1 dessertspoon chopped tomatoes • 1 sprig of parsley, chopped • salt • Tuscan bread

Place the mushrooms in a saucepan with the garlic and chilli, plenty of oil, and salt. Cook over a high heat until the mushrooms shed their moisture, then lower the heat and cook until the moisture evaporates completely. Add the tomato pulp and parsley, and continue cooking for another 10 minutes. Toast slices of Tuscan bread, spread with olive oil, and top with the mushrooms.

CIMBALLO
(Clitocybe geotropa)
In its early stages this mushroom – sometimes known as the Ridestone funnel-cap mushroom – looks like a large nail, then it grows into a tall, scented, coffee-colored funnel. It grows in the mountains and meadows, in coastal areas under hedges, on heaths, and in scrub where it forms zigzag lines. The cap is exquisite; the dried stem is ground into a powder.

DORMIENTE
(Hygrophorus marzuolus)
This spring mushroom – sometimes known as silvery snowbank mushroom – is found in the mountains of Vallombrosa when the snow thaws, and around Siena and Arezzo in February and March. It is protected – only mushrooms larger than ¾ inch (2 cm) can be picked. It has a mild flavor and is excellent fresh, cooked in cream sauces or in flans, or preserved in oil.

CHIOCCIOLE ALLA NEPITELLA (SNAILS WITH CALAMINT LEAVES)

1 large onion • 1 stalk celery • 1 carrot • 1 chilli • 2 cloves garlic • extra-virgin olive oil • 1¼ lb (500 g) peeled tomatoes • calamint leaves • 4½ lb (2 kg) small white snails, ready cleaned • 8 fl oz (200 ml) red wine • meat stock • salt • pepper

Chop the vegetables, chilli, and garlic and fry in a large pan with plenty of oil. When the vegetables have softened, add the tomatoes, calamint, salt, and pepper. Lower the heat and simmer gently for about 10 minutes. Stir in the snails and sprinkle the wine over them. Simmer gently for 1½ hours, adding stock if necessary to prevent it from drying out.

NEPITELLA
(Calamintha nepeta)
Gathered from early spring until the first frosts, calamint is found from the coast to the hills in Tuscany. It flowers in June and July. In Tuscan cooking it is used with mushrooms, snails, artichokes, or lamb. It must be used in very small quantities otherwise the dish will taste of caramel. It is often confused with mint, but the perfume is sweeter and heavier. Use calamint sparingly because it can cause sleeplessness and palpitations.

PIMPINELLA
(Sanguisorba minor)
A curious and unmistakable salad herb, *pimpinella* smells rather like melon peel. It is common at all altitudes, especially on the edges of pathways and vegetable patches. Use it raw in salads or add it to white wine for an intriguing aperitif.

PEPOLINO
(Thymus serpyllum and other varieties)
Wild thyme is the most common wild herb at all altitudes and latitudes. It is a tender plant that covers walls, stumps of trees, and banks between woodland and pasture. The flowered tips are picked between May and October. It is excellent fresh or dried, for roasts, stews, and meat sauces. Fresh thyme can be added to salads.

MORA DI ROVA
(Rubus species)
In Tuscany an abundance of blackberries can be found on the edge of thickets. They have large, flavorsome fruits, especially those growing on the Apennine range. They are ideal for jams and syrups, and children enjoy picking and eating fresh blackberries.

Places of Interest

FLORENCE, AREZZO, AND CASENTINO form a zone that runs the whole length of Tuscany and embraces a large city, cool, shady mountains along the crest of the Apennines, the forests of Casentino, and the Mediterranean coast of the Basso Aretino. Its cuisine is a showcase for the region's food and drink, with outlets of notable quality in the Arezzo area – especially the butchers' shops. In the summer many stores close on Saturday afternoons.

AREZZO

 Macelleria Corrado Falcinelli

Palazzo del Pero, 62/a
📞 0575 369037
⬤ Wed pm

Corrado Falcinelli, the heir to three generations of butchers and producers of salumi, guarantees fine Chianina beef and also offers genuine Tuscan all-pork salumi completely free from preservatives. The pigs are raised in the traditional fashion locally. The excellent lamb sold here comes from local farms.

🐔 Pollo San Marco

frazione San Marco,
via dei Frati, 12
📞 0575 901601
⬤ Sat pm

Here you will find beef, pork, lamb, an assortment of game birds and animals, plus a variety of other local produce including Chianina beef, the firm's own salumi, free-range, yellow-legged chickens from Valdarno (see p35), and ready-to-cook dishes, such as collo ripieno (stuffed neck of beef).

🐂 Macelleria Sestini

via Romana, 130
📞 0575 900067
⬤ Wed pm

Local meat (including Chianina beef) is sold here, along with pork
from the firm's own farm and all kinds of classic salumi. Specialties of the firm include pancettone made from Tuscan bacon and pork, plus suckling pig, stuffed local rabbits, and other prepared meats.

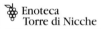 Panificio Tavanti

borgo Santa Croce, 15
📞 0575 352354
⬤ Wed pm

Bread sold here is made in the traditional way and then baked in a wood-fired oven.

🍇 Enoteca Torre di Nicche

piaggia San Martino, 8
📞 0575 352035
○ after 6 pm

This wine shop, bar, and restaurant has a very good selection of Italian wines from all regions and a fine choice of Tuscan produce. Try the salumi and cheese or sample hot or cold dishes cooked traditionally. The cakes are homemade.

BADIA TEDALDA (AR)

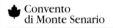 Macelleria Piegai

piazza Bonafede, 23
📞 0575 714246
⬤ Wed pm

You can buy Chianina beef from cattle that grazed on the company's farm at Caprile, an "agriturismo" (a place for farm or wine estate vacations). Likewise, the pork is from pigs from a nearby farm. Other specialties include pork and wild boar sausages.

BIVIGLIANO (FI)

🍁 Convento di Monte Senario

📞 055 406441
⬤ Fri

As well as their famous Gemma d'Abeto liqueur, the monks produce Elixir di China, Amaro Borghini, and Alkermes from an ancient recipe.

PANZANELLA

12 slices stale bread • 2 teaspoons white wine vinegar • 12 anchovy fillets, chopped • 6 tomatoes, cut into wedges • 3 onions, sliced • fresh basil leaves, roughly torn • extra-virgin olive oil • salt • pepper

Soften the bread by soaking it in cold water with the vinegar added. Squeeze it dry and divide it between six plates or bowls. Cover each slice of bread with some of the chopped anchovy, tomato wedges, onion slices, and torn basil leaves. Drizzle olive oil over the top, season with salt and pepper, then repeat to make a second layer.

STRACOTTO ALLA FIORENTINA

2 lb (1 kg) braising steak or brisket in a single piece tied with string • 1 pint (500 ml) Chianti wine • sprigs of rosemary and sage • 1–2 bay leaves • 4 cloves garlic, chopped • 2 onions, chopped • 3 sticks celery, chopped • 3 carrots, chopped • extra-virgin olive oil • 1 lb (500 g) plum tomatoes, chopped • salt • pepper

Put the beef in a bowl with the wine, herbs, and all the vegetables except the tomatoes. Leave to marinate in a cool place for 12 hours. Drain the meat and pat dry. Heat the oil in a flameproof casserole, add the meat and brown all over to seal it. Remove the vegetables from the marinade with a slotted spoon and brown them in a little oil in a second pan, then add to the beef. Pour in the wine from the marinade, add the tomatoes, and simmer for 30 minutes. Remove the vegetables, purée them, and pour the purée back into the pan. Simmer for a further 4 hours, adding water if necessary (but keep the gravy thick). Season with salt and pepper. Untie the meat and serve cut into thick slices, accompanied by the gravy.

CALENZANO (FI)

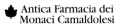 La Pasta di Anna Paola

via Puccini, 237
055 8879505 ● Mon

Here you will find a wide variety of flat and stuffed pasta specialties made from good quality fresh ingredients. The extensive selection varies according to the season and the produce available.

CAMALDOLI (AR)

🍁 Antica Farmacia dei Monaci Camaldolesi

via Camaldoli
0575 556143
● Wed

The Carthusian monks at the monastery produce various liqueurs flavored with different herbs, an aperitif, a dessert liqueur made from fir cones, candies (such as pine, barley, honey, and fruit drops), and a wide variety of honey (with forest honey the local specialty). The monks also make chocolate from their own special recipe.

CAPRAIA A LIMITE (FI)

🍇 Tenuta Cantagallo

località Capraia Fiorentina, via Valicarda, 35
0571 910078

The sea breezes that play over the hillside enable aromatic grapes to be grown successfully here. Alongside the production of the classic Chianti di Montalbano and a Reserve, Carleto is also produced from Rhine Riesling. For a more international style, there is Raffaello made from Sangiovese, Syrah, and Merlot grapes. The olives yield a fine-scented and flavorsome oil – some is bottled as Laudemio and some is used to preserve fresh vegetables. The honey and the grape jam are very good.

CARMIGNANO (PO)

🍇 Fattoria Ambra

via Lombarda, 85
055 8719049

This estate's wine-making technique is based on a policy of separating the different varieties of grape so the wine-makers have more control over the combinations of grapes and are better able to harmonize the final blend. Much of the production is devoted to producing the estate's top wines, Carmignano Vigna Santa Cristina in Pilli and two Reserves: Le Vigne Alte and Elzana, all with good structure and a velvety texture. The Barco Reale makes excellent drinking.

🍇 Fattoria di Artimino

viale Papa Giovanni XXIII, 3
055 8751424

With about 173 acres (70 hectares) of vineyards and twice this area under olive groves, this is one of the most beautiful and interesting Tuscan estates. The Medici villa complex houses a four-star hotel (Hotel Paggeria Medicea) and two restaurants (Biagio Pignatta and Le Cantine del Redi). The vineyard's leading wines are Carmignano and Carmignano Riserva Villa Medicea, as well as Barco Reale and also Vin Santo, the rich sweet dessert wine which is made from Malvasia and Trebbiano grapes.

Fattoria Ambra at Carmignano

FAGIOLI AL FIASCO (BEANS IN A FLASK)

*1 lb (450 g) dried cannellini beans • 1 sprig of sage •
2 cloves garlic, crushed • extra-virgin olive oil •
pepper • salt*

Soak the beans in cold water overnight. The
next day, drain them and put in a pan with all
the other ingredients, adding plenty of oil.
Add enough water to cover, bring to
the boil and simmer for 1–2
hours. In Tuscany, the
beans are cooked in a
Chianti flask placed in
the embers of a fire.
Use fresh Sorana
beans instead, if
available *(see p61).*

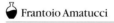

🍇 Tenuta Capezzana

via Capezzana, 100
📞 055 8706005

*This is the largest farm
property in Carmignano
with about 220 acres (90
hectares) of vineyards
and 370 acres
(150 hectares) of olives
surrounding a fine
18th-century Medici
villa. The wines with the
Carmignano label are
Barco Reale, Rosso, and
Vin Santo Riserva. The
rosé Vin Ruspo is
delicious. The Ghiaie della
Furba deserves special
mention: made from
Cabernet Franc, Cabernet
Sauvignon, and Merlot
grapes in equal parts (a
claret blend), it is one of
the most prized wines (a
"Super Tuscan") in Italy.
The extra-virgin olive oil
is excellent.*

🍇 Il Poggiolo

via Pistoiese, 76
📞 055 8711242

*The vineyards here are
scattered over the heart
of the commune and the
estate focuses on the whole
line of Carmignano wines.
This includes a traditional
red (a reserve; a rosé
called Vin Ruspo; and a
younger Barco Reale) and
Vin Santo based on
Trebbiano grapes. These*

*wines
offer very good quality
at reasonable prices.*

CASTIGLION FIORENTINO (AR)

🫒 Frantoio Amatucci

località Noceta, 41/b
📞 0575 657129

*This olive mill produces
and sells the traditional
extra-virgin olive oil
of the Colli Aretini. The
oil is ideal for use in
classic Tuscan soups and
all dishes finished with a
drizzle of good quality
olive oil.*

CORTONA (AR)

🍇 Tenimenti D'Alessandro Luigi

viale Manzano, 15
📞 0575 618667

*This is the former
Fattoria di Manzano
under a new name.
The estate's policy is to
produce wines from
carefully selected grapes.
Notable whites are Podere
Fontarca (Chardonnay
and Viognier) and
Terrazze (Sauvignon
Blanc, Grechetto, and
Chenin Blanc). The
estate's gem is Podere il
Bosco made from Syrah
grapes, followed by
Podere Migliare, from
Sangiovese grapes.*

FLORENCE

🍇 Enoteca Alessi

via delle Oche, 27/29
📞 055 214966
⬤ Sat in July

*This large wine shop has
two levels. The lower floor
contains over 2,000 of the
very finest Italian wines,
subdivided by region and
commune. The serving
counter is on the upper
floor where you can find
Tuscan and house
specialties, particularly
confectionery, as well as a
choice selection of liquors
and liqueurs.*

Il Poggiolo at Carmignano

Boutique dei Dolci

via Fabroni, 18 r
[C] 055 499503
[●] Mon

*An original confectionery
shop founded and run
by an Italian-American.
The recipes are American,
English, French, and
Dutch, all prepared with
organically grown
ingredients. The theme
cakes for kids, made
with original American
cake molds of Disney
and Warner Brothers
cartoon characters, are
one of the shop's
specialties, as is the
classic cheesecake.*

Salumeria
Del Panta

via San Antonino, 49 r
[C] 055 216889
[●] Mon

*This shop features a vast
assortment of traditional
Tuscan salumi and
cheeses, some of them
almost impossible to
find elsewhere. It also
offers excellent
international specialties.
Here you will find the
finest preserved fish –
anchovies, sardines,
herrings, dried or salted
cod. There are all kinds of
pickles, preserves in oil,
flour, pulses, and cereals,
including some very
unusual ones, plus
different kinds of rice,
and spices sold loose.*

Dolci e Dolcezze

piazza Beccaria 8 r,
[C] 055 2345458
[●] Mon

*This confectioner's and
café is renowned for its
very imaginative pastries
and cakes, as well as some
interesting savories. All
ingredients are carefully
chosen from natural
produce and artificial
or chemical products are
rigorously excluded.*

Cantinetta Antinori

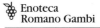 Fernando Primizie

via Don Minzoni, 38 r
[C] 055 587540
[●] Wed pm

*Here you will find a good
variety of vegetables and
fruit, organically grown
or from small local market
gardens. There are also
cheeses and preserves and
a fine selection of wines,
though Tuscans dominate.*

Enoteca
Romano Gambi

via Senese, 21 r
[C] 055 222525
[●] Sun

*All the names that count
among local and Italian
wines, plus wines from
France and the US, can be
found here. There is also a
good selection of whisky
and grappa and a variety
of confectioneries, cakes,
and snacks. Salumi and
cheese are sold at
Christmas. Book for a
tasting. A second shop is
in the town center at Via
Borgo SS. Apostoli, 21-23 r
(055 292646).*

Gelateria Giorgio

via Duccio da Boninsegna, 36
[C] 055 710849
[○] Mon

*This shop is celebrated
throughout Tuscany for its
quality ice cream and the*

torta millefoglie *(vanilla
slice) and* Florentine
schiacciata *(bread).*

Marchesi Antinori

piazza degli Antinori, 3
[C] 055 2359877

*The grapes come from this
winery's various estates to
create a good line of
wines. The stars are the
famed Tignanello from
Sangiovese and Cabernet
grapes (a "Super
Tuscan"), and Solaia
(Cabernet Sauvignon and
Sangiovese grapes). There
are also very good
chiantis, including the
Chianti Classico Peppoli,
and the Reserves: Badia a
Passignano and Tenute
Marchesi Antinori. Note
the white Galestro, a wine
Antinori helped to create.
There is also a spumante:
Marchese Antinori Nature.
The extra-virgin olive oil is
very good, especially from
the Fattoria Peppoli di
San Casciano Val di Pesa.
For purchases apply to:
La Cantinetta Antinori,
Piazza degli Antinori, 3
(055 292234).*

**LAMPREDOTTO
E TRIPPA IN ZIMINO**

*extra-virgin olive oil •
3 cloves garlic , chopped
• 1 lb (500 g) tomatoes,
peeled •1 chilli, deseeded
and chopped • 2 lb
(1 kg) beet leaves, cut
into strips • 2 lb (1 kg)
plain tripe (see below),
cut into strips • salt
• pepper*

Heat some oil in a pan,
cook the garlic briefly,
then add the tomatoes
and cook for about 10
minutes. Add the greens
and cook for 3 minutes.
Add the tripe, season,
and cook for 40–45
minutes. In Italy this dish
is made with half plain
tripe and half *millefoglie*
tripe (which looks like
the leaves of a book).

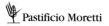 Marchesi de' Frescobaldi

via Santo Spirito, 11
055 27141

Generations of the Frescobaldi family have been making wine in Tuscany for centuries. The Chianti Rùfina Montesodi and Riserva Castello di Nipozzano are well known. Also note the various versions of Pomino: Bianco, Rosso, and Il Benefizio, of which the company is virtually the only producer. For purchases apply to the Enoteca Romano Gambi (see p41).

Pastificio Moretti

via Datini, 22 r
055 685607

On offer here is a wide variety of pasta, and also ready-cooked food.

Gastronomia Palmieri

via Manni, 48 r
055 602081

The variety and quality of its products make this one of Italy's most interesting cheese shops. This fine delicatessen offers an excellent choice of delicacies – caviar, pâté de foie gras, bread baked in a wood-fired oven, preserves, extra-virgin olive oil, salumi, and much more. There is a well-stocked enoteca (wine cellar) with some foreign wines, and there is an excellent selection of ready-made dishes on sale.

Gastronomia Pegna

via dello Studio, 26 r
055 282701
Wed pm

Pegna has been a household name in

BACCALÀ ALLA FIORENTINA

extra-virgin olive oil • 3 cloves garlic, chopped • 1 onion, chopped • 1 lb (450 g) tomatoes, peeled • 2 lb (1 kg) salt cod, presoaked • 1–2 tablespoons chopped fresh parsley • flour • salt • pepper • parsley, to garnish

Heat some oil in a pan, add the garlic and onion, and cook until lightly browned. Add the tomatoes and season with salt and pepper. Meanwhile, bone the cod, leaving the skin on, and cut it into largish squares. Heat plenty of oil in a pan, Flour the pieces of cod, add them to the hot oil, and fry until golden. Remove the fish from the pan, drain on paper towels, and add it to the tomato sauce. Stir in the chopped parsley, and serve garnished with extra parsley.

Florence for 140 years. The products are skillfully selected from Italy and abroad and include a choice of salumi, *cheese, preserves, spices, terrines, and confectioneries.*

Pitti Gola e Cantina

piazza Pitti, 16
055 212704
Mon

Close to Palazzo Pitti, this wine shop boasts a clientèle of Florentine connoisseurs who enjoy the wide range of wines, spirits, preserves, and pickles, all strictly Tuscan produce. Visitors can browse through cookbooks, and there is an area for wine tasting.

Forno di Marcello Pugi

viale De Amicis, 49 r
055 669666
Fri pm

This bakery is famous in Florence and the surrounding area for its delicious schiacciata all'olio *(olive oil bread) and pizza slices. The excellent bread is made using fresh yeast.*

Bar Pasticceria Robiglio

via dei Servi, 112 r
055 212784
Sun

For almost 75 years, Robiglio has delighted gourmets with its traditional confectioneries and excellent coffee. There are two other branches, one on via Tosinghi 11 r (055 215013) and the other on viale Lavagnini 18 r (055 490886). A wide choice of delectable chocolates and snacks is available at the bar.

Salumificio Senese

via Ugnano, 10
055 751611
Wed pm

This firm produces excellent fresh meat from pigs raised on its own farm at Lastra a Signa and by other local breeders. They make their own salumi, *including the Tuscan classics, and serve aromatic sausages from other regions. They do roast suckling pig and cooked meats to order.*

Macelleria Soderi Paolo

interno Mercato Centrale
San Lorenzo
055 2398496
pm

Exceptionally good beef (sometimes Chianina), fine Fanano pork, lamb from the mountains of Pistoia, and various ready-to-cook cuts of meat plus about 30 types of ground beef are sold here. Follow their instructions for grilling the meat.

Sugar Blues

via XXVII Aprile, 46/48 r
055 483666
Wed pm

This shop specializes in macrobiotic foods. Gourmets looking for wholesome, organically grown produce, and both fresh and preserved specialties will find it worth a visit. A selection of natural essences are also sold. Another shop is in Cappalle, in the "I Gigli" shopping center (055 898286).

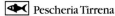 Pescheria Tirrena

via dei Cerchi, 20 r
055 216602
Wed pm

The owner of this shop is a real expert. Every day he selects the pick of the catch, especially shellfish and top-quality white fish.

Fratelli Vettori

borgo San Jacopo, 63 r
055 212797
Wed pm

Fruits and vegetables of outstanding quality, including spring vegetables, are sold here. Prices are high partly because of the quality of the produce and partly because of the shop's well-deserved fame.

Gelateria Vivoli

via Isola delle Stinche, 7 r
055 292334
Mon ☐ Sun

The same family still oversees the high quality of the ingredients used in this ice-cream parlor, which has been famous in Florence for 70 years. Today there are more than 40 ice-cream flavors to choose from. The classics – cream, chocolate, lemon, and torroncino (nougat) – are based on recipes going back to the 1920s. In the café, the breads and desserts are made from natural ingredients.

Macelleria Zagli

via Valori, 6 r
055 587571
Mon pm, Wed pm

This butcher's shop stakes its name on quality Tuscan produce such as Chianina beef (and not just the rib steaks but also the less prized cuts), free-range Valdarno chickens, and pork from Tuscan pigs. Various ready-to-cook dishes are also sold.

FOIANO DELLA CHIANA (AR)

Caseificio Matteassi

via di Cortona, 66a
0575 649101

Here you will find an excellent range of pecorino and ricotta cheeses made from milk produced by local flocks of sheep.

MONTELUPO FIORENTINO (FI)

San Vito in Fior di Selva

località Malmantile
0571 51411

This estate is set in a wonderful panoramic position amid woods just 12 miles (20 km) from Florence. It is farmed organically and produces Chianti Colli Fiorentini, plus Vin Santo, spumante, and grappa. It also produces good extra-virgin olive oil and honey. The estate is one of many agriturismo farms, with vacation apartments for visitors to rent, and it serves a range of good quality refreshments to visiting tourists.

CASTAGNACCIO (CHESTNUT CAKE)

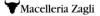

1 lb (400 g) chestnut flour • 4 walnuts, crushed
• 3 oz (75 g) pine nuts • 2 oz (50 g) raisins
• 1 sprig of rosemary • extra-virgin olive oil • salt

Preheat the oven to 400°F (200°C). Put the flour and a pinch of salt into a mixing bowl. Whisk in enough warm water to make a paste. Pour into a greased 8 inch (20 cm) cake pan, and bake in the oven for 5–6 minutes. Scatter the walnuts, pine nuts, raisins, and rosemary leaves over the top and sprinkle with oil. Bake for a further 20 minutes.

MONTEMURLO (PO)

Tenuta di Bagnolo

via Montalese, 156
C 0574 652439

This 16th-century estate belongs to the Marquis Pancrazi, who inherited it from the Strozzi family of Montemurlo. The estate is well-known for its Villa di Bagnolo extra-virgin olive oil. It also produces good quality wine, which is bottled after two months of storage in oak barriques to soften it a little. The wine is made from Pinot Nero grapes. These vines were first planted here when they were mistakenly sold as Sangiovese in the 1970s. The Casaglia extra-virgin olive oil from another family estate at Calamanco is excellent.

PALAZZUOLO SUL SENIO (FI)

Dispensa della Locanda

via Borgo dell'Oro, 1
C 055 8046019
● Wed
○ Sun

Among the firm's own specialities are prosciutto *and* salame *from Cinta pigs – these differ from the standard Cinta Senese breed because they have developed features that help them adapt to high altitudes. The firm also produces cocktail onions preserved in oil, quince jam, liqueurs from fruits and wild herbs, chestnut honey, and various other local delicacies.*

Azienda Agricola Lozzole

frazione Quadalto
Lozzole **C** 055 8043505

A large number of goats, sheep, and pigs that graze freely in chestnut woods are bred here. The estate sells a range of fresh and mature pecorino *and* caprino *(goat's milk) cheeses, some scented with herbs, and chestnuts in season. The farm has not yet received a permit to butcher its own meat, however.*

PIEVE AL BAGNORO (AR)

Villa Cilnia

località Montoncello, 27
C 0575 365017

This medium-sized wine estate in the Aretine Hills offers a good Chianti Colli Aretini and Chianti Riserva. It also produces Mecenate, made from Chardonnay and Sauvignon Blanc grapes, and Vocato made from Sangiovese and Cabernet Sauvignon grapes.

CROSTINI ALLA TOSCANA

extra virgin olive oil • ½ an onion, finely chopped • 12 oz (350 g) chicken livers • 1 oz (30 g) capers • 2 anchovy fillets • ¾ oz (20 g) butter • 1 glass white wine • meat stock • 4 slices Tuscan bread • chopped tomatoes and herbs (optional) • salt • pepper

Heat some oil in a pan, add the onion and cook until softened. Add the livers, pour in the wine, and cook for 5 minutes. Drain the livers and purée with the anchovies and capers. Return to the pan, stir and add enough stock to make a creamy mixture. Season with salt and pepper. Remove the pan from the heat and stir in the butter. Toast the bread, spread with paté and cut each slice into several pieces. Top with chopped tomatoes and herbs.

PONTASSIEVE (FI)

Tenuta di Bossi

via dello Stracchino, 32
C 055 8317830

The estate's star wine is its Mazzaferrata red made from Sangiovese and Cabernet Sauvignon in equal parts. Also interesting is its Chianti Rùfina Riserva Villa Bossi matured in both small and large barrels, and the Colli dell'Etruria Centrale Vin Santo. The extra-virgin olive oil – some of which is bottled as Laudemio – is noteworthy.

Tenimenti Ruffino

via Aretina, 42/44
C 055 83605

This firm is owned by the Folonari family who are involved with a number of estates in Tuscany. The range of wines is good, with some notable highlights, such as Cabreo

di Borgo, made from Sangiovese and Cabernet Sauvignon grapes, and Cabreo La Pietra, from Chardonnay. There are also reds such as Nero di Tondo, a good Pinot Nero, and Romitorio di Santedame from Colorino and Prugnolo. Ruffino also produces Chianti and Vino Nobile di Montepulciano.

🍇 Fattoria di Galiga e Vetrice

località Montebonello
via Vetrice, 5
📞 055 8397008

This estate is among the leading producers of Chianti Rùfina and makes good quality wines. The estate also produces Vin Santo and an excellent extra-virgin olive oil called "Il Lastro."

✳ Gelateria Sottani

località San Francesco,
via Forlivese, 93
📞 055 8368092
⬤ Wed pm

The owner of this ice-cream parlor boasts that only natural products – in particular, good quality fresh milk from the Mugello – go into the ice creams. There is an extraordinary variety of flavors – all the classics plus inzuppato al Vin Santo. Whatever fruit is

Fattoria di Galiga e Vetrice at Pontassieve

in the market – including exotic varieties and wild fruit – is included in the delicious sorbets.

🍇 Fattoria Torre a Decima

località Molino del Piano
📞 055 8317804

This estate's strategy is to promote Malvasia Nera grapes, which are present in the Chianti Colli Fiorentini and the Rosso della Torre, combined with Sangiovese and Cabernet Sauvignon.

PRATO

🍽 Gastronomia Barni

via Ferrucci, 24
📞 0574 607845
⬤ Wed pm

Carefully selected Italian and French cheeses and fine Tuscan salumi are sold here. The wine shop sells wines from around the world and a selection of dessert wines. The ready-made dishes are very good.

✳ Pasticceria Luca

via Lazzerini, 2
📞 0574 21628
⬤ Tues ○ Sun

This shop is owned by Gianluca Mannori, one of Italy's top pastry chefs. He offers numerous eye-catching, delectable specialties, including an Italian celebration cake. The pralines are exceptional, as is the whole chocolate line, especially the highly artistic, hand-painted eggs for Easter.

Oak barrels at the Fattoria Torre a Decima

Oil store at the Frantoio di Santa Tea

Biscottificio Mattei

via Ricasoli, 20/22
055 0574 25756
Mon
Sun

Since 1858, the place to buy cookies in Prato has been "Mattonella," a store named after the firm's founder, Antonio Mattei. Sample the delicious cantuccini *and* cantucci all'anice *cookies.*

Pasticceria Nuovo Mondo

via Garibaldi, 23
0574 27765
Mon Sun

Paolo Sacchetti is a top confectioner. He makes international specialties, and at Christmas, although he is not Milanese or even from Lombardy, he makes one of the very finest panettoni *(a Milanese cake) you can find anywhere.*

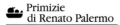

Primizie di Renato Palermo

via Gobetti, 18
0574 30713
Wed pm

This shop offers fruits and vegetables selected for their quality, with the emphasis on organically grown produce, and with trusted market gardeners favored more than official certificates. As far as

possible the produce is Tuscan, but Renato Palermo also looks further afield to other regions where the produce is fresh, in season, and of the finest quality. The same policy guides the selection of various other delicacies: dried pasta, preserves in extra-virgin olive oil, traditional candies, and cakes. Note the local big white beans called schiaccioni *and the exotic and dried fruits.*

Vannucchi Ortofrutta

via Vincenzo da Filicaia, 2
0574 36382
Wed pm

Local produce is sold here in season; a variety of spring vegetables and exotic fruits from leading producers further afield iss also available. Local varieties of beans include capponi *and* schiaccioni.

REGGELLO (FI)

Frantoio di Santa Tea

località Santa Tea, frazione Cascia,
055 868117

The firm's olive oil has an intensely fresh, fruity bouquet and an aroma of newly mown grass. The flavor is strong and bitter with an aftertaste of the salad leaf arugula.

RÙFINA (FI)

Fattoria di Basciano

viale Duca della Vittoria, 159
055 8397034

The estate has about 50 acres (20 hectares) of vines and another 50 acres of olive groves. Its produce is carefully made and the wine in particular is excellent value for money. The focus is on red wines with Chianti Rùfina in a standard version and Reserve, and two finer blends kept in new oak barriques for 12 months: I Pini made with equal quantities of Cabernet Sauvignon and Sangiovese, and Il Corto with a higher proportion of Sangiovese.

CIBREO

2 lb 4 oz (1 kg) chicken livers, hearts, testicles, and rooster's combs or crests • extra-virgin olive oil • 1 onion, chopped • 2 cloves garlic • 2 oz (50 g) salted anchovies, chopped • 6 oz (150 g) tomatoes, peeled • 4 egg yolks • juice of 1 lemon • 1–2 tablespoons chopped fresh parsley • salt • pepper

Clean and cut up the giblets. Heat plenty of oil in a pan and fry the onion, garlic, and anchovies for a few minutes. Add all the giblets and cook until lightly browned. Add the tomatoes and salt and pepper and simmer for 2–3 minutes. Meanwhile, whisk the egg yolks, lemon juice, and parsley with a little warm water in a bowl. Remove the pan from the heat. Still whisking, pour the egg mixture into the pan. Serve the mixture hot with rice or polenta.

Azienda Agricola Colognòle

via del Palagio, 15
055 8319870

This is a family-run firm. The Spalletti name has always been linked with carefully balanced wines that age well, and so the wines marketed are generally a vintage older than average. The grapes from individual vineyards are vinified separately and then blended to make Chianti Rùfina and Chianti Rùfina Riserva del Don. A single white, Quattro Chiacchere, is made from Chardonnay alone. The estate also produces olive oil of excellent quality and offers agriturismo vacation facilities.

Fattoria Selvapiana

località Selvapiana, 43
055 8369848

From a solid family tradition anchored in the land come some of the area's finest Chianti Rùfina. The two single-vineyard wines, Bucerchiale and Fornace, both Chianti Rùfina riserva, are excellent. Fornace contains a small proportion of Cabernet Sauvignon. The extra virgin olive oil is fabulous, and there is also a delicious range of honey.

SANSEPOLCRO (AR)

Erboristeria di Aboca

località Aboca
0575 7461
Mon

This is the sales outlet for one of Europe's most important herbalists. Despite

---

TRIPPA ALLA FIORENTINA

extra virgin olive oil • 2 stalks celery, finely chopped • 2 carrots, finely chopped • 1 onion, finely chopped • 2½ lb (1 kg) tripe, cut into strips • ¾ lb (300 g) tomatoes, peeled and chopped • 4 oz (100 g) Parmesan cheese, grated • salt • pepper

Heat some oil in a pan, add the celery, carrots, and onion and fry until they have softened a little. Add the tripe and cook it for a few minutes. Add the chopped tomatoes, season to taste with salt and pepper and simmer for 25–30 minutes. Stir in the grated Parmesan cheese and serve at once.

---

the firm's size, Valentino Mercatio has retained his passion for exclusively natural products. Sadly, the firm's current policy favors herbal cures over foodstuffs. All the same, in this wonderful old shop you will find essences (sweet and bitter orange) useful in cooking, plus naturally farmed dried herbs, and herbal teas which are ideal for the end of a meal.

Macelleria Betti

via XX Settembre, 98
0575 741077
Wed pm

Here you will find Chianina beef selected from herds in the Val Tiberina; traditional salumi, the firm's own produce (from pigs raised at Porto San Stefano), including excellent loin and sausages in oil. The lamb is from Badia Tedalda.

Gelateria Creperia Ghignoni

via Tiberina Sud, 850
0575 741900
Tues
Sun

Not to be missed; the owner, Palmiro Bruschi,

---

won the Italian ice-cream championship. In addition to assorted ice creams, there are delicious crêpes and mousses to try.

SCANDICCI (FI)

Fattoria Baggiolino

località La Romola,
via della Poggiona, 4
055 768916

This firm produces an excellent extra-virgin olive oil. It is bottled as Laudemio and is one of the best sold under this name.

TERONTOLA (AR)

Mario Baldetti

località Case Sparse,
via Pietraia di Cortona, 21
0575 67143

This winery produces a full-bodied Bianco Vergine della Valdichiana and a white Pietraia from Chardonnay vines. In addition, it makes an interesting red wine – the Rosso Baldetti, made from Sangiovese and Canaiolo grapes.

LUNIGIANA, GARFAGNANA, AND VERSILIA

....

Lunigiana, Garfagnana, and Versilia

RUNNING FROM THE COAST to the highest peaks of the Apennine ridge, this area has something for everyone. Versilia has a long tradition of excellent dishes made with fresh local fish. The Garfagnana offers a very rustic way of life. The Lunigiana has a cuisine that takes elements from the three bordering regions: Tuscany, Liguria, and Emilia-Romagna. In this area farming and the food industry provide the greatest variety of gourmet pleasures. The area also shows great inventiveness in the choice of vines for wine, and it is unrivaled in Italy (or the world) for *porcini* (cèpe mushrooms). Mushrooms are not the only woodland food to play a part in the area's cuisine – chestnuts, bilberries, and raspberries are all widely used. Finally, there is Pescia, not only the center of Italian flower culture but also right in the middle of an area producing wonderful fruits and vegetables.

Passo della Cisa

Pontremoli
FS 🚌

Villafranca in Lunigiana

Licciana Nardi

Fivizzano

Tresana

G a r f a g n a

Podenzana

Aulla
FS 🚌

Fosdinovo

Alpi   Apua

Lag di Va

CARRARA
FS

MASSA
FS

Montignoso FS 🚌

Forte dei Marmi   *Pietrasanta*
FS 🚌

Cama

Lido di Camaiore

VIAREGGI
FS 🚌

TRANSPORT

RAILROAD STATION
- PISTOIA – STAZIONE FS
  0573 21622
- LUCCA – STAZIONE FS
  0583 419689
- VIAREGGIO – STAZIONE FS
  0584 962233

BUS STATION
- MONTECATINI TERME
  0572 772244

The area around Lucca is the most important **wine-making zone** in this region, producing the excellent Montecarlo and other wines. Left, grapes are being harvested for Rosso delle Colline Lucchesi *(see pp52–3)*.

PORCINI
The *porcini* at Garfagnana are among the world's finest, especially those from wooded mountain slopes. They are usually sold from September to November.

◁ **Drying grapes for the "governo" (fortifying) of wine**

Agriturismo (farmhouse vacations) in the Garfagnana are very popular with visitors. The area is dotted with lovely old farmhouses, each with a fascinating history.

Viareggio is not simply a fashionable seaside resort, it is also a very active fishing harbor where a splendid variety of **fresh fish and shellfish** *(see pp54–7)* is landed.

Tuscany's fresh **vegetables** are particularly fine, and they are a vital part of the region's cuisine. Market gardens sweep from the mountains to the coast, giving the area an enormous variety of growing conditions.

STAR ATTRACTIONS

- CAPANNORI (LU): Villa Torrigiani, 0583 928008
- CASTELNUOVO DI GARFAGNANA (LU): National Park of the Apuan Alps, 0583 644354
  National Park of Orecchiella, 0583 619098
- COLLODI (LU): Villa Garzoni, 0572 429590
- LUCCA: Cathedral, 0583 957068
- PISTOIA: Cathedral, 0573 21622

0 kilometers   10

0 miles   10

Abetone

Cutigliano

astelnuovo
Garfagnana

San Marcello
Pistoiese

Barga

Bagni di Lucca

Borgo a
Mozzano

PISTOIA

Agliana

Ponte a Moriano   Collodi   Pescia   Pieve a
                                        Nievole
              Uzzano
LUCCA   Montecarlo Montecatini   Monsummano
                          Terme   Terme
       Capannori
o di
ssaciuccoli   Altopascio   Lamporecchio

• Balbano

Places of Interest pp66–73
Restaurants pp177–180

Wines

THE ALPI APUANE (APUAN ALPS), which run parallel with a stretch of the Tyrrhenian coast between Massa, Carrara, and Viareggio, corral the warm sea breezes and create an ideal climate for vineyards. The same breezes flow up the lower part of the Arno Valley, creating equally good conditions for vines at Lucca. Further inland, toward Pistoia, the influence of the sea wanes, but the Apennine ridge gives shelter from the colder influences of the north and helps to provide a favorable climate for growing flowers. This area produces very respectable white wines from vines like Vermentino and Albarola, a link with nearby Liguria, as well as Trebbiano Toscano, Greco, Grechetto, and Malvasia del Chianti vines. Certain French varieties have long been grown locally and are used in some of the DOC wines, such as Pinot, Sémillon, Sauvignon, and Roussanne. The same is true of reds: alongside Sangiovese, Canaiolo, and rare vines like Ciliegiolo, Colorino, Malvasia Nera, and Pollera Nera are Syrah, Cabernet, and Merlot.

CANDIA DEI COLLI APUANI
This white wine is made in a tiny area at the foot of the Apuan Alps above Massa and Carrara, so production is limited. Made from two Ligurian vines, Vermentino and Albarola, the wine is straw-colored with a fine scent and low alcohol content. It is perfect with *frittelline di cieche* (made with the fry of eels) and delicate fish dishes. There is also a Vin Santo version.

White Colli di Luni is based on Vermentino with some Trebbiano Toscano and other white grapes. It is perfect with fish antipasti and vegetable soups.

COLLI DI LUNI
This is a recent denomination. Its production straddles the two regions of Liguria and Tuscany.

Red Colli di Luni is based on Sangiovese with other black grapes and up to 10 percent Cabernet. It is excellent with roasts and other meat dishes.

SCALOPPINE AI PORCINI

1¹/₂ lb (600 g) porcini (cèpe mushrooms), sliced • 2 cloves garlic • extra-virgin olive oil • 2 oz (50 g) butter • 1 small onion, chopped • 6 veal scallops • white wine • 1 sprig calamint or mint • meat stock • salt • pepper

Fry the mushrooms in a shallow pan with one of the cloves of garlic, some oil, and salt over a high heat until their moisture evaporates. In a separate pan, heat the butter with a little oil. Chop the second garlic clove and lightly fry with the onion in the butter. Add the scallops and cook until browned on both sides. Season with salt and pepper, and moisten with a little white wine. Cook until the meat is almost tender, then cover it with the mushrooms. Add a little stock and the calamint leaves and cook together for 1 minute before serving.

COLLINE LUCCHESI
This denomination applies to wines produced on the hills around Lucca. In addition to the generic whites, rosés, and reds, it includes varietals (wines made from single grape varieties): Vermentino and Sauvignon grapes for whites, Sangiovese and Merlot for the reds which have the Riserva label. The grapes for table wines are also used to make white and red Vin Santo.

CIONCIA

• **2 lb 4 oz (1 kg) veal** *(traditionally flesh from the head, cheeks, tail, but use ready diced pie veal, if necessary)* • **extra-virgin olive oil** • **3 stalks celery, chopped** • **3 carrots, chopped** • **1 onion, chopped** • **8 oz (200 g) tomatoes, peeled** • **chopped fresh parsley** • **chopped fresh basil** • **black olives** • **1 glass white wine** • **chilli pepper** • **salt**

Trim and wash the veal and and cut into small pieces. Place in a pan, cover with water, and simmer for about 30 minutes, then drain well. Heat some oil and fry the meat lightly, then add the chopped vegetables and tomatoes, herbs, olives, and wine. Season with chilli pepper and salt and simmer for 3 hours.

The rosé and red are both made from Sangiovese and Canaiolo Nero. The red resembles a young, very drinkable Chianti and is perfect with suckling pig, fried chicken, or roast rabbit.

The white is made from seven varieties of white grapes, creating a wine with a subtle delicate perfume that is well-suited to soups and vegetable omelettes.

MONTECARLO
This wine is made from traditional Tuscan grapes together with some French ones, which give it a finer perfume and a well-balanced flavor.

The white (Trebbiano Sémillon, Pinot Grigio and Bianco, Vermentino, Sauvignon. and Roussanne) goes with delicate pastasciutte (pasta) and fried fish.

Red Montecarlo (made from Sangiovese and Canaiolo, Syrah, Cabernet, and Merlot) goes with spelt or mushroom dishes.

OTHER WINES WORTH TRYING
In the province of Pistoia you will find DOC **Colli dell'Etruria Centrale** and also DOC **Chianti**, some of which is made using the "*governo*" technique of adding dried grapes or must to the fermented wine to soften it.

WINE TYPE	GOOD VINTAGES	GOOD PRODUCERS
Red Wine		
Super Tuscans *(see p130)*	98, 97, 95, 90	Moretti, Le Murelle di Lucca
Colline Lucchesi	99, 97	Valgiano di Capannori, La Badiola di Capannori
White Wine		
Montecarlo	00, 99	Fattoria del Buonamico Fattoria del Teso

Fish and Seafood

IT IS A PLEASURE to visit the outdoor market at the popular coastal resort of Viareggio when the sea is calm and the fishing boats have been out. With both rocky and sandy seabeds close at hand, and the seas around the island of Gorgona rich with fish, the catch is varied. There are excellent inexpensive fish on sale, as well as the seasonal ones that pass through these waters – fish that are hard to find even in the big city markets. The shellfish are nearly always sold still alive at the market. Viareggio has the same varieties of fish found in other Tuscan seaports: those typical of Livorno's cuisine are described on *pp78–9*, others on *pp14–5* and *p161*. The local cuisine is noteworthy for its use of fewer spices than other regions – the fish is so fresh it does not need to be disguised with sauces or other artifice.

Generally small gilthead or portions of larger fish come from fish farms.

ORATA (GILTHEAD BREAM)
Giltheads are much sought after for their firm white flesh and fine flavor which comes from feeding mainly on shellfish. Those caught at sea, especially if full-grown (quite common in this area), are delectable. They are excellent grilled, baked, and cooked *en papillotte* (in paper).

GALLINELLA
There are various species of gallinella (also called "caponi"), types of gurnard, and they are found on sandy seabeds. Their flesh is white, juicy, and very tasty. They are ideal for soups, and are excellent baked or cooked with vegetables.

Striped bream have dark vertical streaks on the scales.

MORMORA (STRIPED BREAM)
Abundant, especially in summer, this is the most common white fish on the sandy seabed. It is less popular than other white fish because the flesh is not so firm. It can be baked or grilled.

POLPO DI SCOGLIO OR PIOVRA (ROCK OCTOPUS)
These are very common at the markets and are frequently sold alive. Large ones need to be pounded to tenderize the flesh. They are cooked, without water or seasoning, in a saucepan with the lid firmly closed, then seasoned to taste.

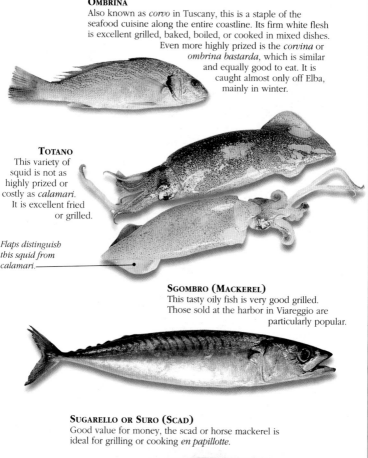

Ombrina

Also known as *corvo* in Tuscany, this is a staple of the seafood cuisine along the entire coastline. Its firm white flesh is excellent grilled, baked, boiled, or cooked in mixed dishes. Even more highly prized is the *corvina* or *ombrina bastarda*, which is similar and equally good to eat. It is caught almost only off Elba, mainly in winter.

Totano

This variety of squid is not as highly prized or costly as *calamari*. It is excellent fried or grilled.

Flaps distinguish this squid from calamari.

Sgombro (Mackerel)

This tasty oily fish is very good grilled. Those sold at the harbor in Viareggio are particularly popular.

Sugarello or Suro (Scad)

Good value for money, the scad or horse mackerel is ideal for grilling or cooking *en papillotte*.

Other Molluscs Worth Trying

Moscardini (small squid) are valued for sauces, especially the fall fry called **fragolini**. There are numerous kinds of shellfish. The finest **cozze** (mussels) are farmed at nearby La Spezia. **Coltellacci** or **cannolicchio** or **cannelli** (razor clams), much appreciated in Versilia, have a long shell which contains a sweet, fleshy mollusc. **Telline** and **arselle** are important in Viareggio's cuisine, but these smooth wedge-shaped clams are very rare. The clams called **vongola grigia** or **cappa gallina** are used in pasta sauces. The **tartufo di mare** (Venus clam), which is very expensive, is sometimes eaten raw. The little cockles called **cuori**, picked up by children on the beaches, have grooved shells and contain a hard red mollusc which is tasty when cooked in seafood sauces. **Capesante** or **pellegrine** (scallops) are good but most are imported. Also popular are the sea snails (**chioccioline di mare**) called **maruzzelle**.

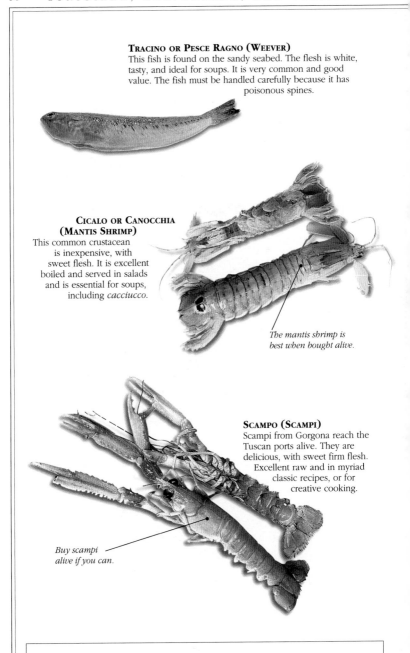

TRACINO OR PESCE RAGNO (WEEVER)
This fish is found on the sandy seabed. The flesh is white, tasty, and ideal for soups. It is very common and good value. The fish must be handled carefully because it has poisonous spines.

CICALO OR CANOCCHIA (MANTIS SHRIMP)
This common crustacean is inexpensive, with sweet flesh. It is excellent boiled and served in salads and is essential for soups, including *cacciucco*.

The mantis shrimp is best when bought alive.

SCAMPO (SCAMPI)
Scampi from Gorgona reach the Tuscan ports alive. They are delicious, with sweet firm flesh. Excellent raw and in myriad classic recipes, or for creative cooking.

Buy scampi alive if you can.

OTHER CRUSTACEANS WORTH TRYING
Gamberetti grigi (brown shrimp) are common at the markets: they are fried and eaten, shell and all. **Astici** (lobsters) are widely eaten but are not caught locally. **Aragoste** (crayfish) are caught off the islands and Argentario, but at the markets you will find mostly fine Sardinian ones. The big red crabs and granseola crabs are more typical of Italy's east coast, while here you find dark **granchi** (crabs) used in soups.

ALICE OR ACCIUGA (ANCHOVY)

These small blue fish are very tasty when freshly caught. In Tuscany, they are eaten fried, marinated raw, or baked in fishcakes, much as elsewhere in Italy. Salted, preserved anchovies are delicious with unsalted Tuscan bread.

Anchovies are more slender than sardines.

ROMBO (TURBOT)

This flatfish is found on the sandy seabed. The white flesh is tasty and firm, and cooks quickly. It is suited to all kinds of recipes. The ones caught in Tuscan waters are very popular.

BRANZINO OR SPIGOLA (SEA BASS)

Sea bass is the most sought-after fish on the market. Actively farmed, it is always excellent, but those caught with a hook and line, especially large ones, are definitely the finest. It is cooked *en papillotte*, baked, or grilled. Tuscans like to cook it with wild fennel.

OTHER FISH WORTH TRYING

Dentice (dentex) are often caught with depth lines. **Occhiata** (saddled bream), which live in schools along the coast, are good grilled. **Tonnetti** (small tunny fish) are sliced and grilled or stewed. **John Dory** (**sanpietro**, in Tuscany, but also **pesce gallo**) has delectable flesh. **Soglioline** (sole) caught along the coast are better than imported ones. **Cernie** (grouper) and **cerniole** (wreckfish) are caught off the islands, as are large fish such as **leccia** (amberjack) and **pesce castagna** (Ray's bream).

Game Birds

GAME BIRDS ARE an important part of Tuscany's gourmet tradition, and the marshlands near Torre del Lago ensure that this is an area rich in birds. The area offers unique recipes using ingredients that are not easy to find elsewhere, such as coot, mallard, and small marsh ducks. In the market at Viareggio, and the ones in other cities in the area, you can buy all kinds of game birds which in other parts of Tuscany can only be found in specialty shops supplying the catering industry.

TORDO (THRUSH)
Songbirds such as song thrush, rock thrush, mistle thrush, and fieldfare are appreciated for their tender, aromatic flesh, especially when the birds have been feeding on the sweet-smelling berries that grow wild. The birds are cooked on a spit, or in casseroles with olives, grapes, and juniper berries, or they are made into pâtés.

Wild duck goes well with fruit, as in this dish of duck breasts with raspberries and vinegar.

This thrush and blackbird terrine includes both the liver and the giblets. Black truffles add extra flavor to the dish.

GERMANO (MALLARD)
Mallard is the most common wild duck in Tuscany. Its flesh is much firmer than that of farm-bred duck, and it has a better flavor, but the birds are interchangeable in recipes.

Little bustard is cooked in a casserole with a sweet-and-sour pickle of sorb apples.

MERLO (BLACKBIRD)
Although blackbirds are widely hunted, they are not as popular as thrushes. They have a good flavor from feeding on berries, but the flesh is tough. The flavor comes out best in *pâtés* and dishes that require lengthy cooking.

FAGIANO (PHEASANT)
The pheasant is the hunters' favorite prey. It is unlikely to be a wild bird, since pheasants are bred for the game reserves. When newly released their flesh is pretty tasteless, but after living in the wild and feeding freely for some time they acquire a gamey flavor. Pheasants are roasted, cooked in casseroles with cream, truffles, and fruit, or in traditional *salmi*, and are made into countless pâtés and terrines.

FOLAGA (COOT)

This water bird is very popular at Torre del Lago. It must be plucked and skinned as soon as it is killed. The coot has a distinctive, slightly fishy flavor and is used to make the classic recipe *folaga alla Puccini*, which dates back to the days of the Italian composer.

Wood pigeon is cooked slowly in a rich gravy with wild cherries, which enhance the flavor of the meat.

COLOMBACCIO (WOOD PIGEON)

The wood pigeon has firm, aromatic, and well-flavored flesh. The bird is widely hunted in Tuscany, where one of the favorite ways of cooking it is in a casserole with olives.

FOLAGA ALLA PUCCINI

- *1 coot • juice of 1 lemon • extra-virgin olive oil • 1 carrot, finely chopped • 2 onions, finely chopped • 1 stalk celery, finely chopped • 4 bay leaves • 1 sprig of thyme • 1 fresh chilli, finely chopped • a few leaves of calamint (or mint) • 1 salted anchovy, boned • red wine • meat stock • 1 dessertspoon flour • 1 sprig of basil • salt • pepper*

Pluck and skin the coot, then soak it for about 2 hours in cold water mixed with the lemon juice. Cut the bird into pieces, discarding the head, wing tips, and the cone of the rump with the tail feathers attached. Heat some oil and fry the carrot, onion, celery, and bay leaves until the vegetables have softened. Add the coot flesh, thyme, chilli, calamint, and anchovy. Brown the meat, then season with salt and pepper. Cover and cook slowly, moistening if necessary first with the wine and then the stock. When the coot is almost cooked, uncover the pan, add a ladleful of stock mixed with the flour, and allow to thicken. Stir in the basil and serve.

BECCACCIA (WOODCOCK)

The woodcock is the most prized of the game birds. It is becoming increasingly rare and is hardly ever seen in any market. It is cooked undrawn and the entrails (apart from the crop) are eaten. There are many regional and international recipes for this bird, but the most popular dish is roasted woodcock with the entrails spread on toast.

OTHER GAME BIRDS WORTH TRYING

Other wild ducks shot in the marshy areas include **alzavola** (teal), **moriglione** (pochard), **fischione** (widgeon), and **codone** (pintail). The **tortora** (turtle dove) is appreciated for its delicate, tender flesh. Partridges are also hunted in Tuscany, both the common gray partridge **(pernice)** and the rock partridge **(coturnice)**, but they are becoming increasingly rare. Wild **quaglia** (quail) are are much tastier than the farm-bred ones usually found in shops. **Beccaccino** (snipe) are smaller than woodcock, but just as tasty, and they can be used in the same recipes.

Traditional Produce

THIS AREA OF northern Tuscany has wonderfully varied landscapes: there are mountains with lakes and woods, and then hills that slope gently to the plains and the sea. The numerous delicacies are closely bound up with these natural settings and the climate, and the produce ranges from Mediterranean olives to spelt (a traditional type of grain) from the mountains. The popularity of the local produce has spread through a mixture of factors: a general concern for traditional qualities, the growth of *agriturismo*, and specialty shops supported by a clientele capable of recognizing quality. It is worth finding trusted stores that specialize in good quality foods.

FILETTO DELLA LUNIGIANA
This dried pork fillet is seasoned with salt and pepper. It combines both Tuscan and Emilian traditions, being less dry and having less salt and pepper than other specialty meats of the region.

LASAGNE BASTARDE
These are *tagliatelle* and *pappardelle all'uovo* made with a mixture of white flour and chestnut flour for extra flavor. They are found in restaurants and on sale in small pasta shops, mainly in Lunigiana and around Monte Amiata.

TORTA DI PEPE
A specialty of Camaiore, this savory pie is made with a *brisée* pastry and filled with beet leaves, rice, eggs, *ricotta*, *pecorino*, Parmesan, and breadcrumbs, all seasoned with plenty of freshly ground pepper *(pepe)*.

BUCCELLATO
Lucca's traditional cake is sold by all *pasticcerie* and bakers in the city. It is a very simple cake, made with flour, sugar, muscatel raisins, and aniseed. Traditionally it was a round loaf, but long shapes are now more common.

PANE DI ALTOPASCIO
This is one of the most prized Tuscan breads and is sold outside the area, reaching supermarkets in northern Italy. Loaves sold locally are normally round; when exported it is usually sold in long broad loaves.

LUCCA OLIVE OIL

The area producing Lucca oil includes the coastal area of Versilia, above all around Carrara, the area north of Lucca along the Serchio, and other smaller zones near Camaiore and Ponte a Moriano. These oils are very fine and fruity. The flavor is of average intensity, full and balanced, sweetish though slightly peppery, with a lingering taste.

CANNELLINI DI SORANA

These white beans are common in Tuscan cooking. Sorana, north of Pescia, produces beans of slightly smaller than average size and these are much sought-after.

DRIED CHESTNUTS

Once a staple ingredient of traditional cooking in many mountain areas, dried chestnuts *(castagne secche)* are now a delicacy used in sweet and savory dishes.

TESTAROLI

A wholewheat flour and water dough is cooked in earthenware pans with lids called *testi*. The dough forms thick sheets which are boiled and served with pesto or tomato and mushroom sauce.

CHESTNUT FLOUR

Chestnut flour *(farina di castagne)* is produced in various areas, including Lunigiana, the Mugello, the Casentino, and Amiata and is an ingredient of many traditional recipes.

NECCI CON LA RICOTTA

1 lb (450 g) chestnut flour • sugar • chestnut leaves
• 1 lb (450 g) fresh ricotta cheese • salt

Mix the flour with a pinch of salt and sugar to taste. Knead in enough water to form a thick but not solid dough. Heat several earthenware *testi* until sizzling hot, then place a chestnut leaf on each one. Spread with a ladleful of paste, then alternate leaves and paste to form layers. Leave to cool. Remove and serve with the cheese and sugar.

PECORINO FROM GARFAGNANA AND LUNIGIANA

This *pecorino* is generally drier than the similar cheese from the Crete to the south. It has a strong milky scent and a distinctive flavor from the mountain grasses the sheep feed on, quite different from that of cheese from the more arid coastal areas.

RICOTTINE DELLA LUNIGIANA

This cheese is eaten very fresh. It is also a traditional cheese for making cakes, especially with chestnuts.

FARRO (SPELT) FROM GARFAGNANA

Spelt is a very ancient cereal which has been cultivated in the Garfagnana for over 7,000 years. Equally ancient is the gastronomic tradition of spelt soup *(minestrone di farro* or *zuppa di farro),* a trademark of this area.

MINESTRONE DI FARRO

8 oz (200 g) dried borlotti beans • ¾ lb (300 g) spelt • 2 oz (50 g) pancetta, chopped • 1 onion, chopped • 1 stalk celery, chopped • 1 carrot, chopped • ¼ of a Savoy cabbage, cut into strips • tomato purée • extra-virgin olive oil • salt • pepper

Soak the beans in cold water overnight. The next day, drain them, put in a pan, and cover with fresh water. Bring to the boil and simmer for 1½ hours. Drain the beans and set aside a quarter of them. Mash the rest with the cooking water, return to the pan, add the spelt, and cook for about 1 hour. Sauté the pancetta, onion, celery, and carrot in some oil. Add the cabbage, the tomato purée diluted in a little water, then the spelt and the whole beans and simmer for 15 minutes. Season and drizzle a little oil over the soup before serving.

TROUT

The Serchio river is celebrated for its fish, which is less commonly eaten now that the number of fishermen has declined. However, the tradition of using the excellent trout from the mountain streams remains strong.

AGNELLO AL TESTO

1 leg of lamb • 4 oz (100 g) lardo (lard) • sage • rosemary • garlic • 2 lb (1 kg) potatoes • extra-virgin olive oil • salt • pepper

Make incisions in the leg of lamb with the tip of a knife. Make a paste with the lard, herbs, and garlic and push it into the incisions. Season with salt and pepper. Put the lamb in a *testo* (earthenware pan with a lid) and cover with plenty of oil. Sink the pan into hot wood embers; heap them over the lid. Cook for 30 minutes, renewing the hot embers frequently.

Rosemary and garlic are often used in curing lardo.

LARDO FROM COLONNATA
Among the pinnacles of Tuscan gastronomy, this *lardo* (lard) is highly rated. The lard is matured in tubs of marble from nearby Carrara. Once removed, it quickly loses its flavor, so it is cut only when needed. It may be used in cooking or thinly sliced and eaten sprinkled with pepper.

ROLLED PANCETTA FROM LUNIGIANA
A combination of the Tuscan style mixed with the traditional styles of the nearby valleys of Parma and Piacenza produces this *pancetta* (bacon cured from belly of pork). Tuscan custom is reflected in the use of herbs, especially rosemary, while the Emilian influence is the technique of rolling the bacon and salting it only lightly, to keep it moist.

WHAT TO SAMPLE
Black-headed lambs, a breed called **Massese** from the Garfagnana and the Lunigiana, are much appreciated and sought-after outside the region. In the Pescia district there is excellent **asparagus** and **fruit** such as **cherries**. Some producers have begun to specialize in herbs. There are a number of **soft fruit** farms. Pistoia has its traditional **cakes** and **candies**, such as **sugared almonds**, **brigidini** (aniseed-flavored wafers), and **berlingozzi** (carnival cakes). The Garfagnana has **truffles**, black and white. Around Abetone there are locally produced **aromatic grappas** scented with berries and herbs. The **table olives** are excellent; many types are small and a brownish-black color, rather like Ligurian *taggiasca* olives. **Biroldo** is a blood sausage, its more authentic versions containing raisins and pine nuts, which is eaten raw if very fresh.

Wild Produce

PRUGNOLO
(Lyophyllum georgii)
Even in antiquity this spring mushroom was prized. Now it is protected and it is forbidden to pick any under ¾ inch (2 cm) high. Whitish with tender flesh and an intense scent of fresh flour, it is sliced and eaten raw on risotto or pasta or cooked quickly in white sauces. It forms circles in mountain meadows or under thorn bushes in the hills.

GRIFOLA
(Polyporus frondosus)
This is a giant fungus that can weigh up to 110 lb (50 kg). From a single stalk growing at the foot of broadleaf trees, it fans out into numerous branches forming a kind of dense bush. When young, it is good preserved in oil.

COLOMBINA
(Russula cyanoxantha)
Easily found, even at markets, this mushroom has distinctive white gills, and is firm and springy to the touch. Commonly known as "the charcoal burner," it grows in woods, especially beech, and is excellent grilled, baked with potatoes, or in deviled dishes.

COCCORA
(Amanita caesarea)
The most expensive mushroom on the market, also known as *ovolo*, grows in broadleaf woods and is protected by a ban on picking specimens under 1½ inches (4 cm). When closed it forms a white ball. If this is cut open, it reveals embryo mushrooms already colored with an orange cap, yellow stalk, and gills. It is not true that they are tastier when closed: open ones have more flavor whether raw or cooked.

COCCORA IN INSALATA (MUSHROOM SALAD)

1 clove garlic • 1 lb (450 g) coccore or ovoli, thinly sliced • juice of 1 lemon
• extra-virgin olive oil • salt • pepper

Cut the garlic clove in half and rub the individual serving plates with the cut surfaces. Arrange the mushrooms on the plates. Mix together the lemon juice, oil and salt. Season with pepper, pour the dressing over the mushrooms, and serve at once.

MINESTRA DI CECI

1lb (450 g) chickpeas • 1 small onion, chopped • 1 small carrot, chopped • 1 small celery stalk, chopped • 2 cloves garlic, chopped • 1 sprig of rosemary • 1 sprig of winter savory • extra-virgin olive oil • grated parmesan cheese (if preferred, mix it with some mature pecorino) • 1 piece of the cotenna (skin) from a prosciutto *• salt • black pepper*

Rinse the chickpeas, then soak in water for 24 hours. The next day, heat some oil and lightly fry the onion, carrot, celery, garlic, and rosemary leaves. Drain the chickpeas, reserving the liquid, and stir them into the vegetables with the cotenna. Strain the soaking water and add enough to the pan to cover the beans. Cover the pan and simmer until the chickpeas are tender. Remove the cotenna and purée the soup in a blender. Return it to the pan and add the savory; season and simmer for 10 minutes. Serve with the cheese and extra oil to drizzle.

SANTOREGGIA (WINTER SAVORY)
(Satureja montana)
Commonly found on dry, stony slopes, this herb is similar to thyme but has different spear-shaped leaves. It has long been noted for its supposed aphrodisiac qualities. It is excellent fresh or dried with sauces, and braised, roasted, or grilled meat.

MIRTILLO NERO (BILBERRY)
(Vaccinium myrtillus)
This summer berry is abundant on the Apennine ridges in high-altitude woods of beech or chestnut. It can be eaten fresh – it has a high vitamin C content – or used in jams and liqueurs.

OLIVELLO SPINOSO (SEA-BUCKTHORN)
(Hippophae rhamnoides)
Wear gloves if you want to pick these orange berries as there are plenty of thorns concealed among the blue-green leaves. However, they are definitely worth the trouble, being rich in vitamin C, and they make exquisite jam. The plants are found in the Apennines on open ground and along escarpments and waterways.

TIMO (THYME)
(Thymus communis)
Thyme is found all over Tuscany and is used a great deal in cooking – in fact, it is a staple of numerous traditional recipes. The flowering sprigs are better than the leaves alone. It is excellent fresh or dried.

Places of Interest

THIS IS A GOOD area for shopping, though prices at Versilia are often inflated because it is such a fashionable tourist spot. The shopkeepers are accustomed to catering to a clientele in search of traditional specialty foods, and many are very knowledgeable. In addition to the addresses given below, the outdoor market at Viareggio is definitely worth a visit.

AGLIANA (PT)

© Arte del Cioccolato di Catinari

via Provinciale, 378
☎ 0574 718506
● Mon am

Roberto Catinari is one of the great Italian and European pastry chefs. Here you will find 120 types of chocolates, such as ones with liqueur centers (grappa, Vin Santo, whisky, Gemma d'abeto, amaretto liqueur, and coffee), or wrapped chocolates weighing 1 oz (30 g) each. The gianduia tortine (chocolate cream cakes) are excellent. Numerous trainees come here from as far away as the US, and Catinari has produced creations to order for famous designers like Armani.

BERLINGOZZO

3½ oz (100 g) butter • 14 oz (400 g) plain flour • 2 eggs • 2 egg yolks • 7 oz (200 g) sugar • grated zest of 1 lemon • 3½ fl oz (100 ml) whole milk • 1 teaspoon baking powder • salt

Preheat the oven to 350°F (180°C). Grease and flour an 8 in (20 cm) cake pan with ¾ oz (20 g) each of the butter and flour. In a bowl, vigorously mix the rest of the flour and butter, eggs and yolks, sugar, zest, milk, baking powder, and a pinch of salt. Pour into the pan and bake for 40 minutes.

🍇 Enoteca Lavuri

via Provinciale, 154/g
☎ 0574 751125
● Tue am

This wine store has a wide selection of the most significant Tuscan wines. Its guiding policy is to comb the region for new products, provided they have a good pedigree. There are also interesting Italian and foreign wines. Lavuri also offers a fine selection of cheeses, coffees, and liquors, including some collector's items.

🔩 Marini

località Ferruccia
via Selva, 313
☎ 0574 718119
● Wed pm
◐ in summer: only am

Marini is a delicatessen and butcher's shop, family run since 1904, selling Chianina beef and local salumi, which includes traditional specialties no longer found elsewhere.

BORGO A MOZZANO (LU)

🐟 Lago la Macchia

frazione Valdottavo
☎ 0583 835444

This fish farm with agriturismo facilities sells the fry of mountain and rainbow trout, sturgeon, eels (including the much prized large female eels called capitoni*), freshwater crayfish, and small trout for frying.*

CAMAIORE (LU)

🔩 Bonuccelli Salumi

via Vittorio Emanuele, 9
☎ 0584 989680
● Wed pm

Here you can find traditional salumi, both local and Tuscan (and some made with wild boar's meat). Particularly interesting products include salt ham, lardo, and biroldo (a Tuscan blood sausage). There is a range of Italian and imported cheeses and a selection of fine wines. The butcher specializes in pork and ham.

🍴 Gastronomia Claudio

via Provinciale, 45
☎ 0584 989069
● Wed pm

Angelo Torciglioni is a great enthusiast for cheeses, scouring Italy for them from Val d'Aosta to Sicily. He makes a point of stocking many fine cheeses produced by small traditional dairies in different regions. The delicatessen also stocks ready-made delicacies (try the torta di pepe *and the* ravioli*), plus various specialties of Torciglioni's own, such as the quite remarkable* cantucci, *as well as much local produce (olives, oil, flour) and delicacies from other regions. Everything is chosen with knowledge and passion. The selection of wines is also excellent.*

🍇 Enoteca Nebraska

strada provinciale per Lucca, bivio per Nocchi
☎ 0584 983805
● Tue ◐ Sun pm

The owners of this wine store are friendly and affable, and they never compromise on the quality

PATTONA AL TESTO

dry chestnut leaves
• 1 lb (450 g) sweetened chestnut flour
• salt

Soak the leaves in warm water for 10 minutes. In a mixing bowl, mix the flour with a little salt and enough water to make a paste. Drain the leaves and pat dry. Pour 2 dessertspoons of the mix onto the smooth surface of two overlapping leaves. Fold the leaves over the mixture and place in an earthenware *testo*. Repeat until the mix is all used up. Cover the *testo* and bake the discs for 30 minutes under smoking embers.

---

of their products. The big names in Tuscan, Italian, and foreign wines can be sampled with excellent cheese and salumi, *and other local products.*

CAMPORGIANO
(LU)

Mulin del Rancone

località Rancone
℡ 0583 618670

This splendid farm, which offers agriturismo *facilities in an old converted watermill on the banks of the Serchio, rescued the local Pontremolese breed of cattle when they were on the verge of extinction. As part of the same philosophy, it produces and sells many traditional local products, such as conserves, lentils, spelt, and fruits and vegetables preserved in oil. Then there are the cookies:* neccini *(made from chestnut flour),* farrini *(spelt flour),* formentini *(maize flour). They also sell* salumi, *cheese, and honey which comes from the Garfagnana.*

CAPANNORI
(LU)

Azienda Agricola La Badiola

località San Pancrazio
℡ 0583 309633

This estate produces an interesting red wine, Vigna Flora, which is made from Cabernet Sauvignon and Merlot grapes, and a promising Stoppielle, from Chardonnay and Pinot Bianco. The extra-virgin olive oil is not bad, if perhaps rather sweet.

Fattoria Colle Verde

località Castello
frazione Matraia
℡ 0583 402310

The estate aims to produce white wines with low acidity, which are well-structured and richly perfumed. A good example is the Brania del Cancello Bianco, made from equal quantities of Trebbiano and Chardonnay grapes. Another notable wine is the Colline Lucchesi Rosso Brania delle Ghiandaie, which is made from a careful selection of red grapes. The estate also produces a very fine extra-virgin olive oil.

Cooperativa del Pastore

via Sarzanese, B45
Castelvecchio di Compito
℡ 0583 979804

The dairy on this estate produces various ewe's milk cheeses best eaten fresh. It also sells, to order, the excellent Massese breed of black-headed lambs.

Fattoria di Fubbiano

località San Gennaro
℡ 0583 978011

This corner of Tuscany enjoys an unusual microclimate and has been chosen for the grafting of experimental varieties of vines by the Regional Authority. These include a Vermentino used to produce Colline Lucchesi Vermentino. The Teroldego grape has been imported to boost the Sangiovese in making the red Pàmpini, which is aged in barriques. *The estate also makes two finer blends of the Rosso delle Colline Lucchesi, from vines with a western exposure for the Villa and a southern for the San Gennaro. The extra-virgin olive oil is excellent. There are splendid* agriturismo *facilities on the estate with farmhouses available to rent.*

The Fattoria di Fubbiano at Capannori

🍇 Fattoria Maionchi

località Tofori,
via di Tofori, 81
☎ 0583 978194

This is a late-17th-century farm with agriturismo accommodation in farmhouses which have been renovated to preserve their original features. Various DOC wines and table wines, traditional extra virgin olive oil from Lucca, olives in brine, conserves from the farm's own fruit (try the pear and grappa jam), and grappas are sold here.

GRAN FARRO (SPELT AND BEAN STEW)

1 lb (400 g) dried borlotti beans • ¾ lb (300 g) spelt • extra-virgin olive oil • 2 cloves garlic • 1 onion • 1 stalk celery • 3 leaves sage • 1 sprig of marjoram • 1 sprig of rosemary • 6 oz (150 g) diced cotenna (skin) of prosciutto • ¾ lb (300 g) ripe tomatoes • salt • pepper

Soak the beans in water for 12 hours. Drain the beans, put in a pan and cover with fresh water, then simmer until tender. Drain, reserving the cooking water. Press the beans through a sieve to purée them. Heat some oil in a pan, add the vegetables, herbs, tomatoes, and cotenna. Season to taste and fry for a few minutes. Add bean purée and the spelt. Simmer for 40 minutes, adding some of the bean cooking water, as necessary. Drizzle with olive oil before serving.

🍇 Tenuta di Valgiano

frazione Valgiano
☎ 0583 402271

This estate produces a range of straightforward, good wines: Bianco delle Colline Lucchesi Giallo dei Muri (from Trebbiano and Chardonnay) and Rosso delle Colline Lucchesi and Rosso dei Palistorti (Sangiovese and Syrah). In addition, there are two regional classics: a single-grape Merlot and the Scasso dei Cesari. The estate also produces excellent extra-virgin olive oil.

CARRARA

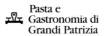 Pescheria Elda

frazione Marina di Carrara
viale Colombo, 9/c
☎ 0585 785060
🌑 Mon pm
🌕 Sun am

Quality counts here, and this depends not just on freshness but also on the origin of the produce. For example, the farmed fish comes from very carefully selected hatcheries: sea bass and bream from Portovenere, mussels from

---

La Spezia, and shellfish from a select group of producers in the northern Adriatic. The fresh fish is all local, coming from Viareggio and La Spezia.

🍴 Pasta e Gastronomia di Grandi Patrizia

via Santa Maria, 1
☎ 0585 72195
🌑 Tues

Here you can buy take-out dishes, most of them typical of Carrara, such as marinated salt cod, stockfish, taglierini ai fagioli (pasta with beans), rice cakes, plus fresh pasta, especially tordelli, and seasonal specialties including fish. On Sunday an interesting, complete menu is offered, from antipasto to dessert, at very reasonable prices.

🍴 Lardo di Colonnata di Giannarelli Marino

frazione Codena
piazza Fratelli Rosselli, 10
☎ 0585 777329

This is a specialty producer of the typical local lardo (cured pork

---

fat), which is processed here but then matured at Colonnata, its place of origin. It is sold at the firm's butcher's shop at number 11 on the piazza.

FIVIZZANO (MS)

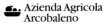 Azienda Agricola Arcobaleno

località Rosara di Sopra
☎ 0585 92508

Organic raspberries, woodland berries, and vegetables are produced here. They are sold fresh or made into liqueurs and conserves. Other organic products, including spelt and various cereals, soups with cereals, pulped tomatoes, and chestnut flour, are also available.

🍁 Farmacia Clementi

via Roma, 109
☎ 0585 92056
🌑 Wed pm

This pharmacy, with its fine old furnishings in Empire style from the late 19th century, is well worth visiting even if you are not in search of medicine. The Elixir

di China is made to a recipe belonging to the great-grandfather of the present owner, and the fruit syrups are made of berries from the local woods or fruit cultivated on the firm's own soft fruit farm.

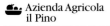

Azienda Agricola Giardino

Colle di Cerignano, 1
☎ 0585 92441

This estate produces organically grown fruit and vegetables, potatoes, cherries, apples, apricots, pears, and San Giovanni plums, a local variety.

Azienda Agricola il Pino

località Pastena di Ceserano
☎ 0585 982355

This farm grows and sells organic zucchini and strawberries.

FOSDINOVO (MS)

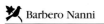

Barbero Nanni

località Fornello
via Fravizzola, 17
☎ 0187 68410

This agriturismo offers accommodation in five bedrooms, in a hillside setting. The owner selects a clone of the Vermentino grape for the Colli di Luni Vermentino di Fravizzola and puts Mammolo grapes to use in the Colli di Luni Rosso del Fornello.

LAMPORECCHIO (PT)

⊛ Pasticceria Carli - da Pioppino

piazza Berni, 20
☎ 0573 82177
● Wed ☐ Sun

For well over a century now, this confectionery shop has made authentic brigidini and berlingozzi to the same recipe.

LICCIANA NARDI (MS)

Apicoltura Dell'Amico e Amorfini

località Amola
☎ 0187 471502

Local honey – aromatic chestnut, dandelion, acacia, honeydew, and meadow – is produced and sold here, along with jars of local dried fruit preserved in honey.

🐦 Montagna Verde

località Apella
☎ 0187 421203

This is an agriturismo where refreshments are available. Chestnuts, chestnut flour, honey, pecorino cheese, and mushrooms (from the estate's woods) are sold.

LIDO DI CAMAIORE (LU)

Gastronomia Giannoni

viale Colombo, 444
☎ 0584 617332
● Wed pm

Ready-to-eat dishes made only from fresh produce, including fish, can be found here. There is a fine selection of salumi, including well-matured prosciutto di Langhirano.

LUCCA

Antica Bottega di Prospero

via San Lucia, 13
● Wed pm

This 200-year-old shop sells all kinds of different beans, spelt, and other cereals, plus pulses and chestnut flour.

🌳 La Cacioteca

via Fillungo, 242
☎ 0583 496346
● Wed pm

On sale here is a wide range of Tuscan pecorino, especially from the Garfagnana, some of it matured by the owner Aldo Pieracci by storing in caves and barrels. There is also a selection of Tuscan salumi, oil, and wine from around Lucca and cheeses from all over Italy.

TORDELLI LUCCHESI

2 lb 4 oz (1 kg) plain flour • 7 eggs • ¾ lb (300 g) loin of pork • rosemary • 1 lb 2 oz (500 g) rump steak • 6 oz (150 g) veal brain • 4 oz (100 g) beet leaves • thyme • 1 slice Tuscan bread • meat stock • grated nutmeg • grated Parmesan cheese • extra virgin olive oil • pepper • salt

Preheat the oven to 350°F (180°C). Make incisions in the pork and insert rosemary leaves. Place the pork and the steak in a roasting pan, brush with a little oil, and season. Roast for 30 minutes, basting with stock, if necessary. Meanwhile, steam the beet leaves and brains until cooked. Soak the bread in some meat stock. Dice all the meat and the leaves. Mix with the bread, 1 egg, the cheese, thyme, and nutmeg. Season. Mix the flour, 6 eggs, and salt, knead the dough and roll it out. Fill with the meat to form large ravioli. Cook in boiling salted water for 4 minutes. Serve with butter and cheese.

Piazza del Mercato in Lucca, once a Roman amphitheatre

mainly based on non-native vines: Sauvignon Blanc and Chardonnay for whites and a blend of Cabernet and Sangiovese for the red. The estate has recently started renting out renovated farmhouses on its land.

✹ Taddeucci

piazza San Michele, 34
☎ 0583 494933
● Thurs ○ Sun

This pasticceria has been in the same family for 120 years. Specialties are buccellato (Lucca cake, which looks more like bread than cake) and traditional vegetable pies (spicy but sweet, made with beet leaves).

🖳 Delicatezze di Isola

via San Giorgio, 5/7
☎ 0583 492633
● Wed pm

A wide range of delicacies, some typical of Lucca and others from all over the world, including cheese and some unusual salumi (made from game and turkey), smoked fish, and wines are sold here.

🍶 Tenuta di Forci

via per Pieve San Stefano, 7165
☎ 0583 349001

This 14th-century farm offers its fine extra-virgin olive oil under the label Olio dell'Antico Frantoio di Forci.

🖳 Lucca in Tavola

via San Paolino, 130/132
☎ 0583 581022
● Wed pm

Here you will find all the specialties of the Lucca area, chosen by the owner, a sommelier and oil taster,
including wines, oils, spelt and spelt products, honey, preserves, and olives.

🌾 Azienda Agricola Moretti Daniele-Le Murelle

località Cappella, via per Camaiore, traversa V
☎ 0583 394055

This estate has 74 acres (30 hectares) of vineyards, olive groves, and woodland. Wine production is

🍇 Enoteca Vanni Giulietta

piazza San Salvatore, 7
☎ 0583 491902
● Mon am

Within the stone walls and vaulted ceilings of this shop is a wide choice of local and other Italian wines. One section is devoted to whisky (including collector's items) and grappas. Book for a tasting. Lucca olive oil is also sold.

ZUPPA FRANTOIANA (BEAN SOUP)

1¼ lb (600 g) dried cannellini beans • 3 cloves garlic • sprigs of sage • extra-virgin olive oil • 1 onion, sliced • 4 oz (100 g) rigatino (bacon), sliced • 1 lb (400 g) black cabbage (cavolo nero), sliced • 2 potatoes, chopped • 2 carrots, chopped • 1 stalk celery, chopped • 8 oz (200 g) pumpkin, chopped • 1 head chicory, chopped • 1 bunch of mixed herbs, chopped • 6 slices crusty bread • salt • pepper

Soak the beans in water overnight. The next day, drain and place in a pan with 2 garlic cloves and the sage. Cover with water and simmer for 2 hours. Drain the beans and reserve the water. Heat some oil in a pan, add the onion and bacon and fry until browned. Add the vegetables and the bean water and cook for 30 minutes. Crush half the cooked beans and add the crushed and the whole beans to the soup. Season with salt and pepper. Rub the bread with the remaining garlic and sprinkle with oil. Place the slices in a tureen and pour the soup on top.

Polleria Fratelli Volpi

via San Paolino, 42
☎ 0583 56689
● Wed pm

Free-range chickens, ducks, and pigeons, rabbits from the Garfagnana, wild game, Pratomagno hams, pork sausages, wild boar, goose, and game from small local producers can all be found here. There are also various poultry and game dishes prepared, ready for cooking in the oven.

MASSA

❋ Gelateria Eugenio

località Ronchi,
Marina di Massa, via Pisa
☎ 0585 240369
● Mon in winter
○ Sun

This ice-cream parlor is famed for the excellent quality and the sheer variety of its many ice creams, some of them sublime.

❦ Podere Scurtarola

via dell'Uva, 3
☎ 0585 831560

This is one of the few producers that still bottles the rare white wine Candia dei Colli Apuani in both the dry and the semisweet versions. The Scurtarola Rosso is made from almost local vines such as Massaretta and Buonamico plus Ciliegiolo and a fair proportion of Sangiovese. It is drunk young. A small quantity of Vermentino Rosso wine is made from the local grapes. The farm also sells two different kinds of honey (chestnut and acacia flavors) as well as olive oil.

TORTA DI ERBE (HERB PIE)

4½ lb (2 kg) mixed green leaves and herbs • 2 oz (50 g) cured pork fat (lardo) • 2 oz (50 g) mortadella (or local salami) • 2 oz (50 g) pecorino cheese • 4 fl oz (100 ml) extra-virgin olive oil • 8 oz (200 g) flour • extra-virgin olive oil • pepper • salt

Preheat the oven to 400°F (200°C). Cook the leaves and herbs in boiling water until tender. Squeeze dry and chop with the pork fat and mortadella. Mix in the cheese and oil and season. Mix the flour, water, a little oil, and salt into a dough. Line a pie pan with half the dough, add the cooked leaves and herbs, and cover with the rest of the dough. Bake for 10 minutes then lower the temperature to 350°F (180°C) and cook for a further 20 minutes. Serve warm.

⬛ Drogheria Caffè gli Svizzeri

via Cairoli, 53
☎ 0585 43092
● Wed pm

This long-established grocery store has two main sections: a choice selection of local produce from the land – spelt, testaroli (pasta disks like pancakes), chestnut flour, ricotta cheese – and, in response to consumer demand, a rich choice of pulses and cereals. They also sell teas and spices.

MONSUMMANO TERME (PT)

ⓖ Slitti Caffè e Cioccolato

via Francesca sud, 268
☎ 0572 640240
● Sun

In Italy, chocolate confectioners are rare, but Monsummano has a world champion. Andrea Slitti has won countless awards, cups, and championships, in well-earned recognition of the taste and attractive appearance of his creations, which are true works of art. This shop and café has wonderfully luscious and imaginative chocolates, chocolate bars, Arabian coffee beans swathed in chocolate, chocolate teaspoons for stirring coffee, creamy spreads, and flavored chocolate sculptures.

MONTECARLO (LU)

❦ Carmignani

località Cercatoia
via della Tinaia, 7
☎ 0583 22381

Lorenzo and Gino Carmignani produce Duke Vermiglio, made with Syrah, Merlot, and Sangiovese grapes and aged in wood. There is also a Vin Santo version, Le Notti Rosse di Capo Diavolo, plus Montecarlo Rosso Sassonero and Bianco Pietrarchiara. Output is limited to a few thousand bottles of each. There is agriturismo accommodation to rent in the summer.

⚜ Fattoria del Buonamico

località Cercatoia
via Provinciale di
Montecarlo, 43
📞 0583 22038

This is a leading producer of Montecarlo Bianco and Rosso, backed up by a white, Vasario, from Pinot Bianco fermented in wood and aged in barriques. *There are also two reds: Cercatoia, with a good proportion of Sangiovese Grosso followed by Cabernet Sauvignon, Merlot, and a little Syrah; and Il Fortino, from pure Syrah grapes from a 30-year-old vineyard.*

⚜ Fattoria del Teso

località Teso
via Poltroniera
📞 0583 286288

Montecarlo Bianco and Rosso are offered at this estate, both excellent quality for the price.

MONTIGNOSO (MS)

🏛 La Bottega di Adò

via Vecchia Romana Est, 66
📞 0585 348315
⏺ Wed pm

The traditional Tuscan hams and sausages of this long-established salame *producer have a slightly sweet flavor, in the Emilian style. The*

company pursues a policy of high quality and is best known for its sausages, made to the highest standards. They should be eaten fresh and raw. Note also the firm's salamis – traditional soft Tuscan mortadella, *its* biroldo *(a blood sausage similar to* buristo*),* soppressata, *excellent* cotechini *plus, of course, Colonnata lardo.*

🏛 Gastronomia Osvaldo

località Cinquale
via Gramsci, 32
📞 0585 309193
⏺ Wed pm

Here you can find a well-chosen line of often very exclusive delicacies from every corner of Tuscany. There are wonderful specialties, like the salumi *and pecorino cheeses, always of the very highest quality.*

PIEVE A NIEVOLE (PT)

🏺 Frantoio Del Ponte

via Poggio alla Guardia, 12
📞 0572 67095

The Del Ponte Gold extra-virgin olive oil is this firm's premium product. The oil is made from olives from the Val di Nievole and Monte Albano. The estate has its own olive presses.

🌾 Panetteria Capecchi

via Dalmazia, 445
📞 0573 400208
⏺ Wed pm

This firm claims that a brick oven using gas, not wood, bakes the best cakes and bread, and sampling their wares it is impossible to disagree. The Tuscan bread and other types of traditional Italian bread are excellent, as is the schiacciata *baked on the floor of the oven. The* cantucci, *made with natural ingredients of high quality, are exceptional. The range of foods is completed with various Italian cheeses and* salumi.

🛒 Primizie e Funghi Sauro e Assunta

piazza della Sala, 11
📞 0573 21663
⏺ Wed pm

Excellent local fruit and vegetables are stocked by this greengrocer, plus best quality produce from further afield, including an unusual range of exotic fruits. In addition, all kinds of dry fruit, a large assortment of pulses, cereals, flour, mushrooms from Abetone, and a selection of gastronomic specialities are sold.

PONTREMOLI (MS)

🐂 Macelleria Mori

via Pietro Bologna, 23
📞 0187 830858
⏺ Wed pm

The meat sold by this specialty butcher's shop includes very fine lamb, raised locally. Mutton is also sold, but only in the winter months.

The Fattoria del Teso at Montecarlo

TRESANA (MS)

🛥 Tomà Rita

località Groppo, via Bola, 41
📞 0187 477946

This is the place for fresh chestnuts in season, plus dried chestnuts and chestnut flour.

VIAREGGIO

🌾 Forno Benzio e Pancaccini

via Mazzini, 75
📞 0584 962439
⬤ Wed pm

Many excellent kinds of bread are sold here, especially pane brutto (the Tuscan name for oddly shaped loaves), ciabatta (loaves containing lard), and ciabatta polesana (loaves made with a flour that can be left to rise for a long time). Cookies like anicini and pratolini are also available.

🎯 Rolando Bonini

via Mazzini, 181
📞 0584 44175
⬤ Wed pm

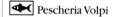
Il Puntodivino wine store

Seemingly a small butcher's shop opposite the celebrated Ristorante Romano, but in reality this is a shop run by a great game expert who sells game caught by various hunters in this area and also the Maremma, and who has contracts (contratti) with the forestry guards. As well as fresh game birds and animals (plus all cuts of free-range Hungarian geese), it has a selection of dry meats and bottled sauces based on game.

✳ Gelateria Mario

via Petrolini, 1
📞 0584 961349
⬤ Mon

The specialties of this shop are whipped ices and fresh fruit sorbets. It also sells fruit that is filled with ice cream flavored with the same fruit. A second shop on via dei Lecci 132 sells semi-freddi (ice cream and sponge desserts) and cakes.

🍇 Il Puntodivino

via Mazzini, 229
📞 0584 31046
⬤ Mon
◻ Sun

This is a particularly charming wine shop with tasting counter and an excellent restaurant run by Roberto and Cristina Franceschini. It stocks 700 wines and liquors from all over the world. It also has very fine extra-virgin olive oil. Snacks made with Colonnata lardo are served with the wines.

Pescheria Volpi

Mercato Centrale
📞 0584 32221
⬤ Mon

At the well-stocked fish market of Viareggio this is the most interesting fishmonger, with scampi from Gorgona, Sardinian crayfish, local red prawns sold live, and all the fish you need to make a real cacciucco (fish soup).

VILLAFRANCA IN LUNIGIANA (MS)

🌾 Pan Art

località Filetto,
via San Genesio, 21
📞 0187 495124
⬤ Wed pm

This the place to buy real testaroli (pasta disks like pancakes), torta d'erbe (herb pie), and, above all, Carsenta flat peasant bread cooked on chestnut leaves in a testo.

CACCIUCCO ALLA VIAREGGINA

extra-virgin olive oil • 4 cloves garlic • 1 fresh chilli, seeded and chopped • 1lb (500 g) octopus • 1 lb (500 g) cuttlefish • 1 glass red wine • 1½ lb (800 g) ripe tomatoes, chopped • 1½ lb (800 g) mixed fish (scorpion fish, gurnard, hake, weever, white bream, small ombrine) • 1¼ lb (600 g) shark steaks and conger eel • 10 razor clams • slices of bread • 1–2 tablespoons chopped fresh parsley • salt

Heat some oil in a pan. Chop two of the garlic cloves and lightly fry with the chilli. Cut the octopus and cuttlefish into largish pieces and stir into the pan. Add the wine and cook over a low heat until the wine has evaporated. Add the tomatoes; cook for 15 minutes. Add all the other fish, cutting up the large ones so they cook uniformly. Cover with hot water and simmer without stirring. When the fish is nearly cooked, add the razor clams and cook until all the fish is tender. Season with salt. Toast the bread, rub with the remaining garlic, and use to line a tureen. Pour in the soup, garnish with parsley and serve.

PISA
AND
LIVORNO

Pisa and Livorno

THE PROVINCES of Pisa and Livorno are strongly influenced by the sea, for better or for worse. On the plus side is the fact that Livorno (which is still known by its anglicized name of Leghorn in many tourist brochures) is one of the most important fishing harbors on the Tyrrhenian and that means plenty of fresh fish. It owes its prosperity to Cosimo I, who chose Livorno – a tiny fishing village in 1571 – as the site for Tuscany's new port when Pisa's harbor silted up. The other plus is that the sea air suits some types of vegetables and fruits. On the minus side, the salt air has an unfavorable effect on the quality of the extra-virgin olive oil produced along the coast. However, the benefits of the sea are felt further inland where the warm air from the sea, the hilly ground, and the quality of the soil make for good growing conditions. The flourishing undergrowth in the extensive woodlands along the coast and inland is rich in scents and wildlife, as well as mushrooms and berries. This is an area where agriculture, food production, and gastronomic tradition reflect a marriage of land and sea and a balance between agriculture and nature.

There is a plentiful supply of excellent **fish** at Livorno thanks to the good quality of the water and the sheer abundance of fish in the seas of Vada, Formiche Grosseto, Gorgona, and the other islands (*see pp 78–79*).

TRANSPORT

RAILROAD STATION
- PISA – STAZIONE FS
  050 500707
- LIVORNO – STAZIONE CENTRALE
  0586 898111

BUS STATION
- VOLTERRA
  0588 86099

STAR ATTRACTIONS

- PISA: tower and Cathedral, ⟦ 050 560921
  Baptistry and Camposanto, ⟦ 050 560464
  Santa Maria della Spina, ⟦ 050 910510
- SAN MINIATO (PI): Cathedral, ⟦ 0571 42745
- SAN PIERO A GRADO (PI): church of San Piero
- TENUTA DI SAN ROSSORE (PI): nature park,
  ⟦ 050 525500
- VOLTERRA (PI): Museo Etrusco Guarnacci,
  ⟦ 0588 86347
  Roman amphitheater, ⟦ 0588 86150
  Gallery and civic museum, ⟦ 0588 87580

◁ **Drop nets at Bocca d'Arno**

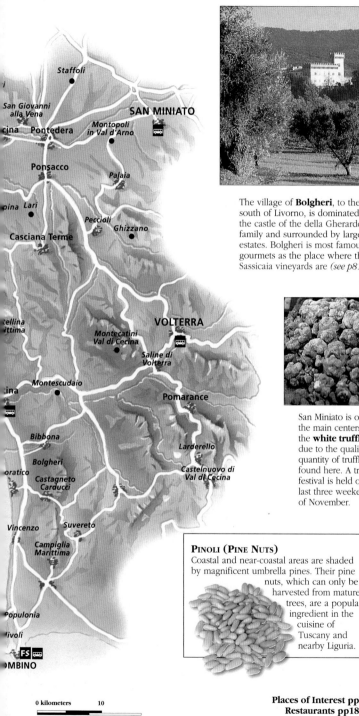

Staffoli

San Giovanni
alla Vena

SAN MINIATO

cina Pontedera   Montopoli
                   in Val d'Arno

Ponsacco

                Palaia

pina Lari

              Peccioli
                      Ghizzano

Casciana Terme

cellina
ittima
                VOLTERRA
          Montecatini
          Val di Cecina
                   Saline di
                   Volterra

cina Montescudaio

              Pomarance

Bibbona
                      Larderello
Bolghieri
oratico   Castagneto   Castelnuovo di
          Carducci   Val di Cecina

Vincenzo   Suvereto

           Campiglia
           Marittima

Populonia

livoli

FS

MBINO

The village of **Bolgheri**, to the
south of Livorno, is dominated by
the castle of the della Gherardesca
family and surrounded by large
estates. Bolgheri is most famous to
gourmets as the place where the
Sassicaia vineyards are *(see p81)*.

San Miniato is one of
the main centers for
the **white truffle**,
due to the quality and
quantity of truffles
found here. A truffle
festival is held on the
last three weekends
of November.

PINOLI (PINE NUTS)
Coastal and near-coastal areas are shaded
by magnificent umbrella pines. Their pine
nuts, which can only be
harvested from mature
trees, are a popular
ingredient in the
cuisine of
Tuscany and
nearby Liguria.

0 kilometers   10

0 miles   10

Places of Interest pp88–95
Restaurants pp180–185

Fish

FRESH FISH IS LANDED at Livorno harbor from all types of fishing grounds
nearby – the sandy shallows, especially those at Vada, and the deep
waters with seabeds of stone or gravel off the islands. But Livorno is
not the only fishing harbor on this part of the coast: fishing is also an important
industry in the islands. The waters around Elba, in particular,
contain many rare fish in season, such as ombine meagers and amberjack.
Piombino also has a busy fishing harbor, and some small boats call in
along the Riviera degli Etruschi.

PALOMBO OR NICCIOLO (SMOOTH-HOUND SHARK)
This shark has delicate flesh which is always tasty
and firm, and Italians consider it suitable for children.
Palombo is a basic ingredient in the local
cacciucco (fish soup). It is sold ready-skinned.
Often other sharks are passed off for *palombo*,
which is acceptable in the case of *spinarolo*
(spur dog) or *smeriglio* (porbeagle shark)
because they are also tasty, but the *gattuccio*
(lesser spotted dogfish) is far inferior.

RAZZA OR ARZILLA (SKATE)
Various kinds of skate
are caught in these waters.
Only the wings are eaten.
Some regional recipes
suggest boiling the
fish and serving it with
a sauce or stewing it.

GRONGO (CONGER EEL)
This typical coastal fish is similar
to the ordinary eel but it is
bonier and the flesh is less
fatty. It grows to an enormous
size and is used in soups
and sauces.

CODA DI ROSPO OR RANA PESCATRICE (MONKFISH)
Fierce-looking *(see lower part of
the photograph)* but delicious, this
is one of the most versatile fish in
the kitchen. Usually only the tail
end is sold in slices, which is a
pity since it makes a splendid soup
when cooked whole. The liver
is regarded as a delicacy.

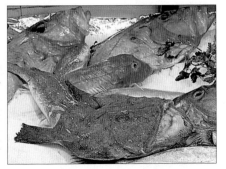

STRIGLIA DI SCOGLIO (RED MULLET)

This fish is a prime ingredient of Tuscan fish cuisine. Freshly caught and lightly cooked, smaller red mullet are always cooked whole. Larger red mullet are excellent grilled or baked in paper; or they may be fried or filleted as an *antipasto* (appetizer or starter). The related, very similar *triglia di fango* is a duller color, but has a stronger flavor. Red mullet liver is highly regarded.

SARAGO (A TYPE OF BREAM)

This white fish is typical of the coast and is highly prized. Its flesh is very tasty. *Sarago* is usually grilled or baked.

*Hake have numerous relatives. Small hake (*merluzzetto*) are delicious when fried.*

NASELLO OR MERLUZZO (HAKE)

Some fine specimens of hake are sold at the markets of Viareggio and Livorno, and when the fish is that fresh, it is excellent in all kinds of recipes. Hake is a delicate fish, easy to digest.

SEPPIA (CUTTLEFISH)

The most common of the squid family, *seppie* is usually inexpensive in markets. Cuttlefish is very versatile and is used in numerous regional recipes and special-occasion dishes. It is excellent boiled and dressed for a salad, or it can be grilled or baked. Pick one with the dark outer skin intact, and avoid those already cleaned. The ink sac is used for coloring and flavoring risottos and fresh pasta, although this is not a Tuscan tradition.

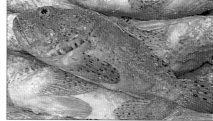

SCORFANO (SCORPION FISH OR RASCASSE)

This fierce-looking fish, considered the best fish for soup, is also delicious baked with rosemary. The flesh is white, tender, and juicy.

Wines

THE WEATHER IN the provinces of Pisa and Livorno is affected by the warm air currents of the Tyrrhenian Sea and, consequently, the wines produced along the coast have always been fair but not excellent, light-bodied, and rather short on bouquet. The lack of first-rate wines changed in 1968 with the creation of Sassicaia, the most influential of modern Italian red wines, and the one which paved the way for the creation of other wines based on Cabernet Sauvignon. As in most parts of Tuscany, local vines are cultivated alongside foreign vines imported in the late 19th century.

The traditional whites include Trebbiano Toscano, Vermentino, Malvasia del Chianti, and Bianco Pisano di San Torpé, with Sauvignon as an import. Among the local reds are Sangiovese, Canaiolo Nero, Malvasia Nera, and the imports Cabernet Sauvignon and Merlot. Elba with its iron-rich soil and briny breezes produces wines rich in flavor but lacking in perfume. Also, the difficulty cultivating the vines means that the wine is more expensive. Typical white grape vines grown on the island include Trebbiano Toscano (Procanico), Ansonica, and Moscato; the red grape vines include Sangioveto or Sangiovese and Aleatico.

The red (Rosso) goes well with pork chops and spare ribs; the Rosso Superiore with grilled red meats.

The whites and the rosé (Rosato) are the perfect accompaniments for first courses with light sauces.

BOLGHERI
The Bolgheri area is limited to the region of Castagneto Carducci. It produces Bianco from Trebbiano Toscano, Vermentino, and Sauvignon, with Sauvignon and Vermentino from the same vine contributing at least 80 percent; Rosato, Rosso, and Rosso Superiore from Cabernet Sauvignon, Merlot, and Sangiovese grapes; and a Vin Santo Occhio di Pernice, ordinary and Riserva, from Sangiovese and Malvasia Nera.

MONTESCUDAIO
This wine is produced in the hills, where the soil gives it a special fragrance.

The white, from Trebbiano Toscano, Malvasia, and Vermentino grapes, goes well with full-flavored fish dishes and eels.

The red, based on Sangiovese, is very similar to Chianti. It differs by having an intensely fruity perfume and because it is aged for only a short time, no more than about four years. Serve it with meat stews, mushrooms, and pasta with meat sauces.

BIANCO PISANO DI SAN TORPÉ
The Arno valley around Pisa and Livorno produces this delicately perfumed light white wine. Its name comes from a variety of Trebbiano named after the first holy martyr of Pisa. This wine is ideal as an aperitif and with vegetable dishes. The Vin Santo and Vin Santo Riserva versions are perfect with sweet cookies.

CHIANTI COLLINE PISANE
This wine is subtly perfumed with a lighter body than other Chiantis, so it makes an excellent accompaniment to a wider range of dishes, including white meats with sauces. It is also produced in Superiore and Riserva versions.

BOLGHERI SASSICAIA
This is the great wine of the Super Tuscan category. It owes its success to the Cabernet Sauvignon vine which develops an unusual bouquet and body in the soil in this area. The wine has to age at least two years in wood, of which at least 18 months is spent in small casks holding no more than 50 gallons (225 liters). It is good with *bistecca alla fiorentina*, but its perfect match is game.

CACCIUCCO ALLA LIVORNESE

extra-virgin olive oil • 2 onions, finely chopped • 1 carrot, finely chopped • 1 stalk celery, finely chopped • 4 cloves garlic • 1 handful of chopped parsley • 2½ lb (1 kg) small reef-fish suitable for soups, including a few mullet • 1 larger fish (scorpion fish, weever, gurnard, slices of conger, and palombo) • 1 lb (400 g) octopus, cut into pieces • 1 lb (400 g) cuttlefish, cut into pieces • a few scampi, cockles, and slices of squid (optional) • 1 lb (400 g) mantis shrimps • 2½ lb (1 kg) ripe tomatoes, peeled and seeded • chilli pepper • 3 glasses red wine • 3 dessertspoons wine vinegar • slices of Tuscan bread • salt

Heat some oil in a large pan (preferably a terra-cotta one) and lightly fry the chopped vegetables, garlic, and parsley. Clean the small fish and add them with the chilli. Fry lightly and season with salt. Add the vinegar and let it evaporate, then add the wine and the tomatoes. Simmer for 10 minutes then pass the mixture through a sieve. Heat some oil and fry the cuttlefish, octopus, and squid, if using, then add the sieved mixture and gradually all the other fish, calculating the cooking time for each (adding mantis shrimp, scampi, and cockles last). Add water, if necessary. Toast the bread and line a tureen with the slices. Pour the cooked soup over the bread and serve.

ELBA ANSONICA
Made with at least 85 percent Ansonica grapes, this is a dry white wine with a good body. It is well suited to a fish *antipasto* and delicately flavored first courses. There is also a sweet *Passito* (raisin wine) version.

ELBA BIANCO
This dry white wine, which is made chiefly from Trebbiano grapes, goes well with the island's traditional herb soups. There is also a spumante version.

ELBA ALEATICO
Considered the pearl of Elba's output – partly because of the difficulty of working the grapes – this is a pleasantly sweet red wine. Drink it with *torta ubriaca*, a fruit cake that is sprinkled with Elba Aleatico.

ELBA ROSSO AND ROSSO RISERVA
Sangiovese predominates, with small quantities of other red grapes in these wines. The young Rosso is good with white meats, especially rabbit in sauce, while the Riserva goes well with game – try it with hare.

WINE TYPE	GOOD VINTAGES	GOOD PRODUCERS	WINE TYPE	GOOD VINTAGES	GOOD PRODUCERS
Red Wine			**Red Wine**		
Bolgheri	97, 96, 90	Podere Grattammacco di Castagneto Carducci, Ornellaia di Bolgheri, Le Macchiole di Bolgheri	Montescudaio	97, 96, 90	Sorbaiano di Montecatini Val di Cecina
Bolgheri Sassicaia	97, 96, 90	Tenuta San Guido di Bolgheri	Supertuscans *(see p.130)*	98, 97, 95, 90	Tua Rita di Suvereto, Tenuta del Terriccio di Castellina Marittima, Michele Satta di Castagneto Carducci
Chianti delle Colline Pisane	97, 90	Tenuta di Ghizzano			

Traditional Produce

MOST OF TUSCANY grows excellent vegetables but the rural areas of Livorno and the Arno Valley between Pisa and Florence are particularly productive. One of the reasons market gardening here is so successful is the length of the growing season, which covers almost every month of the year except perhaps dry periods in high summer. The most distinctive Tuscan dishes are the soups *(minestre* and *zuppe)*, and fresh vegetables are such an important ingredient in local cooking that nearly all the *trattorie* grow their own produce. The areas around San Miniato and Volterra are renowned for white truffles.

BLACK-EYED PEAS

These peas were widely used in Europe before the discovery of America. In Italy they have been replaced by *cannellini* and *borlotti* beans, but they are still grown in Tuscany, in the area around Pistoia.

ELVERS

Elvers, the fry of eels (*cée* in the local dialect), have long been caught in Tuscan river estuaries. In local recipes they are cooked quickly in a covered pan or used to make stuffed omelettes. Elvers are now protected in Italy but not in Spain, where they are called *angulas.*

Cée alla pisana *is a Viareggio-style dish of elvers, cooked with garlic and sage.*

CÉE ALLA PISANA

extra-virgin olive oil • 4 cloves garlic, crushed • 4 sage leaves , chopped • just over 1 lb (500 g) elvers • 1 piece of fresh chilli, chopped • salt

Heat plenty of oil in a pan and sauté the chopped garlic and the sage leaves. Add the elvers and cover the pan at once, holding the lid down firmly and shaking the pan to prevent them from sticking. After a few seconds, uncover the pan and stir the elvers. Add the chilli and season with salt. Re-cover the pan and cook the elvers on a low heat for a few minutes.

OLIVE OIL FROM THE LIVORNO MAREMMA

The area of production for this oil lies inland from the Tyrrhenian coast and comprises Castagneto Carducci, Bibbona, Sassetta, and Monteverdi Marittimo. The oil is light and fruity with floral notes and a hint of the aroma of hay. It has a balanced flavor without marked intensity.

GOBBI IN GRATELLA

2¼ lb (1 kg) cardoons
- *extra-virgin olive oil*
- *wine vinegar • salt*
- *pepper*

Cut the cardoons into
pieces about 4½
inches (12 cm) long
and cook in boiling
water until tender.
Drain and rinse under
cold running water,
then remove the strings.
Season with plenty of
oil, salt and pepper, and
a few drops of vinegar.
Leave for 2 hours and then
grill the cardoons over
very hot charcoal.

GOBBI (CARDOONS)
Cardoons with their silvery
white stalks look like prickly
celery. Those from the Arno
Valley – the area bordering the
province of Florence – are
particularly sought-after.

OIL FROM THE HILLS OF PISA
Oil from olive
groves south of Pisa
and east of Livorno
has a delicate, yet
somewhat peppery
and fruity flavor.
It has a flowery
scent and a
sweetish aftertaste
of almonds.

PASTA SECCA (DRIED PASTA)
Lari produces some of the finest
dried pasta in Italy. The pasta is
sent to specialty shops all over
the world.

Tagliatelle

Pappardelle

Tagliolini

PASTA SECCA ALL'UOVO (DRIED EGG PASTA)
Many small
producers make
different egg-
based long
pastas. Although
these pastas are
dried, they have all the
flavor of fresh pasta.

WHAT TO SAMPLE
The **wild game**, especially boar, hare, wood pigeons, and woodcock, in this area – and
especially in the Maremma around Livorno – is as fine as that found in Grosseto. Inland,
and on Elba, there are areas that are good for vegetables and for **fine fruit**, including
yellow freestone peaches, white peaches (on Elba), figs, table grapes, and cherries (on
Monte Pisano and in the Lari area). In the hill areas there is excellent **prosciutto crudo**,
ham from shoulder of pork, and **pecorino** cheese at Volterra. The **farinata di ceci**
(chickpea polenta) is a speciality of Livorno. Local confectioners make and sell marzipan
fruits. On Elba the production of **honey** and **extra-virgin olive oil** is considerable.

At the start of the season, the early artichokes do not have any spines.

CARCIOFINI SOTT'OLIO

36 artichokes (late-season ones) • 2 pints (1 liter) wine vinegar • 2 bay leaves • 1 clove • 4 juniper berries • 1 dessertspoon black peppercorns • extra-virgin olive oil • salt

Clean the artichokes, removing the tough outer leaves. Dilute the vinegar with 3 pints (1½ liters) of water and pour it into a tall saucepan. Add the spices and plenty of salt. Bring to the boil, add the artichokes, and simmer for 6–7 minutes. Drain carefully and leave to cool. Dry the artichokes and transfer to one or more clean jars. Cover with oil, taking care not to trap air bubbles inside. Store in a cool dry place.

By the time the cold weather sets in, the artichokes have developed spines.

CARCIOFI (ARTICHOKES)
Artichokes are an essential ingredient in many traditional dishes, including fish ones, in the area; *Violetto* artichokes are a traditional Tuscan variety.

CAVOLFIORE (CAULIFLOWER) FROM CASCIANA
Casciana is a spa town renowned for cultivating cauliflowers, some of which grow to a very large size.

SPINACI (SPINACH)
Inland from Livorno, tasty spinach grows all the year round. In the springtime it is eaten raw in salads; the rest of the year it is cooked in traditional dishes.

OTHER PRODUCE WORTH TRYING
All summer the vegetables in this area are full of flavor, and the **eggplant is** exceptional. Look out for **fennel, peas, potatoes** from Santa Maria a Monte, **white asparagus** from the Valle d'Arno, **zucchini**, and **celery**. Along the coast there are sweet, juicy **tomatoes**. The **basil**, both the large-leaved variety and small-leaved Ligurian basil, has a wonderful scent. Specialty producers grow **garlic**, **onions,** and **shallots**.

Wild Produce

MILK-CAP MUSHROOM
(Lactarius sanguifluus)
This mushroom is called *pineggiole* locally, but *sanguinello* in the rest of Italy. Easily recognized because the gills shed a thick, red liquid, it is an orangey color with green patches, and has chalky flesh. They are common in woods along the coast, and the best ones are found under pine trees. Excellent preserved in oil, they can also be grilled or cooked in pasta sauces.

BLACK MOREL
(Morchella conica)
When the spring flowers bloom, these mushrooms *(spugnole)* sprout along the coast under pine and heathland trees, and inland in vineyards, orchards, and wherever there have been fires in pine woods. They are exquisite, fresh or dried, in risottos, sauces, savory pies, and casseroles.

TRIPPA CON LE SPUGNOLE

extra-virgin olive oil • 18 oz (500 g) morels, sliced • 1 sprig of calamint (or mint) • 3 cloves garlic, finely chopped • 1½ lb (700 g) tripe, cut into strips • light meat stock • salt • pepper

The traditional recipe uses *porcini* (cèpe mushrooms) but morels are better. Heat plenty of oil, add the mushrooms, calamint, and garlic, and season with salt and pepper. Cook until the mushrooms shed all their water. Lower the heat, add the tripe, and cook until all the liquid has evaporated and the tripe is tender, moistening with a little meat stock, if necessary. Adjust the seasoning.

YELLOW MOREL
(Morchella esculenta)
The yellow morel *(spugnola gialla)* is highly prized in international cuisine. It is common in the coastal scrub of Tuscany in springtime, then in damp inland valleys under elm and ash trees and in vineyards. Usually sold dried at the markets, this morel is excellent in pies, risottos, soups, and with eggs or meat.

SADDLE FUNGUS
(Helvella monachella)
In spring this mushroom forms clusters under poplars where the ground is sandy, especially at the coast. It is picked along with morels. While the perfume and taste are not exceptional, it adds a pleasant flavor to sauces.

SUMMER BOLETUS
(Boletus lepidus)
Distinguished from other cèpes by its yellow stalk
and scaly surface, this mushroom has rubbery
yellow flesh when ripe, but turns a pinkish color
when cut. It is nothing special but is picked
because of the thrill of finding a cèpe in summer,
when no other boletus mushrooms are to be
found. If young, they are very good fried.

BORAGE
(Borago officinalis)
One of the best-known and prettiest of the
wild herbs, borage *(borraggine)* grows on
waste ground on the Tuscan plains. It has a
pleasant taste of cucumber, and the leaves
are cooked in many of the classic soups of
the region and added to spinach dishes.
The pretty blue flowers add a lovely splash
of color to leafy salads.

CAPERS
(Capparis spinosa)
Caper plants *(capperi)* scramble
over sea-facing rocks and walls.
Their flower buds, salted and
pickled, are one of the classic
Mediterranean condiments.

PINE NUTS
(Pinus pinea)
Pinoli are found in abundance all year
round in Tuscany, growing inside the
cones of the majestic umbrella pines. Sadly,
they are harvested by machine, which is
very damaging to the undergrowth and
threatens to kill off the coastal pine woods.
Left on the tree, the large cones fall as they
open, so the pine nuts can be picked up
from the ground.

BACCALÀ IN DOLCEFORTE (SALT COD IN SWEET-AND-SOUR SAUCE)

*1 glass white wine • 1 small glass wine vinegar • 2 dessertspoons pine nuts •
2 dessertspoons sugar • 1 dessertspoon sultanas • a few calamint (or mint) leaves • extra-
virgin olive oil • 1¾ lb (800 g) salt cod, presoaked and cut into pieces • plain flour*

Put the wine, vinegar, pine nuts, sugar, sultanas, and calamint in a pan. Bring to the boil
and boil until the liquid is reduced by half. Heat the oil in a separate pan. Coat the cod
pieces in flour and fry in the oil for 6–7 minutes on each side. Drain the cod and put in
another pan with a little of the oil and the sauce. Sauté over brisk heat for 3–4 minutes.

Places of Interest

THE FOLLOWING PLACES sell an extensive range of foods produced in this region – fruits, vegetables, meat, fish, cheeses, pasta, honey, and preserves. They also have excellent wine-makers. In addition, it is always worth stopping wherever you see a hand-written sign outside a farm, as many farmers will sell their produce directly to visitors. You may even find some who will let you pick fruit from the trees and gather vegetables from their kitchen gardens.

ASCIANO (PI)

🍷 Fattoria di Asciano

via Possenti, 87
📞 050 855924

This large estate has its own olive press, once the property of Lorenzo il Magnifico. It produces Monti Pisani Colle di Bellavista extra-virgin olive oil, which is one of the finest olive oils in Italy. More versatile than the classic Pisan oils, it is very good for making mayonnaise and dressing fish grilled over charcoal or poached.

BIBBONA (LI)

🐟 Fattoria San Anna

località Sette Fattorie
via Aurelia Sud
📞 0586 670230

The fruits and vegetables grown on the farm here are used for making preserves, jams, and fruit in syrup. Sauces and soups are sold ready to heat up and serve. All the products are carefully packaged in glass jars, and they are guaranteed to keep well.

BOLGHERI (LI)

🍇 Tenuta Belvedere

località Belvedere
📞 0565 749735

This property is owned by Piero Antinori, who uses it for growing local vines. His Bolgheri Bianco Belvedere and Bolgheri Rosato Vigneto Scalabrone are notable wines. The best known, however, is a red, Guado al Tasso. The wines can be bought at Enoteca Tognoni (see opposite page).

🍇 Azienda Agricola Le Macchiole

via Bolgherese, 189/A
📞 0565 766092

By tending the vines and careful wine-making this estate has produced a line of fine wines. The prime one is Bolgheri Rosso superiore Paléo Rosso, well supported by Paléo Bianco (Sauvignon, Chardonnay, and Vermentino) and two single-grape reds: Messorio (Merlot) and Scrio (Syrah).

🍇 Tenuta dell'Ornellaia

via Bolgherese, 191
📞 0565 7181

Owned by the Marquis Lodovico Antinori, this estate is known for a good wine, Ornellaia (from

The gateway to Bolgheri

Cabernet Sauvignon, Merlot, and Cabernet Franc), accompanied by other noteworthy wines – Masseto (from Merlot alone), Le Volte (Sangiovese, Cabernet Sauvignon, and Merlot), and Poggio alle Gazze (Sauvignon Blanc). The extra-virgin olive oil is also excellent. Purchases can be made at Enoteca Tognoni (see opposite).

🍇 Tenuta San Guido

località Capanne, 27
📞 0565 762003

This estate gave birth to the first wine to be called a "Super Tuscan," Sassicaia. The owner, the Marquis Niccolò Incisa della Rocchetta, assisted by his skilled staff, chose Cabernet Sauvignon vines and achieved excellent results. At present this is the only wine made here, with the 180,000 bottles always booked well in

The cellar of the Tenuta dell'Ornellaia at Bolgheri

advance. *The extra virgin olive oil is not always of the highest quality – it depends on the year. Purchases can be made at Enoteca Tognoni (see below).*

Enoteca Tognoni

via Giulia, 6
■ 0565 762001
● Wed
○ Sun

This wine store stocks a good selection of the great wines of Bolgheri and Tuscany, as well as various other Italian wines. You can sample and buy cheeses, Maremma salumi, and other local delicacies. Hot and cold dishes are served: the former include soups made with spelt.

CALCI (PI)

 Il Colletto

località Par di Rota
via dei Pari, 14
■ 050 939320

The excellent extra-virgin olive oil sold at Il Colletto is produced from the firm's own organically grown olives.

CAMPIGLIA MARITTIMA (LI)

Azienda Agricola Jacopo Banti

località Citerna
■ 0565 838802

The small range of red and white wines sold here includes a noteworthy Val di Cornia Bianco Il Peccato made from Vermentino grapes alone, and Ceragiolo, an unusual red from Ciliegiolo grapes alone. The olive oil comes from the olive groves dotted on the hillsides.

The Elixir China Calisaja shop at Castagneto Carducci

CAPOLIVERI – ELBA (LI)

Azienda Agricola Mola

località Gelsarello, 2
■ 0565 958151

This is a mixed farm, producing a range of vegetables, fruits, oil, and wine. The wines produced here are Elba Bianco Vigna degli Aiali, Elba Rosso Gelsarello, a pure Sangiovese, and two sweet wines: Elba Aleatico and Passito di Moscato.

CASTAGNETO CARDUCCI (LI)

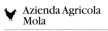 Enoteca Il Borgo

via Vittorio Emanuele, 25/27
■ 0565 766006
● Mon
○ Sun

Only Italian wines – the premier wines of the Bolgheri area and the leading estates – are stocked by this wine shop. The range includes a selection of grappas and liquors and olive oil from local producers.

Elixir China Calisaja

via Garibaldi
■ 0565 766017
● Wed pm in winter

This is the sales outlet for a long-established firm. It imports quinine bark, which is then processed by hand in the traditional way, by pounding in a mortar and soaking in alcohol. The resulting elixir is then stored in wood. The firm also produces an infusion made from vanilla pods, sugar, lemon, and milk, which is called "Gran liquore del Pastore." The shop sells a wide range of local produce, including honey, preserves, and pasta, much of it organically produced.

SEPPIE IN ZIMINO

extra-virgin olive oil
• *1 onion, chopped*
• *2 stalks celery, chopped*
• *2¼ lb (1 kg) beet leaves, sliced into large pieces* • *2¼ lb (1 kg) cuttlefish, cut into strips*
• *10 oz (300 g) tomatoes, peeled*
• *chopped fresh parsley*
• *salt* • *pepper*

Heat some oil in a pan, add the onion and celery, and cook until softened slightly. Add the beet leaves, cover and cook for about 15 minutes. Add the cuttlefish, cook for a few minutes, and then add the tomatoes. Season with salt and pepper and simmer until the cuttlefish is tender. Garnish with the parsley.

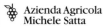

Podere Grattamacco

località Grattamacco
0565 763840

The peak of this estate's wine production is the Bolgheri Rosso Superiore Grattamacco from Cabernet Sauvignon, Merlot, and Sangiovese grapes, followed by Bolgheri Bianco Grattamacco from Vermentino, Trebbiano, and Sauvignon. The estate produces a fine oil, one of the best in the district.

Fattoria Poggio Lamentano

località Lamentano, 138/b
0565 766008

This estate is owned by a Scot called Michael Zyw, who devotes himself to painting and the land. He produces a fine, intense, fruity extra-virgin olive oil, which is well-known abroad and appreciated by leading restaurateurs in Italy.

Azienda Agricola Michele Satta

località Vigna al Cavaliere
0565 763894

Reconciling style with a commitment to quality is the goal of this estate. The Bolgheri Rosso Piastraia blends four types of grape: Merlot, Cabernet, Syrah, and Sangiovese. The red Il Cavaliere is from Sangiovese alone. Among the whites, Bolgheri Vermentino La Costa di Giulia is of note.

CASTELLINA MARITTIMA (PI)

Tenuta del Terriccio

via Bagnoli
050 699709

The Lupicaia '95 available here is a well-structured red made from Cabernet and Merlot grapes. There is also its younger brother, Tassinaia, containing some Sangiovese. The Montescudaio Bianco and the Saluccio, from Chardonnay and Sauvignon Blanc, and fermented in wood, are also noteworthy.

CASTIGLIONCELLO (LI)

Gelateria Dai Dai

via del Sorriso, 8
0586 753390

Delicious ice creams made from good quality ingredients are offered here. Try the ice cream bricks, tartufini, cassatas, vanilla ice-cream, sorbets, and bocconcini.

CAVO – ELBA (LI)

Apicoltura Ballini

strada provinciale della Parata
0565 949836

Here is a leading breeder of queen bees, exported worldwide, and a producer of outstanding honey from unusual flowers, mostly aromatic herbs: rosemary, lavender, cardoons, heather, arbutus (strawberry tree), helichrysum, eucalyptus, sweet chestnut, and wild flowers. There is another shop at via Michelangelo 11 in the village.

CRESPINA (PI)

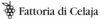

Fattoria di Celaja

località Cenaja
via Lustignano, 4
050 643949

Production here is based on two main lines, Chianti and a Bianco Pisano di San Torpé from Trebbiano grapes alone.

DONORATICO (LI)

Maestrini

via Aurelia, 1
0565 775209
Mon Sun

BACCALÀ IN ZIMINO (SALT COD IN TOMATOES)

$1^3/_4$ lb (800 g) salt cod, soaked in water for 2 days • $1^3/_4$ lb (800 g) beet leaves • $1^1/_4$ lb (500 g) tomatoes • extra-virgin olive oil • 3 green onions, chopped • 2 cloves garlic, chopped • salt • pepper

Rinse the cod, remove the skin, and cut it into pieces. Wash the beet leaves and put them in a pan with just the water that adheres to the leaves. Cover and cook over a low heat for about 10 minutes. Drain, squeeze out the water, and chop coarsely. Scald the tomatoes in boiling water, peel while still warm, and cut into pieces. Heat some oil in a pan and gently fry the green onions, garlic, and cod for 5 minutes. Using a slotted spoon, remove the cod and set aside. Add the tomatoes to the pan, season with salt and pepper, and simmer gently for 30 minutes. Add the greens and the pieces of cod and stir gently for about 10 minutes. Serve piping hot.

TELLINE ALLA LIVORNESE (LIVORNO COCKLES)

*extra-virgin olive oil • 1 onion, chopped • ³/₄ lb (350 g)
tomatoes, peeled and chopped • 1 fresh chilli, seeded and
chopped • 2¹/₂ lb (1.2 kg) cockles (telline) • 3 eggs
• chopped fresh parsley • salt • pepper*

Heat some oil in a pan, add the onion, and fry until
slightly softened. Add the tomatoes and chilli and season
with salt and pepper. Cook over a moderate heat for 10
minutes. Add the cockles in their shells and cook until
they have all opened. Beat the eggs in a bowl, then add
them to the pan with the parsley. Stir to mix all the
ingredients and serve at once.

*A medium-to-high quality
selection of Tuscan,
Italian and foreign wines,
especially DOCG wines
from central Tuscany
are sold here. Wines can
be tasted accompanied
by salumi and excellent
cheeses in a relaxed
atmosphere with
background music.*

GHIZZANO (PI)

🍇 Tenuta di Ghizzano

Piccioli, via della Chiesa, 1
📞 0587 630096

*The main effort of this
estate is focused on the
extra-virgin olive oil from
its 15,000 olive trees. It is
a very active estate which
has enhanced the wine
production of the Pisan
hills with a very
respectable Chianti and
Veneroso, a red wine from
Sangiovese, Cabernet, and
Merlot grapes.*

LARI (PI)

🐗 Agriturismo Le Macchie

località Usigliano
via delle Macchie, 2
📞 0587 685327

*Cinta Senese pigs graze
half-wild on this farm.
The meat and salumi the
farm produces are less
salty and spicy to suit the
taste of non-Tuscans. It*

*has lardo (lard), which
is processed at Colonnata
in marble molds,
fegatelli (pig's liver
wrapped in caul fat), and
sausages in oil, as well
as jams, preserves, and
fresh vegetables. There is
also a restaurant and
farmhouse vacation
accommodation.*

🌾 Martelli Artigiani Pastai

via S. Martino, 3
📞 0587 684238

*This family firm welcomes
visitors (it is popular with
Americans) and readily
answers questions about
its working methods. The
Martelli family's pasta
(in a wide range of
shapes, all dried at low
temperatures and
extruded through bronze)
is excellent, and though
output is limited, it is
found in leading stores
on every continent.*

LIVORNO

🍇 D.O.C. Parole e Cibi

via Goldoni, 40/44
📞 0586 887583
🌑 Mon. ⏻ Sun.

*An exceptional range
of wines – over 2,000
from all over the world –
can be found at this
wine shop. There is also
a wide selection of
grappas, whisky, and
other liquors. The store
has a very lively wine bar
offering tasty snacks to
accompany the wines,
and there is a restaurant
(serving in the evenings
only) which is open until
the wee hours.*

🍇 Cantina Nardi

via Leonardo Cambini, 6/8
📞 0586 808006
🌑 Sun.

*A good selection of both
Italian and Tuscan wines
is sold here, with the
emphasis on Val di Cornia
and Bolgheri, plus the
latest vintages of the
"Super Tuscans." They
also sell olive oil and a
range of liquors. During
the day they run a small
osteria (hostelry) in the
wine cellar with a limited
number of traditional
Tuscan dishes prepared to
perfection. The cacciucco,
(fish soup) is very popular,
and you need to order it
in advance.*

Fishing boats in Livorno harbor

Azienda Agricola Cecilia at Marina di Campo on Elba

MARCIANA – ELBA (LI)

🍂 Walter Ciangherotti

località La Zanca
☎ 0565 908281

*Here there are excellent
organic honeys, such as
lavender, rosemary,
blackberry, heather,
chestnut, and field honey.*

BAVETTINE
SUL PESCE

¾ lb (300 g) scampi
• 6 small mullet • ¾ lb
(300 g) clams • 6 mantis
shrimp • extra virgin olive
oil • 8 oz (200 g)
monkfish • 8 oz (200 g)
small cuttlefish • 1¼ lb
(500 g) bavettine (ribbon
pasta) • 2 cloves garlic,
chopped • 1 lb (400 g)
tomatoes, chopped
• chopped fresh parsley
• salt • pepper

Peel the scampi and
fillet the mullet. Use the
heads to make stock and
cook the shrimp and
clams in it for 5 minutes.
Strain the stock; reserve
the clams and shrimp.
Stir-fry the monkfish,
cuttlefish, fillets, scampi,
and garlic in some oil.
Add the tomatoes, salt,
pepper, and parsley and
simmer. Cook the pasta
in the stock. Add the
shrimp and clams to the
sauce and serve.

MARINA DI CAMPO – ELBA (LI)

🍇 Azienda Agricola Cecilia

località La Pila
☎ 0565 977322

*The complete range of this
firm's Elba DOC wines
includes an outstanding
Ansonica, Rosso, and a
sweet Aleatico wine. Skins
and seeds of grapes from
wine-making produce two
kinds of grappa, one from
Ansonica grapes, the other
from a blend of Ansonica,
Moscato, and Aleatico.*

MONTECATINI VAL DI CECINA (PI)

🍇 Fattoria Sorbaiano

località Sorbaiano
☎ 0588 30243

*Two types of grape typical
of central Italy, Sangiovese
and Montepulciano
d'Abruzzo, and two
foreigners, Cabernet
and Syrah (not common
in Italy but recently
introduced to various
regions) are carefully
balanced in the estate's
Montescudaio Rosso delle
Miniere. Equally well-
balanced is the blend of
Trebbiano, Vermentino,
Chardonnay, and Riesling
for the Montescudaio
Bianco Lucestraia
matured in barriques.
The Vin Santo wine is
made the old way. The
estate makes an excellent
organically produced
extra-virgin olive oil. It
has a lively program
of agriturismo (farm and
estate vacations).*

MONTESCUDAIO (PI)

🦪 Azienda Agricola da Morazzano

via di Morazzano, 28
☎ 0586 650015

*Quality conserves, fruits,
vegetables, and extra
virgin olive oil are all
produced by this firm.
The many items include
shallots in oil, tomato
purée, and low-sugar jams.*

PISA

Ⓒ Cioccolateria De Bondt

via Turati, 22
☎ 050 501896
⏺ Mon; from June to
September

Delicacies from the Cioccolateria De Bondt

Azienda Agricola Acquabona

About 30 types of chocolates – some made in molds while others are handcrafted like real works of art (there are even Christmas trees and Easter eggs in season) – and 15 kinds of chocolate bars are all the work of Paul De Bondt, a skilled Dutch confectioner who settled in Pisa for love.

⊛ Pasticceria Salza

via Borgo Stretto, 46
☎ 050 580144
◉ Mon ◯ Sun

A confectionery shop renowned for the freshness of its raw materials and top-of-the-line products, from chocolates to cookies, cakes, ice creams, chilled cream desserts, and traditional Sienese fruit cakes including panforte and ricciarelli.

PONTEDERA (PI)

⚊ Pastificio Caponi

via Verdi, 16
☎ 0587 52532
◉ Sat

This small, family-run pasta-maker is one of the leading firms still using traditional methods to produce limited quantities of an excellent egg pasta, which is dried at low temperatures. It has been famous throughout Italy and Europe for 40 years for its good quality

ingredients and the care devoted to all phases of production. In addition to dried pasta, it sells various other gastronomic specialities.

◄◄ Pescheria Toti

via Marconcini, 72
☎ 0587 53921
◉ Wed and Sat pm

Here you have a wide selection of excellent fresh fish, which comes mainly from the Livorno and Viareggio harbors.

PORTOFERRAIO – ELBA (LI)

🍇 Azienda Agricola Acquabona

località Acquabona
☎ 0565 933013

This is one of the largest vineyards and wineries on the island, with 37 acres (15 hectares) of the traditional Elba vines including Ansonica,

which it produces in more limited quantities. The Aleatico is interesting, with about 1,000 18 ounce (half-liter) bottles produced a year. It also produces small quantities of grappa.

⚊ La Bottega del Pane

viale Elba, 13
☎ 0565 914165
◉ Wed pm

Well-known locally for its fine focaccia reflecting the sunny flavors of the Mediterranean and a wide variety of modern filled rolls, this bakery also sells excellent standard white and brown bread.

🍇 Azienda Agricola La Chiusa

località Magazzini, 93
☎ 0565 933046

Long-established on Elba, this estate's fine vineyards slope down to within a few yards of the sea. It principally makes Elba Bianco, but its most interesting products are two dessert wines, Elba Ansonica (made from partly dried grapes) and Elba Aleatico. The extra-virgin olive oil produced by the estate merits separate mention because it is excellent quality and, unhappily, there is not enough to satisfy the very high demand for it.

CÉE ALLA LIVORNESE (LIVORNO-STYLE EELS)

2¼ lb (1 kg) elvers • extra-virgin olive oil • 1 sprig of sage, chopped • 3 cloves garlic, chopped • 8 oz (250 g) tomatoes, peeled • chopped fresh chilli • salt • pepper

Wash the elvers carefully and pat dry. Heat some oil in a pan, add the sage and garlic, and fry gently until the garlic has softened. Add the elvers to the pan and cook for 5 minutes over a moderate heat. Add the tomatoes and a small amount of chopped chilli. Season with salt and pepper. Simmer for another 10 minutes before serving.

TRIPPA ALLA LIVORNESE

extra-virgin olive oil
• *3 cloves garlic , chopped*
• *2¼ lb (1 kg) tripe,*
cut into strips • *4*
dessertspoons vinegar
• *chopped fresh parsley*
• *salt* • *pepper*

Heat some oil in a pan, add the garlic, and fry gently for a few minutes. Add the tripe and cook for 3–4 minutes. Pour in the vinegar and a glass of hot water. Cook until the liquid has evaporated and then remove from the heat. Taste and adjust the seasoning. Sprinkle with the chopped parsley and serve at once.

PROCCHIO – ELBA (LI)

 Macelleria Mazzarri

via Centrale
📞 0565 907289
🔴 Wed pm

In the open season, Mazzarri butchers local wild boar; the rest of the year he has excellent meat, mostly Tuscan (including Chianina beef), otherwise Piedmontese.

SALIVOLI DI PIOMBINO (LI)

🍴 Romeo Formaggi

via dei Cavalleggeri, 5
📞 0565 44455

The region's best salumi, as well as authentic culatello di Zibello and Norcia hams, are sold by this shop, which specializes in salumi. It also has a rich selection of cheeses from central and northern Italy: formaggi ubriachi from the Veneto, various types of robiola from the Langhe, pecorino di fossa from Soliano al

Rubicone, and the famous Piedmontese Castelmagno.

SAN GIOVANNI ALLA VENA (PI)

 Macelleria Bernardini

via Garibaldi
📞 050 799375
🔴 Wed pm

Prosciutto crudo *and* salumi *made from pork or game are produced here. The* Boccone del buttero *is an intriguing specialty made from strips of boar meat seasoned with olives.*

SAN MINIATO (PI)

🍇 Frantoio Sanminiatese

via Maremmana, 8
📞 0571 460528

This estate produces excellent extra virgin olive oil and spicy table olives. It is open daily except during the olive-pressing season (this is usually from mid-October to mid-January).

SUVERETO (LI)

🍇 Azienda Agricola Gualdo del Re

località Notri, 77
📞 0565 829888

The unusual DOC Val di Cornia range of wines – Bianco, Rosso, and Rosso Riserva – are the staples of this estate. They are backed up by other notable wines, like the red Federico Primo (Sangiovese and Merlot in equal parts) and the white Vermentino Vigna Valentina.

TRIGLIE ALLA LIVORNESE

3¼ lb (1.5 kg) red mullet, cleaned • *4 cloves garlic, finely chopped* • *extra-virgin olive oil* • *2¼ lb (1 kg) tomatoes, peeled and chopped* • *1 fresh chilli (misleadingly called* zenzero *- ginger - in Tuscany), seeded and finely chopped* • *handful of parsley, chopped* • *salt* • *pepper*

Arrange the red mullet in a single layer in a greased pan. In a second pan, sauté the garlic in a little oil, add the tomatoes, and simmer. When the tomatoes are half-cooked, add the chilli and season to taste with salt and pepper. Once the sauce is well cooked, pour it over the mullet and simmer over a low heat, taking care that the sauce does not dry out (add a little hot water to the pan, if necessary). When the fish are cooked, sprinkle in the chopped parsley and serve.

Oil jars at the Azienda Agricola Orlando Pazzagli

Azienda Agricola Orlando Pazzagli

via Cavour, 40
0565 829333

With its own olive groves and press, this estate covers the whole cycle of production. Its La Piastrina extra-virgin olive oil is typical of the area and is outstanding.

Azienda Agricola Tua Rita

località Notri, 81
0565 829237

On the borders of the provinces of Livorno and Grosseto, this estate's wines are designed to highlight both traditional local vines and imported ones. Especially notable are the reds Giusto di Notri (from Merlot and Cabernet) and Perlato del Bosco Rosso from Sangiovese alone. There are three whites: Perlato del Bosco Bianco (Ansonica and Clarette), Sileno (Gewürztraminer, Riesling, Chardonnay), and Val di Cornia.

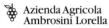

Azienda Agricola Ambrosini Lorella

località Tabarò, 96
0565 829301

This estate's Riflesso Antico demonstrates how to make a great wine from a local vine, Montepulciano d'Abruzzo. The Val di Cornia Rosso and Bianco are also very good.

VOLTERRA (PI)

Agriturismo Lischeto

località San Giusto
0586 670346

The owner of this estate is one of many Sardinians who have moved to this region; his wife is Tuscan. The estate has a milking herd of 1,000 ewes and

PICCHIANTE

2 lb (800 g) lights (pork or lamb lungs), cleaned • extra-virgin olive oil • 2 cloves garlic, chopped • 1 onion, chopped • 2 carrots, chopped • 1 sprig of rosemary, chopped • 1 sprig of sage, chopped • basil leaves, torn • 1 glass white wine • 6 oz (150 g) tomatoes, peeled and chopped • salt

Cut the lights into pieces. Heat some oil in a pan and lightly fry the garlic, vegetables, and herbs. Add the lights and fry until browned. Pour in the wine and tomatoes. Season with salt, cover and simmer for about 45 minutes, then uncover the pan and cook until the sauce has thickened.

their milk is used to produce excellent pecorino *cheeses, both fresh and mature, and also fresh and baked* ricotta *cheeses. A second family estate not far from the sea produces very good extra-virgin olive oil, and the honey is excellent. The agriturismo facilities on the estate include apartments to rent with meals of typical Sardinian and Tuscan dishes available.*

View of the countryside from the heights of Volterra

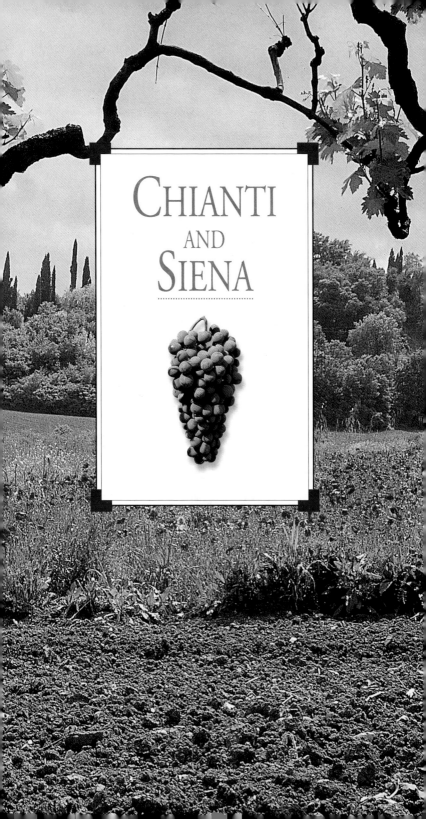

CHIANTI
AND
SIENA

Chianti and Siena

ITALY'S BEST-KNOWN WINE comes from this region. The geographical region of Chianti, which had the name long before the wine, is only one part of the winegrowing area of the same name. Chianti wine is produced over a huge area of central Tuscany. The area that gave birth to Chianti wine now sports the Chianti Classico label on its bottles of wine, to indicate that it comes from the classic heartland of Chianti. This heartland, a hilly district stretching across the provinces of Florence and Siena, does not look like a wine-producing area. The woodlands are studded with ancient towns and villages, whose long history is visible at every gateway. On the hilltops, often screened from the main roads, stand country houses set in estates where the olive groves and vineyards are separated by extensive woodland. These villas and castles bear witness to the splendors of past nobility and prosperity, but also to bloody wars.

The old rivalry between Florence and Siena still smolders, and, in fact, has helped to spur on the revival of wines that were produced in the past, and which have now regained much of their original character and vitality.

FLOR

San Casciano in Val di Pesa

Montespertoli

Mercat Val di Pe

Castelfiorentino

Certaldo

Tavernelle Val di Pesa

Barberino Val d' Elsa

San Gimignano   Poggibonsi

Castellin in Chian

Colle di Val d'Elsa

Castel di San Gimignano

Monteriggioni

0 kilometers   10

0 miles   10

Cinta Senese pigs, which are easily distinguished by their dramatic markings, browse freely with herds of other pigs in the oak woods and meadows in Val di Pesa. In Tuscany the breed dates back to antiquity and you can spot them in celebrated Renaissance paintings, including those of Luca Signorelli.

STAR ATTRACTIONS

- MONTERIGGIONI (SI): Town wall, 0577 280551
- SIENA: Palazzo Pubblico, 0577 292263 Cathedral, 0577 47321 Piazza del Campo
- SAN GIMIGNANO (SI): Cathedral, Palazzo del Podestà, 0577 940340 Museo Civico, 0577 940008

◁ **Spring landscape at Incisa Val d'Arno**

CHIANTI
The famous red wine was once identified by its distinctive straw-padded bottle. Nowadays, this bottle has fallen out of favor because of the high cost of production and difficulties of transportation and storage.

The vineyards in this area are often estates with large old country houses. The Cusona estate belongs to the noble Guicciardini Strozzi family and produces an excellent Vernaccia di San Gimignano.

Incisa in Val d'Arno

Figline Valdarno

Greve in Chianti

San Giovanni Valdarno

nzano Chianti

Montevarchi

Radda in Chianti

Arno

Gaiole in Chianti

Bucine

Pergine Valdarno

C h i a n t i

Castelnuovo Berardenga

ENA

Monte San Savino

Panforte, the rich fruitcake, is a symbol of Siena's gastronomic pleasures. Its origins lie in the honey breads of the Middle Ages *(see p106).*

(see p106)

TRANSPORT

FS RAILROAD STATION
• SIENA – STAZIONE FS
  0577 280551
• COLLE DI VAL D'ELSA
  0577 922791

BUS STATION
• SAN GIMIGNANO
  0577 940008
• CASTELFIORENTINO
  0571 629049

Chianti extra-virgin olive oil is the most famous and celebrated of Tuscany's oils in other parts of the world. The quality is excellent, but it is not produced in the same quantities as the oil from other regions, and it is expensive.

Places of Interest pp112–123
Restaurants pp185–187

Wines

The CHIANTI AREA is very extensive, covering six of the region's provinces, all with very different terrains and microclimates. Its beauty is reminiscent of a magical Renaissance atmosphere, and the area has attracted many foreign investors and businessmen from northern Italy who have settled here, invested in vineyards, and made an essential contribution to reviving the region's wine. This is the realm of the Sangiovese vine, which seems to have originated here. It is used for making numerous wines, often in large quantities, especially the Chianti DOCG.

Other important red grapes are Canaiolo Nero and Colorino. The main whites are Trebbiano Toscano and Malvasia del Chianti or Malvasia Bianca, used in small amounts in Chianti but more important for wines such as Vin Santo. Vernaccia di San Gimignano, a very compact thin-skinned white grape is an important grape which gives its name to the wine it is used for.

The properties of the soil and climate in this area make it possible to get good results from Cabernet Franc, Chardonnay, Merlot, Syrah, and Pinot Nero red grapes, and Chardonnay and Sauvignon white grapes. Formerly, grapes were dried on racks and then added to the must while it was still young to make Chianti mellow (a practice known as *"governo"*), but this technique is very rare nowadays.

Sangiovese, also called Sangioveto, is the most important red grape vine not only of the Chianti area but of all of Tuscany.

CHIANTI

The label on a bottle of this wine may say Chianti or it may have the name of one of seven subdenominations: Colli Aretini, Colli Fiorentini, Montalbano and Rùfina *(see pp24-6)*, Colline Pisane *(see p81)*, Colli Senesi, and Montespertoli. This last one goes back only to 1997 and has just reached the market. Chiantis from the various subzones differ in body, bouquet, and the length of the aging time.

With Chianti Superiore there is a lower yield per acre; Chianti Superiore Riserva is aged for at least two years and is stored in the bottle for three months.

CHIANTI COLLI SENESI

This wine has many of the qualities of Chianti Classico but is not as full-bodied and mellow. It can be served with the same dishes as a young Chianti Classico.

CHIANTI CLASSICO

The Chianti Classico area was defined in 1932 as the "most ancient area of origin" whose boundaries were laid down by the Grand Duke Cosimo II in 1716. The label Chianti Classico distinguishes the Chianti made in this historical area from the Chianti produced elsewhere in Tuscany. The wines made here are full-bodied and suited to lengthy aging.

Young Chianti Classico goes well with the traditional local antipasti, and with pollo alla diavola (spicy chicken) and spit-roasted pork.

The Riserva complements red meat dishes such as bistecca alla fiorentina and the strong flavor of mature pecorino cheese.

THE GALLO NERO COMMUNES

The Chianti Classico area stretches between Florence and Siena and comprises the communes of Castellina, Gaiole, Greve, and Radda, and part of Castelnuovo Berardenga, Barberino Val d'Elsa, Poggibonsi, San Casciano, and Tavernelle Val di Pesa. Only 10 percent of this area is earmarked for Chianti Classico DOCG. In 1924, the producers of Chianti Classico founded a consortium and chose as its emblem a black rooster *(gallo nero)*, the historic badge of the Chianti military league. In 1966, Chianti Classico received independent DOCG status.

San Casciano
Val di Pesa

Greve
in Chianti

Tavernelle
Val di Pesa

Barberino
Val d'Elsa

Radda
in Chianti

Poggibonsi

Castellina
in Chianti

Gaiole
in Chianti

Castelnuovo
Berardenga

GALESTRO
This is a fairly recent white wine, born from the marriage of Tuscan vines such as Trebbiano and Malvasia and foreign varieties that may include Chardonnay and Pinot Blanc.

VERNACCIA RISERVA
This wine has to age for at least a year, with four months' storage in the bottle. Some producers age the wine in wood, others do not. This results in a wide variety of different and very interesting styles. It is good served with baked fish and white meats.

VERNACCIA DI SAN GIMIGNANO
One of Tuscany's most famous wines, this white DOCG is produced on the hills of San Gimignano. It has a dry, harmonious flavor which has been greatly enhanced by modern techniques of processing at low temperatures. The young wine is ideal with first courses and shellfish dishes.

Grapes for Vernaccia di San Gimignano wine

CINGHIALE AL VINO BIANCO

2¼ lb (1 kg) leg of wild boar • 1 glass red wine vinegar • 1 glass white wine • 3 cloves garlic • 1 lemon • chilli pepper • extra-virgin olive oil • salt • pepper

Crush one of the garlic cloves and mix it with the vinegar. Season with pepper. Marinate the meat in this mixture overnight. The next day, heat the oven to 325°F (160°C). Dry the meat and sprinkle with the remaining garlic, chopped, and the chilli pepper and salt. Place the meat in an earthenware dish greased with olive oil and baste with the white wine. Cook in the oven until it begins to sizzle, then add the lemon cut in slices. Roast for 3 hours, adding a little more white wine if necessary. Serve the leg cut in slices. Skim the fat off the cooking juices and serve the juices as gravy.

SAN GIMIGNANO ROSATO
This is one of the seven new varieties of DOC San Gimignano, comprising three reds (Riserva and Novello), two rosés (one from Sangiovese alone), and two types of Vin Santo (white and rosé).

Grapes hung to dry for making Vin Santo

VIN SANTO

Vin Santo almost certainly originated in Tuscany and possibly in Chianti, although it is produced in other regions as well – there are about 20 different types. It owes its distinctive flavor to grapes that are hung up or set on racks to dry. Vin Santo is sold either as a dry wine (though it is never perfectly dry) or as a dessert wine, for which demand is falling. It is particularly well suited to the dry confections of the Siena area, such as *biscotti* or *cantuccini (see p34)*.

VIN SANTO
DEL CHIANTI

The Vin Santo of Chianti Classico has earned its own DOC label, and from the 1997 vintage also that of Chianti. However, the leading estates avoid using the DOC appellation and continue to label their products as "Vino da tavola" (table wine).

WINE TYPE	GOOD VINTAGES	GOOD PRODUCERS
Red Wine		
Chianti Classico	98, 97, 95, 93, 90	Fonterutoli di Castellina in Chianti, La Massa di Panzano in Chianti
Super Tuscans *(see p130)*	98, 97, 95 90	Felsina di Castelnuovo Berardenga, S. Giusto & Rentennano di Gaiole in Chianti, Fattoria di Nozzole di Greve in Chianti, Vicchiomaggio di Greve in Chianti
White Wine		
Vernaccia di San Gimignano	99, 97, 95	Montenidoli di San Gimignano, Panizzi di San Gimignano

OTHER WINES WORTH TRYING

Combining the traditional local vines with foreign varieties has produced a profusion of original wines. They include the so-called Super Tuscans *(see p130)*, many of which are very expensive. The DOC **Colli dell'Etruria Centrale** is a range of wines, labeled Bianco, Rosato, Rosso, Novello, Vin Santo. A less successful initiative is the creation of four new-style Tuscan wines identified by the term **Capitolato**: **Muschio** (Chardonnay and Pinot Bianco) and **Selvante** (Sauvignon) for the white wines, **Biturica** (Cabernet and Sangiovese) and **Cardisco** (Sangiovese) for the reds.

Cinta Senese Pork

CINTA SENESE PIGS are a very old local breed with a long history in the area's art as well as its cuisine. They appear in paintings dating back to the 14th century, including Ambrogio Lorenzetti's celebrated fresco of the *Effetti del Buongoverno* (Results of Good Government) in Siena. Cinta Senese pigs have a dark coat with a white belt round their forequarters. They are not, as most people will tell you, a cross between a wild boar and a pig. Some years ago the breed was almost extinct because the pigs can only be reared semiwild in lightly wooded areas; today local breeders are working hard to save the breed. The pigs graze freely on tubers, roots, truffles, and acorns. Although they look leaner than other breeds, they have a thick layer of fat, and their flesh is very firm with a delicate flavor. Inevitably, the quality of the meat, both fresh and cured, combined with the high cost of breeding the pigs, makes Cinta pork products much more expensive than those from other types of pig.

BURISTO DI CINTA

This pork specialty is made from the flesh of the pig's head, including the tongue and some of the skin. The meat is boiled and ground, then spices, pig's blood, and boiled fat are added. The mixture is stuffed into a natural casing made from the pig's small intestine and slowly boiled.

Two Cinta pigs grazing in an oak wood

The hoof of the Cinta hindquarter is black.

CINTA PROSCIUTTO

Prosciutto crudo from Cinta pigs is seasoned with plenty of pepper in the traditional Tuscan way. It is then left to mature for at least 18 months, resulting in a very tasty ham. Unlike other hams, the foot and hoof are always left on this one.

GRIFI

2¼ lb (1 kg) meat from the muzzle of a Cinta pig, cubed • 2 cloves • 1 onion, chopped • 1 clove garlic, chopped • 1 sprig of thyme, chopped • 1 sprig of rosemary, chopped • 2 glasses Chianti • 1 dessertspoon tomato purée • 1 sprig of tarragon, chopped • salt • pepper

Put the meat in a flameproof earthenware casserole, add the cloves, and cover with water. Bring to the boil, then simmer until the water has evaporated. Add the onion, garlic, thyme, and rosemary. Stir in the wine mixed with the tomato purée and season with salt and pepper. Cover and simmer gently, adding a little hot water if it starts to dry out. When the meat is almost tender, add the tarragon and cook for a further 5 minutes.

The hoof of the forequarter is usually a light color.

SPALLA (SHOULDER)
Cured shoulder is drier and saltier than the ham made from a leg of pork and tastes more peppery. It costs much less than *prosciutto crudo*.

ARISTA (CHINE OF PORK)
Salted *arista* has a thick layer of fat, which makes it look almost like pig's cheek.

RIGATINO
This is a very peppery *pancetta* (bacon) used a great deal in Tuscan cooking. It is also excellent in *antipasti* and Tuscan unsalted bread.

SOPPRESSATA DI CINTA
This salami is much the same as ordinary *soppressata* except that the meat used to make it is high-quality Cinta.

CINTA SALAME
Drier and firmer than normal Tuscan *salame*, but seasoned in the same generous way, this type is generally a medium-to-small in size.

Coarsely ground meat is mixed with fat chopped with a knife.

OTHER CINTA PORK PRODUCTS WORTH TRYING
The **fresh meat**, which is sold in the usual pork cuts, can be found only at a few specialized butchers. The tasty meat is very fashionable in Tuscany and much in demand among restaurateurs. Apart from the *salumi* illustrated above, the meat is used to make **capocollo** (dry-cured sausage), **lardo,** and **fresh and cured sausages**.

Sienese Fruit Cakes

Sienese cakes are made with dried and candied fruits – candied pumpkin is especially popular – and sometimes contain nuts. They are bound together with egg whites and sweetened, at least originally, with honey. Nuts and dried figs were once high-energy foods for the poor, and these cakes were nourishing as well as being a good way of using up egg whites when the yolks had been used in other dishes. The cakes have the added advantage of keeping well, so they can be made in advance. Recipes date back to the Middle Ages: *panforte* dates from the 13th century, when it was originally a variant of *pan pepato* (pepper cake), and *dolceforte,* made with spices and honey, was a medieval staple. Arab influences are also evident in some of the spices and other flavorings. These cakes are worth sampling freshly made, if possible: fresh *panforte,* in particular, tastes very different from the commercial product.

The flat cake is dusted with confectioner's sugar, sometimes mixed with a little ground cinnamon.

PANFORTE DI SIENA
This is Siena's most famous cake, made from flour, almonds, egg whites, sugar, and honey. It is flavored with dried and candied fruits – especially pumpkin and citrus fruits – and scented with vanilla, cloves, cinnamon, nutmeg and, occasionally, a little cocoa powder.

PAN PEPATO
This cake is older than *panforte,* and there are many different recipes in existence from various parts of Italy. In the Siena area it is often called *panforte scuro.* It contains larger quantities of cocoa powder and more spices, including pepper, than *panforte.*

CAVALLUCCI
These pale cookies are made with almonds, dried fruit, flour and egg whites, and are sweetened with sugar and honey.

TORTA NATALIZIA RUSTICA

6 eggs, separated • 8 oz (200 g) flour • 1¼ lb (500 g) dried figs, finely chopped • 1¼ lb (500 g) walnuts, crushed • 8 oz (200 g) caster sugar • 4 oz (100 g) lard, melted

Preheat the oven to 325°F (160°C). Whisk the egg whites until stiff. Sift the flour and gradually add to the egg whites. Beat the yolks, sugar, and lard and fold into the whites. Stir in the figs and nuts. Spoon into a greased cake pan and bake the cake for 30 minutes.

CANTUCCI OR TOZZETTI
These crisp cookies are almost identical to the *biscottini* or *cantuccini di Prato (see p34)*, except these cookies sometimes contain aniseed, in which case they are called *anicini*. They are made with flour, eggs, almonds, sugar, and pine nuts. The dough is shaped into a long loaf, baked and cut into slices. The slices are returned to the oven to dry. They are eaten dipped in Vin Santo.

PANE CON I SANTI
This large, shallow loaf is made from sweetened bread dough flavored with raisins, nuts, and pepper.

The cookies are sprinkled with confectioner's sugar.

RICCIARELLI
These cookies are made from a simple almond paste mixed with sugar and egg whites to soften them. They are flavored with vanilla, lemon zest, and honey, then baked on a wafer base made from rice flour.

The dough is cut into lozenge shapes.

SCHIACCIATA CON L'UVA OR CIACCINO CON L'UVA
This sweet *focaccia* covered with raisins probably came originally from Gaiole in Chianti.

OTHER FRUIT CAKES WORTH TRYING
Schiacciata di Pasqua is a raised sweetened loaf flavored with aniseed that is made for Easter. **Torta di Cecco** or **torta al cioccolato** is taller than *pan pepato*, has more candied than dried fruit, and is covered with chocolate icing. A popular recent innovation is **ricciarelli**, covered with chocolate. Also typical of Siena is **torrone** (nougat) in jaw-breaking or softer versions, both covered in chocolate. The **torta natalizia rustica** (rustic Christmas cake) made by peasant families from nuts and dried figs is probably the origin of most modern-day Sienese fruit cakes.

Traditional Produce

IN FLORENCE EVER SINCE the Middle Ages there has been the saying: "You're as rich as if you had a farm in Chianti" because this was the wealthiest area of the countryside around Florence. Here, the old, established families of Florence and Siena still have their farms and estates, together with people from all over the world. In the shops, restaurants, and the *agriturismi* of Chianti you hear dozens of languages spoken, not just because of the visiting tourists but because many foreigners live and work here, most of them from other parts of Europe and the United States. They share a great love of Tuscan history and traditions. And, paradoxically, it is these newcomers, together with some of the younger members of the old families, who struggle to preserve the area's traditional products. As long as farms avoid specializing and continue to produce a wide range of foodstuffs, they will enable small local firms to obtain genuine local produce, from pork and vegetables to cheese, oil, and vinegar.

BLACK CABBAGE
Cavolo nero is the prince of Tuscan vegetables, cultivated throughout Tuscany. With its long, dark, crinkly leaves and delicate, sweetish flavor, it is essential for *ribollita* (vegetable soup) and many of the more celebrated regional soups.

PICI
The typical Sienese pasta is a kind of thick *spaghetti* made of ordinary wheat flour (not the hard durum wheat) and water. The dough is cut into long strips which are then rolled with the flat of the hand to make them thinner and rounded. *Pici* are sold both fresh and dried in the shops.

MARZOLINO
At one time this cheese was made only in the spring from the milk of ewes that had been grazing on the first fresh grass of the year.

This cheese is oval.

PESTO TOSCANO

1¼ lb (500 g) black cabbage
• young extra-virgin olive oil (produced in November and December) • 3 cloves garlic • 2 dessertspoons mature grated pecorino • 1 dessertspoon pine nuts • salt • pepper
Plunge the cabbage into a pan of boiling water and leave until the water boils again. Drain, cool, then process in a blender with the garlic and pine nuts until finely chopped. Stir in the pecorino and add salt and pepper. Stir in enough oil to give a creamy consistency. Spread on bread croutons.

VINEGAR
Many celebrated wine-making estates offer excellent single-grape or Chianti vinegars, often aromatized with herbs.

CHIANTI OLIVE OIL
This comes from the territory south of Florence comprising Greve, Radda, Gaiole, Castellina, Figline, Cavriglia, and San Giovanni. These oils are very fruity with a fresh scent, full-bodied, and astringent. They have medium fluidity, with a slightly bitter and intensely pungent aftertaste, some herbal notes and a faint tinge of sour tomato.

BREAD FROM WOOD-FIRED OVENS
In Chianti you still find Tuscan bread baked the traditional way in wood-fired ovens.

GRAPPA
The skins and seeds of grapes left from making Chianti wine are used to produce very fashionable, modern grappas.

TONNO DEL CHIANTI
Despite its fancy name of "Chianti tuna," this is steam-cooked, brine-cured pork, produced by Cecchini, an unusual butcher's shop in Panzano in Chianti (see p119).

WHAT TO SAMPLE
Though rare, you can still find **pecorino** made the local way from a fresh paste curdled with the flower tufts of the wild artichoke. It is rich in milk fat and usually matured before eating. This area also has the most authentic producers of Tuscan *salumi*: they make excellent traditional **guanciale**, **finocchiona**, **prosciutto crudo**, **salame,** and **sausage**, as well as some innovative variations. The meat is excellent, especially **pork** from **Grigio** pigs, **lamb**, and **Chianina beef** (more likely to be found in shops here than the rest of Tuscany, but nearly all imported from the Arezzo area). San Gimignano has **white truffles**. Val di Pesa has fine fruits, especially **peaches**.

Wild Produce

GRISETTE
(Amanita vaginata)
Grisette *(fungo gentile)* is one of the most common amanita mushrooms found in woods from May to November. The colors vary, but it can be identified by the furrowed edge of the cap and the absence of a ring on the stalk; however, it should always be shown to an expert before eating. It is a very delicate mushroom and is excellent cooked with garlic and parsley.

MAN-ON-HORSEBACK MUSHROOM
(Tricholoma equestre)
Common in mixed pine woods in the fall, this yellow mushroom *(equestre)* adds a delicious flavor to sauces or savory pies and goes well with garlic and parsley. It can also be preserved in oil. There is a poisonous mushroom that looks very similar, so this one must be checked by an expert before it is eaten.

GRAY WAX-CAP MUSHROOM
(Hygrophorus limacinus)
This handsome mushroom *(limaccioso)* has a gray cap with thick, fleshy white gills and a white stalk covered in gray viscous gluten. It is common in pine woods in the fall. The white flesh, with its rich aroma, is excellent in pies and stuffings, or preserved in oil.

DOVE-COLORED TRICHOLOMA
(Tricholoma columbetta)
It takes experience to recognize these fleshy white mushrooms *(columbetta)*, which sometimes have green patches at the foot of the stalk. They are common in chestnut and oak woods in the fall. They are excellent with meat or bottled in oil, and go well with man-on-horseback mushrooms and the related gray tricholoma mushroom *(see opposite)*.

TAGLIATELLE AI FUNGHI

extra-virgin olive oil • a bunch of parsley • 3 cloves garlic • small piece of chilli, chopped • 1¼ lb (600 g) mixed mushrooms, sliced • 4 oz (100 g) fresh sausages, chopped • 18 oz (500 g) tomatoes, peeled • 18 oz (500 g) tagliatelle *• salt*

Heat some oil in a pan and add the mushrooms, parsley, garlic, chilli, and sausage. Season. Cook over a high heat until the mushrooms have shed their water. Lower the heat and cook until the liquid has evaporated. Add the tomatoes and simmer until cooked. Meanwhile, cook the *tagliatelle*. Serve the sauce with the pasta.

MARMELLATA DI ROSA CANINA (ROSE HIP JAM)

• *dog rose hips* • *sugar*

Cut open the hips and remove the seeds and bristles inside. Wash the hips well in running water. Pour enough water into a preserving pan to come 1–2 inches (2.5–5 cm) up the side. Weigh the rose hips and put them in the pan with half their weight in sugar. Cook until all the water has evaporated and the fruit is soft. Sieve the fruit, return it to the pan, and continue cooking until it reaches the desired density. Bottle at once.

DOG ROSE
(Rosa canina)
Dog rose *(rosa di macchia)* hips, picked after the first frosts, are excellent in jams, sweet sauces, fortified wines, and liqueurs. The bristles around the seeds need to be removed before cooking.

BLACKTHORN
(Prunus spinosa)
The blackthorn *(marruche)* is a common tree on the edges of woods and fields. Its very astringent fruit, sloes, can be eaten after the first frosts. They are very good in liqueurs and syrups.

GRAY TRICHOLOMA MUSHROOM
(Tricholoma terreum)
Little gray tricholoma mushrooms *(moretta)* spread through pine woods in their thousands in the fall. The mushroom cap is covered in what looks like mouse fur, and the gills and stalks are a grayish white. Always have them checked by an expert before eating since they are similar to poisonous tricholomas. They are exquisite in sauces, savory pies, and with fish. They can also be preserved in oil.

BUTCHER'S BROOM
(Ruscus aculeatus)
In springtime the young shoots of this attractive bush *(pungitopo)* are delicious, though slightly bitter. They can be preserved in oil, or simmered and served with egg sauces. Here, they are shown growing with the true wild asparagus *(Asparagus acutifolius)* – both are picked and eaten.

Places of Interest

THE RUSTIC ORIGINS of many of the gastronomic suppliers listed here are preserved intact. The farmhouses, for instance, are nearly all historic mansions crammed with colorful works of art. When shopping you can hear a mixture of many languages from all the French, American, German, and Japanese visitors mingling with the local Italian population. Despite the high numbers of tourists, the quality of the regional food produce has hardly suffered at all – unlike the situation in some of the big cities. Often, in fact, the foreigners shopping in Chianti are even more discerning than the local customers.

BARBERINO DI VAL D'ELSA (FI)

Casa Emma

località Cortine
055 8072859

The Merlot Soloìo produced on this estate is very fine, with unusual body and bouquet. There is also a mellow Chianti Classico Riserva, which is very good.

Fattoria Isole & Olena

località Isole, 1
055 8072763

From a truly skilled professional comes a series of wines of the greatest interest: Chianti Classico, Cepparello (based on Sangiovese), Eremo (on Syrah), and Cabernet Sauvignon Collezione De Marchi. The extra-virgin olive oil is very fine.

Castello di Monsanto

via Monsanto, 8
055 8059000

This estate can justly claim to have played an important role in the region's wine-making revival by its foresight and enterprise. Its wines are excellent: the Chianti Classico, elegant and full-bodied, plus the reds Fabrizio Bianchi (Sangiovese) and Nemo, based on Cabernet.

Fattoria Pasolini Dall'Onda

piazza Martini, 10
055 8075019

Extra-virgin olive oil with an intense fruity flavor is produced from olives grown and pressed on the estate. Olive oil production goes back a long way here – it has been made on the estate since 1573.

Wine aging in barrels at the Cecchi winery at Castellina in Chianti

PAPPA COL POMODORO

⅔ lb (300 g) stale bread
• *4 cloves garlic, chopped*
• *2 lb (900 g) small ripe tomatoes, peeled*
• *a few basil leaves, torn*
• *extra-virgin olive oil*
• *vegetable stock* • *salt*
• *pepper*

Soak the bread in cold water for a few hours, then lightly squeeze out the water with your hands. Put the bread in a pan with the garlic, tomatoes, basil, and plenty of olive oil. Bring up to simmering point, then simmer gently for at least 30 minutes until the bread is well mixed with the other ingredients. Remove from the heat and season to taste with salt and pepper. Serve with extra-virgin olive oil to drizzle over the top.

CASTELLINA IN CHIANTI (SI)

Casa Vinicola Cecchi

località Casina dei Ponti
0577 743024

Wines made from a range of grapes are offered here. Of particular interest is the Chianti Classico Messer Pietro di Teuzzo and Spargolo made from Sangiovese grapes. A recent addition is Arcano made from organic Sangiovese grapes. The group has other estates, including Castello di Montauto which makes a good Vernaccia di San Gimignano.

Castello di Fonterutoli

località Fonterutoli
0577 73571

This is an old-established wine estate with a great

tradition behind its Chianti Classico: it retains all its vigor in the regular version and in the Riserva Castello di Fonterutoli, and the Riserva Ser Lapo. Note the two other excellent wines in Concerto (Sangiovese and Cabernet Sauvignon) and Siepi (Sangiovese and Merlot).

Azienda Agricola Villa Cerna at Castellina in Chianti

🍇 Gagliole

località Gagliole, 42
☎ 0577 740369

The favorable position of these vineyards and their organic cultivation have produced excellent results in both the Gagliole Rosso (Sangiovese with Cabernet Sauvignon) and Gagliole Bianco (Trebbiano with a little Chardonnay).

🐝 Apicoltura Lecchini

località La Piazza
☎ 0577 733560

Local honey, especially from chestnut, acacia, and wild flowers, as well as honey-based energy-boosters and beauty products are sold here.

🍇 Castello di Lilliano

località Lilliano
☎ 0577 743070

The Chianti Classico and Riserva, both wines of distinctive, forceful character, are backed up by Anagallis, a red wine from Sangiovese and Colorino grapes matured in oak barriques.

🍇 Rocca delle Macìe

località Le Macìe
☎ 0577 7321

An attractive, dynamic estate with a carefully gauged production centered on the red wines of the region. The Chianti Classico is vinified from various crus, including La Tenuta Sant'Alfonso. The Fizzano Riserva is notable. Also interesting is

the Roccato (Sangiovese and Cabernet) and Ser Gioveto (Sangiovese). It also has a mellow grappa and extra-virgin olive oil.

🐂 Macelleria Stiaccini

via Ferruccio, 33
☎ 0577 740558
⬤ Wed pm.

This butcher's shop sells its own fresh sausages, as well as a good selection of Tuscan salumi with some Sienese specialities as well. It has Chianina beef plus various other cuts of meat, all from animals which have been carefully selected by the owners from herds in the province. It also offers ready-to-eat spiedini (kebabs), fegatelli, and other seasoned meats.

🍇 Azienda Agricola Villa Cerna

località Villa Cerna
☎ 0577 743024

This estate is owned by the Cecchi family. It offers a Chianti Classico with a good structure and a Riserva matured in wood, both in large barrels and oak barriques. The estate also makes a Vin Santo which is allowed to ferment in casks.

PANFORTE

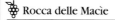

6 oz (150 g) caster sugar • 6 oz (150 g) honey • 1 dessertspoon cocoa powder • 6 oz (150 g) each of peeled almonds and hazelnuts, roasted and halved • 2 oz(50 g) chopped nuts • pinch each of ground cinnamon, cloves, and nutmeg • vanilla essence • 3 oz (70 g) flour • ½ lb (250 g) diced candied fruit • confectioner's sugar • rice flour wafer or rice paper

Preheat the oven to 325°F (160°C). In a pan (preferably copper), heat the sugar and honey over a gentle heat until a drop of the mixture forms a soft ball when dropped into cold water. Remove from the heat and add the cocoa, nuts, fruit, spices, few drops of essence and 2 oz (60 g) of the flour; stir carefully. Pour into a shallow cake pan lined with the wafer or rice paper. Mix the remaining flour with 2 dessertspoons confectioner's sugar and a little cinnamon. Sprinkle it over the mixture, then bake in the oven for 30 minutes. Cool, turn out, and sprinkle with confectioner's sugar mixed with cinnamon.

CASTELNUOVO BERARDENGA (SI)

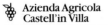

Azienda Agricola Castell'in Villa

località Castell'in Villa
0577 359074

The wine here is of a consistently high quality, thanks to the skilled hand of a wine-maker on this estate who excels at the production of Chianti Classico as a young wine and a Riserva. Also worth noting are the Poggio delle Rose, made from Sangiovese alone, and the Vin Santo.

Fattoria di Felsina

strada Chiantigiana, 484
0577 355117

This is one of the most interesting cellars in Tuscany, containing a wide range of fine wines, from Chianti Classico to the Berardenga and Rancia selections (at their best in the Riserva version). The Fontalloro (from pure Sangiovese) and Maestro Raro (Cabernet) are equally excellent. The estate also produces a very good Vin Santo and two whites: I Sistri (Chardonnay) and Pepestrino (made from Trebbiano, Sauvignon, and Chardonnay grapes).

FAGIOLI ALL'UCCELLETTO

2 cloves garlic, chopped • sprigs of sage, chopped • extra-virgin olive oil • 3¼ lb (1.5 kg) fresh beans or 1 lb (450 g) dried beans, soaked overnight • 1¼ lb (600 g) tomatoes, sliced • salt • pepper

Lightly fry the garlic and sage in the oil. Add the beans, tomatoes, and about 14 fl oz (400 ml) water. Season to taste with salt and pepper and simmer for about 30 minutes.

Pasticceria Lodi Pasini

via Fiorita, 6
0577 355638
Mon
Sun am

Traditional Sienese cakes and fresh stuffed pasta are the two specialities here – try their lemon-scented ravioli filled with a mixture of ricotta and other cheeses.

Fattoria di Petroio

località Querciagrossa
0577 328045

The two classic wines of this part of Tuscany are produced on the richly endowed land of this small estate – Chianti Classico and Chianti Classico Riserva.

Agricola San Felice

località San Felice
0577 359087

This estate has produced good results with some of its wines, such as the Riserve di Chianti Classico Poggio Rosso, Il Grigio, and the Vigorello red, which is made from Sangiovese plus small amounts of Cabernet Sauvignon grapes. The olive oil is very good.

COLLE VAL D'ELSA (SI)

Frantoio Roncucci

località Mensanello
0577 971080

The oil comes exclusively from the estate's own groves (70 percent Correggiolo olives) and is sold by measure straight from the press while it is operating. As the oil is not

The Castello di Brolio of the Tenuta Ricasoli

bottled, you need to take a suitable container with you to carry your oil home.

GAIOLE IN CHIANTI (SI)

Agricoltori del Chianti Geografico

via Mulinaccio, 10
0577 749489

This cooperative winery, run by a great wine-maker, is based on two estates. The Gaiole estate produces the red wines, especially Chianti Classico with the Contessa di Radda selection, the Riserva Montegiachi, and the Capitolare di Biturica (based on Cabernet Sauvignon and Sangiovese). The San Gimignano estate principally produces whites, including Vernaccia.

Apiari Floridea

località Badia a Coltibuono
L'Osteria, 27
0577 746110

This apiarist is rigorous about the production of honey by natural methods. Honeys include ones made from pollen from chestnut trees, woodland flowers, broad-leaved trees, acacia, and heather.

Badia a Coltibuono

località Badia a Coltibuono
0577 749498

This estate, with its old monastery buildings dating from the 11th century, favors a traditional approach to production with particular emphasis on Sangiovese vines. Its star product is Sangioveto, made from Sangiovese alone. Another noteworthy wine is the Chianti Classico Riserva.

Badia a Coltibuono

Barone Ricasoli – Castello di Brolio

località Brolio
0577 7301

This is one of the oldest and most renowned of the Chianti Classico wineries. Much of the production is Chianti Classico Brolio, which also comes in a Riserva version. This is followed in volume by Casalferro, a Sangiovese from a particular clone with the Merlot grape. In recent years the Sangiovese vine used for producing the Casalferro has been used to make Formulae, a young wine that offers very good value for money.

Castello di Ama

località Ama
0577 746031

Only a small number of vines are grown on this particular estate, but all of them are of the highest quality, from Chianti Classico onward. In the best years, the estate also produces Vigneto La Casuccia and Bellavista selections. The most applauded wine is Vigna l'Apparita, based on Merlot grapes. The extra-virgin olive oil is also excellent. For purchases, apply to the Enoteca Rinaldi, Lecchi in Chianti (0577 746021).

Castello di Cacchiano

località Cacchiano, frazione Monti in Chianti
0577 747018

The Ricasoli Firidolfi family has drawn on expert help to enhance the Sangiovese grapes in the Chianti Classico, the Riserva, and the Rosso R.F. from Merlot, Sangiovese, and Canaiolo, matured in small casks. The Vin Santo is very good.

Macelleria Chini

via Roma, 3
0577 749457
Mon and Wed pm

The Chini family has worked in the meat trade since the 17th century. Their products are of the highest quality – there is salumi made from pure-bred Cinta Senese pigs, plus meat from other local animals.

POLLO ALLA DIAVOLA

1 free-range chicken
• *marinade of sliced garlic, rosemary leaves, and extra-virgin olive oil*

Cut the chicken down the backbone, open it out, and flatten with a meat mallet. Pour over the marinade and leave for 1 hour. Grill over hot embers, turning it every 6–7 minutes until tender.

Fattoria Pile e Lamole and Fattoria di Vistarenni

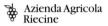

località Vistarenni
📞 0577 738186

These two estates produce a Chianti Classico Lamole di Lamole and Villa Vistarenni, both very good value for money, and an interesting Lamole di Lamole selection, again Chianti Classico. Other notable products are an excellent extra-virgin olive oil; Lamole di Lamole, an aqua-vitae, and Codirosso, from Sangiovese and Cabernet Sauvignon matured for six months in barriques.

Azienda Agricola Riecine

località Riecine
📞 0577 749098

This property has changed hands and at present it seems that the previous style is continuing with just a few excellent wines: Chianti Classico, Chianti

POLLO CON LE OLIVE

3 spring chickens, each cut into 8 pieces • 10 oz (300 g) pitted green olives • 3 bay leaves • flour • 3 cloves garlic • extra-virgin olive oil • about 14 fl oz (400 ml) dry white wine • chicken stock • salt • pepper

Coat the chicken pieces in flour. Heat some oil in a frying pan, add the chicken and fry over a brisk heat to seal on all sides. Add the bay leaves, garlic, and wine and cook until the wine has evaporated. Add the olives and a little stock. Cover and continue cooking until the chicken is tender, adding more stock if required. Adjust the seasoning and serve.

Vineyards of the Fattoria Pile e Lamole at Vistarenni

Classico Riserva, and La Gioia di Riecine, from Sangiovese alone.

Rocca di Castagnoli

località Castagnoli
📞 0577 731004

Two vineyards belong to this estate, one at Gaiole and the other at Castellina. The wine most representative of the "Super Tuscan" style is Stielle, made from Sangiovese and Cabernet grapes, followed by Buriano, made from Cabernet Sauvignon alone. Chianti Classico Riserva, Poggio a' Frati, and Capraia are all produced in the traditional style.

Fattoria di San Giusto a Rentennano

località Monti in Chianti
📞 0577 747121

This estate limits its wines to three different types, all of them of very high quality. The Chianti Classico is a powerful wine with complex perfumes, especially the Riserva. Percarlo, from Sangiovese alone, has good character, and the estate's Vin Santo is held to be one of the best in the whole of Tuscany.

Le Antiche Delizie del Bianchi

via Ricasoli, 72
📞 0577 749501
🕐 Tues pm

This bakery offers a very varied line of specialties which reflect its basic principle: to keep a close rapport with the surrounding district and use natural ingredients. It has bread made with fresh yeast and kneaded by hand, especially the classic Tuscan loaf and what is called "Etruscan bread," made with spelt and a mixture of flours. It also sells traditional cakes and some of the firm's own creations, like the Torta Chiantigiana, made with extra-virgin olive oil. Their ice cream is made with good quality natural ingredients. The delicatessen has a select range of local specialties, and the small restaurant, Lo Sfizio del Bianchi, offers real local cuisine.

GREVE IN CHIANTI (FI)

Gelateria Cabana

località Strada in Chianti
via Mazzini, 32
📞 055 8588659
🕐 Wed pm.

Very fine cream and fruit ice creams in a variety of

flavors, all from natural ingredients, are sold in this ice-cream parlor. It also has ice-cream cakes and pastries – the zuccotto and the millefoglie both merit a special mention.

🍇 Casa Vinicola Carpineto

località Dudda
☎ 055 8549062

A good Chianti Classico, also in a Riserva version, is produced here as well as Cabernet Sauvignon Farnito.

🐂 Antica Macelleria Falorni

piazza Matteotti, 69
☎ 055 853029
🔓 daily, including Sun

This large store has a wine cellar and wine-tasting shop. It sells a wide range of salumi which can be sampled with the wine. The family firm has long been closely associated with traditional Tuscan products, including Chianina beef, Cinta pork, wild boar, and local salumi. It also has a modern outlook, producing best-selling items like zampone (stuffed pig's feet) and packaging its own sliced hams and other meats in sealed containers. However, the traditional spirit and methods remain, evident in the excellent fresh meat and local game, and salumi from both Cinta and ordinary pigs and wild boar.

🍇 Tenuta di Nozzole

località Passo dei Pecorai
☎ 055 2385901

The Folinari family owns this splendid villa and the vineyards, which produce great wines. Especially try the Chianti Classico Nozzole and the Riserva La Forra. The estate also makes a Cabernet Sauvignon, Il Pareto, and Chardonnay, Le Bruniche. The Fattoria di Nozzole is the sales point for all the Folonari estate's various products.

🍇 Castello di Querceto

località Dudda
☎ 055 85921

This family firm produces Chianti – the younger version and the Riserva il Picchio are noteworthy – and draws on Sangiovese vines for its La Corte red.

🍇 Azienda Agricola Querciabella

località Ruffoli
via S. Lucia a Barbiano, 17
☎ 055 853834

A professional and far-sighted approach to the estate's objectives is the key to the success of its outstanding wines. The Chianti Classico produced here is one of the finest in the area and also comes in a Riserva version. Equally fine are the Camartina, made from Sangiovese and Cabernet Sauvignon grapes, and the Batàr, produced from equal parts of Pinot Bianco and Chardonnay grapes.

🍇 Azienda Agricola Poggio Scalette

località Ruffoli
via Barbiano, 7
☎ 055 8546108

Vittorio Fiore, one of Tuscany's best-known wine-makers, owns this small estate. It has old vines, and its production is select and of the very highest level. At present it offers only one wine, Carbonaione, produced from Sangiovese grapes alone, and a fine extra-virgin olive oil.

RIBOLLITA (VEGETABLE SOUP)

10 oz (300 g) dried cannellini beans • 3 zucchini • 3 carrots • 1 stalk celery • 10 oz (300 g) potatoes • 3 tomatoes • 12 oz (350 g) onions • 4 oz (100 g) guanciale (pig's cheek) • extra-virgin olive oil • 8 oz (200 g) peas • ½ black cabbage, cut into strips • a few sprigs of parsley • meat stock • stale Tuscan bread, sliced • salt • pepper

Rinse the beans, soak overnight, and then cook them in the same water over a very low heat. Meanwhile, chop the zucchini, carrots, celery, potatoes, tomatoes, half the onions, and the *guanciale* and fry them in oil in a large pan until softened. Add the peas, cabbage, and parsley, moisten with the bean cooking water and some stock. Add salt and pepper. Simmer for 1 hour. Purée some of the beans in a vegetable mill and add to the soup with the whole beans. Arrange the bread slices in an ovenproof dish. Pour the soup over the bread and leave to cool. Preheat the oven to 350°F (180°C). Finely slice the remaining onions and add them to the soup with more oil. Bake in the oven until the oil simmers and the onion forms a golden crust.

Azienda Agricola Vecchie Terre di Montefili

via San Cresci, 47
055 853739

Refined Chianti Classico matched by the Sangiovese Colli della Toscana Centrale Anfiteatro is produced by this estate. Also of great interest is the Colli della Toscana Centrale Bruno di Rocca, from Cabernet Sauvignon and Sangiovese, and Vigna Regis, a white wine from Chardonnay, Sauvignon, and Traminer.

Tenuta Vicchiomaggio

via Vicchiomaggio, 4
055 854079

A splendid, intensely fruity extra-virgin olive oil, one of the best in the whole region, is produced by this estate. It also makes Chianti Classico and grappa.

Fattoria Viticcio

via San Cresci, 12/A
055 854210

This small estate in Chianti is interesting because it adds Nebbiolo grapes to the Cabernet Sauvignon and

Sangiovese in its Monile red. Its other very good reds are Prunato from Sangiovese grapes and Chiantis.

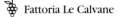
MERCATALE VALDARNO (AR)

Fattoria Petrolo

località Galatrona
055 9911322

The line of extra-virgin olive oil is excellent and can be purchased directly at the estate together with its Vin Santo. The wines (Torrione from Sangiovese alone, Galatrona from Merlot alone, Terre di Galatrona from Sangiovese with a little Merlot) are found only in wine shops, and they are expensive.

MERCATALE VAL DI PESA (FI)

Castelli del Grevepesa

località Ponte di Gabbiano
via Grevigiana, 34
055 821101

This large cooperative winery has a wide variety of good wines. Notable among them is the Chianti Classico Clemente VII

because of its very reasonable price for the quality of the wine. There are numerous estate wines: among the line of Chianti Classici, the Vigna Elisa and Sant'Angiolo Vico l'Abate are noteworthy.

MONTESPERTOLI (FI)

Fattoria Le Calvane

via Castiglioni, 1/5
0571 671073

A Chianti Colli Fiorentini Il Quercione, a Riserva Il Trecione, and Vin Santo Zipolo d'Oro are all offered here. There are also wines made from vines not traditional to the area, including Borro del Boscone, from Cabernet Sauvignon matured in new oak barriques, Sorbino from Chardonnay grapes, and Colle Cimoli made from Chardonnay, Sauvignon Blanc, and Traminer.

Azienda Agricola Poggio Tizzaoli

via Barrucciano, 1/2
0571 671379

A good extra-virgin olive oil, very typical of the area, is produced at this estate.

The splendid hill panorama of Montespertoli

PANZANO IN CHIANTI (FI)

🍇 Enoteca Baldi

piazza Bucciarelli, 25
☎ 055 852843
◷ daily, including Sun

This is a first-rate wine bar, offering an excellent selection of Italian and international wines and, above all, a wide range of the delicacies of central Tuscany. There are good gourmet savories to sample with the wines.

🐂 Antica Macelleria Cecchini

via XX Luglio, 11
☎ 055 852020
● Wed
◷ Sun am

At first glance you seem to have entered an ordinary butcher's shop when you go in. Then you notice the classical music playing softly in the background,

The Antica Macelleria Cecchini

CARNE IN GALERA

2¾ lb (1.2 kg) sirloin or fillet of beef • **1 sprig of sage, finely chopped** • **2 or 3 sprigs of rosemary, finely chopped** • **1 clove garlic** • **4 fl oz (100 ml) white wine vinegar** • **8 fl oz (200 ml) hot beef stock, plus extra, if necessary** • **extra-virgin olive oil** • **salt**

Heat some oil in a pan, add the beef, and fry until well browned and sealed on both sides. Add the garlic and herbs and fry for 1–2 minutes. Lower the heat, add the vinegar and stock. Cover and cook over a low heat until the liquid has evaporated. Add salt when the meat is half cooked. Add more stock if it evaporates before the meat is tender.

---

and behind the counter a second room opens out with a fine table for sampling wine and hams, with other local and traditional specialties hanging from the ceiling. Then you start to browse through the large, elegant 16-page menu (at present reduced for renovation), which looks more like a restaurant menu than a butcher's price list. It offers 22 cuts of Tuscan lamb ready to cook (seasoned, dressed, and packaged); nine types of meat for roasting (from Chianina beef to pigeons); 12 stuffed-meat dishes; 13 different meats for grilling; 12 kinds of sausage, 12 meat preparations for cooking in a saucepan; 10 for cooking in a frying pan; 18 unusual sauces and delicacies, all of them made by the firm; nine pork products; 12 terrines and pâtés; and eight different cuts of cold meats (tongue, boned calf's head, galantines). In addition, there are chestnuts, traditional pulses, extra-virgin olive oil, Vin Santo, herbs, and fresh produce from the firm's farm. These quality products are presented with an almost maniacal devotion to tradition, a careful search for the oldest recipes (some are reprinted on the menu), and a careful choice of authentic ingredients. All these factors add a cultural dimension to the gourmet extravaganza, making it an unmissable experience for meat lovers.

🍇 Azienda Agricola Cennatoio

via San Leolino, 35
☎ 055 852134

The star product from this estate is its Vino Etrusco from Sangiovese grapes. The Chianti Classico Riserva and the Rosso Fiorentino, made from Cabernet Sauvignon, are also good.

🍇 Tenuta Fontodi

via San Leolino, 89
☎ 055 852005

This carefully managed estate produces high quality wines, starting with its Chianti Classico Riserva Vigna del Sorbo, which is among the finest in its class. Outstanding among the varietals are the Colli della Toscana Centrale Flaccianello della Pieve, from Sangiovese, and a great Colli della Toscana Centrale Pinot Nero Case Vie. It also makes a good extra-virgin olive oil.

🍇 La Massa

via Case Sparse, 9
☎ 055 852701

This estate has focused on only two wines, with the goal of giving Chianti the same dignity as the great international wines, and it has succeeded with its Chianti Classico and the Giorgio Primo selection.

RICCIARELLI (ALMOND COOKIES)

**9 oz (250 g) peeled almonds • 10 oz (300 g) caster sugar
• 1 egg white • 1 dessertspoon honey • pinch
of ground cinnamon • grated zest of
1 lemon • confectioner's sugar
• 1 rice flour wafer or rice paper**

Preheat the oven to 275°F (140°C). Crush the almonds in a blender and mix them with the sugar. Beat the egg white and mix it into the almonds with the honey, cinnamon, and lemon zest. Mix well. Roll out the dough on a work surface sprinkled with confectioner's sugar until it is ¾ inch (2 cm) thick. Cut out lozenge shapes 3 inches (7.5 cm) in length. Place each on a slightly larger piece of wafer or on rice paper. Bake in the oven for about 15 minutes, taking care not to let the cookies brown.

Fattoria Villa Cafaggio

via San Martino in Cecione, 5
055 8549094

Besides an interesting Chianti Classico, this estate makes two wines of unique character from the area's most important red grapes, blended in different proportions: Sangiovese dominates in the San Martino and Cabernet Sauvignon in the Cortaccio.

POGGIBONSI (SI)

Melini

località Gaggiano
0577 989001

On one of the largest Chianti Classico estates, half the estate provides the grapes for its Chianti Classico La Selvanella Riserva, possibly its most renowned product. There is also a good white wine, Vernaccia di San Gimignano Le Grillaie. The estate also produces an interesting olive oil.

RADDA IN CHIANTI (SI)

Castello d'Albola

via Pian d'Albola, 31
0577 738019

Belonging to the Zonin family, this estate is known for two innovative classics – the Acciaiolo from Sangiovese and Cabernet Sauvignon grapes, and Le Fagge from Chardonnay. The Chianti Classico Riserva and the Novello Sant'Ilario are both very good.

Enoteca Arte Vino

viale XI Febbraio, 21
0577 738605
Tues ☐ Sun

This wine bar specializes in local wines and serves hot and cold dishes with them, including crostini, local salumi, and pecorino.

Azienda Agricola Il Poggerino

via Poggerino, 6
0577 738232

The professional skill and passion with which this

fairly small vineyard is managed have produced interesting results in the Chianti Classico and the Riserva Bugialla.

Casa Porciatti

via IV Novembre, 1
0577 738055
Wed pm
Sun am May to October

All kinds of good things can be found in this food store-cum-butcher's-cum wine shop. Apart from the fine wares on display, the staff will procure all kinds of specialties on request. It has real Chianina beef, Sienese cakes bearing the shop's own hallmark, local marzolino cheese matured in the store's cellars, and its own salumi, including its own creation "tonno di Radda" (dried lean pork) and sausage flavored with black truffles (not the synthetic aroma). It also has a rich selection of the region's olive oils, wines, and local honey.

Azienda Agricola Terrabianca

località San Fedele a Paterno
0577 738544

The star wine here is definitely Campaccio, which also comes in a Riserva version, from Sangiovese and Cabernet Sauvignon. It is backed up by one of the finest Tuscan whites, Piano della Cappella. Try the Chianti Classico Vigna della Croce and the estate's other white, Fior di Fino, from Malvasia and Trebbiano.

Castello di Volpaia

località Volpaia
0577 738066

The village of Castello di Volpaia

One of the finest estates in Tuscany, this has excellent agriturismo (farm vacation) facilities and quality products. The Chianti Classico Riserva, the Coltassala from Sangiovese grapes, and the Balifico from Sangiovese and Cabernet are all noteworthy. The estate has excellent extra-virgin olive oil and a whole line of vinegars.

SAN CASCIANO IN VAL DI PESA (FI)

 **Tenuta Castello il Corno**

via Malafrasca, 64
📞 055 8248009

This is an ancient farm, producing wines and, above all, an excellent extra-virgin olive oil.

Fattoria Corzano e Paterno

località San Vito
📞 055 8249114

Located close to the boundary of the Chianti Classico area, this firm produces a fine Terre di Corzano Chianti and a very good Vin Santo, one of the best in the region.

 Oleificio Giachi

località Mercatale in Val di Pesa via Campoli, 31
📞 055 821082

This firm bottles excellent extra-virgin olive oil, mostly from local olive presses, including its own blend, Colle dei Giachi.

Azienda Agricola Massanera

via di Faltignano, 76
📞 055 8242360

Free-range Cinta Senese pigs are raised here and turned into fine salumi, but prices are high. The estate also makes very good, but expensive, oil and wine.

 **Antica Fattoria Niccolò Machiavelli**

località San Andrea in Percussina
📞 0577 989001

This estate is owned by the Gruppo Italiano Vini (group of wineries in key regions), which has recently attracted praise for its wine. One example is the Chianti Classico Riserva Vigna di Fontalle, but the best known is Ser Niccolò, from Cabernet Sauvignon grapes.

SAN GIMIGNANO (SI)

Azienda Agricola Il Casale-Falchini

via di Casale, 40
📞 0577 941305

This estate was one of the first to revive production of Vernaccia, a policy that has produced the excellent wines Vigna al Solatio, enriched with a little Chardonnay, and Vinea Doni. Among its other wines, Càmpora, a red from pure Cabernet Sauvignon, is very good.

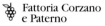 **Fattoria di Cusona**

località Cusona, 5
📞 0577 950028

The Guicciardini Strozzi firm owns this centuries-old property. It makes a good Vernaccia, which also comes in a Riserva version, made from grapes gathered late in the harvest and then fermented in barriques. There is also a spumante version. Among the red wines is Sodole, which is produced from Sangiovese grapes.

The towers of San Gimignano

PAPPARDELLE SULLA LEPRE (PASTA WITH HARE)

4 dessertspoons olive oil • 1 onion, chopped • 1 carrot, chopped • 1 stalk celery, chopped • a few sage leaves • a handful of parsley, chopped • 6 oz (150 g) guanciale (pig's cheek), chopped • shoulder, neck, and breast of a hare, cut into pieces • hare giblets (lights, heart, liver) and blood • 2 glasses Chianti • vinegar • beef stock • 4 fl oz (100 ml) milk • 1¼ lb (600 g) fresh pappardelle • grated Parmesan cheese • salt • pepper

Heat the oil in a pan (preferably earthenware) and fry the onion, carrot, celery, sage, parsley, and *guanciale* lightly. Gradually add pieces of hare and the lights and stir-fry until browned. Add the red wine and allow it to evaporate. Moisten with the blood and a little vinegar. Simmer gently for 10 minutes. Add salt and pepper. Warm the milk and add to the pan, cover and simmer for 1 hour, adding a little stock if it starts to dry out. Bone the pieces of hare and return them to the pan with the chopped heart and liver. Simmer for another 5 minutes. Meanwhile, cook the *pappardelle*. Drain the pasta and serve it with the sauce and Parmesan cheese.

Azienda Agricola Fontaleoni

località Santa Maria, 39
0577 950193

With its 37 acres (15 hectares) of vines and 7 acres (3 hectares) of olives, this estate focuses on the area's classic wines. There are two styles of Vernaccia, the normal and the Vigna Casanuova.

Montenidoli

località Montenidoli
0577 941565

A small estate with a very good Vernaccia. The traditional version is good value for money, and there are two choices, Carato and Fiore.

Fattoria di Pietrafitta

località Cortennano
0577 943200

Four kinds of Vernaccia: normal, Riserva, and two selections are produced

here. The firm has 988 acres (400 hectares) of vines and produces Chianti Colli Senesi and has recently begun making DOC San Gimignano wines, with an interesting Rosato. Its 54 acres (22 hectares) of olives yield excellent, fruity extra-virgin olive oil.

Azienda Agricola Panizzi

località Santa Margherita, 34
0577 941576

The estate's care for its vines and the quality of its wines is apparent in the Vernaccia with a Riserva version partly fined in

barriques. The Chianti Colli Senesi is more full-bodied and structured than the others.

Teruzzi & Puthod – Ponte a Rondolino

località Casale, 19
0577 940143

This is the domain of Enrico Teruzzi, who reinvented Vernaccia di San Gimignano. The estate is a leading producer of the very finest Vernaccia, in a normal version and in the Terre dei Tufi selection matured in barriques. The table wines include an excellent Carmen, a Sangiovese vinified as a white wine.

Fattoria San Quirico

località Panicole, 39
0577 955007

From an area ideally sited for vineyards comes a pure Vernaccia and the Riserva I Campi Santi, a notable wine not aged in wood. The Chianti Colli Senesi is also very good.

SIENA

Pasticceria Buti

via Vittorio Emanuele II, 53
0577 40464
● Mon ◐ Sun

Sienese cakes, including an authentic spicy pan pepato, *are sold here.*

The Teruzzi & Puthod estate at Ponte a Rondolino

Enoteca Italiana

Fortezza Medicea, 1
📞 0577 288497
⬤ Sun
🕐 12noon–10pm

This interesting wine shop has an enormous range of Italian wines – there are over 900 names from all regions plus 400 Tuscans, chosen by an expert committee. A dozen wines are opened in turn daily for tasting with assorted snacks.

 Forno dei Galli

via dei Termini, 45
📞 0577 289073

Bread, fresh pasta, and traditional Sienese cakes are sold here.

❊ **Bar Impero**

via Vittorio Emanuele, 10/12
📞 0577 47424
⬤ Mon
🕐 Sun

Excellent ice cream is made and sold here all year round.

🍶 **Drogheria Manganelli**

via di Città, 71/73
📞 0577 280002
⬤ Wed pm

The original furnishings date back 120 years in this real old-fashioned grocer's shop. It makes its own traditional Sienese cakes and has a choice selection of products from all over Italy, as well as some imported delicacies, all from high quality producers. There is a good range of wines.

 Gastronomia Morbidi

via Banchi di Sopra, 75
📞 0577 280268
⬤ Wed pm

This is a delicatessen for gourmets, selling a small, select range of wines with choice grappas, plus the firm's own traditional salumi *and an array of hams and sausages from other regions. It also has an assortment of cheeses from its own dairy and other parts of Italy, and a range of international dishes, both fresh and ready-cooked.*

😊 **Bar Nannini**

Banchi di Sopra, 97
📞 0577 247013
🕐 daily, including Sun

At this long-established café, it is possible to sample nearly all the traditional Sienese cakes.

😊 **La Nuova Pasticceria di Iasevoli**

via Dupré, 37
📞 0577 41319
⬤ Mon
🕐 Sun am

Fine traditional Sienese confections, including cantucci *(cookies) and* pane con i santi *(sweet bread containing fruit), can be found here.*

😊 **Pasticceria Pierini**

via Mencatelli, 2
📞 0577 283159
⬤ Mon
🕐 Sun am

This confectionery shop makes excellent Sienese cakes to sell.

 Enoteca San Domenico

via del Paradiso, 56
📞 0577 271181
🕐 daily, including Sunday

A selection of Italian wines is sold here – not just the big names but also fine wine from smaller producers – plus a choice of liquors, champagne, Tuscan olive oil, and the firm's own traditional cakes.

TAVARNELLE VAL DI PESA (SI)

 **Azienda Agricola Poggio al Sole**

località Badia
a Passignano
📞 055 8071504

The area's classic red grapes can be found in the juicy Seraselva, *produced from Merlot and Cabernet, and the full-bodied Chianti Classico Casasilia, which is from Sangiovese.*

AGNELLO IN FRICASSEA (LAMB FRICASSÉE)

1 leg and 1 shoulder of lamb • 2 onions • 1 carrot, chopped • 1 stalk celery, sliced • 2 dessertspoons flour • 4 egg yolks • juice of 1 lemon • a few calamint (or mint) leaves • extra-virgin olive oil • salt • pepper

Bone the lamb. Slice 1 onion. Put the bones, sliced onion, carrot, and celery in a pan of water and cook for 2 hours to make stock. Cut the meat into pieces 2–2½ inches (5–6 cm) long. Finely chop the remaining onion. Flour the pieces of meat and brown them in the oil with the onion. Add salt and pepper and moisten with the stock. Cover and simmer until the meat is cooked. Add enough stock to make a sauce. Beat the egg with the lemon juice, pepper, and calamint. Remove the pan from the heat, add the egg and stir briskly. The sauce should have the consistency of mayonnaise. Serve hot or cold, but do not reheat.

MONTALCINO
AND THE
SIENESE CRETE

Montalcino and the Sienese Crete

IN THIS GOURMET GUIDE, the southern part of the province of Siena has been separated from the north because the zone of Chianti Classico wine and the zone of Brunello and Vino Nobile deserve separate treatment. A corner of the province of Arezzo has been added to this section because Lucignano and Monte San Savino are influenced more by Sienese gastronomic habits than by their own.

The clay hills known as the Crete have fine truffles, rounded and regular, without knobby bits or cracks, especially San Giovanni d'Asso, Trequanda, Buonconvento, and Asciano. In fact, the commune of San Giovanni d'Asso has the highest production of truffles in Italy. There is nothing smooth and regular about the eroded hillocks that give the Crete its name. The sunny rolling hills have tremendous, jagged gashes in them, spectacular gulleys denuded of topsoil by heavy rain so they are bare of vegetation. Great slashes suddenly open in wheat fields, vineyards, olive groves, and young oak scrub. The Crete, like the wooded areas of Montalcino, the valley of the Merse and the Val d'Orcia, is studded with ancient farms set in woods rich with mushrooms, herbs, and fruits. The farms often have a complete food production cycle (cereals, cattle, sheep, and pigs, cheese-making, olive groves, and presses).

Colle di Val d'Elsa

Monterigg

Casole d'Elsa

Sovic

Colline Metallifere

Chiusdino

Monticiano

STAR ATTRACTIONS

- CHIUSI (SI): National Etruscan Museum, ☎ 0578 227667
- MONTE OLIVETO MAGGIORE (SI): Abbey, ☎ 0577 707017
- MONTEPULCIANO (SI): Cathedral, Madonna di San Biagio, ☎ 0578 75887
- MONTE S. SAVINO (AR): Loggia dei Mercanti, ☎ 0575 843098
- PIENZA (SI): Cathedral, ☎ 0578 749071
- SANT'ANTIMO (SI): Abbey, ☎ 0577 835659

Pecorino cheese made in the Crete – especially the mature *pecorino* of Pienza – is world-famous *(see pp132–3)*.

Beekeeping at Montalcino has reached very high quality levels with a whole range of unusual honey-based products *(see pp134–5)*.

WHITE TRUFFLES
The Sienese Crete area is blessed as far as truffle lovers are concerned because it has a rich supply of the white truffle *(Tuber magnatum)*. San Giovanni d'Asso is the truffle center and holds a truffle fair every November.

◁ **The Tuscan hills dominated with cypresses**

Large old estates in this area often produce the celebrated Brunello di Montalcino DOCG, one of the great internationally famous wines. These farms were once bustling villages: around the main landowner's house were a wine cellar, an olive press, shops and workshops, a herbalist, dairy, butcher, and church. In many cases, such as Fattoria dei Barbi at Montalcino, the estate pictured here, these activities still continue.

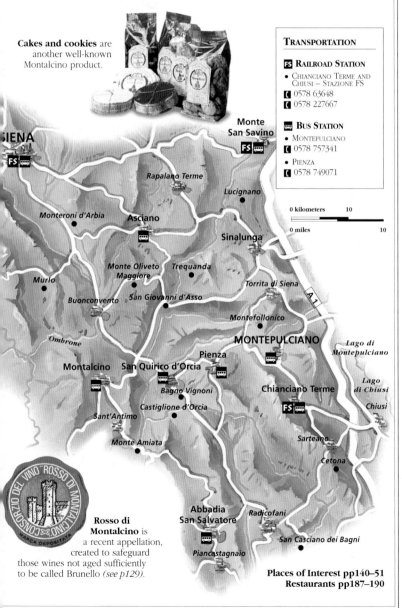

Cakes and cookies are another well-known Montalcino product.

TRANSPORTATION

FS RAILROAD STATION
- CHIANCIANO TERME AND CHIUSI – STAZIONE FS
[0578 63648
[0578 227667

BUS STATION
- MONTEPULCIANO
[0578 757341
- PIENZA
[0578 749071

0 kilometers   10

0 miles   10

Monte San Savino

SIENA

Rapalano Terme

Lucignano

Monteroni d'Arbia   Asciano

Sinalunga

Monte Oliveto Maggiore   Trequanda

Murlo

Torrita di Siena

Buonconvento   San Giovanni d'Asso

Montefollonico

Ombrone

MONTEPULCIANO   Lago di Montepulciano

Pienza

Montalcino   San Quirico d'Orcia   Lago di Chiusi

Bagno Vignoni   Chianciano Terme   Chiusi

Castiglione d'Orcia

Sant'Antimo

Monte Amiata   Sarteano

Cetona

Rosso di Montalcino is a recent appellation, created to safeguard those wines not aged sufficiently to be called Brunello *(see p129).*

Abbadia San Salvatore   Radicofani

San Casciano dei Bagni

Piancastagnaio

Places of Interest pp140–51
Restaurants pp187–190

Wines of Montalcino

THE MAJESTIC RED WINE grown around Montalcino, south of Siena, is one of Italy's greatest wines. Brunello di Montalcino DOCG dates from the late 19th century, which is relatively recent compared with other noble wines. Its fortune and that of all Sienese wine-making lies with the Sangiovese Grosso vine, the only grapes used to make this wine. The same is true of the Rosso di Montalcino. The great Sienese reds were born out of patient effort and a careful eye on the market, and the work of Tuscan and foreign vine-growers who have preserved the link with the local tradition.

There are subtle variations in the bouquet and flavor of Montalcino wines, depending on where they come from. The area around the city is like a large pyramid with four sides sloping to the valleys. On the north side, the wines are elegant and have good body; to the east, the cooler climate confers a more austere structure and great potential for aging; to the south, the body is sustained but the perfume is less elegant; to the west, the wines are especially well balanced and pleasant to drink.

MOSCADELLO
DI MONTALCINO
Few estates produce this wine, so it is not easy to find on the market. In the most common versions it is liqueurlike, but it can also be sweet and sparkling. It is a pale yellow or golden color and has the typical muscatel scent. It is perfect with the sweet dry cookies of Siena and with fruit. It should be made from the ancient Moscadello vine, which has largely disappeared; attempts are being made to nurture some of the original vines. Moscato Bianco is widely used in its place.

The Sangiovese grape grown in Montalcino is called Brunello.

The oldest wines are sometimes called "wines for meditation."

BRUNELLO
DI MONTALCINO
Described in Tuscany as the king of wines, this wine has found worldwide fame. It is aged for at least four years before it is sold; five years if it bears the Riserva label. The high price is justified by this lengthy aging process. The wine's ruby-red color takes on a garnet red hue as it ages. The elegant bouquet is intense and the taste very well balanced. It is a great wine to drink with roasted or braised meats and strong, mature cheeses.

WINE TYPE	GOOD VINTAGES	GOOD PRODUCERS
Red Wine		
Brunello di Montalcino	97, 95, 94, 90	Siro Pacenti, Capanna, Salvioni La Cerbaiola, Lisini, Fattoria del Casato, Caparzo di Montalcino
Rosso di Montalcino	97, 95, 90	Altesino di Montalcino, Argiano di Montalcino
Super Tuscans (see p130)		Argiano di Montalcino

PICI CON L'ANATRA MUTA

1 muscovy duck • 1 carrot • 1 red onion • 1 bunch of parsley • extra-virgin olive oil • 1 glass red wine • 2¼ lb (1 kg) tomatoes, peeled and chopped • 2 tablespoons tomato purée • salt • pepper

Bone the duck, leaving the neck, legs, and wings complete. Use the bones and the neck to make stock. Grind up the rest of the duck meat, giblets, carrot, onion, and parsley. Fry this mixture slowly in the olive oil with the whole parts of the duck. Season to taste. Continue cooking slowly, moistening with the red wine. When the wine has all evaporated, add the fresh tomatoes and the tomato purée, then simmer gently for 3 hours. Check from time to time and add some of the duck stock if it looks as if it is becoming dry. Serve the duck sauce on the local *pici* pasta. (At Trequanda this pasta is also known as *pinci* or *lunghetti*).

ROSSO DI MONTALCINO

Brunello grapes are used to make this younger, less austere wine. Very dry with an intense ruby-red color, it is a versatile table wine which goes with Sienese cuisine's many savory dishes, such as first courses with meat sauces and second courses of pork, stewed meats, and meat with sauces.

NOVELLO

Many estates are successfully making this young wine, which has earned a place for itself in the market. Produced by the *macération carbonique* method, where grapes are fermented whole in a closed vat, it is richly perfumed and suited to drinking with all courses. However, it can be expensive for the quality and does not age well.

The Azienda Col d'Orcia at Montalcino

Other Wines from South of Siena

The province of Siena boasts the richest and most diverse wine production in the whole of Tuscany. The area south of Siena produces not only Brunello but also two great DOCG wines, Vino Nobile di Montepulciano and Chianti Colli Senesi made from Sangiovese Grosso grapes. In the Montepulciano area the Sangiovese Grosso vine is called Prugnolo Gentile, because of the elongated shape of its grapes and their plummy blue color and scent. This vine attains its full potential in the Colli Senesi, either with the grapes used alone or in combination with other reds such as Cabernet Sauvignon, Cabernet Franc, Pinot Nero, and Merlot. Sangiovese Grosso forms up to 80 percent of Chianti while it varies from 60 percent to 80 percent in Vino Nobile and Rosso di Montepulciano. Other red grapes are also added to these wines, including Canaiolo for mellowness and Mammolo for its bouquet.

The Sienese region also has a long tradition of white grape vines. The most common is Trebbiano Toscano, but the present trend is to reduce the quantity of this grape and gradually replace it with other grapes such as Chardonnay, Pinot Bianco, Sauvignon, Traminer Aromatico, Rhineland Riesling, Pinot Grigio, and Muller Thurgau, which have long been grown here. The second traditional white grape is Malvasia Toscana, then there are other lesser varieties like Grechetto Bianco, also called Pulcinculo because of the dark spot found on the tip of the grape.

VIN SANTO DI MONTEPULCIANO

This highly prized traditional Vin Santo is made with Pulcinculo in addition to the other traditional grapes. It can be labeled Riserva after it has aged for at least five years in wood. Served as a dessert wine, it goes well with sweet dry cookies. The price varies, but it can be very expensive. Some estates produce it in a *"Vendemmia Tardiva"* version, from grapes left to dry on the vines instead of picking them and drying them on racks.

The white version from white grapes.

This attractive amber-colored Vin Santo, called Occhio di Pernice, is made from at least 50 percent Sangiovese grapes.

THE SUPER TUSCANS

Many Tuscan estates have long been engaged in producing wines outside the rules of the DOC or DOCG wines. The choice of vines and methods of production aim at the very highest quality. The techniques vary from one estate to another – they may be based on traditional Tuscan vines alone or combined with noble vines like Cabernet Sauvignon and Merlot. Some excellent wines have been produced and they are much in demand internationally. These wines are called Super Tuscans, an appellation which indicates prized wines much sought-after abroad.

CHIANTI E CHIANTI DEI COLLI SENESI

Chianti is made from Tuscan grapes vinified in the Siena area; Chianti dei Colli Senesi is made from grapes that have been grown and vinified locally.

VINO NOBILE DI MONTEPULCIANO

This DOCG wine can be one of Italy's most impressive reds. The area of production for the wine stretches west from Valdichiana and east into another small area. Specific areas that produce superior wine include Argiano, Caggiole, Canneto, Casalte, and Valiano. The wine is aged for two years in casks, or three years in the case of the Riserva. It is a deep red color, with an intense, balanced bouquet, excellent with *bistecca alla fiorentina*, grilled meats, and mature cheeses.

ROSSO DI MONTEPULCIANO

This red wine, which has practically no aging, was created to bring Montepulciano wine closer to the general public. It is a bright ruby red with an intense bouquet and a pleasant dry flavor. It is ideal as a general table wine with full-bodied dishes, such as grilled meats.

VAL D'ARBIA

Made mainly from Trebbiano Toscano and Malvasia grapes, this dry white wine is a pale yellowish color with a hint of green. Fruity and fresh-tasting, it makes a good aperitif or it can be served with fried or baked fish.

Wine Type	Good Vintages	Good Producers	Wine Type	Good Vintages	Good Producers
Red Wine			**Super Tuscans** (see p130)	98, 97, 95, 90	Avignonesi di Montepulciano
Rosso di Montepulciano	97, 90	Avignonesi, Poliziano, Dei di Montepulciano	**White Wine**		
Chianti *and* Chianti dei Colli Senesi	98, 97, 95, 93, 90	Farnetella di Sinalunga, Fattoria del Colle di Trequanda	Vino Nobile di Montepulciano	97, 95, 90	Avignonesi, Fattoria del Cerro, Poliziano di Montepulciano

Pecorino from the Sienese Crete

SOUTH OF SIENA, in the primeval landscape of the Crete, shepherds tend sheep whose milk is used to make *pecorino* cheese. The ancient craft of cheese making is now largely practiced by Sardinian shepherds who have settled here in recent decades, but this has not altered the traditional quality of the cheese – the Sardinians have preserved their own sheep-tending skills, while absorbing the habits and tastes of the Sienese people. The Crete and the southern part of the province of Siena produce the most prized *pecorino* in Tuscany.

MATURE PECORINO DI PIENZA
This is the most prized and famous of Tuscan *pecorini*, prepared with milk solely from the Crete and Montalcino areas. The secret of its quality lies in the use of fresh, unpasteurized milk and a covering of olive oil lees (skins after the olives have been pressed) to keep the inside soft and slightly mellow. (Avoid cheeses covered with plastic film, which ruins the cheese.) These cheeses are matured for anything from 5 to 18 months.

The whitish color of the crust is due to the olive oil lees.

MATURE PECORINO
The area of production for this cheese is the same as for the traditional Pienza cheese and the two are quite similar, except that this cheese does not have the olive oil crust, so the inside has a drier texture and a stronger flavor.

This cheese has a hard, deep yellow crust.

SEMIMATURE PECORINO
After 90–120 days of maturing, *pecorino* is still beautifully mellow, ideal for eating with *salumi*, with pears, or in thin slices on meat, *crostini*, or baked vegetables. Sometimes chillies, black pepper, or black truffles are incorporated into the cheese. It is rare, however, to find a cheese-maker who uses pieces of fresh truffle; most use semiprocessed truffles or the synthetic aroma, resulting in an inferior product.

A coating of extra-virgin olive oil on this white cheese keeps the inside soft.

This cheese is covered in tomato purée which keeps the inside soft and enhances its scent, giving it a red crust.

FRESH PECORINO

Sweet and creamy, with a markedly milky flavor, fresh *pecorino* is eaten within 90–120 days of being made. It is popular with all age groups and can be eaten at the end of the meal or as an *antipasto* dressed with extra-virgin olive oil from the Crete region and seasoned with salt and black pepper.

CIPOLLE IN FORNO

12 red onions • extra-virgin olive oil • white wine vinegar • 2 oz (50 g) pecorino, grated • 4 oz (100 g) breadcrumbs • salt • pepper

Preheat the oven to 400°F (200°C). Peel the onions, cut two slits to form a cross at the top of each and put them in a baking pan. Brush with oil and season with salt and pepper. Roast in the oven until well cooked. Moisten with the vinegar and return to the oven to evaporate the liquid. Mix the cheese and crumbs, sprinkle them over the onions and serve.

FRESH PECORINO WITH HERBS OR NUTS

Fresh *pecorino* may have herbs or nuts added to it. The cheese should be eaten within a week and is excellent as an *antipasto* or as a snack with a little extra-virgin olive oil from the Crete drizzled over it.

Chopped arugula in fresh pecorino is a recent innovation.

Adding small pieces of walnut to the cheese is an old tradition.

PECORINO SOTT'OLIO

In some families and farmhouses there is a tradition of preserving mature *pecorino* in olive oil mixed with herbs or spices.

OTHER EWE'S MILK PRODUCTS WORTH TRYING

Raviggiolo is a fresh curd cheese eaten within four days of making. Traditionally it is salted and eaten as an antipasto or sugared as a dessert. It is very delicate and should be kept in a sealed container in the refrigerator. The **ricotta** in this area is delectable, especially when made from raw milk: it is eaten on ribbon pasta or made into fillings for stuffed pasta such as ravioli. Another product of this area is **marzolino** *(see p108)*.

Honey

THROUGHOUT TUSCANY – from the mountains to the coast, where the Mediterranean landscape is dotted with wonderfully aromatic plants – honey *(miele)* is produced. Renowned for its therapeutic properties, honey is thought to help with disorders in all parts of the body, from liver to lungs to circulation. At Montalcino beekeeping (apiculture) has a long history, originating with the skill of the foresters who used to gather wild honey from hollow trees, and are still capable of hiving swarms of wild bees. Traditional honey production in Montalcino and the surrounding area is based on the flowering chestnut woods on the Apennine slopes. Many local firms take hives to other parts of Italy, so they can extend the honey-producing season.

Chestnut honey is a rich, dark brown color.

CHESTNUT HONEY

The aroma and slightly bitter taste of chestnut honey *(miele di castagno)* make it good for cooking and in confectioneries. It is believed to be useful for intestinal disorders and helpful in regulating the nervous system and in cases of anemia.

SUNFLOWER HONEY

This honey *(miele di girasole)* is thought to be mildly effective at soothing pain or fever and is a mild diuretic.

Sunflower honey is very dense with an opaque yellowish color.

CANTUCCI DI MONTALCINO

8 oz (200 g) unpeeled almonds • 1¼ lb (500 g) plain flour • 4 eggs • 1 teaspoon baking powder • ¾ lb (350 g) sugar • 4 oz (100 g) chestnut honey • few drops of vanilla essence • butter • salt

Preheat the oven to 350°F (180°C). Roast the almonds for 4 minutes. Heap the flour on a work surface and make a well in the center. Beat the eggs and pour into the well with the baking powder, sugar, honey, vanilla essence, and a pinch of salt. Knead until the dough is smooth, then add the almonds. Roll out the dough and shape into long fingers. Transfer to a buttered and floured baking sheet and bake for about 20 minutes. Cut the fingers diagonally into ¾ inch (2 cm) slices and leave to dry.

WOODLAND HONEY

Rich in mineral salts and iron, woodland honey *(melata do bosco)* is very fortifying.

Woodland honey is a deep golden color.

SULLA CLOVER HONEY
Because it has a faint aroma, this honey *(miele di sulla)* can be used for sweetening foods without affecting their flavor. It is thought to help purify the liver and keep the intestines in good order.

This clear honey is a light golden color.

HEATHER HONEY
Delicately scented heather honey *(miele di erica)* is good for coughs and colds, as it helps to soothe sore respiratory organs.

Jellylike heather honey is brownish-orange.

ARBUTUS HONEY
Arbutus honey *(miele di corbezzolo)*, from the wild strawberry tree, is quite bitter. It is thought to be good for the circulation and blood.

Arbutus honey is a mustard color, or milky white if very pure. It is very thick and granular.

PRESERVES IN HONEY
The classics – hazelnuts, almonds, or walnuts in honey *(vasetti "sotto miele")* – are found in most parts of Tuscany. There is also the unusual delicacy of boiled chestnuts flavored with vanilla and conserved in acacia honey.

OTHER VARIETIES OF HONEY WORTH TRYING
Acacia honey, clear and very fluid, is probably the variety most commonly seen. It is not strong and suits a range of tastes. Rich in energy, it is fortifying and has mild laxative properties which are thought to help purify the liver. **Tiglio** (linden) honey, excellent for problems with the respiratory tract, is also useful for inducing sleep. **Millefioro** (wild flower) is versatile and very nourishing. **Eucalipto** (eucalyptus), helpful in disorders of the respiratory tract, is a decongestant and emollient for smokers. **Lavanda** (lavender) is richly scented and helps to calm the nervous system. **Rosmarino** (rosemary) has a strong flavor and is a mild diuretic. **Timo** (thyme), rich in fructose, is believed to be good for the circulation, as is **trifoglio** (clover) honey. At Montalcino, other honey specialities include grappa, candies, fruit cakes, and preserves.

Traditional Produce

THERE ARE PLENTY of genuine Tuscan specialities for the gourmet in this area, and they are nearly always produced with due respect for the environment. The *prosciutti* and *salumi*, cèpe mushrooms and truffles, extra-virgin olive oil, game birds and animals, Chianina beef, lamb, and fine vegetables produced in this part of Tuscany all have their own very distinctive character.

OSSI DI MORTO
These very hard cookies, made from egg whites and chopped almonds, are typical of Montalcino.

GRAPPA
In recent years a lot of work has gone into improving the grappa made by distilling the grape skins and seeds left over from the wine-making process. Leading wine-makers have staked their names on these grappas, some of interest to true connoisseurs.

COLLI SENESI OLIVE OIL
The Colli Senesi is a broad, homogeneous area south of Siena, from Montalcino toward the northeast, comprising Asciano, San Quirico d'Orcia, San Giovanni d'Asso, Pienza, Montepulciano, Trequanda, Rapolano Terme, Lucignano, and Sinalunga. The olive oils produced here are of medium-to-high fruitiness, and generally full-bodied. They vary in taste, but all are peppery when young, usually with a slightly bitter aftertaste.

POLLASTRELLA AL DRAGONCELLO

1 young free-range pullet • 1 apple • a large bunch of tarragon • 1 knob of butter • 1 dessertspoon plain flour

Preheat the oven to 350°F (180°C). Brown the pullet, then stuff it with the apple and tarragon. Sew up the bird with kitchen twine, wrap in wax paper, and roast in the oven for about 40 minutes. Remove the paper and pour off the cooking juices. Roast the bird for another 5 minutes until it is a golden color, then remove from the pan. Thicken the juices in the pan with the butter and flour; serve with the bird.

TARRAGON
One of the classic herbs of international cuisine, tarragon (*persia* in Tuscany, elsewhere *dragoncello* or *estragone*) is a common aromatic in the Siena area, where it is widely used in sauces and meat dishes.

PLAGA DI MONTALCINO OLIVE OIL
This intensely fruity olive oil is produced throughout the whole Montalcino area. It has a fresh scent of herbs and a rounded taste, rather astringent and pungent. The strong flavor has a markedly bitter, peppery aftertaste.

For this salami the meat is coarsely ground and the fat is chopped with a knife.

MORTADELLA

The local name for Tuscan salami encased in pig's large intestine is *mortadella* (while the smaller size is usually called *salame*). This salami is slightly less fatty than some types and its medium-to-high quality is due to the good local pork.

This meat is finely ground and rather fatty.

FINOCCHIONA

This salami, which is cured for eating raw, contains aromatic fennel seeds or flowers. It is similar to Florentine *sbriciolona*, but usually cured for longer.

Wrapped in straw paper, lombo can breathe.

LOMBO

Chine of pork is boned and salted and scented with fennel seed to add even more flavor to the good quality meat. If fresh, *lombo* is served dressed with olive oil and lemon.

BURISTO

Typical of the Siena area, *buristo* (blood pudding) is made from the flesh of the pig's head – including the tongue and some of the skin – finely ground and mixed with spices, pig's blood, and boiled fat. The meat is encased in the pig's stomach and slowly boiled. It is traditionally eaten strewn with chopped raw onion.

WHAT TO SAMPLE

Rigatino, salted belly of pork, is indispensable in local cooking. There are numerous traditional cakes, especially at Montalcino, where you can find Sienese classics such as **ricciarelli** and **panforte**. Specialities peculiar to Montalcino and the Crete are **pane coi santi**, bread dough with nuts, raisins, and aniseed mixed into it; **torta di Montalcino**, a soft cake containing raisins and covered with chocolate, hazelnuts, and almonds; **morselletti**, aniseed cookies (the original recipe also calls for olive oil); **pinolata**, made of pastry with cream and raisins, covered with pine nuts to look like a pine cone; **schiacciata di Pasqua**, a bread flavored with mint, rosewater, saffron, aniseed, and citrus peel. The local pasta, **pinci**, is like large spaghetti. **Saffron** grows wild in this area, and the medieval village of Murlo has grown **rice** for centuries.

Wild Produce

WHITE WAX CAP
(Hygrophorus penarius)
Late in the season this mushroom *(lardaiolo bianco)* is abundant in thick stands of evergreen and deciduous oaks. It remains white and fleshy after cooking and is good in sauces with white meats.

LESSER BOLETUS
(Boletus duriusculus)
The sturdiest and most prized of this group of *porcini*, the lesser boletus *(oppiarello)* grows under poplars along the coast. It is good cooked with garlic and parsley (it darkens when cooked). When young, these mushrooms are preserved in oil; mature ones are dried.

CHANTERELLE
(Cantharellus cibarius)
This mushroom *(giallarello)* has adapted to virtually all cuisines and is popular in many countries. Chanterelles grow in all kinds of woodland but in this area are found mainly under holm oaks. Less perfumed than the Alpine chanterelles that grow under beech and spruce, they are excellent fried with garlic and parsley, in cream, and in sauces.

PARASOL MUSHROOM
(Lepiota procera)
Common in both the coastal scrub and on grassy hillsides, this popular mushroom *(bubbola)* is very conspicuous because of its height – up to 20 inches (50 cm) – and the drumstick shape of its cap. It is excellent raw in salads or preserved in oil when young. When ripe, the cap is very good grilled, fried, or deviled. The woody stalk is dried and made into an aromatic powder.

FUNGHI CON LA NEPITELLA (MUSHROOMS WITH CALAMINT)

1¾ lb (800 g) mixed mushrooms, sliced • 3 cloves garlic, chopped • 1 sprig of calamint (or mint) • 1 dessertspoon tomato purée • extra-virgin olive oil • salt • pepper

Put the mushrooms in a pan with the garlic, sprig of calamint, plenty of oil, and salt and pepper. Cook over a high heat until the mushrooms shed their water, then lower and cook till the liquid evaporates (the oil should be clear again). Add the tomato purée and cook over a moderate heat for 10 minutes.

COMMON SOW THISTLE
(Sonchus oleraceus)
One of the best-known edible wild plants, sow thistle *(crespigno)* grows abundantly on the edges of vegetable patches and paths, on waste ground, and in orchards. Sweet and tasty when young, it is good raw. As it matures, it is eaten in mixed salads, stuffings, and omelettes.

WILD ASPARAGUS
(Asparagus acutifolius)
Plentiful early in spring growing by hedgerows, ditches, and on the edge of woods, picking wild asparagus *(asparago selvatico)* is a pleasant pastime. It is used in the same way as the cultivated variety.

WILD LETTUCE
(Lactuca serriola)
This salad vegetable *(lattuga di campo)* is well known to country people in Tuscany, who go looking for it. Check with an expert before you pick it: the rosettes at the base of many spring plants can look similar and not all are edible. Wild lettuce is very good raw or cooked and dressed with oil, lemon juice, or vinegar.

PENNE IN SALSA D'ERBETTE DI PRIMAVERA

1 young wild fennel plant • a few calamint (or mint) leaves • 1 rosette of common poppy leaves • 1 young borage plant • 1 small bunch of parsley • 20 basil leaves • 1 handful nettle tips • 1 handful of field eryngo • 1 head of wild chicory leaves • 2 heads of wild lettuce leaves • 3 young sow thistle plants • 1 sprig tarragon • 10 leaves lemon balm • 1 sprig marjoram • 6 walnuts • extra virgin olive oil • 1 chilli • 2 cloves garlic • 1¼ lb (500 g) tomatoes, peeled • 1¼ lb (500 g) penne • salt

Make sure the herbs are dry. Chop them in a blender or food processor with the walnuts. Put them in a jar, cover with olive oil, and leave for at least 2 days. Heat a little oil in a pan, add the chilli and garlic, and fry until softened slightly. Add the tomatoes and season with salt. Cook over a brisk heat. Add the herbs and walnuts and cook for a further 5 minutes. Meanwhile, cook the pasta. Drain well and serve with the tomato and herb sauce, mixing thoroughly.

STRAWBERRY TREE (ARBUTUS)
(Arbutus unedo)
The strawberry tree *(corbezzolo)* is common in Mediterranean thickets, where its colorful appearance – green leaves, white flowers, and red fruit – enlivens the scenery. When ripe, the fruit is creamy rather than juicy, and is very sweet. It can be eaten fresh (in moderation) or used in preserves.

Places of Interest

As with the Chianti region, the well-informed, polyglot clientele of this area want the genuine flavors of the past, thus helping to ensure the survival of these foods. There are fewer shops here, but there are many interesting farms, as well as some of the finest wine producers. The farms have such a wide range of products that they are almost self-sufficient: they offer not only olive oil and wine but also *salumi*, cheese, fresh vegetables, and local honey, all of them excellent.

ASCIANO (SI)

 Tenuta Monte Sante Marie

località Monte Sante Marie
📞 055 700020

This farm, which offers agriturismo facilities, makes a marvelous extra-virgin olive oil. In years when they have a bumper crop of fruit, they make and sell excellent cakes and jams as well.

BUONCONVENTO (SI)

La Bottega del Pane

via del Taia, 21
📞 0577 806800

The Tuscan bread made the old traditional way with fresh yeast by this shop keeps well for several days. The shop also sells a wide range of Sienese cakes, and its illustrious clientele includes the Queen of the Netherlands.

CASTIGLIONE D'ORCIA (SI)

Podere Forte

località Petrucci
📞 0577 887488

At present this young estate produces an outstanding extra virgin olive oil. However, it is preparing to begin wine production with the help of an international staff of experts.

CHIUSI (SI)

Azienda Agricola Colle di Santa Mustiola

via delle Torri, 86/A
📞 0578 63462

A single wine, Poggio di Chiari from Sangiovese grapes alone, matured in French and Slavonian oak, is produced here. The owner, a supporter of local products, has reintroduced the cultivation of spelt and breeds Cinta Senese pigs.

LUCIGNANO (AR)

 Apicoltura Nocciolini

località Selva, 50a
📞 0575 836097

All types of honey, from this and other areas, gathered by itinerant beekeepers is sold here.

 Panificio Redi

località Croce
📞 0575 837037
🔴 Sat pm

CINGHIALE IN AGRODOLCE (BOAR IN SWEET AND SOUR SAUCE)

3¼ lb (1.5 kg) lean boar's meat • 3 pints (1.5 liters) red wine • 8 fl oz (250 ml) wine vinegar • juniper berries • 3 bay leaves • 1 dessertspoon plain flour seasoned with salt and pepper • extra-virgin olive oil • 2 carrots, finely chopped • 1 onion, finely chopped • 1 stalk of celery, finely chopped • meat stock • 4 oz (100 g) chopped panforte • 3 cavallucci (sweets) • 4 oz (100 g) dark chocolate • 1 oz (25 g) butter • 2 oz (50 g) raisins • 2 oz (50 g) pine nuts • 2 oz (50 g) chopped walnuts • salt • black peppercorns and ground pepper

Marinate the boar's flesh for 24 hours in the wine, half the vinegar, the juniper berries, bay leaves, and a few peppercorns. Remove the meat, reserving the marinade. Cut the meat into small cubes and coat with the seasoned flour. Heat some oil in a pan, add the meat, and brown on all sides. Add the vegetables and cook until they are tender, then moisten with a little stock. Simmer gently adding the marinade a little at a time. Meanwhile soak the *panforte* and *cavallucci* in the stock until they crumble, add the chocolate, butter, dried fruit, nuts, and the rest of the vinegar. When the boar is cooked, remove it from the pan and keep warm. Add the *panforte* mixture to the cooking juices and heat, stirring until it forms a thick, smooth sauce. Pour the sauce over the meat and serve.

The Azienda Agricola Argiano at Montalcino

A very varied range of wines is produced on this estate – not surprising, as it is probably the largest estate in the district. The castle has been restored by the large American corporation, Banfi, and it houses a valuable collection of antique wine bottles and glasses, which is open to the public.

Here Tuscan bread is made the old-fashioned way, kneading by hand before leaving it to rise.

🐂 Franco Scarpelli

via Matteotti, 121
📞 0575 836016
⬤ Mon, Wed, Thurs

The owner of this butcher's is an expert on Chianina beef and is guided by an innate passion for the breed. He raises and butchers mostly Chianina beef following traditional methods. He also makes his own excellent hams and sausages from local pigs. The poultry comes from nearby farms.

MONTALCINO (SI)

🍇 Azienda Agricola Altesino

località Altesino
📞 0577 806208

This is one of the very few estates to produce brandy from Brunello. It takes courage to distill a wine destined to become Brunello. All the same, in less generous years, this is a good way to obtain something different. Production is limited and the brandy is aged in barrels for a minimum of 10 years. Outstanding among the wines is the Brunello di Montalcino Alte d'Altesi, based on

Sangiovese grapes with a small amount of Cabernet Sauvignon, and Quarto d'Altesi, a pure Merlot.

🍇 Azienda Agricola Argiano

località Sant'Angelo in Colle, 54
📞 0577 844037

On one of the most attractive estates in Montalcino, a staff of wine-making experts have produced a widely praised Brunello and a Riserva version. Other wines with harmonious aromas and flavors produced here are the Rosso di Montalcino and the Solengo, from Cabernet Sauvignon, Merlot, Syrah, and Sangiovese grapes.

🍇 Banfi Spa

Castello di Poggio alle Mura
📞 0577 840111

🍇 Fattoria dei Barbi

località Barbi
📞 0577 848277

Not so much a farm as a village for gourmets: this ancient hamlet southeast of Montalcino produces one of the most famous Brunello wines. There is a cheese dairy and a building where salumi are made. In the best years, as well as Brunello DOCG, an excellent special selection is produced: Brunello di Montalcino DOCG Vigna del Fiore. Other notable products are Rosso di Montalcino, Chianti dei Colli Senesi, Brusco dei Barbi, Grappa di Brunello, and extra-virgin olive oil.

🏛 Batignani Roberto

via Delle Caserme, 7
📞 0577 848444

This family beekeeping business has honey from sulla clover, sunflowers, wild flowers, chestnut, and many others.

Barrels in the cellar of the Fattoria dei Barbi at Montalcino

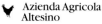

🍇 Biondi Santi Spa

via Panfilo dell'Oca, 3
☎ 0577 847121

*A single firm distributes
the wines produced by
the Biondi Santi family's
various estates. From the
Greppo estate come the
Brunello and Rosso di
Montalcino, wines that
reflect a traditional style,
a tribute to Tancredi,
son of Ferruccio who, a
century ago, made
Brunello world famous.
From Villa Poggio Salvi
comes the Lavischio
(Merlot) and some of
the grapes used for the
"Super Tuscans,"
including Sassoalloro
(Sangiovese). The
Tenuta Greppo olive
oil is very good.*

🍇 Azienda Agricola Capanna

località Capanna, 333
☎ 0577 848298

*This small family-run
vineyard has made a
name with its Brunello di
Montalcino Riserva and
Rosso di Montalcino.*

🍇 Azienda Caparzo

località Torrenieri,
☎ 0577 848390

*The decision to make
wine with Brunello
grapes only in the best
years has been rewarded
by significant results,
especially in the Brunello*

*La Casa selection. Also
excellent is the Rosso La
Caduta and Ca' del
Pazzo, from Sangiovese
and Cabernet Sauvignon,
a success since it was first
made in 1982. Among
the new generation of
wines there is an
outstanding Val d'Arbia
Le Crete, made from
Trebbiano, Malvasia, and
Chardonnay.*

🍇 Fattoria del Casato

località Podernovi
☎ 0577 849421

*An integral part of
Fattoria dei Barbi (see
p141) until 1998, the
Fattoria del Casato, now
run by Donatella Cinelli,
has become independent
and is connected with the
Fattoria del Colle di
Trequanda (see p151)
where the Rosso and
Brunello di Montalcino
produced here can be
purchased. Its cellar will
remain combined with
the Barbi estate's until its
own facilities are finished.
The star wine is Brunello
Prime Donne, made by
an all-female staff.*

🍇 Azienda agricola Case Basse

località Villa
Santa Restituta
☎ 0577 848567

*Only three wines are
produced here, and all of
them are excellent. They*

*are the Brunello di
Montalcino, Brunello di
Montalcino Riserva, and
Intistieti, made from
Brunello grapes in less
favorable years. The wines
can be purchased from
Drogheria Franci (see
p144).*

🍇 Castel Giocondo

località Castelgiocondo
☎ 0577 848492

*New vineyards facing
south in a breezy climate
are a productive bonus
which the Marchesi de'
Frescobaldi firm manages
with great care. The
Brunello di Montalcino
Riserva is one of the most
sought-after, followed
by the Rosso di Montalcino
and the Lamaione, based
on Merlot. Recently, in a
joint venture with the*

Harvesting Brunello grapes at the Azienda Caparzo

Some of Hubert Ciacci's hives

Picchio Pacchio

extra virgin olive oil
* *1 small onion, chopped*
* *3¼ lb (1.5 kg) ripe tomatoes, peeled*
* *vegetable or meat stock*
* *6 eggs • Tuscan bread, sliced • salt*

Heat the oil in a pan, add the chopped onion, and cook until softened. Add the tomatoes, lower the heat, and simmer for 30 minutes. Cover the mixture with plenty of stock. As soon as it boils, beat the eggs and add them to the soup, stirring briskly. Arrange the sliced bread in soup plates and ladle the soup on top of it. Drizzle a little extra-virgin olive oil over each dish and serve at once.

American wine-maker Robert Mondavi, it has produced two "Super Tuscans": Luce and Lucente from Sangiovese and Merlot grapes in different proportions. The wines can be purchased from Enoteca La Fortezza and Drogheria Franci (see p144).

and the practice of traveling to other parts of the country with the hives, has resulted in a wide variety of honeys (including bitter arbutus honey). Other delicacies include jams made with honey, chestnuts preserved in honey, liqueurs, and traditional confectionery.

🍇 Azienda Agricola Cerbaiona

località Cerbaiona
📞 0577 848660

Diego Molinari, a former airline pilot, has successfully turned to the production of wines. His star wine is Brunello, at an above-average price, and Cerbaiona, based on Sangiovese grapes.

🐝 Hubert Ciacci

via Traversa dei Monti, 227a
📞 0577 848640

Here there is beekeeping of the highest quality; great respect for the natural qualities of honey,

🍇 Azienda Agricola Col d'Orcia

località Sant'Angelo in Colle
📞 0577 808001

Many of the vines here are Brunello and the estate's Poggio al Vento vineyard produces its finest Brunello. Equally good are the classic Brunello di Montalcino and the Rosso di Montalcino. This estate is one of the few to produce Moscadello di Montalcino, offered in the "Vendemmia Tardiva" (late harvest) version of the Pascena selection. Olmaia, from Cabernet Sauvignon, is a "Super

Tuscan." The Novello Novembrino is made from traditional Sangiovese.

🍇 Azienda Agricola Collemattoni

località Sant' Angelo in Colle
via del Capannino
📞 0577 844127

Father and son share the work on this estate, one of the smallest in the area, the former working in the vineyard and the latter in the wine cellar. They produce excellent Brunello and an even finer Rosso di Montalcino.

The Azienda Agricola Col d'Orcia at Montalcino

 Costanti

località Colle
al Matrichese
📞 0577 848195

*The vines on this estate
are carefully tended,
down to the rose bushes
planted at the ends of the
rows as a useful indicator
of any possible disease in
the vines. The results are
attractive: the Brunello
di Montalcino is excellent
in the two versions,
regular and Riserva.*

Enoteca La Fortezza

piazzale Fortezza
📞 0577 849211
⬤ Mon
⭕ Sun

*Inside the fortress of
Montalcino, in what was
once the garrison tower,
there is a wine shop that,
together with the local
government, stocks
produce from all the local
producers. Hundreds of
firms are represented,
almost all wineries,
together with the few
major producers of
cheese and various
pecorini, salumi and
finocchiona, salami, and
cured ham suppliers. The
oil comes from the few
producers that guarantee
consistent quality. There
is a charge for tasting.*

Drogheria Franci

piazzale Fortezza, 5
📞 0577 848191.
⬤ Wed pm
⭕ Sun

*This firm's apiary has
been one of the area's best
known for over three
generations. It has 10
types of honey, including
bitter arbutus honey,
dried fruit preserved in
honey and honey candies.
The shop has a wine section
that specializes in
Montalcino wines but also
has a pleasing selection of
other wines, not all of*

*them Tuscan. It also sells
various local gastronomic
specialties, with salumi
and cheeses to accompany
the wine tasting.*

 Forno Lambardi

via Soccorso Saloni, 24
📞 0577 848084
⬤ Wed pm

*On sale here are fresh
bread and traditional
cookies – ossi di morto,
morselletti, brutti e buoni,
and many others – made
from natural ingredients,
sold loose or prepackaged.*

Lisini

località Sant'Angelo in
Colle
📞 0577 844040

*Its favorable position
and the richness of the
soil make this estate one
of the finest in the area.
It produces a Brunello di
Montalcino of great body
and elegance. The Ugolaia
selection is interesting.*

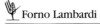 Pasticceria Mariuccia

piazza del Popolo, 29
📞 0577 849319
⬤ Mon ⭕ Sun

*Pasticceria Mariuccia
produces traditional
Montalcino cakes such
as torta di Montalcino,
bacio di Montalcino (a
cold dessert made from
a very old recipe), and
pane coi santi.*

CAVOLO
SULLE FETTE

*2¼ lb (1 kg) black
cabbage • 12 slices of
Tuscan bread • 2 cloves
garlic • extra-virgin olive
oil • 2 tablespoons
vinegar • salt • pepper*

Wash the cabbage leaves
and remove the central
rib. Cook the leaves in
boiling water. Toast the
bread, halve the garlic
and rub the toast with
the cut surfaces. Place in
a soup tureen. When the
cabbage is cooked, put
the leaves on the bread
with a little cooking
water. Season with oil,
vinegar, salt, and pepper.

Mastrojanni

località Castelnuovo
dell'Abate
Podere Loreto
📞 0577 835681

*Despite the fact that this
estate is unable to satisfy
the growing demand for
its wine, it continues the
policy of producing
Brunello only in the best
years. The result is an
excellent Brunello, which
has been appreciated
for many years. The
table wines combine
Sangiovese and Cabernet
Sauvignon grapes to
make Rosso San Pio.*

Siro Pacenti

località Pelagrilli, 1
📞 0577 848662

Vineyards around Montalcino

A highly interesting Brunello and Rosso di Montalcino are being made by an estate that is growing significantly through careful renewal of the vines and the cellar.

🍇 La Poderina

località La Poderina Castelnuovo dell'Abate
☎ 0577 835737

This is the second estate owned by the Saiagricola company (it also owns the Fattoria del Cerro at Montepulciano). Here the company's energies are concentrated on trying to get the very best out of the Sangiovese grape in the form of its most tantalizing product, Brunello di Montalcino.

🍇 Poggio Antico

località Poggio Antico
☎ 0577 848044

The output is focused on Brunello, which in its best years achieves a notable level and also comes in a Riserva version. The estate's small wine shop contains a selection of its finest vintages, which are difficult to find even in specialty shops.

🍇 Il Poggione

località Sant'Angelo in Colle
☎ 0577 844029

The estate's best wine is definitely Brunello, but the Rosso di Montalcino is also of great interest. In addition, the estate produces a small amount of Moscadello in a sparkling version and traditional Vin Santo.

🍇 Salvioni Azienda Agraria Cerbaiola

piazza Cavour, 19
☎ 0577 848499

This estate produces a great Brunello and an excellent Rosso di Montalcino. The quality of the wine is very high but so, unfortunately, are the prices – without apparently discouraging the wine connoisseurs: there is always limited availability of this wine. The small amount of olive oil they produce is also excellent.

🍇 Talenti

località Sant'Angelo in Colle-Pian del Conte
☎ 0577 844043

Pierluigi Talenti has worked hard on his Sangiovese vines and, after years of careful selection in the vineyard, he has created a great Brunello. There was nothing immodest in his dedication of a wine to himself: the Rosso Talenti, which is made from Sangiovese grapes combined with the

Tuscan Colorino and the French Syrah, is a great success.

⊛ Pasticceria Ticci

località Torrenieri, via Romana, 47
☎ 0577 834146
⊙ Sun am

This is a great café and confectioner's with a wide range of excellent traditional cakes, including panforte and ciambelline made with red Montalcino wine.

MONTEFOLLONICO (SI)

♣ Caseificio Putzulu

località Fattoria in Posto, 1
☎ 0577 669744

Sheep are raised here and there is a dairy producing ricotta and a selection of other excellent ewe's milk cheeses which are aged for varying periods.

LESSO RIFATTO

1¼ lb (500 g) leftover boiled meat (beef, veal, and chicken)
• extra-virgin olive oil • 1 onion, chopped
• 1 carrot , diced • 1 stalk celery, diced • 2 oz (50 g)
pancetta, diced • 1 glass red wine • 12 oz (300 g)
tomatoes, pulped • 1 oz (25 g) dried porcini (cèpes)
• salt • pepper

Cut the beef and veal into slices and the chicken into strips. Heat the oil in a pan, add the onion, carrot, celery, and pancetta and fry gently until browned, then add the meat and wine. Add the tomatoes and season to taste with salt and pepper. Cover and simmer for 15 minutes. Meanwhile, soak the porcini in warm water for 15 minutes, then add to the pan. Continue to cook gently for 20 minutes. Arrange the meat on a serving dish, pour the sauce over it and serve.

MONTEPULCIANO (SI)

🍇 Avignonesi

Via di Gracciano
del Corso, 91
📞 0578 757872

This company has four
estates producing wine:
two at Montepulciano
and two at Cortona.
Its flagship wine is
the Vino Nobile di
Montepulciano, but
another wine that has
made a name for itself
is Toro Desiderio, from
pure Merlot, Cabernet
Sauvignon, and Prugnolo
Gentile grapes. Other
pearls are the Vin Santo,
from white grapes, and
the Occhio di Pernice
from Prugnolo Gentile.
The careful selection of
grapes and the lengthy
aging of these dessert
wines inevitably means
that they will never be
cheap to buy. The extra-
virgin olive oil produced
by the company is also
excellent.

🍇 La Braccesca

strada statale, 326
località Gracciano
di Montepulciano
📞 0578 707058

Since most of its vines are
Sangiovese, this estate's
output has been limited to
two wines, the Vino Nobile
and Rosso di
Montepulciano Sabazio,
but they have recently
added an important
Merlot variety. It has only
recently become known
on the market but it has
attracted considerable
interest. The credit is due
to the staff and the
philosophy of Antinori,
who took over the estate in
1990. Purchases can be
made at Enoteca Borgo
Buio, Montepulciano
(0578 717497) and
Enoteca di Ghino, Pienza
(0575 748057) (see p149).

🍇 Fattoria del Cerro

località Acquaviva
via Grazianella, 5
📞 0578 767722

This is probably the biggest
private producer of Vino
Nobile di Montepulciano.
Most of the vines, owned
by the Saiagricola group,
are reserved for the Vino
Nobile, on which the estate
is staking a lot, especially
on the Riserva, but it also
has a splendid Rosso di
Montepulciano. The white
wines are Braviolo, based
on Trebbiano, and Cerro
Bianco from Chardonnay.

The Azienda Avignonesi at Montepulciano

🍇 Azienda Agricola Contucci

via del Teatro, 1
📞 0578 757006

The centuries-old cellars,
which have belonged to
the family since the 13th
century, contain large
and small casks in which
the Vino Nobile ages for
the Pietra Rossa label. The
Vin Santo is produced in
the traditional manner in
very small casks that hold
from 11–22 gallons (50–
100 liters) and the wine is
allowed to settle naturally,
without being filtered.

🧀 Caseificio Cugusi Silvana

strada statale per Pienza
via della Boccia, 8
📞 0578 757558

Outstanding pecorino
cheeses matured for
varying periods, including
the dark kind typical of
Pienza, can be found
here. The fresh pecorino
is delectable, almost juicy
in texture, somewhere
between a caciotta and a
mozzarella. Also unusual
are the more mature types
for grating which are
always mellow and never
dry. There are also
excellent fresh cheeses
with arugula or walnuts.

🍇 Dei

località Villa Martiena
📞 0578 716878

At this small property, very
respectable Vino Nobile
di Montepulciano and
Rosso di Montepulciano
wines have been created.
Recently it has introduced
French vines which are
used in its Sancta
Catharina, a red made
from Syrah, Cabernet
Sauvignon, and Petit
Verdot together with
Prugnolo Gentile.
Purchases can be made
from Terra Toscana
(see p148).

ZUPPA DI LENTICCHIE CON FAGIANO

1¼ lb (500 g) lentils • 1 carrot • 1 onion, halved
• 1 stalk celery, halved • 2 cloves garlic • 1 sprig of winter
savory • 2 bay leaves • 1 pheasant • 4 oz (100 g) lardo
(pork fat), finely sliced • 1 sprig of rosemary • 1 sprig of
sage • extra-virgin olive oil • chicken stock • salt • pepper

Preheat the oven to 475°F (250°C). Put the lentils in a pan of water with the carrot, onion, celery, garlic, winter savory, bay leaves, a little oil, and salt. Cover and simmer over a moderate heat until the lentils are soft, adding more boiling water if necessary. Grease the inside of the pheasant with olive oil, tuck the sage and rosemary into the cavity, and season with salt and pepper. Lard it with the pork fat and tie with kitchen twine. Place in a greased roasting pan and roast for 30 minutes, turning and basting with the cooking juices from time to time. Remove the fat, return the pheasant to the oven, baste with the juices, and cook until golden. Remove the pheasant and chop the flesh. Deglaze the pan juices with a little oil and chicken stock. Drain the lentils, remove the vegetables, garlic, and bay leaves. Return the meat to the pan with the lentils. Warm through and serve.

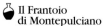

Fassati

località Gracciano
via di Graccianello, 3/A
0578 708708

Enhancing Vino Nobile was the objective of the Sparaco family, owners of the Fazi Battaglia firm that purchased this estate in 1969. Today the line includes red wines from traditional grape varieties. Of note is the Vino Nobile di Montepulciano Riserva Salarco, the Rosso di Montepulciano Selciaia, the Novello Fontago (from Prugnolo Gentile, Canaiolo Nero, and Mammolo grapes), the Chianti Le Caggiole, and Torre al Fante, this last one from Prugnolo Gentile alone, presented on various occasions as a "Super Tuscan."

Il Frantoio di Montepulciano

piazza Pasquino
0578 758732

This is a cooperative olive mill producing fine extra-virgin olive oil, in particular the product denominated IGP

Toscano, which is produced exclusively in this area from the output of the cooperative's 600 members.

Il Macchione

località Caggiole
via Provinciale, 12
0578 758595

The Swiss owner of this small estate, formerly a dentist, has done things properly. With meticulous care and attention he has produced a Vino Nobile di Montepulciano, Le Caggiole (also in a Riserva version), which has great texture and elegance. The main problem is laying one's hands on it, since the output never meets the

demand. Also excellent is the young Rosso di Montepulciano.

Enoteca Oinochoè

via Voltaia del Corso, 82
0578 757524

A wide range of the best Tuscan wines is sold in this wine shop, with nearly all the estates of the Montepulciano area represented. In addition to a line of regional products, including dessert wines such as Moscadello and Vin Santo, there are classics from Piedmont, Friuli, the Veneto, and Lombardy. A selection of Tuscan oils and vinegars is also sold.

Poliziano

località Montepulciano
Stazione, via Fontago, 11
0578 738171

Only in the best years is Vino Nobile di Montepulciano Vigna Asinone made. This wine shows its fine qualities early but also ages well. The same Sangiovese vines but from selected grapes from different vineyards are used to make Elegia, while Cabernet Sauvignon is used with a small amount of Merlot to make the much prized Le Stanze di Poliziano, a tribute to the famous poet and humanist. You can buy the wines from Enoteca Borgo Buio (0578 717497) and Enoteca Oinochoè, Montepulciano.

The winery at Fattoria Poliziano

The countryside around Pienza

🛥 Azienda Agricola San Benedetto

strada per Chianciano, 25
☎ 0578 757649

This estate, set amid very beautiful hills, sells fruit (peaches, apricots, quinces, and grapes) and organically grown plums and figs, natural jams (some made without sugar), and wild flower honey.

🍇 Terra Toscana

via Ricci, 14/A
☎ 0578 757708

Situated just 55 yards (50 meters) from Piazza Grande is this winery, representing 35 estates in the Montepulciano area. Many of them are essentially vineyards making only wine and grappa. The others have been chosen for the traditional quality of their regional produce: organically produced pasta, honey, truffles, and mushrooms from Monte Amiata, and excellent pecorino cheese. A daily selection of wines is offered for tasting.

🍇 Vecchia Cantina di Montepulciano

via Provinciale, 7
☎ 0578 716092

This winery is responsible for over half the volume of wine produced in the area. The extent of the vineyards, spread over a wide area, has made it possible to make some interesting wines, five or six altogether, that form a line of products marketed under the Cantina del Redi label. They include Vino Nobile di Montepulciano, Rosso di Montepulciano, and a Vin Santo, while the greatest success of the Vecchia Cantina trademark is its Vino Nobile di Montepulciano.

MONTERONI D'ARBIA (SI)

♠ Azienda Agricola Santa Margherita

località Ville di Corsano
via del Colle,711
☎ 0577 377101

This farm makes fresh and matured goat's milk cheese, packaged French-style in various forms. The cheeses are produced organically, and some of them are flavored with fresh herbs.

MURLO (SI)

🐝 Apicoltura Quercioli Sonia

piazza Benocci,
frazione Vescovado
☎ 0577 814255

All the local Sienese varieties of honey, including wild flower, arbutus, and sunflower are produced by this apiarist.

PIENZA (SI)

🍇 La Cornucopia

piazza Martiri
della Libertà, 2
☎ 0578 748150
🕐 daily

This wine store and gourmet shop sells all kinds of preserves from Tuscany and other Italian regions. It has a wide range of wines, mostly Tuscan labels but with a good selection from other regions. There are also grappas, mainly Tuscan, and various other national and international liquors. The store also sells a variety of vinegars.

SUGO DI CHIOCCIOLE (SNAILS IN SAUCE)

extra-virgin olive oil • 1 stalk celery, sliced • 1 carrot, chopped • 1 onion, chopped • 2 cloves garlic, sliced • 1 chilli, deseeded and chopped • sprig of rosemary • 1¼ lb (500 g) snails, prepared for cooking, boiled and removed from shells • 3½ lb (1.5 kg) tomatoes, peeled • ¾ lb (300 g) ground beef • chopped parsley • white wine • vegetable stock • salt

Heat some oil in a pan, add the vegetables, chilli, garlic, and rosemary, then add the beef and fry until the meat is browned. Add the tomatoes and salt and cook for 30 minutes. Add the snails and parsley and cook for another hour, adding a little wine and stock from time to time.

L'Enoteca di Ghino

via del Leone, 16
0578 748057
Sun

Since customers coming from abroad would be disappointed if they found this wine shop closed when they arrived, Ghino Poggianini decided to live over his shop so he could always be on call for his customers. He concentrates on wine and has over 2,000 labels, with wines ranging in price from a few euros up to several hundred a bottle. He even has fine old wines and collectors' items. The shop also has a selection of extra-virgin olive oils, which come from about 15 producers.

Forno Sacchi Danilo

via delle Mura, 16/18
0578 748545
Wed pm

This baker and pastry cook is renowned for Tuscan bread and traditional cakes, especially ricciarelli, *made from coarsely ground almonds. He also makes* ossi di morto *from almonds and egg whites, and other confections based on almond paste enriched with dried fruits and chocolate, such as* pinolati, pizzicotti, *and* serpe. Tarts *and* ciambelloni (ring-shaped cakes) *complete the product line.*

Caseificio Solp

località Poggio
Colombo, 40
0578 748645

Pecorino *matured for various periods is sold here, plus* caciotta *from a mix of cow's and ewe's milk, and* raviggiolo (see page 133) *made to order.*

RADICOFANI (SI)

Cooperativa Agricola Produttori latte Val d'Orcia

località Contignano
strada dell'Orcia, 15
0578 52012
Wed pm

This cooperative makes pecorino *and* ricotta *cheeses from the milk produced by its 80 members. It makes small* caciotte *from a mixture of cow's and ewe's milk.*

SAN QUIRICO D'ORCIA (SI)

Macelleria Bassi Raffaello

piazza della Libertà, 1
0577 895077
Wed pm

Raffaello Bassi chooses his beef from small farms which devote special care to the feeding of their animals. He sells Chianina beef and lamb

from local farms. His poultry and pork come from trusted breeders. He makes a variety of salumi, *sausages, and hams.*

SARTEANO (SI)

Prodotti Tipici

via Di Fuori, 73
0578 267020
Wed pm

The traditional food specialities of the area are stocked here – in particular, a wide range of pecorino *cheese.*

SINALUNGA (SI)

Barbieri

via Trieste, 102
0577 678256
Wed pm

Fresh meat, prosciutti, *and pork sausages all from the firm's own pigs are sold here.*

The Enoteca di Ghino at Pienza

RIVOLTI CON RICOTTA

extra-virgin olive oil • 2 cloves garlic • 1 handful parsley, chopped • 1 carrot, chopped • 1 onion, chopped • 1 stalk celery, chopped • ¾ lb (300 g) ground beef • 2 fresh sausages, chopped • 4 oz (100 g) prosciutto crudo, chopped • 2 glasses white wine • 1¼ lb (500 g) tomatoes, peeled • 1 egg • ¾ lb (300 g) plain flour • ¾ lb (300 g) cooked spinach, chopped • 8 oz (200 g) ricotta • 4 oz (100 g) grated Parmesan cheese • ground nutmeg • salt • pepper

In a large pan, heat some oil and fry the garlic, parsley, vegetables, and meat over a moderate heat until the meat is browned. Add the wine, cook until it evaporates, then add the tomatoes. Simmer gently for about 3 hours; stir frequently. Meanwhile, beat the egg and mix with 18 fl oz (500 ml) water and the flour to make a batter. Season with salt. Warm a pan that has been lightly greased with oil. Pour in a ladle of batter and smooth out to make a pancake. Cook on both sides until golden, then remove from the pan. Repeat until all the batter is used. Stir the spinach into the pan with some oil, the ricotta, half the Parmesan, and the nutmeg. Season. Use to fill the pancakes. Arrange in an ovenproof dish, cover with the meat sauce, sprinkle with the rest of the Parmesan, and cook in the oven at 350°F (180°C) until the cheese melts.

Purchases can be made at La Cornucopia di Pienza (see p148).

 **Frantoio Mazzarrini**

frazione Rigomagno
0577 663624

Excellent extra-virgin olive oil, typical of the Colline Senesi, is produced here. Their olive press works on a continuous system, keeping temperatures low, to the benefit of the oil.

 Pa. Ri. V.

frazione Guazzino
via XXV luglio, 4
0577 624061
Sun pm

There is a retail sales point for Tuscan bread and traditional Sienese cakes at this wholesale bakery.

TREQUANDA (SI)

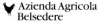 **Azienda Agricola Belsedere**

località Belsedere
0577 662307

Agriturismo *facilities are available at this farm. The lamb is certified organically produced,*

Tenuta Farneta

località Farneta
0577 631025

Although it has a significant range of Chianti, this estate's most successful wines are its Bentivoglio and Bongoverno, two finer wines from Sangiovese grapes aged by different methods. The Bentivoglio is matured for 16–18 months, partly in large casks and partly in small ones, while Bongoverno is matured for 21 months in small oak casks (barriques) alone. The difference in maturing methods and the use of barriques for maturing makes the Bongoverno the more expensive of the two wines.

Azienda Agricola Castello di Farnetella

località Farnetella
0577 663520

This firm's star product is its Chianti Colli Senesi, a quality wine which is

very good value for money. They also produce wines made from non-Tuscan vines that give their best here, such as the Pinot Nero, vinified in red to create Nero di Nubi, and Sauvignon Blanc, used in a richly perfumed and very elegant wine. The Castello trademark is marketed by the Fattoria di Felsina (see p114), Giovanni Poggiali's other estate at Castelnuovo Berardenga.

The Fattoria del Colle at Trequanda

as is the ricotta *and* pecorino, *made by hand from fresh milk. It has excellent pork and* salumi *which, though not certified organic, are produced completely naturally. In addition to Tuscan* prosciutto *and* spalla, *there is excellent* buristo, mortadella, soppressata, lombo, finocchiona, *and other meat specialities which can be purchased in small quantities.*

🌳 Azienda Agricola San Polo

Podere San Polo
☎ 0577 665321

Pecorino *of Pienza is matured for different lengths of time here. Some of the cheese is wrapped in walnut leaves and left to mature.*

🍇 Fattoria del Colle

via Torta, 7
☎ 0577 662108

The remarkable vivacity of one of Italy's leading oenologists (winemakers), Donatella Cinelli, guarantees quality and superior hospitality on this farm with its expanding agriturismo facilities. She devised the Movimento Turismo del Vino, which organizes Open Cellars – days when hundreds of the leading cellars all over Italy welcome visitors like guests to a party, with tastings, guided tours, and general pageantry. The brand-new osteria (inn) has tastings and sells excellent extra virgin olive oil, pecorino cheeses, truffles, Chianti DOCG, Vin Santo, a white wine from Traminer grapes, and other wines. Donatella Cinelli's policy is to produce everything in an environmentally friendly manner.

ZUPPA DI CECI (CHICKPEA SOUP)

10 oz (300 g) chickpeas, soaked overnight • extra-virgin olive oil • 2 cloves garlic • rosemary • 1 dessertspoon tomato purée • 10 oz (300 g) Tuscan bread • salt

Preheat the oven to 200°C (400°F). Cook the chickpeas in a pan of water until tender, then press through a sieve to purée them, adding the cooking water. In an earthenware pan, heat some oil and lightly fry the garlic, rosemary, and the tomato purée diluted in half a glass of warm water. Add the chickpeas to the pan, season with salt, and stir for some minutes to absorb the flavors. Slice the bread into croutons and brown them in the oven. Put them into soup plates and pour in the chickpea purée. Drizzle with a little olive oil and serve.

🏺 Cooperativa Agricola Il Lecceto

via della Trove
località Castelmuzio
☎ 0577 665358

This cooperative brings together 65 small olive growers from the village of Trequanda and the neighboring communes who produce an extra-virgin olive oil that is very typical of this area. The olive oil can also be purchased at the Pro Loco in Piazza di Trequanda.

🌾 Il Panaio di Cinzia e Roberto Mancini

via di Diacceto, 16
☎ 0577 662288
🕐 Wed pm

Traditional Tuscan bread and cakes typical of this region are sold here. The cantucci, pinolata, panforte, *and* schaiccciata di Pasqua *are all well worth trying.*

🐂 Macelleria Ricci

viale Rimembranze
☎ 0577 662252
🕐 Mon, Tues, Wed pm
🕐 Sun in summer

A fine butcher's shop with scrupulous hygiene methods, this is run by the Azienda Agricola

---

Trequanda. It sells the estate's Chianina beef. The complete cycle for producing meat from birth to butchering is covered, faithfully following traditional methods. Also on sale are pecorino *cheeses from the estate of Sorano (GR) which raises sheep and has its own dairy.*

FRITTATA FINTA

2¼ lb (1 kg) potatoes, cut into cubes • 1 sprig of sage •3 cloves garlic • extra-virgin olive oil • salt

Cook the potato cubes in salted boiling water until tender. Drain the potatoes, then purée by passing them through a vegetable mill. Chop the sage and garlic in the vegetable mill. Heat some oil in a nonstick frying pan, add the sage and garlic, and fry briefly over a gentle heat. Add the puréed potatoes, stirring constantly to blend them with the sage and garlic. Using a fork, press the mixture to shape it into a flat, compact cake. Continue cooking, carefully turning the cake over a number of times until it is golden brown on both sides. The potato cake can be eaten hot or cold.

MAREMMA
AND
MONTE
AMIATA

Maremma and Monte Amiata

THE MAREMMA AND MONTE AMIATA region is the wildest part of Tuscany. Impenetrable scrub, crisscrossed by foresters following the wild boar tracks, alternates with the majestic forests of Monte Amiata and coastal pine woods studded with rosemary – especially those in the breathtaking park, Monti dell'Uccellina. The area covers the province of Grosseto, including Monte Amiata which is the highest mountain peak in southern Tuscany, and some communes from the province of Siena. For centuries human activities have been adapted to nature, which has bestowed rich gifts but which has equally been very hostile in the marshlands. Maremma cattle are raised here, looking like buffaloes with their wide horns. This is a land of strong flavors, with game a specialty on every restaurant menu and plenty of fresh fish in the fishing harbors of Porto San Stefano and Castiglione della Pescaia and the prolific lagoon of Orbetello. Old traditions endure, and it is a region of organic farming and farmhouse hospitality, in a land where there are still open spaces for men and animals.

Maremma cattle were mainly bred as draft animals, as they gave little milk or meat, though their meat tastes good. Some herds, tended by *butteri* (cowherds), graze half-wild on the edge of the stunningly beautiful Parco dell'Uccellina.

Monte Argentario, once an island, is now a promontory, rich in vegetation, with two ancient fishing ports, Porto Ercole and Porto San Stefano. It is joined to the coast by two strips of land enclosing the lagoon of Orbetello.

Massa Marittima

Roccastrad.

Follonica

Montepescali

Vetulonia

Punta Ala

Castiglione della Pescaia

GROSSETO

Marina di Grosseto

Ombrone

Marina di Alberese

Monti dell'Uccell

Talamone

0 kilometers   10

0 miles   10

Alb

ORBETELL

Giglio

Porto San Stefano

Giglio Castello

Monte Argentario

Giglio Campese   Giglio Porto

Po Er

◁ **The medieval city of Pitigliano**

STAR ATTRACTIONS

- Massa Marittima (GR): Cathedral, ☎ 0566 902766
- Pitigliano (GR): Museo Palazzo Orsini, ☎ 0564 615568
- Sovana (GR): Etruscan necropolis, ☎ 0564 414303
- Ansedonia (GR): Museo di Cosa, ☎ 0564 881421
- Alberese (GR): Uccellina National Park, ☎ 0564 407098

HERBS

The abundance of herbs, cultivated in most gardens and frequently found growing wild in thickets and along the coast, has influenced the cuisine of all Tuscany. In the Maremma, foods are nearly always flavored with herbs, particularly game dishes.

The wild boar, which is an indigenous variety, is the symbol of the Maremma. Its flesh is much prized. A Wild Boar Festival is held at Capalbio in September (*see pp158–9*).

Monte Amiata's rugged sides are covered in chestnut woods rich with tasty mushrooms. The area is also famous for its fauna, especially the great variety of birds seen here.

Hare is a much-loved ingredient in many traditional Tuscan dishes. However, nowadays Italians usually have to import them as no hunters will give up the few hares they manage to shoot.

TRANSPORTATION

RAILROAD STATION

- Grosseto – Stazione FS
  0564 414303

- Orbetello – Stazione FS
  0564 860447

BUS STATION

- Massa Marittima
  0566 902016

Places of Interest pp164–169
Restaurants pp190–191

Wines

THE MAREMMA USED to be considered a difficult area which produced rather lackluster wines. Today there is a growing appreciation of some of its wines, and the Maremma now appears to be a land whose winegrowing potential needs exploring. It is claimed, in fact, that the very first Sangiovese vines grew here, though some experts favor the Chianti area. Sangiovese is the main component of the area's reds, which may contain small amounts of local red grapes, including Canaiolo, Ciliegiolo, Malvasia Nera, Alicante, and even Montepulciano. White wines are nearly always based on Trebbiano Toscano mixed with Greco, Grechetto, Verdello, Malvasia del Chianti, and the local Ansonica. Imported vines are now grown here: Cabernet Sauvignon and Merlot for reds and Pinot, Chardonnay, Sauvignon, and Riesling for whites.

BIANCO DI PITIGLIANO

This wine is named after the picturesque town in the heart of the area of production. The wine is produced from Trebbiano Toscano plus numerous other white grapes which can make up to 50 percent of the grape quantity. It has a pleasant, slightly bitter flavor and is ideal with artichokes and savory vegetarian dishes. There are also Superiore and spumante versions.

The Morellino di Scansano Riserva is aged for at least two years and goes well with game.

MONTEREGIO DI MASSA MARITTIMA

The name refers to several different types of wine. The Bianco is made from Trebbiano Toscano with up to 50 percent of other white grapes, including Malvasia di Candia. The Vermentino has to contain at least 90 percent of the grape from which it gets its name. Both wines make good accompaniments for delicate fish and vegetable dishes. The Rosato, the Rosso Riserva, and Rosso Novello contain at least 80 percent Sangiovese, plus other red grapes. The Rosato goes well with white meats, the Rosso with red meats and game. The Vin Santo, in ordinary and Occhio di Pernice versions, is perfect with honey cakes and sweet dry cookies.

MORELLINO DI SCANSANO

The vines on the hills have the advantage of being exposed to cool breezes. Sangiovese grapes (here known as Morellino) from the hills are mixed with local grapes such as Alicante to produce this red wine. Its distinctive spicy perfume, full-bodied flavor and good acidity make the wine an ideal accompaniment for food in a spicy marinade.

ANSONICA COSTA DELL'ARGENTARIO

A recent appellation for a white wine from Ansonica grapes, this has subtle fruity scents. Light and fresh, it is suited to delicate fish *antipasti* or vegetable first courses. There is a sweet Passito wine, which is excellent with sweet dry cookies. The wine produced on the island of Giglio has a brinier taste and a higher alcohol content: ideal with fish baked or cooked in a sauce.

CORATA DI CINGHIALE

4 oz (100 g) lardo (lard), diced • extra-virgin olive oil • 1 onion, chopped • heart, spleen, lights, and liver of a wild boar • 1 sprig of calamint • 1 sprig of wild thyme • 1 chilli, diced • 1¼ lb (600 g) ripe tomatoes, sliced • 4 fl oz (100 ml) red wine • salt

Put the *lardo* in a pan with some oil and the chopped onion. Cook until the onion is browned. Cut the heart, spleen, and lights into pieces and add to the pan with the calamint leaves, thyme, and chilli. Cook until the meat is browned on all sides. Add the tomatoes and season with salt. Simmer briskly for 10 minutes. Chop the liver into small pieces and stir into the pan. Pour in the wine and cook over a brisk heat for another 5 minutes.

PARRINA ROSSO

This wine is produced from 80 percent Sangiovese with some Canaiolo and Montepulciano grapes. It goes well with white and red meats, roulades and medium-ripe cheeses.

PARRINA BIANCO

This white wine is made with at least 50 percent Trebbiano Toscano grapes, with some Malvasia del Chianti and Ansonica. It is good with *antipasti* and vegetable or egg dishes.

The Rosato version, made from at least 70 percent Sangiovese grapes, is drunk young. It is ideal with shellfish in sauce.

The Riserva version is very good with traditional Tuscan roasted meats, especially roast guinea fowl.

OTHER WINES WORTH TRYING

The **Montecucco** DOC wine was first marketed with the 1998 vintage. There are four types : **Bianco**, **Vermentino**, **Rosso**, and **Sangiovese**. The **Rosso di Sovana** DOC (Sangiovese or Ciliegiolo) was first marketed with the 1999 vintage.

WINE TYPE	GOOD VINTAGES	GOOD PRODUCERS
Red Wine		
Morellino di Scansano	98, 97, 95, 90	Le Pupille di Magliano, Moris Farm di Massa Marittima
Monteregio di Massa Marittima	98, 97, 90	Massa Vecchia di Massa Marittima
Super Tuscans *(see p130)*	98, 97, 95, 90	Rascioni e Cecconello di Orbetello, La Stellata di Manciano, Moris Farm di Massa Marittima

Wild Game

ONCE THE MAREMMA was so well known as "wild boar country" that the protected native Italian breed of boar was called the "maremmana." Its meat was not just an attraction in restaurants, but was commonly eaten in homes, and there was a flourishing business of making wild boar *salumi* to sell as a souvenir of the region. Wild boar was not the only game to populate the inaccessible undergrowth of this area, either – there were also deer, hares, and porcupines. The foresters, who for decades were also poachers, caught whatever came their way, cooking it over a wood or charcoal fire and creating the robust recipes that were the origins of the game cuisine of today, rich not only in flavor but also in imagination.

**IL CINGHIALE
(WILD BOAR)**
A characteristic feature
of Tuscan cooking,
wild boar is now
found all over Italy.

**COSTOLETTE DI CINGHIALE
(WILD BOAR CHOPS)**
With wild boar chops, the gamey taste
is not pronounced, so they appeal to
those who prefer delicate flavors.
They are excellent grilled and
should be served rare.

SALSICCE (SAUSAGES)
Made from a mixture of finely
ground boar meat and pig fat,
these sausages are dried
before they are eaten.

POLPA DI CINGHIALE (CUBED BOAR MEAT)
"*In scottiglia,*" a rich stew of meat in a
sweet and sour sauce made with things
like olives and apples, is a traditional
Tuscan recipe. Leg or shoulder of wild
boar, cut into cubes, is a popular
ingredient for this sort of stew.

PROSCIUTTO DI CINGHIALE

Cured ham made from wild boar is drier and less fatty than the local *prosciutto* made from pigs, and is usually less salty and peppery. Traditionally, the fur was left on the skin, but EU regulations no longer allow this.

Small sausages (called cacciatorini*) are made from boar in the same way as from pork.*

SALAME DI CINGHIALE (WILD BOAR SALAME)

Salame made from lean boar's flesh and pig's fat (*pancetta* and *lardo*) is generally drier and has a stronger taste than pure pork salami.

Shoulder of venison is ideal for traditional Tuscan stews.

IL CAPRIOLO (VENISON)

Found all over Tuscany, venison was traditionally eaten only in a stew, *salmi*, or sauces for pasta. A newer idea is to grill the chops or pan-cook them with herbs, or roast a leg until rare.

OTHER GAME MEAT WORTH TRYING

Wild boar is also used to make **soppressate** (matured salami), often with chilli, **salt pork,** and **pork preserved in oil. Fallow deer** are common: they come from farms or graze in the open after being released into game reserves. The meat is usually stewed. A recent innovation is **salumi** (*salame, cacciatore, bresaoline*) made from **roe deer, red deer,** and **fallow deer**. These meats are also found preserved in oil with olives, garlic, chilli, and herbs. **Hare** is a basic ingredient of Tuscan cooking, but now, regrettably, it is impossible to find fresh hare. However, frozen ones are imported. Porcupine meat was once much prized, but it is now a protected animal.

Traditional Produce

THE LAGOON AT ORBETELLO adds wonderful variety to the foods produced in the province of Grosseto, making this region one of the richest in typical Tuscan foods. *Porcini* (cèpe mushrooms) can be found everywhere, especially on Monte Amiata, where picking them is a local industry. Amiata is one of the chestnut capitals of Italy. There is plentiful sea fish, with Porto San Stefano taking its catch mainly from the reefs called the Formiche di Grosseto and around the islands. With some of the Tuscany's largest olive presses in this area there is plenty of olive oil, and truffles, especially the March truffle *(see p18)*, are abundant along the coast.

MAREMMA GROSSETANA OLIVE OIL

Practically the whole province makes this type of olive oil. Communes producing significant quantities are Orbetello, Capalbio, and Magliano in southern Tuscany, and Massa Marittima in the north. These are fruity oils of average intensity, with herbal and, at times, floral fragrances. They have excellent fluidity, firmly structured flavors and a pungent aftertaste, sometimes with a tinge of bitterness.

TABLE OLIVES

Tuscany is not famed for its table olives, but the Santa Caterina variety, cured in brine while green, is sold throughout Italy. All the farmhouses still salt a small part of their olive crop, dry them in the oven to reduce the bitterness, and preserve them in oil, preferably Leccino oil. Olives are also an important ingredient in many of the traditional dishes of this area.

Carré (rib) of lamb is common in Tuscan restaurants. The chops are generally served in a mixed grill.

AGNELLO TOSCANO (TUSCAN LAMB)

The real Tuscan lamb comes from herds that move from pasture to pasture: they are driven from Maremma to Chianti, then Mugello and finally to Casentino. They are highly prized because the aromatic herbs they graze on flavors the meat.

WHAT TO SAMPLE

Large organically farmed estates, often offering farmhouse hospitality (*agriturismo*), make the Maremma one of the leading producers of **honey**, preserved **fruits**, and **vegetables**. The **pecorino** and **ricotta cheeses** are important, both in quantity and quality. The **table grapes** are excellent, as are the **peaches**, **pears**, and **yellow cherries** from Seggiano, and **walnuts** from Amiata. In addition to **game animals** there are numerous **wood pigeons** and **woodcock**.

ANGUILLA (EEL)

Excellent quality eels are abundant in the lagoon of Orbetello so there is no need to farm them in this area.

SCAVECCIO

2¼ lb 4 oz (1 kg) eels • flour • extra-virgin olive oil • 18 fl oz (500 ml) wine vinegar • 4 cloves garlic, sliced • 2 sprigs of rosemary • peppercorns • 1 chilli, deseeded and chopped • salt

Clean the eels and cut them into smallish pieces. Roll the pieces in flour. Heat the oil, add the eel pieces, and fry until tender. Dry the pieces on absorbent paper towels and then pack them into a clean jar. Pour the vinegar into a pan, dilute it with a glass of water, and add the chilli, the pepper, salt, garlic, and rosemary. Bring it to the boil, then pour it into the jar of eels, taking care to cover the pieces. Leave at room temperature for 3 or 4 days.

LE COPPIETTE (DRIED MEAT)

These are strips of meat salted, seasoned and hung up to dry on cords or slender sticks. The meat may be pork, beef, boar, mutton, donkey, or horse.

CEFALO OR MUGGINE (GRAY MULLET)

This fish is caught in the sea at the mouths of rivers and in lagoons. It is strongly associated with the resort of Orbetello in the middle of the Laguna di Orbetello, and is eaten both fresh and cured.

OTHER FISH WORTH TRYING

At Orbetello fish farms raise excellent **branzini** (sea bass) and **orate** (gilthead bream) in troughs fed either by warm subterranean waters or by seawater. **Latterini** (sand smelt), excellent fried or eaten raw with lemon and olive oil (*in carpione*), are caught in the sea, the lagoon of Orbetello, and the Lake of Chiusi. Fishing for **cieche** (elvers – eel's fry) is traditional at river mouths. **Anguilla sfumata** (smoked eel) is a Spanish dish adapted through the centuries to local tastes: the eels are marinated and then smoked. They are sautéed in extra virgin olive oil before eating. The **cefalo** (gray mullet) raised at Orbetello is smoked to a recipe of Spanish origin. For at least 1,000 years its roe has been dried and sold as **bottarga**, a custom that may be even older here than in Sardinia.

Wild Produce

LARDAIOLO ROSSO
(Hygrophorus russula)
In the late fall this white mushroom, with its burgundy-colored marbling and gills that are waxy to the touch, is very common under evergreen oak and Turkey oak. Foresters consider it one of the best mushrooms for preserving in oil.

SAMPHIRE
(Crithmum maritimum)
Samphire grows on cliffs. The narrow fleshy leaves, which have a distinct taste of iodine, are pickled before eating.

FUNGAGNELLO
(Lyophyllum fumosum)
Found in abundance in woods of broad-leaved trees, this mushroom often forms large tufts with numerous caps growing from a single base. It is much sought-after, despite the fact that it is very similar to a poisonous fungus. Firm and fleshy, it is eaten fried with garlic and parsley, in sauces and bottled in oil.

ACQUACOTTA CON I FUNGHI

extra-virgin olive oil • 2 cloves garlic, chopped • 2 stalks celery, sliced • 1¼ lb (600 g) mixed mushrooms, sliced • 14 oz (400 g) tomatoes, chopped • 1 small piece of chilli, chopped • 1¾ pints (1 liter) boiling water • 12 slices Tuscan bread • 6 eggs • grated mature pecorino • salt

Heat some oil in a pan and fry the garlic and celery until soft. Leave to cool, then add the mushrooms, and season with salt. Return the pan to the heat and cook until the mushrooms have released their water and it has evaporated. Add the tomatoes and chilli. Cook for 20 minutes. Pour in the boiling water and simmer for 10 minutes. Toast the bread and put it in a pan with the eggs and *pecorino*. Pour the boiling soup over them and serve.

CICCIOLE
(Pleurotus eryngii and Pleurotus ferulae)
These winter mushrooms grow underneath eryngo and giant fennel. Widespread in Puglia, Sicily, and Sardinia, where they are the most common mushrooms, they are well-known to the foresters of Tuscany, who usually eat them grilled.

CASTAGNOLO
(Tricholoma acerbum)
In the fall this mushroom can be found in the thick undergrowth and the chestnut woods of Monte Amiata. It has a distinctive yellowish cap with a flanged edge always turned downward. Tasting of unripe fruit, it is much in demand for preserving in oil.

ARISTA DI MAIALE ARROSTO

2¼ lb (1 kg) chine of pork • 2 cloves garlic, sliced • rosemary • fennel seeds • extra-virgin olive oil • salt • pepper

Make incisions in the meat, especially near the bone, and insert garlic, fennel seeds, and rosemary leaves. Tie sprigs of rosemary around the part opposite the bone. Season with salt and pepper and smear with oil. Leave for several hours. Preheat the oven to 325°F (160°C). Put the meat in a greased roasting pan containing a little water. Cook for about 1½ hours, turning frequently and basting with the juices.

RAMERINO (ROSEMARY)
(Rosmarinus officinalis)
Parts of the coastal scrub are overrun with wild rosemary, loved for its heady scent and robust flavor.

CIAVARDELLO
(Sorbus torminalis)
The fruits of this tree are called sorbs. Smaller and less well-known than those of the domestic tree, they ripen on the plant and can be picked and eaten from the tree. They are excellent for making gelatin desserts and liqueurs. They were one of the ingredients of some ancient Celtic beverages.

OLOLO BIANCO
(Amanita ovoidea)
Among the sand dunes and pine woods by the sea you can find this mushroom, which looks a large white ball. When it opens it turns into a sturdy white mushroom with a large bulb at the base of the stalk and a ring with the texture of butter. It is good fried with garlic and parsley. Always check with an expert before eating, as the genus includes some very poisonous species.

Places of Interest

THERE IS MUCH to explore in the wild Maremma region: great areas of woodland separate the villages and conceal farms of different sizes, often offering unusual gastronomic delights. The following establishments are all tried and tested, but if visiting the region you will probably be able to make other exciting discoveries of your own. Look out for handwritten notices offering agricultural produce. In this ideal setting, there is an increasing number of small properties run by enthusiasts of organic farming who breed cattle in the traditional way.

ALBINIA (GR)

 Tenuta La Parrina

località La Parrina
0564 862636

This farm produces a wide range of goods. Wine is an essential part of it, with the various types of Parrina including an enjoyable Bianco Podere Tinaro and Rosso Riserva. Among the other wines, there is an interesting Ansonica Costa dell'Argentario. The olive oil, honey, and cheese are very good. The farm has recently added agriturismo *to its attractions.*

 Azienda Bioagricola La Selva

località San Donato
0564/885669

Situated near the sea, this estate has agriturismo *facilities and sells fresh vegetables, especially tomatoes, various kinds of preserves, and both classic sauces and a modern, creative range.*

ARCIDOSSO (GR)

Agriturismo Sorripe

frazione Montelaterone
0564 964186

Agriturismo facilities with a restaurant are available at this estate. It produces and sells fresh and dried chestnuts, chestnut flour, and extra-virgin olive oil.

CASTEL DEL PIANO (GR)

Corsini

via Cellane, 9
0564 956787
Sat pm

For three generations the bread made here has been famous in southern

The farmhouse of the Tenuta La Parrina at Albinia

CALDARO

extra-virgin olive oil
• 1 onion, chopped • 1 chilli, chopped • 1 glass white wine • ½–¾ lb (250 g) tomatoes, peeled • ¾ lb (300 g) octopus, ready prepared, rinsed and cut into pieces • ¾ lb (300 g) squid, cleaned and sliced • 2 scorpion fish • 1 John dory • 1 weever • 1 gurnard • 1 sea bream • a few cockles • 6 prawns • ¾ lb (300 g) sliced conger eel • ¾ lb (300 g) sliced moray eel • 1 stale loaf of bread • 2 cloves garlic, halved • chopped fresh parsley • salt

Heat some oil in a large pan, add the onion and chilli, and cook until the onion has browned. Add the octopus and squid and cook until nearly tender. Stir in the wine, tomatoes, and a little water, cook briefly, then add the other fish and season with salt. Slice the bread and rub the slices with the garlic. Arrange the bread in soup plates. As soon as the soup is fairly thick, pour it over the bread slices to serve.

Tuscany. Both classic Tuscan and other Italian cakes are made from natural ingredients in the traditional way.

CASTIGLIONE DELLA PESCAIA (GR)

Enoteca Castiglionese di Luciano Lenzi

piazza Orsini, 18
0564 933572
Tues, Wed pm
Sun

A broad, carefully chosen range of the best Tuscan DOC and DOCG wines, including 200 types of Chianti, 70 of Brunello, and 20 of Vino Nobile can

be found here. Practically all the producers of Bolgheri are found here, plus other significant Italian wines. There is also honey and local preserves in oil, and a selection of carefully chosen varieties of olive oil.

FOLLONICA (GR)

🍇 Ilia Enogastronomia

via Bicocchi, 83/85
📞 0566 40093
🌑 Wed pm

Traditional rustic soups, tortelloni maremmani, and other stuffed pasta dishes are the specialities of this well-known delicatessen. It also offers a wide range of Tuscan wines and liquors. The store has an interesting selection of its own fresh and preserved produce and some imported goods. Recently it has opened a wine-tasting room.

🛢 Massai Drogheria e Pizzicheria

via Roma, 35
📞 0566 263269
🌑 Wed pm

This food shop has been in the same family certainly since 1867, when – as the proprietor likes to say – "round here it was all a swamp and the people lived in houses on stilts." Then, as now, it made its own classic Tuscan cakes and the recipes have not changed. Eugenio Massai selects the very best of the region's wines and foods. The delicatessen offers specialties made only from fresh produce and only to order.

 Pescheria Pallino

Mercato coperto di piazza XXIV Maggio
📞 0566 40322 ⏰ From Mon to Sat, am

Cellar of the Azienda Agricola Val delle Rose

This fish shop sells fresh fish from the nearby ports of Argentario and Castiglione della Pescaia as well as from its own fish farms.

GROSSETO

🌾 Corsini

via Matteotti, 12/14
📞 0564 416242
🌑 Only on Sun

This is the sales point for the Corsini bakery at Casteldelpiano.

🏛 Apicoltura Rossi

viale Caravaggio, 62
📞 0564 20459

An most original fragrant blackthorn honey is one of kinds of honey produced here. There are honey confectioneries in various flavors, including pine buds and woodland fruits.

🐓 Azienda Agricola La Tartaruga-Motta

località Banditella di Alberese
📞 0564 405105

The estate's main wine is Morellino di Scansano, also available in a Riserva version. The other wines are based on local vines: Giove, a red made from Ciliegiolo grapes alone; and white Tartaruga from Trebbiano and Ansonica with a little Chardonnay.

Its honey, made from blackthorn, sunflowers, and chestnut trees, is delicious.

🍇 Azienda Agricola Val delle Rose

località Poggio La Mozza
📞 0564 409062 🅶

This estate has been taken over by the Cecchi family, which has widened the production line with wines from other parts of Tuscany. In this case they have added Morellino di Scansano, in both the regular and Riserva versions.

TOTANI RIPIENI

1 loaf of bread • white wine • extra-virgin olive oil • 1 egg • 6 squid, cleaned • fresh thyme leaves • fresh parsley • 1 onion • 2 cloves garlic • 1 chilli • salt • pepper

Preheat the oven to 375°F (190°C). Mix a little wine and oil with the egg and season with salt and pepper, then soak the bread in it. Cut off the squid tentacles and chop together with the vegetables and herbs. Mix with the bread and use to stuff the squid. Close the opening with wooden toothpicks. Arrange in a dish, pour over a little more oil and wine, and bake for 20 minutes. Cool, then slice to serve.

A view of Moris Farms

 Fattoria Le Pupille

località Pereta
☎ 0564 409517

The policy of this estate is research and innovation without neglecting the area's classic wine, Morellino di Scansano, also produced in a Riserva version. One of their innovations is Saffredi (from Cabernet Sauvignon, Merlot, and Alicante). The estate's other produce includes various blends of extra-virgin olive oil and preserves bottled in the estate's own oil under the "Solo Maremma" brand name.

ISOLA DEL GIGLIO (GR)

 **Azienda Agricola Danei**

via G. Di Vittorio, 15
☎ 0564 863935

This is the island's only estate of any size. The wines are based on Ansonica. The dry wines come in two versions: a more rustic, traditional one and a mellower version called Fior d'Ansonica. The sweet Passito is a rare wine sold in small 18 fl ounce (500 ml) bottles. The estate's headquarters are at Orbetello, via Bolgia 53.

MAGLIANO IN TOSCANA (GR)

 **Azienda Agricola Mantellassi**

località Banditaccia
☎ 0564 592037

The best best wine here is the Morellino di Sansano Riserva. Also worth noting is the red Querciolaia, from Alicante grapes.

MANCIANO (GR)

Caseificio Sociale

località Piano di Cirignano
Podere Fedeletto
☎ 0564 609137
◐ Afternoons daily

Here you can find pecorino at various degrees of maturity from the Maremma's biggest cheese dairy.

Azienda Agricola La Stellata

via Fornacina, 18
☎ 0564 620190

Careful selection of the grapes guides the limited output of this small estate, which boasts one of the finest whites of the region, the Bianco di Pitigliano Lunaia. Also interesting is the Lunaia Rosso from Sangiovese, Ciliegiolo, and Montepulciano d'Abruzzo, as well as the Grappa Lunaia, distilled from the leftovers after white grapes have been pressed. Its agriturismo facilities include accommodation in apartments.

MASSA MARITTIMA (GR)

Azienda Agricola Massa Vecchia

località Rocche
Podere Fornace
☎ 0566 904144

This estate has two lines of production: one is innovative, embodied in La Fonte di Pietrarsa,

---

SCOTTIGLIA (MEAT AND TOMATO STEW)

extra-virgin olive oil • 3 stalks celery, chopped • 3 carrots, chopped • 2 onions, chopped • 3 cloves garlic , chopped ³/₄ lb (1.5 kg) mixed meat (chicken, duck, rabbit, pigeon, lamb), cut into large pieces • 14 oz (500 g) tomatoes • 18 fl oz (500 ml) red wine • 1 fresh chilli, chopped • salt

Heat some oil in a pan, add the celery, carrots, onions, and garlic, and fry lightly. Add the meat and fry until browned. Stir in the tomatoes, wine, chilli, and salt. Cover the pan and simmer until the meat is tender, adding hot water if it becomes too dry.

BUGLIONE

3¼ lb (1.5 kg) mixed cuts of lamb (such as leg, shoulder, and loin), cut into pieces • 1 onion, chopped • 2 cloves garlic, chopped • 1 fresh chilli, chopped • 1 sprig of rosemary, chopped • 1 glass Chianti • 1¼ lb (600 g) tomatoes, peeled • 1 loaf of homemade bread • extra-virgin olive oil • salt • pepper

Put the meat in a pan with some oil and the chopped onion, garlic, chilli, and rosemary. Brown the meat on all sides, then add the wine and cook until it evaporates. Add the tomatoes and dilute with a little hot water as the mixture cooks. When the meat is cooked, slice the bread and toast it. Dip the slices in the sauce and place them in a tureen. Pour the meat over them and serve.

from Cabernet Sauvignon; the other uses traditional vines for Le Veglie di Neri from Aleatico and a good Terziere from Alicante. Stone-ground wholemeal flour from an ancient local variety of grain is also produced.

 Moris Farms

località Curanuova
📞 0566 919135

One of the Maremma's most important estates by reason of its size – about 198 acres (80 hectares) of vines – and also by the praise lavished on its wines. They include a great Morellino di Sansano Riserva and an equally great younger Morellino. Also notable are the Avvoltore, from Cabernet Sauvignon and Sangiovese, and the Monteregio Rosso Moris. Its "La Mazzina" farm at Poggio Le Mozzine also produces extra-virgin olive oil.

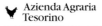 **Azienda Agraria Tesorino**

località Valpiana
📞 0566 55606

This farm's main product and the only one on sale to visitors is an excellent, traditional extra-virgin olive oil. For tourists using the agriturismo facilities, there is no restaurant, only accommodation in houses and apartments and vegetables in season.

MONTEMERANO (GR)

 **Enoteca Perbacco**

via della Chiesa, 8
📞 0564 602817
🔴 Wed, Thurs am
⭕ Sun

This is the sales point for the Caino restaurant next door. It stocks the wines

on the restaurant's very fine wine list, with about 900 labels and ample space devoted to Tuscany. There are also cakes made in the restaurant kitchens, pickles and preserves in oil, coffees, and olive oil.

MONTENERO D'ORCIA (GR)

🫒 **Frantoio Franci**

via Grandi, 5
📞 0564 954000

This olive mill produces a wide and varied range of oils: a light, fruity oil for fish and delicate salads; medium fruity oil for all uses; and Villa Magra, the estate's own blend, which is intensely fruity and ideal for typical Tuscan dishes. This last one comes only from the Montenero and Montalcino olive groves, the other two come from neighboring zones.

MONTEPESCALI SCALO (GR)

🫒 **OLMA – Collegio Toscano Olivicoltori**

località Madonnino, 3
📞 0564 329090

This mill presses the olives from its 870 member estates in the Maremma. The Madonnino, an excellent, intensely fruity oil with a distinctive bitter tinge, is bottled here.

The Azienda Agraria Tesorino at Massa Marittima

SPAGHETTI ALL'AMMIRAGLIA

*4¹/₂ lb (2 kg) mussels, scrubbed • 1¹/₄ lb (600 g) spaghetti •
extra-virgin olive oil • 2 cloves garlic, chopped
• ³/₄ lb (300 g) ripe tomatoes, sliced into strips • ¹/₂ fresh
chilli, deseeded and chopped • 1 oz (25 g) chopped fresh
parsley • salt*

Put the mussels in a pan with some water, cover and
cook until they all open. Remove the mussels from their
shells and strain the water. Cook the pasta. Meanwhile,
heat plenty of oil in a large pan and fry the garlic. Add
the tomatoes, chilli, parsley, and ¹/₂ glass of the mussel
water. Drain the spaghetti and add to the pan with the
mussels plus more of the water. Sauté briskly, stirring.

ORBETELLO (GR)

 Pescheria Covitto

via Volontari del Sangue, 15
0564 862632
Sun am

*Excellent fresh fish from
the Tuscan sea and the
lagoon, purchased daily
at local markets, is on
sale here.*

 Pasticceria Ferrini

via Carducci, 8/10
0564 867265
Tues
Sun

*With great bravura,
Rita Ferrini continues
the tradition begun by
her grandfather in this
quality patisserie, which
sells classic fresh cakes*
*and pastries, including
fruit parcels, apple tarts,
and ricotta cakes. Ice
creams are also sold.*

 Orbetello
Pesca lagunare

via Leopardi, 9
0564 860288
Mon to Sat, mornings
only

*Fresh fish from both sea
and lagoon is available
here, as well as various
preserved delicacies, such
as bottarga (gray mullet
roe), smoked fillets of gray
mullet, and smoked eel.*

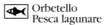 Azienda Agricola
Rascioni e
Cecconello

località Poggio Sugherino,
frazione Fonteblanda
0564 885642

*The Poggio Capitana
made from Sangiovese
and Poggio Ciliegio from
Ciliegiolo are wines that
merit attention because
of the skill of the estate's
owners in bringing out
the best in two traditional
Tuscan vines.*

PAGANICO (GR)

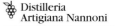 Distilleria
Artigiana Nannoni

Fattoria Aratrice
0564 905204
Sat.

*This distillery works for
outside customers and
also specializes in making
its own grappa from
Fragolino, a strawberry-
scented grape – the estate
has 62 acres (25 hectares)
of vines. However, its
most appealing products
are fruit vinegars (plum,
woodland berries, pear,
orange) matured in
small oak casks with the
addition of small amounts
of a distillate of the same
fruit and beech shavings.*

PITIGLIANO (GR)

 Cantina Cooperativa
di Pitigliano

via Nicola Ciacci, 974
0564 616133

The Castle of Montepò near Scansano

This cooperative winery has about 700 members producing the grapes for the Bianco di Pitigliano and Duropersico, a white from an ancient local vine. It also produces a kosher wine for Jewish communities.

 Macelleria Polidori

via Roma, 139
0564 616108
Wed pm
Sun

Fresh local meats are sold here, as well as their own salumi – the one made from wild boar is very popular. Other specialties include dried boar's meat (coppiette), which is called "carne secca" here; schiacciata, also from boar; and turkey ham, a specialty of Jewish origin.

SATURNIA (GR)

Macelleria Vito Passalacqua

via Ciacci, 4
0564 601269
Mon–Thurs only mornings; Fri, Sat all day

This butcher's shop sells high quality beef and lamb exclusively from local breeders. The firm's own hams and salumi are also extremely good.

SCANSANO (GR)

Fratelli Andreini

frazione Poggioferro
via Amiatina, 25
0564 511002

The Mignola extra virgin olive oil, exclusively from local olive groves, is an excellent oil with a medium fruity bouquet, fairly versatile and well suited to all local dishes.

POLLO ALLA CACCIATORA (HUNTER'S CHICKEN)

extra-virgin olive oil • 2 onions, chopped • 3 cloves garlic, chopped • 3 spring chickens, each cut into 8 pieces • 1 glass white wine • 10 oz (300 g) tomatoes, peeled • chopped fresh chilli to taste • salt

Heat the oil in a pan and lightly fry the onions and garlic. Add the chicken and brown on all sides. Pour in the wine and cook until it evaporates, then add the tomatoes, chilli, and salt. Simmer until the chicken is cooked, adding hot water if the sauce starts to dry out.

 **Azienda Agraria di Montepò**

Località Montepò
frazione Pancole
0564 580231

The winery is set in a 16th-century castle perched on an imposingly rugged hill top and surrounded by vines. The estate has been actively producing wine only since the 1995 vintage. It immediately made its name due to the quality of its Morellino di Scansano and Rosso San Venanzio. It also produces fine meat from its select breed of Apennine sheep.

Erik Banti

località Fosso dei Molini
0564 508006

This is one of the leading producers of Morellino di Scansano in the Ciabatta, a wine of excellent texture. The Aquilaia '95, made from Alicante and Morellino grapes, is also of interest.

Cantina Cooperativa Morellino di Scansano

località Saragiolo
0564 507288

This hardworking cooperative winery makes a very fine Riserva version of the Morellino di Scansano wine. The younger versions of two special blends, Vignabenefizio and Roggiano, are extremely good.

SORANO (GR)

 Azienda Agricola Sassotondo

frazione Sovana
località Pian di Conati, 52
0564 614218

Set amid meadows and attractive woods, this organically farmed estate offers agriturismo with bedrooms and a shared kitchen. It is a new wine producer (its first wine was the 1997 vintage), but already it guarantees a product of good quality. The underground cellar, hewn out of tufa, holds a Bianco di Pitigliano, a Rosso Franze from Sangiovese grapes matured in barriques, and a Rosso which, since the 1999 vintage, qualifies for the new DOC Rosso di Sovana label. The estate also produces good extra-virgin olive oil.

TRAVELERS' NEEDS

Restaurants

THE ADDRESSES THAT FOLLOW include the most celebrated restaurants in the region, as well as less well-known ones that are recommended for their careful presentation of the region's cuisine and its wines, in keeping with the philosophy of a gourmet guide. The list is based on such factors as the quality of the food and wine in relation to the kind of restaurant, the general standard of the food, and the exclusivity of the produce or the setting. For the price guide, €, see the inside back cover. The following criteria in each restaurant have been rated on a scale of 1 to 5.

Cellar: variety, quality, and originality of the wine list.
Comfort: level of service, space between tables, the view, location, ease of parking, standard and cleanliness of the restrooms.
Tradition: conformity to local traditions and skill in choosing local ingredients.
Q/P: quality:price ratio (value for money).
   Cooking pot: a special merit for restaurants offering classic regional dishes cooked to perfection, and for the quality of the preparation and faithfulness to local traditions.
   Gourmet rosette: a special merit mark for the quality of the cuisine, character of the dishes (authentically Italian), courteous staff, and good service.

FLORENCE, AREZZO AND CASENTINO

ANGHIARI (AR)

Locanda Castello di Sorci

località San Lorenzo
☎ 0575 789066
● Mon. €

This restaurant is run by Primetto, a friend of various well-known people, such as the political cartoonist Forattini, who drew the amusing wine labels. It is a must if you want to eat well and spend little. The tagliatelle is splendid, cut from enormous sheets of dough worked by the skillful chefs in a kitchen in full view of the customers.

CELLAR	●			
COMFORT	●			
TRADITION	●	●	●	●
Q/P	●	●	●	●

AREZZO

Antica Osteria L'Agania

via Mazzini, 10
☎ 0575 295381
● Mon. €

Home-style cooking covering all the regional traditions, with the emphasis on game, can be found at this restaurant in the center of Tuscany (don't miss the grifi con polenta*). The restaurant shows great flair in its use of wild herbs and the host is a great connoisseur of mushrooms (available from spring to winter).*

CELLAR	●	●		
COMFORT	●	●		
TRADITION	●	●	●	●	●
Q/P	●	●	●	●

Il Saraceno

via Mazzini, 6a
☎ 0575 27644
● Wed. €

You can enjoy authentic Arezzo cuisine at this small rustic restaurant. There is genuine Chianina beef, dishes of the local pork, game, mushrooms, and classic soups. Everything is made on the premises. The cellar has a fascinating selection of all the best Tuscan wines.

CELLAR	●	●	●	
COMFORT	●	●	●	
TRADITION	●	●	●	●
Q/P	●	●	●	●

BADIA TEDALDA (AR)

L'Erbhosteria del Castello

frazione Rofelle
☎ 0575 714017
● Wed. €

This charming trattoria *is in a village high in the Apennines between Tuscany and Emilia Romagna. Its specialties are mushrooms and truffles and dishes based on wild herbs, such as omelettes with borage, or pastry cakes with alpine yarrow or thyme. There are good first and second courses of game and excellent beef from local pastures. The desserts are homemade, and there are unusual wild herb and fruit liqueurs.*

CELLAR	●	●		
COMFORT	●	●	●	
TRADITION	●	●	●	●
Q/P	●	●	●	

BORGO SAN LORENZO (FI)

Ristorante degli Artisti

piazza Romagnoli, 1
☎ 055 8457707
● Wed. €€

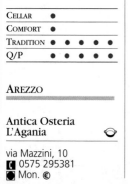

Here, in an elegant late 19th-century ambience, Tuscan dishes feature on the richly traditional menu. There is Chianina beef from Cecchini and Cinta Senese pork from Massanera. Note the tortelli di patate al ragù, a speciality of the Mugello. All the food is prepared on the premises.

CELLAR	● ●		
COMFORT	● ● ●		
TRADITION	● ● ● ●		
Q/P	● ● ●		

CAPRESE MICHELANGELO (AR)

Buca di Michelangelo

via Roma, 51
📞 0575 793921
🕐 Wed, Thu.
€

Real Tuscan mountain cuisine – unpretentious but with all the authentic flavors – is offered at this simple restaurant. The desserts merit a special mention: they are very simple, but utterly delicious. The restaurant offers accommodation in a number of hotel rooms.

CELLAR	● ●		
COMFORT	● ●		
TRADITION	● ● ● ●		
Q/P	● ● ●		

CARMIGNANO (PO)

Biagio Pignatta

località Artimino
via Papa Giovanni XXIII
📞 055 8718086
🕐 Wed, Thurs midday.
€€

Fairly traditional Tuscan cooking is served at this restaurant, with the meat grilled over a wood fire. It also serves some fish

dishes. The fresh pasta and delicious pastries are all made on the spot. The restaurant's wine list is good, with a careful selection of local vintages from which to choose.

CELLAR	● ● ●		
COMFORT	● ● ●		
TRADITION	● ● ●		
Q/P	● ● ●		

Da Delfina

località Artimino
via della Chiesa, 1
📞 055 8718074
🕐 Mon, Sun evening.
€€€

This restaurant offers traditional Tuscan cuisine with some occasional variations on the basic theme. The classic dishes are all here, from ribollita to pigeon. It is one of the few restaurants to make real panzanella. There are also good desserts. The wine list has a large selection of premium Carmignano wines. In the summer you can eat outside on the attractive terrace with a wonderful view over the nearby Tuscan hills.

CELLAR	● ● ●		
COMFORT	● ● ● ●		
TRADITION	● ● ● ●		
Q/P	● ● ● ●		

CASTELFRANCO DI SOPRA (AR)

Vicolo del Contento

via Ponte a Mandri, 38
📞 055 9149277
🕐 Mon, Tues, midday all weekdays.
€€€€

This restaurant is one of the jewels of the Valdarno. It serves excellent sea fish cooked in Mediterranean style and fine local meat.

Fresh seasonal produce is carefully selected for the fish and vegetable dishes (all dressed with the right oil). When they are in season, there are porcini, ovoli, *and artichokes.*

CELLAR	● ● ●		
COMFORT	● ● ● ●		
TRADITION	● ●		
Q/P	● ● ●		

FIESOLE (FI)

45 Piazzo Mino

piazza Mino da Fiesole, 45
📞 055 599854
🕐 Mon, midday
€€€€

This restaurant offers regional dishes and, in particular, fish dishes. There is an extensive wine list which includes useful and entertaining information. Wines are also sold by the glass.

CELLAR	● ● ● ●		
COMFORT	● ● ● ●		
TRADITION	● ●		
Q/P	● ● ●		

CORTONA (AR)

Tonino

piazza Garibaldi, 1
📞 0575 630500
🕐 Wed, Mon evening (always open in summer).
€€€

Elegant in Art Nouveau style, this restaurant serves a rich range of antipasti, first courses of pasta, and more or less classic second courses. The pasta, bread, and desserts are all homemade.

CELLAR	● ● ●		
COMFORT	● ● ● ●		
TRADITION	● ● ●		
Q/P	● ● ●		

EMPOLI (FI)

La Panzanella

via dei Cappuccini, 10
📞 0571 922182
🕐 Sun, Sat.
€€

*This is an old, family-run
Florentine trattoria with
period décor. The menu
features the traditional,
classic, hearty dishes of
real home cooking, such
as* stracotto alla fiorentina.
The pasta is homemade.

CELLAR	•	•			
COMFORT	•	•			
TRADITION	•	•	•	•	•
Q/P	•	•	•	•	

FLORENCE

Caffè Concerto

lungarno Cristoforo
Colombo, 7
📞 055 677377
🕐 Sun.
€€€

*Gabriele Tarchiani's
eclectic décor and the
"Nouvelle Cuisine" here
are a distinct innovation
compared with the
traditional style found in
other restaurants in the
area. The view of the river
Arno from the veranda
alone makes a visit
worthwhile. Meat and fish
are skillfully combined
with seasonal vegetables in
a choice of dishes. Their
desserts are especially
tempting.*

CELLAR	•	•	•	•	
COMFORT	•	•	•		
TRADITION	•				
Q/P	•	•	•	•	

Cibreo

via Andrea del Verrocchio
(corner with via dei Macci)
📞 055 2341100
🕐 Sun, Mon
€€€€€

*This famous, elegant
restaurant belongs to
Fabio Picchi, who is very
skillful at enhancing quite
simple, traditional Tuscan
dishes with his own
special touch (there is no
printed menu). The wide-
ranging and richly
inventive Tuscan dishes
are made on the premises
from quality ingredients.
Note the cuttlefish and
other seafood dishes.
The desserts are especially
attractive. There is an
international wine list
with plenty of Tuscan
wines. The restaurant's
annex, the Vineria del
Cibreino, is popular and
always crowded due to its
very reasonable prices
(though the cooking is of
the same standard).*

CELLAR	•	•	•	•	
COMFORT	•	•	•	•	
TRADITION	•	•	•	•	
Q/P	•	•	•		

Cinghiale Bianco

borgo San Jacopo, 43r
📞 055 215706
🕐 Wed. €€

*This small restaurant is
near the Ponte Vecchio on
the Arno's "rive gauche."
Try the first courses dressed
with vegetables and good
quality olive oil. The
bistecca alla fiorentina
and* tagliata di manzo
*are both excellent. If you
plan to go with someone
special, book the table in
the romantic niche on the
second floor.*

CELLAR	•	•			
COMFORT	•	•			
TRADITION	•	•	•	•	•
Q/P	•	•	•	•	

Del Carmine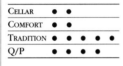

piazza del Carmine, 18
📞 055 218601
🕐 Sun. €

*All the classic Florentine
dishes, with occasional
detours to other Italian
provinces, are served here.
The ribollita is notable,
as are the various other
soups. There are first
courses of pasta, and
fish is served on Friday.
Don't miss the Florentine-
style tripe.*

CELLAR	•	•			
COMFORT	•	•	•		
TRADITION	•	•	•	•	•
Q/P	•	•	•	•	

Il Latini

via dei Palchetti, 6r
📞 055 210916
🕐 Mon. €€

*The setting here is a
typical old-fashioned
trattoria with Florentine
and Chianti dishes, such
as* ribollita, pappa col
pomodoro, *spelt soup,
pork, rabbit, and
Chianina steaks. Some of
the ingredients come from
local suppliers, and the
wine and oil come from
the owners' estate. The
wine list has a selection of
good Tuscan labels, and
there is a house wine
served in flasks.*

CELLAR	•	•			
COMFORT	•	•	•		
TRADITION	•	•	•	•	•
Q/P	•	•	•	•	

Le Mossacce

via del Proconsolo, 55r
📞 055 294361
🕐 Sat, Sun. €

*The menu prices are not
excessive when you think
of the delicious Florentine
food being served here.
The restaurant only seats
35 at a time, and its name
alludes to the rapid
rotation of diners as they
give up their places to
others waiting their turn.
A good house wine
(Chianti Colline
Fiorentine) is served in
flasks and other Chianti
labels are also available.*

CELLAR	●				
COMFORT	●				
TRADITION	●	●	●	●	●
Q/P	●	●	●	●	

Pane e Vino

via San Niccolò, 70, a/r
055 2476956
Sun, midday.
€€€

As the name suggests, the wine here is particularly good. The restaurant has a wide range of very attractive regional dishes that are far from predictable. There is a choice selection of cheeses and the desserts are all prepared on the premises.

CELLAR	●	●	●	●
COMFORT	●	●	●	
TRADITION	●	●	●	
Q/P	●	●	●	

Enoteca Pinchiorri

via Ghibellina, 87
055 242777
Sun, Mon, Tue lunch.
€€€€€

Giorgio Pinchiorri and Annie Feolde fully deserve their worldwide fame for this restaurant. Every detail of the setting and service – its elegance, quality, and sheer cachet – put it at the very top of the class in Italy and the rest of Europe. The cuisine is delectable and full of character, the ingredients are the very best the market offers, the cellar is among the finest in Europe. And the bill will reflect this.

CELLAR	●	●	●	●
COMFORT	●	●	●	●
TRADITION	●			
Q/P	●			

Ruggero

via Senese, 89r
055 220542
Tues, Wed. €

A classic Florentine trattoria in both the décor and the menu, which includes traditional crostini with regional salumi, various soups and minestroni, ribollita and pappa col pomodoro, with old-fashioned stews.

CELLAR	●				
COMFORT	●	●			
TRADITION	●	●	●	●	●
Q/P	●	●	●		

FUCECCHIO (FI)

Le Vedute

frazione Ponte a Cappiano
via Romana Lucchese, 121
0571 297498
Mon. €€€€

Quality fish dishes are the backbone of the menu, alternating with meat, and in particular game, all following the cycle of the seasons – mushrooms and truffles come in October, spring brings fresh vegetables, and so on. There is a careful selection of salumi – a wider choice in winter – and cheese. Pasta and desserts are homemade.

CELLAR	●	●	●	
COMFORT	●	●	●	
TRADITION	●			
Q/P	●	●	●	

LASTRA A SIGNA (FI)

Sanesi

via Arione, 33
055 8720234
Mon, Sun evening.
€€

This historic restaurant in a lovely rustic setting has been in the same family for 170 years. It serves classic Tuscan home cooking, especially meat grilled over charcoal, such as bistecca alla fiorentina accompanied by beans.

CELLAR	●	●			
COMFORT	●	●			
TRADITION	●	●	●	●	●
Q/P	●	●	●	●	

MARRADI (FI)

Cucina il Camino

viale Baccarini, 38
055 8045069
Wed. €€

Lovers of quality home cooking will enjoy this restaurant. The dishes are not always strictly Tuscan because geographically this is in Romagna. Worthy of note are the mushrooms in season, fresh pasta, meat roasted in the wood-burning oven, and tasty desserts made with the celebrated local chestnuts.

CELLAR	●	●			
COMFORT	●	●	●		
TRADITION	●	●	●	●	●
Q/P	●	●	●		

PALAZZUOLO SUL SENIO (FI)

Locanda Senio

via Borgo dell'Ore, 1
055 8046019
Tues, Wed, midday on weekdays. €€€

Sample traditional dishes of wild herbs and fruits, as well as ancient recipes handed down from memory by the old folks of the town, in this very interesting and original restaurant. Set in a 14th-century town in the Mugello, it uses local ingredients and the basic dishes are creatively assembled. There are some pleasant rooms available.

CELLAR	●	●	●		
COMFORT	●	●	●	●	
TRADITION	●	●	●	●	●
Q/P	●	●	●		

PRATO

Enoteca Barni

via Ferrucci, 22
📞 0574 607845
● Sun, Sat midday.
€€

This pleasant, cheerful restaurant grew out of the success of a delicatessen, which at first offered meals only at midday. For several years now it has opened in the evenings as well and has retained its lively atmosphere. Three young chefs create tasty meat and fish dishes using plenty of fresh ingredients (including some unusual game). Everything is made on the premises, including the bread, fresh pasta, and desserts. There is an international wine list.

CELLAR	●	●	●	●
COMFORT	●	●	●	●
TRADITION	●	●		
Q/P	●	●	●	

Osvaldo Baroncelli

via Fra Bartolomeo, 13
📞 0574 23810
● Sun, Sat midday.
€€€€

Good food is served in elegant surroundings at this attractive restaurant. They use good-quality meat and fish, some from outside the region but mostly local. Many of the dishes are inspired by traditional Tuscan ones. The desserts are delicious.

CELLAR	●	●	●	
COMFORT	●	●	●	
TRADITION	●	●		
Q/P	●	●	●	

Il Piraña

via Valentini, 11
📞 0574 25746
● Sun, Sat midday.
€€€€

Fish dishes are the speciality of this popular restaurant. The simple Mediterranean-style dishes rely on high-quality fresh ingredients for their excellent flavor. The homemade desserts are equally good.

CELLAR	●	●	●
COMFORT	●	●	●
TRADITION	●		
Q/P	●	●	●

PRATOVECCHIO (AR)

Accaniti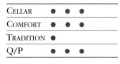

via Fiorentina, 14
📞 0575 583345
● Tues. €

This is one of the rare restaurants with the courage to offer porcini *exclusively when they are found locally. The home-style cooking uses local ingredients, prepared in a way that maintains the wholesome quality.*

CELLAR	●	●		
COMFORT	●	●		
TRADITION	●	●	●	●
Q/P	●	●	●	

Quattro Cantoni

via Uffenheim, 10
📞 0575 582696
● Mon. €

This trattoria *serves good traditional cooking. There is a wide choice of first course dishes, including* tagliatelle, tortelli di patate, *and* tortelli di carne, ravioli di magro *(ravioli stuffed with spinach and ricotta),* gnocchi, *and* strozzapreti. *For a second course there are roasted and grilled meats.*

CELLAR	●	●		
COMFORT	●	●		
TRADITION	●	●	●	●
Q/P	●	●	●	

SANSEPOLCRO (AR)

Balestra

via dei Montefeltro, 29
📞 0575 735151
● Mon, Sun evening.
€

This is a classic Tuscan restaurant in a modern setting. The restaurant gets its name from the fact that all the members of the family who own it are expert marksmen with crossbows. Creative cooking enhances the regional ingredients (plus a few from neighboring Umbria and Marche). The pasta is handmade and fresh Italian mushrooms and truffles are served when they are in season.

CELLAR	●	●	●	
COMFORT	●	●	●	
TRADITION	●	●		
Q/P	●	●	●	

Da Paola e Marco Mercati all'albergo Oroscopo

località Pieve Vecchia
via Togliatti, 68
📞 0575 734875
● Sun, midday.
€€€€

Set in a lovely 19th-century building, this small restaurant has a rustic yet elegant quality. The fine cuisine consists partly of regional dishes and partly of innovative modern recipes. The desserts are excellent, and there is a choice wine list, which includes some notable wines. The restaurant also has some attractive rooms available.

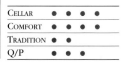

CELLAR	●	●	●	●
COMFORT	●	●	●	●
TRADITION	●	●		
Q/P	●	●	●	

Da Ventura

via Aggiunti, 30
[C] 0575 742560
[●] Sat.
€€

Reflecting influences from three different regions – Tuscany, Romagna, and Umbria – this restaurant serves simple, tasty traditional dishes from all their cuisines. Alongside Chianti beef there is suckling pig and shin of pork, freshly made pasta (wonderful tagliolini *with truffles), and good desserts. The restaurant has accommodation in six bedrooms.*

CELLAR	●	●		
COMFORT	●	●	●	
TRADITION	●	●	●	●
Q/P	●	●	●	●

TERRANUOVA BRACCIOLINI (AR)

Ristorante Pin Rose

località Cicogna
via La Pineta, 38
[C] 055 9703833
[●] Mon, Tues.
€€€

The owner belongs to a family of fish wholesalers, and this restaurant specializes in Tuscan fresh fish dishes. The huge restaurant is situated in an enormous wood of ancient pine and oak trees. The fish comes mostly from Porto Santo Stefano, Piombino, and Viareggio. The cellar has a good selection of wines from the Veneto, Friuli, Alto Adige, Tuscany, and Sardinia.

CELLAR	●	●		
COMFORT	●	●	●	
TRADITION	●			
Q/P	●	●	●	

LUNIGIANA, GARFAGNANA AND VERSILIA

CAMAIORE (LU)

Ristorante Conca Verde da Tiziano

via Misciano, 22
[C] 0584 984700
[●] Tue. €€

Following the success of his wife's cooking for their wine shop, Encota Nebraska, the owner embarked on this restaurant. The menu combines the authentic, traditional specialities of Lucca with a more innovative cuisine.

CELLAR	●	●	●
COMFORT	●	●	●
TRADITION	●	●	●
Q/P	●	●	●

Ristorante Emilio e Bona

località Lombrici, 22
[C] 0584 989289
[●] Mon. €€€

In an old olive mill by a mountain stream, Tuscan and classic Italian dishes are served. The food is prepared with a light touch, and the meals finish with a few carefully chosen homemade desserts. The wine list is Tuscan and Italian with some French.

CELLAR	●	●	●
COMFORT	●	●	●
TRADITION	●	●	●
Q/P	●	●	●

Ristorante Vignaccio

località Santa Lucia
via della Chiesa
[C] 0584 914200
[●] Wed. €€

Flavorsome traditional dishes are served at this restaurant in the hills. Classic regional specialties are combined with other dishes made from quality Italian and international ingredients. A rich selection of Italian and French cheeses and excellent desserts follows. The cellar has many delightful regional wines.

CELLAR	●	●	●
COMFORT	●	●	●
TRADITION	●	●	●
Q/P	●	●	●

CAPANNORI (LU)

La Cecca

località Coselli
[C] 0583 94130
[●] Mon, Wed evening.
€€

Here, the dishes take their theme, in rotation, from Garfagnana and Lucchesia, with rustic dishes like biroldo *(blood pudding) or a polenta of chestnut flour and other more elaborate dishes. There is meat grilled over charcoal, good* salumi, *and rural desserts. The wines are mainly regional.*

CELLAR	●	●		
COMFORT	●	●	●	
TRADITION	●	●	●	●
Q/P	●	●	●	●

CARRARA

Da Venanzio

località Colonnata
[C] 0585 758062
[●] Thurs, Sun evening.
€€€

The cuisine here is mainly regional and confined to seasonal produce. Everything is made in the kitchens, including a rich selection of desserts. The cellar is mostly Tuscan

*with various notable
Italian or foreign wines.
But Venanzio is above all
the undisputed king of
lardo: his lardo di
Colonnata, seasoned with
herbs is world famous.
Venanzio cures his beef
for the carpaccio in brine
left over from the lardo.*

CELLAR	●	●	●	●	
COMFORT	●	●	●		
TRADITION	●	●	●	●	
Q/P	●	●	●	●	

CUTIGLIANO (PT)

Trattoria da Fagiolino

via Carega, 1
☎ 0573 68014
● Wed, Tues evening.
€€

*Classic Tuscan mountain
dishes are served here,
with mushrooms and
game in season, plus kid
and steak. There are first
courses with homemade
pasta and various soups.
The menu finishes with a
wide range of desserts.*

CELLAR	●	●			
COMFORT	●	●			
TRADITION	●	●	●	●	●
Q/P	●	●	●	●	

FORTE DEI MARMI (LU)

Lorenzo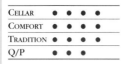

via Carducci, 61
☎ 0584 84030
● Mon. €€€€

*This elegant restaurant,
run with passion and skill
by Lorenzo Viani, is a
shrine to Tuscan and
Italian gourmets. All the
ingredients are
exceptional, especially the
fish which Viani gets twice
daily from trusted sources.
The chef, who does not
lack creativity when
needed, often holds back
to keep things simple to*

*highlight the freshness
and quality of the food.
There are specialties like
"bavette sul pesce,"
spaghetti with tiny squid
scented with sage, or
bocconcini di pescatrice
with slivers of artichokes.
For meat-lovers there is
equally good fare. The
wine list is one of the
finest in Italy.*

CELLAR	●	●	●	●	●
COMFORT	●	●	●	●	
TRADITION	●	●	●		
Q/P	●	●	●		

LUCCA

Buca di Sant'Antonio

via della Cervia, 1/3
☎ 0583 55881
● Mon, Sun evening.
€€

*There was an inn on this
site as long ago as the
17th century. Nowadays
it is an elegant rural
restaurant featuring
regional specialties with
certain innovations. The
meat and vegetable dishes
are imaginative, and the
desserts reflect the town's
gastronomic traditions.
There is a good choice of
wines at reasonable prices.*

CELLAR	●	●	●	●	
COMFORT	●	●	●	●	
TRADITION	●	●	●	●	
Q/P	●	●	●		

Canuleia

via Canuleia, 14
☎ 0583 467470
● Sun. €

*This very attractive
restaurant is in an
ancient vault behind
piazza dell'Anfiteatro.
Great care is evident in
the choice of ingredients,
from the vegetables to the
oil, and from the breads to
the meat. The dishes reflect
the traditions of Lucca with
some modern touches.*

CELLAR	●	●			
COMFORT	●	●	●		
TRADITION	●	●	●	●	
Q/P	●	●	●		

Da Giulio - in Pelleria

via delle Conce, 45
☎ 0583 55948
● Sun, Mon. €

*The menu here features
the classic dishes of
Lucca, starting with
antipasti of crostini,
salumi, and other rustic
specialties, and
continuing with local
minestre and soups,
meat and game, almost
all in rustic style.*

CELLAR	●	●			
COMFORT	●	●			
TRADITION	●	●	●	●	
Q/P	●	●	●	●	●

MONTIGNOSO (MS)

Il Bottaccio

via Bottaccio, 1
☎ 0585 340031 €€€€€

*An enchanting Relais &
Châteaux (historic hotel),
set in an old oil mill,
has a restaurant which
is acquiring an
increasingly leading role
thanks to the quality and
character of the cuisine.
The menu includes fresh
seafood, good meat
(especially the game),
and extremely good
cakes and pastries.*

CELLAR	●	●	●	●	
COMFORT	●	●	●	●	●
TRADITION	●	●			
Q/P	●				

PESCIA (PT)

Cecco

viale Forti, 96
☎ 0572 477955
● Mon. €€

This restaurant has always been a shrine to the green asparagus of Pescia, the most prized in all of Tuscany – but only in springtime. The rest of the year try the local mushrooms, truffles, Sorana beans, and whatever else the season offers. Everything is made on the premises and there is a marked preference for local produce. The house specialty is chicken "al mattone." The wine list is largely Tuscan with some whites from Friuli.

CELLAR	●	●			
COMFORT	●	●	●		
TRADITION	●	●	●	●	●
Q/P	●	●	●	●	

PIETRASANTA (LU)

L'Enoteca Marcucci

via Garibaldi, 40
☎ 0584 791962
● Mon, midday daily.
€€€

This is somewhere half-way between a wine bar and a restaurant. It presents simple country and seafood dishes with a regional accent, chosen especially to accompany the excellent wines in the cellar.

CELLAR	●	●	●	●	●
COMFORT	●	●			
TRADITION	●	●	●		
Q/P	●	●	●	●	

PISTOIA

Trattoria dell'Abbondanza

via dell'Abbondanza, 10/14
☎ 0573 368037
● Wed, Thu lunch. €

Here you will find Tuscan cuisine prepared the old way – no cream or frozen foods, and only seasonal produce fresh from the kitchen garden. Among the regular dishes are bollito misto, chicken and fried vegetables with good oil, and fish (on Fridays). The desserts are homemade. There is no wine list, just the house red and white.

CELLAR	●				
COMFORT	●	●	●		
TRADITION	●	●	●	●	●
Q/P	●	●	●	●	●

Il Castagno di Pier Angelo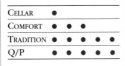

località Piteccio
via del Castagno, 46/b
☎ 0573 42214. ● Mon, midday on weekdays.
€€€

Set in a glade of chestnut trees, this restaurant provides good service with its three menus, featuring meat, fish, and creative dishes. They are all based on traditional cuisine, but with innovative touches. The imagination shown in the fish cuisine is truly admirable, as is the originality shown in finding ingredients from Tuscany and the rest of Italy. The wine list prices are reasonable.

CELLAR	●	●	●	●	
COMFORT	●	●	●	●	●
TRADITION	●	●	●		
Q/P	●	●	●	●	

PODENZANA (MS)

La Gavarina d'Oro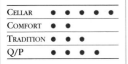

via Castello, 13
☎ 0187 410021
● Wed. €

This is the right place to sample the famous panigacci, once a simple dish of Lunigiana, now a traditional delicacy: focaccine cooked between two testi (earthenware pans) and flavored with pesto or mushrooms. There is also chargrilled meat, testaroli, and other fresh pasta and simple traditional dishes.

CELLAR	●				
COMFORT	●				
TRADITION	●	●	●	●	●
Q/P	●	●	●	●	●

PONTE A MORIANO (LU)

La Mora

via Sesto di Moriano
☎ 0583 406402
● Wed. €€€

La Mora means "the stopover," and this is the place to stop if you want to eat good Tuscan food or simply eat and drink well. The well-established restaurant is Sauro Brunicardi's jewel (his family has run it since 1867). He is a passionate lover of his region and of good wine. This is apparent in the excellent cellar which has everything from the Lucca area and much from the other regions of Italy and the world, as well as a distinctive choice of liquors and liqueurs. The Garfagnana cuisine – modernized where necessary – is equally good and the restaurant has an elegant, hospitable atmosphere. Try the gran farro *and local porcini.*

CELLAR	●	●	●	●
COMFORT	●	●	●	●
TRADITION	●	●	●	●
Q/P	●	●	●	

UZZANO (PT)

Mason

via Parri, 56
☎ 0572 451363
● Wed, midday Sat.
€€€

The chef's skill is displayed to best advantage in the fish and game bird dishes in this restaurant, which is tucked away in the hills between Pescia and Montecatini. The cuisine is traditional, local Tuscan but it has a very distinctive personal touch that serves to show off the produce at its best.

CELLAR	●	●	●		
COMFORT	●	●	●		
TRADITION	●	●	●	●	
Q/P	●	●	●		

VIAREGGIO (LU)

Gusmano

via Regia, 58
📞 0584 31233
🔴 Tues, lunchtime on weekdays in summer.
€€€

Situated in the heart of Viareggio, this pleasant restaurant is distinguished by its excellent fish cuisine. Importantly for a seafood restaurant, fresh fish is delivered twice a day thanks to the good rapport between the restaurant owner and the fishermen who cast their nets in the waters off Viareggio.

CELLAR	●	●	●	
COMFORT	●	●	●	●
TRADITION	●	●	●	
Q/P	●	●	●	●

Oca Bianca

via Coppino, 409
📞 0584 388477
🔴 Tues, lunchtime.
€€€€

Upstairs with a view over the sea and the harbor, in a luxurious setting with a very distinctive décor, is a traditional restaurant. The cuisine is mainly seafood with a tried and tested menu. The fish is local, the

cellar huge (2,000 wines) and excellent. Downstairs at the Bistrot dell'Oca the mood changes. There are wines by the glass, great dishes of oysters and other French-style raw shellfish, steam-cooked seafood, Catalan-style lobsters, soups according to the season, and a choice of over 100 international cheeses, all at very reasonable prices.

CELLAR	●	●	●	●	●
COMFORT	●	●	●	●	●
TRADITION	●	●	●		
Q/P	●	●	●		

Romano

via Mazzini, 120
📞 0584 31382.
🔴 Mon.
€€€€

This is one of the best seafood restaurants in Italy. Romano and Franca Franceschini cook wonderful dishes from high-quality fresh fish. Their menu is a stunning mixture of simplicity and creativity, with harmonious colors, aromas, and accompaniments. Trying to choose between stuffed baby squid, sparnocchi *(mantis shrimp) with honey, or* cacciucco alla viareggina *(Viareggio-style fish soup) is hard because all the dishes are an inspiration. The excellent extra-virgin olive oil and perfectly fresh vegetables only serve to enhance the dishes. The style of the desserts is just as good, and the quality and variety of the cellar puts it on the same level. Try the Montecarlo wine from the restaurant's own vineyard, a white well above average.*

CELLAR	●	●	●	●	●
COMFORT	●	●	●	●	●
TRADITION	●	●	●		
Q/P	●	●	●		

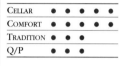

PISA AND LIVORNO

BIBBONA (LI)

La Pineta

località Marina di Bibbona
via dei Cavalleggeri, 27
📞 0586 600016
🔴 Mon. €€€

The owners of this seafront restaurant have no fewer than three fishing boats in the family, which augurs well for the fresh fish which is its staple fare. The fish comes to the table perfectly fresh in simple dishes, accompanied by equally fresh vegetables. Other dishes on the menu are either made on the premises or by local producers – even the mayonnaise is made on the spot with extra-virgin olive oil. The cellar contains a wide selection of mostly Italian wines with the odd French label.

CELLAR	●	●	●
COMFORT	●	●	
TRADITION	●	●	●
Q/P	●	●	●

CAPOLIVERI – ELBA (LI)

Il Chiasso

vicolo Sauro, 13
📞 0565 968709. 🔴 Tues, lunchtime. 🔲 April-Oct.
€€€

The layout of this restaurant is unusual. Situated in a small street in the town, it has tables set outside and two rustic dining rooms at the side. The affable host, Luciano, serves octopus with potatoes (minestrone di polpo), *Livorno-style mullet in a pot, spaghetti with amberjack roe or served* alla Chiasso *(with sea urchins, prawns, and*

tomatoes), and other seafood dishes, with both local and regional recipes.

CELLAR	● ● ●			
COMFORT	● ● ●			
TRADITION	● ● ● ● ●			
Q/P	● ● ● ●			

Da Pilade

località Marina di Mola
🄲 0565 968635
⭘ Easter–Oct. €€

Tuscan fish and meat dishes are served here – grilled meat, game in season, fresh fish, and the island's mushrooms. Desserts include sorbets and schiacciata (fruit bread). This is a hotel as well as a restaurant.

CELLAR	● ● ●		
COMFORT	● ● ●		
TRADITION	● ● ●		
Q/P	● ● ●		

CASTAGNETO CARDUCCI (LI)

Ristorante Da Ugo

via Pari, 3
🄲 0565 763746
⬤ Mon. €

This restaurant offers traditional Tuscan and Maremma cooking with particular emphasis on mushrooms and game. Wood pigeon, pork, and rabbit are served, plus some seafood, especially in summer. The owner also runs the Enoteca Il Borgo opposite the restaurant.

CELLAR	● ● ●			
COMFORT	● ●			
TRADITION	● ● ● ● ●			
Q/P	● ● ●			

Zi' Martino

località San Giusto, 264
🄲 0565 763666
⬤ Mon. €

This inexpensive rustic trattoria is typically Tuscan. You can find wild boar, lamb, and grilled meats and tortelli on the menu.

CELLAR	● ●			
COMFORT	● ●			
TRADITION	● ● ● ●			
Q/P	● ● ● ●			

CECINA (LI)

Antica Cecina

via Cavour, 17
🄲 0586 681528
⬤ Sun.
€€

The setting here is very pleasant with the atmosphere of an old inn. The day's menu depends on the market, especially for fish. Dishes include homemade pasta, fresh local fish, tripe, and salt cod cooked in a sweet-and-sour sauce with onions and potatoes. The desserts are all made on the premises.

CELLAR	● ●			
COMFORT	● ●			
TRADITION	● ● ● ●			
Q/P	● ● ● ● ●			

LARI (PI)

Castero

località Lavaiano
via Galilei, 2
🄲 0587 616121
⬤ Sun evening, Mon.
€€

A must for its meat dishes grilled over charcoal, this pleasant family-run restaurant features typical, simple Tuscan cuisine. The pork, beef (not Chianina), lamb, and much else are all choice quality, and the ingredients (especially the salumi) are local.

CELLAR	● ● ●			
COMFORT	● ● ●			
TRADITION	● ● ● ●			
Q/P	● ● ● ●			

LIVORNO

Antico Moro

via Bartelloni, 59
🄲 0586 884659
⬤ Wed.
€€

The classic local fish dishes – the usual grilled fish and fritto misto – are available here, but there is also steak for dedicated meat-eaters.

CELLAR	● ●			
COMFORT	● ●			
TRADITION	● ● ● ●			
Q/P	● ● ●			

La Barcarola

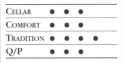

viale Carducci, 39
🄲 0586 402367.
⬤ Sun.
€€

The family that owns this restaurant has run it for over 60 years, so they have built up a close relationship with their suppliers. This ensures good-quality local fish, which is the mainstay of the menu. Cacciucco is one of the traditional dishes found all year round. There is a good choice of first and second courses, which are exclusively seafood.

CELLAR	● ● ●		
COMFORT	● ● ●		
TRADITION	● ● ● ●		
Q/P	● ● ●		

Ciglieri

frazione Ardenza
via Franchini, 38
🄲 0586 508194
⬤ Wed.
€€€€€

This elegant restaurant uses good-quality regional ingredients (including fresh vegetables, pigeons, and Chianina beef) to produce creative traditional recipes. The bread, pasta, and pastry are all homemade.

CELLAR	●	●	●	●
COMFORT	●	●	●	●
TRADITION	●	●		
Q/P	●	●		

MARCIANA – ELBA (LI)

Publius

località Poggio
piazza del Castagneto
☎ 0565 99208
● Mon. ⬛ Mar–Nov.
€€

Fine regional cooking and courteous service can be found here. Many of the dishes are based on fresh fish, such as stoccafisso all'elbana, but there are also meat and game dishes. The restaurant is good value for money, and the terrace has a fine sea view.

CELLAR	●	●	●	
COMFORT	●	●	●	
TRADITION	●	●		
Q/P	●	●	●	●

MARCIANA MARINA – ELBA (LI)

Capo Nord

località La Fenicia
☎ 0565 996983
● Mon. ⬛ April–Dec.
€€€€

Elba's classic dishes, such as stock fish with potatoes, are alternated with fresh fish cooked very simply in salt at this seafront restaurant. There are plenty of creative ideas for using the produce from the island and nearby

areas. The desserts, presented in a separate menu, are good. There is an international wine list.

CELLAR	●	●	●	
COMFORT	●	●	●	●
TRADITION	●	●	●	
Q/P	●	●	●	

Rendez Vous – Da Marcello

piazza della Vittoria, 1
☎ 0565 99251/99298
● Wed. ⬛ Mar–Oct.
€€

At this restaurant fish and other seafood are cooked both in simple, tasty dishes and in more sophisticated forms, including potato stuffed with a mixture of polpa di pesce (filleted fish) and shellfish roasted in a wood-burning oven (along with other kinds of fish).

CELLAR	●	●	●	
COMFORT	●	●	●	
TRADITION	●	●	●	
Q/P	●	●	●	

MONTOPOLI VAL D'ARNO (PI)

Quattro Gigli

piazza Michele, 2
☎ 0571 466878
● Mon, Sun evening (10 Jan–31 Mar).
€€

Here flavor is wedded to culture. Many of the traditional dishes are taken from ancient – mostly Renaissance – Florentine recipe books, the fruit of careful historical research. The results are some excellent savory dishes with fruit as one of the ingredients. More recent tradition is not neglected: there is ribollita, classic Tuscan meat dishes, and also stock fish and salt cod. In season there are truffles

and mushrooms from San Miniato. The wine list has a good selection of Tuscan labels. The restaurant has some bedrooms available.

CELLAR	●	●	●	●
COMFORT	●	●	●	●
TRADITION	●	●	●	●
Q/P	●	●	●	●

PISA

Artilafo

via Volturno, 38
☎ 050 27010
● Sun.
€€€

International cuisine – revisited and revised in some cases – and simple but creative meat and fish courses are on the menu at this tasteful restaurant. There is no printed wine list but the cellar contains about 300 wines from all over Italy.

CELLAR	●	●	●	
COMFORT	●	●	●	
TRADITION	●			
Q/P	●	●	●	

Bruno

via Bianchi, 12
☎ 050 560818
● Tues, Mon evening. €€

Enjoy typical Pisan cooking at this rustic family-run restaurant. Dishes include salt cod with leeks, Pisan-style stock fish, and seppie in zimino (cuttlefish soup).

CELLAR	●	●			
COMFORT	●	●			
TRADITION	●	●	●	●	●
Q/P	●	●			

Cagliostro

via del Castelletto, 26
☎ 050 575413
● Tues. €€
This highly unusual trattoria is in an ancient

monastery which has been renovated in a modern, airy style and is also used for art exhibitions. The creative seasonal cuisine is based on produce from the land. Traditional Tuscan dishes are not listed on the menu but patrons can order them. The desserts are home-made, and the chocolate ones deserve a special mention, especially the steamed chocolate pudding. The wine bar has about 300 Italian wines. There are selections of Italian and foreign cheeses and salumi *from the Marches.*

CELLAR	●	●	●
COMFORT	●	●	●
TRADITION	●		
Q/P	●	●	●

Osteria dei Cavalieri

via San Frediano, 16
📞 050 580858
🌑 Sun, Sat lunchtime. €

Interesting Tuscan cuisine offers very good value for money here. Ingredients are fresh, seasonal, and mostly local. The cellar has a good selection of Italian wines and the extra-virgin olive oil comes from a small producer nearby. The restaurant offers three "tasting menus": fish, meat, and vegetarian.

CELLAR	●	●	●
COMFORT	●	●	●
TRADITION	●	●	●
Q/P	●	●	●

PONTEDERA (PI)

La Polveriera

via Marconcini, 54
📞 0587 54765
🌑 Sun.
€€
This restaurant is rich in character and culinary

intuition, producing interesting seafood dishes combined with the region's herbs and vegetables.

CELLAR	●		
COMFORT	●	●	●
TRADITION	●		
Q/P	●	●	●

PORTOFERRAIO – ELBA (LI)

La Barca

via Guerrazzi, 60
📞 0565 918036.
🌑 Wed. €€

This small restaurant on the seafront offers high-quality dishes made with fresh ingredients, all at reasonable prices. The cuisine is mainly seafood, grilled over a wood fire.

CELLAR	●	●		
COMFORT	●	●		
TRADITION	●	●	●	●
Q/P	●	●	●	●

RIO MARINA – ELBA (LI)

La Canocchia

via Palestro, 3
📞 0565 962432
🌑 Mon (except summer).
🗓 Mar–Oct. €€

For some years this has been the premier restaurant on Elba, one not to miss. The menu features local recipes plus original ideas based on fresh seafood. There is a broad range of first courses and a good selection of the island's wines.

CELLAR	●	●		
COMFORT	●	●	●	
TRADITION	●	●	●	●
Q/P	●	●	●	●

SAN MINIATO (PI)

Il Convio

località San Maiano
📞 0571 408114
🌑 Wed.
€€

This elegantly rustic restaurant is deep in the countryside. The cuisine is traditional with regional recipes. It specializes in both classic and modern, creative dishes made with the local white truffles. The wine from the owner's estate (Alto Desco) is particularly good.

CELLAR	●	●	●
COMFORT	●	●	●
TRADITION	●	●	●
Q/P	●	●	●

SAN VINCENZO (LI)

Il Bucaniere

viale Marconi
📞 0565 705555
🌑 Tues.
🗓 Only in the summer season.
€€

In a wooden cabin on stilts by the sea, Fulvietto Pierangelini, son of the well-known restaurateur Fulvio, who owns the Gambero Rosso (see p184), runs this restaurant. Open only in the evenings, it offers real seafood delicacies. There are one-course meals, antipasti and first courses, and both traditional and creative modern dishes, all using good quality ingredients. The cheese trolley has fine Tuscan cheeses, the desserts are interesting, and the wine list (only Tuscan and French) is small but carefully chosen.

CELLAR	●	●			
COMFORT	●	●	●		
TRADITION	●	●	●		
Q/P	●	●	●	●	

Gambero Rosso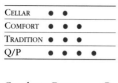

piazza della Vittoria, 13
☎ 0565 701021
🔴 Mon, Tues in winter.
€€€€€

Fulvio Pierangelini is the owner and chef of this splendid, unforgettable, small restaurant – one of the most famous in Italy – serving fine food. He has an unerring instinct for flavors and scents, and a quite exceptional ability to improvise. Everything at the Gambero Rosso is perfect: carefully chosen raw materials from all over Europe combined with fresh meat and fish from his own region. The dishes are light and full of flavor, with the cooking beautifully timed. Tasteful tables are laid under the watchful eye of Emanuela, the padrona di casa. The cellar, which contains an international range of wines, is one of the most outstanding in Italy. Even the price:quality ratio is very good if you choose the "tasting menu."

CELLAR	●	●	●	●	●
COMFORT	●	●	●	●	●
TRADITION	●	●			
Q/P	●	●	●		

STAFFOLI (PI)

Da Beppe

via Livornese, 35/37
☎ 0571 37002
🔴 Mon, Sun evening.
€€€€

Located in the hills, this restaurant traditionally offered a meat-based menu when the present owner's father ran it. Nowadays, fish is favored

on the menu, but there is still a small space for the style of the past. The dishes are based on local produce, with ideas from other regions and countries. There is a good wine list with an eye to the whites.

CELLAR	●	●	●	●	
COMFORT	●	●	●	●	
TRADITION	●	●			
Q/P	●	●	●		

SUVERETO (LI)

Eno-oliteca Ombrone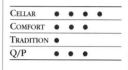

piazza dei Giudici, 1
☎ 0565 829336
🔴 Mon. €€€€

This restaurant is in a renovated 14th-century olive mill. Giancarlo Bini was one of the first – if not the first – to provide in his restaurant (formerly at Grosseto) an informative list of types of olive oil and combine each dish with the right oil. In his new premises he has continued along the same lines, offering a choice of no fewer than 168 kinds of extra-virgin olive oil from all over Italy. The cuisine is excellent and definitely regional. Note particularly the wild boar (in the traditional recipe alla bracconiera) and the game. The restaurant's salumi and desserts are excellent.

CELLAR	●	●	●	●	
COMFORT	●	●	●		
TRADITION	●	●	●		
Q/P	●	●	●		

TIRRENIA (PI)

Dante e Ivana

via del Tirreno, 207/c
☎ 050 32549
🔴 Sun, Mon lunchtime.
€€€€

This fish restaurant offers shellfish from the markets at Viareggio and Livorno. The dishes, which reflect the day's catch, do full justice to the fish.

CELLAR	●	●	●	●	
COMFORT	●	●	●		
TRADITION	●				
Q/P	●	●	●		

ULIVETO TERME (PI)

Osteria Vecchia Noce

località Noce
☎ 050 788229
🔴 Wed, Tues evening.
€€

Set in an 18th-century olive mill in a medieval town, this restaurant serves traditional Tuscan cuisine with a very light touch. It uses only local and seasonal produce and fish brought to the nearby ports. Everything is homemade. The anatra in dolceforte (sweet-and-sour duck), marinated boar with polenta, and the suckling pig are especially interesting dishes to try. The wines are Italian – mainly Tuscan – with the occasional foreign wine.

CELLAR	●	●	●		
COMFORT	●	●	●		
TRADITION	●	●	●	●	
Q/P	●	●	●	●	

VADA (LI)

Il Ducale

piazza Garibaldi, 33
☎ 0586 788600
🔴 Mon. €€€

Situated in an elegant 19th-century building, this restaurant serves its customers traditional seafood cuisine. Its fish is supplied almost exclusively by local fishermen. The homemade bottarga (dried,

salted fish roe) uses roe from various kinds of fish.

CELLAR	●	●	●
COMFORT	●	●	●
TRADITION	●	●	●
Q/P	●	●	●

VOLTERRA (PI)

Vecchio Mulino

Saline di Volterra
via del Molino
[0588 44060.
● Mon, Sun evening (winter).
€€

The setting for this delightful restaurant is a renovated old mill. The restaurant's sophisticated cuisine is based on meat (game in the fall and winter), with plenty of fresh vegetables in season, and mushrooms depending on the time of year. The dishes have a regional flavor with some added personal touches. There are some rooms available for people to stay.

CELLAR	●	●	●
COMFORT	●	●	●
TRADITION	●	●	●	●
Q/P	●	●	●

CHIANTI AND SIENA

CASTELLINA IN CHIANTI (SI)

Antica Trattoria La Torre

piazza del Comune, 15
[0577 740236
● Fri. €€

The tables and chairs at this restaurant are set out in the attractive medieval piazza, and the food is cooked on an open spit. The cuisine is typical of Chianti with ribollita, homemade pasta, crostini,

---

Chianina beef and pigeon, plus a good choice of homemade desserts. The restaurant's cellar stocks a good range of the top Tuscan wines plus a selection of other wines from northern Italy.

CELLAR	●	●	●
COMFORT	●	●	●
TRADITION	●	●	●	●
Q/P	●	●	●

Pietrafitta

località Pietrafitta
[0577 741123
● Thu. €

This hospitable small restaurant with its period furnishings serves a few classic Tuscan dishes, such as local salumi and bistecca alla Fiorentina. Everything is homemade.

CELLAR	●	●	●
COMFORT	●	●	●
TRADITION	●	●	●	●
Q/P	●	●	●

CASTELNUOVO BERARDENGA (SI)

Antonio

via Fiorita, 38
[0577 355321
● Mon. In summer daily at lunchtime.
€€€€

This fine restaurant is celebrated for its excellent seafood dishes. The menu is rewritten each morning, after the dawn purchases at the meat, fruit, and vegetable markets. The host, Antonio Farina, has an excellent cellar with prestigious wines from all over the world.

CELLAR	●	●	●	●	●
COMFORT	●	●	●
TRADITION	●
Q/P	●	●

Bottega del 30

località Villa Sesta
via Santa Caterina, 2
[0577 359226
● Tues, Wed, lunchtime on weekdays.
€€€€

This small restaurant is set in a 17th-century farmyard above an ancient monastery and is surrounded by vines. Elegant without being too formal, it offers interesting, creative cooking based on old Tuscan recipes. Choose the versatile "tasting menu," which includes some of their specialties.

CELLAR	●	●	●
COMFORT	●	●	●
TRADITION	●	●	●
Q/P	●	●	●

Poggio Rosso

località Santa Felice
[0577 359260
€€€€€

Set in the farming hamlet of San Felice, where there is also a fascinating historic hotel with well-appointed rooms, this is a stylish restaurant. It serves good, fairly creative, meat-based dishes with special emphasis on the farm's own produce, especially the excellent extra-virgin olive oil. The restaurant also serves some seafood dishes.

CELLAR	●	●	●
COMFORT	●	●	●	●	●
TRADITION	●	●
Q/P	●

COLLE DI VAL D'ELSA (SI)

Arnolfo

via XX Settembre, 50
[0577 920549
● Tues.
€€€€€

This restaurant is housed in a 500-year-old building in a charming village. There are two menus – one is traditional and the other innovative modern – both featuring excellent, tasty dishes. The service reflects great courtesy and professionalism. The dishes range from fish to local meat, as well as a choice selection of ingredients from other areas of Tuscany. The pastries are not to be missed. The markups on the wine list are very reasonable. There is accommodation available in five bedrooms, which all have a pleasant, relaxed atmosphere.

CELLAR	●	●	●	●	●
COMFORT	●	●	●	●	●
TRADITION	●	●			
Q/P	●	●	●		

GAIOLE IN CHIANTI (SI)

Ristorante Badia a Coltibuono

località Badia
a Coltibuono
📞 0577 749031
€€

A splendid medieval abbey is the setting for this restaurant, which is run by the Stucchi Prinetti family (their mother, Lorenza de' Medici, is in charge of the kitchen). As a showcase for their wines, the restaurant's owners serve traditional Tuscan dishes, which are sometimes enriched with modern personal touches. Dishes are made with choice ingredients such as Cinta Senese pork and fresh produce either from their own market garden, or supplied by small local growers. The interesting wine list includes fine wines from the family estate together with a selection of other Tuscan and Italian wines.

CELLAR	●	●		
COMFORT	●	●	●	●
TRADITION	●	●	●	●
Q/P	●	●	●	

GREVE IN CHIANTI (FI)

Da Padellina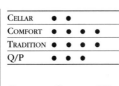

strada in Chianti
corso del Popolo
📞 055 858388
🍴 Thu.
€€

This pleasant country trattoria in Chianti serves purely classical cuisine. The ribollita and bistecca alla fiorentina are excellent, while the peposo alla fornacina, an old Impruneta recipe for meat stew, is worth trying. Desserts are homemade and include a traditional zuccotto.

CELLAR	●	●	●		
COMFORT	●	●	●		
TRADITION	●	●	●	●	●
Q/P	●	●	●		

MERCATALE VAL DI PESA (FI)

Il Salotto del Chianti

via Sonnino, 92
📞 055 8218016. 🍴 Wed, lunchtime on weekdays.
€€€

The fish cuisine of this small stylish restaurant is more Mediterranean than Tuscan. However, for the meat dishes the approach is definitely regional, both in style and ingredients. Fresh vegetables are an essential part of the fish and the meat dishes. The bread and desserts are made on the premises.

CELLAR	●	●	●	
COMFORT	●	●	●	●
TRADITION	●	●	●	
Q/P	●	●	●	

PASSIGNANO (FI)

Osteria di Passignano

badia a Passignano
📞 055 8071278.
🍴 Sun. €€€

The fish cuisine at this small, stylish restaurant is more Mediterranean than Tuscan, but the meat dishes are definitely regional. The bread and desserts are made in the restaurant's kitchens.

CELLAR	●	●	●
COMFORT	●	●	●
TRADITION	●	●	
Q/P	●	●	●

PANZANO IN CHIANTI (FI)

Il Vescovino

via Ciampolo da Panzano, 9
📞 055 852464
🍴 Tues. €€€

A wood-burning oven and a medieval fireplace are two of the attractions of this restaurant. The menu includes updated Tuscan dishes plus recipes from other regions. Fresh fish is served. The bread, pasta, and desserts are homemade. There is a wide choice of wines in an ancient cellar which you can visit.

CELLAR	●	●	●
COMFORT	●	●	●	●
TRADITION	●	●	●
Q/P	●	●	●

SAN CASCIANO IN VAL DI PESA (FI)

La Tenda Rossa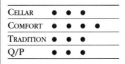

località Cerbaia
piazza del Monumento, 9/14
📞 055 826132
🍴 Sun, Mon lunchtime.
€€€€€

A busy family team runs this stylish, but very friendly restaurant, which offers innovative versions of the Tuscan classics as well as new ideas for fish and meat. The starting point is the local market, as reflected in the menu, which is rewritten almost daily. Everything is homemade, including the bread, the service is impeccable, and there is a fine cellar.

CELLAR	●	●	●	●	●
COMFORT	●	●	●	●	
TRADITION	●	●			
Q/P	●	●			

SIENA

Botteganova

strada di Montevarchi statale, 408, 29
[0577 284230
● Mon. €€€

The Sicilian chef at this chic restaurant knows how to get hold of perfect ingredients. He adapts the local cuisine to produce his own personal version of Mediterranean dishes, with an especially creative approach to seafood. The desserts are skillfully prepared, and there is a choice selection of cheeses.

CELLAR	●	●	●	●
COMFORT	●	●	●	
TRADITION	●	●		
Q/P	●	●	●	

Osteria del Fico Mezzo

via dei Termini, 71
[0577 222384
● Sun. €

This cheerful osteria (inn), is as imaginative and informal with its furnishings as it is with the food. Fresh vegetables, salumi, cheeses matured to different degrees of ripeness, and excellent house honey are used.

CELLAR	●	●	●
COMFORT	●	●	
TRADITION	●	●	●
Q/P	●	●	●

Guido

vicolo Pier Pettinaio, 7
[0577 280042 €€

Tuscan cuisine with some personal touches can be found in this restaurant set in a 15th-century building. The bistecca alla fiorentina and the game merit special mention.

CELLAR	●	●	●
COMFORT	●	●	●
TRADITION	●	●	●
Q/P	●	●	●

Le Logge

via del Porrione, 33
[0577 48013
● Sun, lunchtime on Mon. €€€

Set in the oldest palace in Siena, Palazzo Piccolomini, next to the Logge del Papa, this restaurant is popular with artists. It offers typical Tuscan cuisine (plus some fish dishes) with plenty of traditional recipes and homemade fresh pasta. The wines are mainly regional.

CELLAR	●	●	●
COMFORT	●	●	●
TRADITION	●	●	●
Q/P	●	●	●

Antica Trattoria Papei ☺

piazza del Mercato, 6
[0577 280894
● Mon. €

This is probably the only trattoria in town with a real family atmosphere. The sauces and the pasta are made on the premises: the pappardelle with hare is really special. The dishes

are authentic Sienese cuisine – nothing is frozen or prepackaged.

CELLAR	●	●	●		
COMFORT	●	●			
TRADITION	●	●	●	●	●
Q/P	●	●	●		

MONTALCINO AND THE SIENESE CRETE

BAGNO VIGNONI (SI)

Antica Osteria del Leone

piazza del Muretto
[0577 887300
● Mon. €

This attractive restaurant is in the center of this medieval town, which is famous for its hot spa, a pool in the main square. Its four rooms are set in a 14th-century building with exposed beams and a terra-cotta floor. Homemade pasta such as pici and pappardelle served with a sauce of wild boar, hare or all'aglione (garlic). Other specialities include tripe, guinea fowl with Vin Santo, and mushrooms in season. The desserts are also good.

CELLAR	●	●	●	
COMFORT	●	●	●	
TRADITION	●	●	●	●
Q/P	●	●	●	●

Osteria della Parrata

via del Moretto, 40
[0577 887559
● Wed.
€

A 15th-century barn with a fine panoramic garden is the attractive setting for this restaurant. Grilled food is its specialty. The pecorino cheeses are excellent, as is the lombo bagnato (loin) with balsamic vinegar. Fresh vegetables are widely used in the first courses.

CELLAR	•	•			
COMFORT	•	•			
TRADITION	•	•	•	•	
Q/P	•	•	•	•	

BUONCONVENTO (SI)

Osteria di Duccio

via Soccini, 76
📞 0577 807042
🔴 Wed. €

There is a very welcoming family atmosphere at this restaurant. The food is typical Sienese cuisine with numerous rustic dishes, including crostini *and* salumi, tagiolini ginestrati *(with local chicken and saffron),* ravioli *of potatoes,* ribollita *seasoned with oil and onion,* pappardelle sulla lepre *(only in the open season for hare),* faraona in crosta tartufata *(guinea fowl in a crust),* saddle of rabbit with herbs, purée of chickpeas, patate alla fattoressa *(country-style potatoes),* porcini *specialities (in summer and early fall), and homemade desserts. The produce is always fresh with ingredients bought in daily. There is house wine or Rosso di Montalcino.*

CELLAR	•				
COMFORT	•	•			
TRADITION	•	•	•	•	•
Q/P	•	•	•	•	

CETONA (SI)

Frateria di Padre Eligio

convento di San Francesco
📞 0578 238015
🔴 Tues.
€€€€€

Intriguingly situated in a medieval monastery, this restaurant is surrounded by a park housing a community of young people who work in the restaurant and hotel.

The traditional Italian cuisine, with a personal touch, is very good. Most of the ingredients are produced by the community. The menus are hand-painted. Prices are steep, however – think of them as a contribution to this community.

CELLAR	•	•	•	•	
COMFORT	•	•	•	•	•
TRADITION	•	•			
Q/P	•				

CHIUSI (SI)

Zaira

via Arunte, 12
📞 0578 20260
🔴 Mon (except summer).
€€

This simple pleasant family-run restaurant in the town center serves classic local cuisine, which is closely linked to the seasons. It has a fascinating cellar (20,000 bottles) that stretches into Etruscan tunnels hewn out of the rock.

CELLAR	•	•	•		
COMFORT	•	•	•		
TRADITION	•	•	•	•	•
Q/P	•	•	•		

LUCIGNANO (AR)

Osteria da Totò

piazza del Tribunale, 6
📞 0575 836763
🔴 Tues. €

Over the years Lorenzo Totò has become a TV star, appearing on numerous shows and describing his grandparents' recipes, especially the ones with wild herbs. He is also kept busy teaching the secrets of Tuscan cuisine to Japanese pupils. When they are not his guests in

Italy, he is off to Japan. His wife and children, Boris and Beatrice, help to run the rustic restaurant, set on an ancient square at the top of the town. The son and daughter follow in the footsteps of their imaginative father, serving up wonderful sauces and soups. The family's extra-virgin olive oil is excellent.

CELLAR	•				
COMFORT	•	•			
TRADITION	•	•	•	•	•
Q/P	•	•	•		

MONTALCINO (SI)

Osteria del Vecchio Castello

località Poggio alle Mura
📞 0577 816026
🔴 Tues. €€€€

The little convent of the 13th-century Pieve di San Sigismondo housed a restaurant of the same name until March 2000. Now, in its place Susanna Fumi (in the kitchen) and her husband Alfredo Sibaldi (sommelier) have taken over, bringing with them all the history and experience of the Osteria del Vecchio Castello di Roccalbenga which they used to run. Despite the change of location – no longer among the woods at the foot of Monte Amiata but amid the celebrated vines of Montalcino – there are still only 16 covers and the food is as wonderful as ever. The cooking serves only to enhance the excellent regional and seasonal ingredients in harmonious flavor combinations. The wine lists have been increased from two to three: Italian, regional, and foreign. Adjacent to the restaurant are a wine store and six large suites.

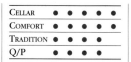

CELLAR	●	●	●	●	●
COMFORT	●	●	●	●	●
TRADITION	●	●	●	●	
Q/P	●	●	●	●	

Poggio Antico

località I Poggi
🔴 0577 849200
⬤ Mon, Sun evening.
€€€€

Diners have a panoramic view of the countryside at this charming restaurant. The regional cuisine is adapted intelligently, as in the fried vegetables and the gnocchetti di ragù bianco di cinghiale. There are excellent desserts.

CELLAR	●	●	●		
COMFORT	●	●	●		
TRADITION	●	●			
Q/P	●				

Porta al Cassero

Rocca della Fortezza
🔴 0577 847196
⬤ Wed. €

A small osteria offering Montalcino cuisine, with classic pinci (or pici) and traditional dishes, from pappa col pomodoro (bread and tomato soup) to a purée of chickpeas and zuppa alla scottiglia di cinghiale (wild boar stew), with the occasional dish from other regions.

CELLAR	●	●			
COMFORT	●	●	●		
TRADITION	●	●	●	●	●
Q/P	●	●	●		

Il Pozzo

località Sant' Angelo in Colle 🔴 0577 844015
⬤ Tues. €

Nestling in the hills five minutes from Montalcino, this traditional trattoria serves a selection of superb dishes. There is a limited choice of regional wines.

CELLAR	●	●			
COMFORT	●	●			
TRADITION	●	●	●	●	
Q/P	●	●	●		

Taverna dei Barbi

località Pordenoni
🔴 0577 841111
⬤ Tues, Wed evening. €€

This restaurant is next door to the famous Barbi wine store. The décor is rustic yet elegant and the food served is typical Montalcino cuisine.

CELLAR	●			
COMFORT	●	●	●	
TRADITION	●	●	●	
Q/P	●	●	●	

MONTEFOLLONICO (SI)

La Chiusa

via della Madonnina, 88
🔴 0577 669668
⬤ Tues. €€€€€

Situated in an ancient farmhouse, this is one of the most celebrated restaurants in the region. Dania Masotti presents regional food in a cuisine that is full of character but inspired by tradition. There are charming, but very expensive, rooms too.

CELLAR	●	●	●	
COMFORT	●	●	●	●
TRADITION	●	●	●	●
Q/P	●			

MONTEPULCIANO (SI)

Diva e Maceo

via di Gracciano nel Corso, 90/92
🔴 0578 716951
⬤ Tues. €

This simple restaurant is very popular with locals and visitors alike, who enjoy its Tuscan dishes.

These range from classic antipasti to pappardelle al cinghiale, pici all'aglione (considered the best in the area), and grilled or roasted meat. The desserts are homemade.

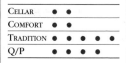

CELLAR	●	●			
COMFORT	●	●			
TRADITION	●	●	●	●	●
Q/P	●	●	●	●	

La Grotta

località San Biagio, 15
🔴 0578 757607
⬤ Wed. €€€

This restaurant, opposite the church of San Biagio, is renowned for its meat, especially the tagliata di Chianina and bistecca alla fiorentina. The rest of the menu offers regional specialties such as antipasti with bruschetta and crostini, homemade pasta, and second courses such as duck, stuffed pigeon, and rabbit. Everything is delicious. The wine list has some French wines.

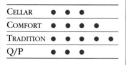

CELLAR	●	●	●	
COMFORT	●	●	●	●
TRADITION	●	●	●	●
Q/P	●	●	●	

PIENZA (SI)

Il Prato

via Santa Caterina, 1/3
🔴 0578 749924
⬤ Tue. €

Recently taken over by the owners of Silene at Seggiano (see p191), this restaurant is run with the same professionalism. The cuisine and wine list are unchanged. There is a very pleasant garden.

CELLAR	●	●	●		
COMFORT	●	●	●		
TRADITION	●	●	●	●	●
Q/P	●	●	●		

La Taverna di Moranda

frazione Monticchiello
via di Mezzo, 17
📞 0578 755050
🔴 Mon. €€

*About 6 miles (10 km)
from Pienza, toward
Monte Amiata, you can
find real Tuscan cuisine
at this restaurant. The
pasta is made by hand
and the menu changes
with the seasons. The
antipasti are based on
local salumi; the first
courses are pici served
with simple tomato sauces,
or richer meat sauces;
and the second courses
are meat, including
stuffed pigeon, the house
specialty, and agnello a
scottadito (rabbit with
olives) and steak dishes.*

CELLAR	●	●	●		
COMFORT	●	●	●		
TRADITION	●	●	●	●	●
Q/P	●	●	●		

SINALUNGA (SI)

Locanda dell'Amorosa

località Amorosa
📞 0577 679497
🔴 Mon, Tues lunchtime.
€€€€€

*This is one of the most
important and fascinating
Tuscan restaurants,
situated in a 400-year-old
town. The excellent
cuisine draws on tradition
but is also innovative. The
menu gives a lot of space
to meat dishes but there
is no lack of fish. The
desserts are very good.
The cheeses from the Crete
are noteworthy, as is the
salumi produced by a
local firm. Splendid suites
and rooms in the
medieval town's towers
and walls are available.*

CELLAR	●	●	●	●
COMFORT	●	●	●	●
TRADITION	●	●		
Q/P	●	●		

Osteria delle Grotte

via Matteotti, 33
📞 0577 630269.
🔴 Wed. €€€

*Set in an old lemon grove,
this restaurant has a
fixed-price "tasting menu"
(including Tuscan wine)
with seasonal produce,
meat, game, and excellent
handmade fresh pasta.*

CELLAR	●	●		
COMFORT	●	●	●	
TRADITION	●	●	●	●
Q/P	●	●	●	

SOVICILLE (SI)

Trattoria Cateni   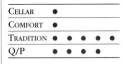

via dei Pratini, 23
📞 0577 342028
🔴 Wed. €

*This restaurant has a
panoramic terrace
overlooking Siena. The
arched interior and
antique furniture give it a
traditional feel. The
scottiglia is excellent, as
are the specialties based
on wild boar (pappardelle,
cinghiale alla cacciatora)
and mushrooms (zuppa,
vitella). The pasta and
desserts are homemade.*

CELLAR	●			
COMFORT	●			
TRADITION	●	●	●	●
Q/P	●	●	●	●

TREQUANDA (SI)

Locanda del Colle   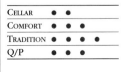

via Torta, 7
📞 0577 662108
🔴 Wed in the low season.
€

*The dining room of this
restaurant is painted with
floral frescoes, reminiscent
of the old verandas on
Sienese country houses a
century ago. The décor is
Art Nouveau with original
period furniture. Here
you can taste simple
dishes, such as picchio-
pacchio, homemade
lunghetti with nana
(muscovy duck), zuppa
Trequanda, Chianina beef,
or beef in Brunello wine.
The homemade jams
turn up in excellent tarts.
To sample the food, you
are set a task – a farm
chore, or a guided tasting
of oil or wine.*

CELLAR	●			
COMFORT	●	●	●	
TRADITION	●	●	●	●	●
Q/P	●	●	●	●

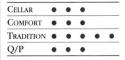
MAREMMA AND
MONTE AMIATA

CAPALBIO (GR)

Maria

via Comunale, 3
📞 0564 896014
🔴 Tues. €€

*Politicians and media
personalities are often
found among the tourists
sampling Maurizio Rossi's
Maremma specialties.
While wild boar dominates
the menu, the tortelli with
truffles, the acquacotta
(soup), and the fried
vegetables are noteworthy.*

CELLAR	●	●	●	
COMFORT	●	●	●	
TRADITION	●	●	●	●
Q/P	●	●	●	

CASTIGLIONE DELLA
PESCAIA (GR)

Osteria del Buco

via del Recinto, 11
📞 0564 934460
🔴 Mon. €

*This restaurant is in an
opening in the ancient
walls of the medieval town.
The cuisine, like the décor,
is pure Maremma. Dishes*

include bruschette *(some with long-forgotten toppings), vegetable and pulse soups, game, and very good fish (including some little-known kinds unusual in a restaurant).*

CELLAR	●	●			
COMFORT	●	●			
TRADITION	●	●	●	●	●
Q/P	●	●	●	●	

GROSSETO

Buca di S. Lorenzo

viale Manetti, 1
📞 0564 25142
🔴 Sun. €€

This restaurant serves fish cuisine when local fish is available. At other times it offers traditional Tuscan dishes, including homemade pasta.

CELLAR	●	●	●		
COMFORT	●	●	●		
TRADITION	●	●	●	●	●
Q/P	●	●	●		

ISOLA DEL GIGLIO (GR)

La Margherita

località Giglio Porto
via Thaon de Revel, 5
📞 0564 809237. 🔴 Mon.
⬜ from Easter–Sept. €

Good home-cooked simple fresh fish dishes are served at this restaurant. Note the delicious first course dish cavatelli *(pasta) with* mazzancolle *(mantis shrimp) and* pecorino.

CELLAR	●	●		
COMFORT	●	●		
TRADITION	●	●	●	
Q/P	●	●	●	

Trattoria Da Maria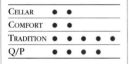

località Giglio Castello
📞 0564 806062
🔴 Wed. ⬜ Mar–Dec.
€€

This family restaurant is set in the hills with a delightful view over the Baia di Campese. The restaurant serves a choice of fine fish and meat dishes, including the island's traditional rabbit recipe.

CELLAR	●	●	●	
COMFORT	●	●	●	
TRADITION	●	●	●	
Q/P	●	●	●	

Da Santi

località Castello
via Marconi, 20
📞 0564 806188
🔴 Mon (except summer).
€€

Here in this restaurant, you can enjoy excellent fish cuisine with the type of fish dependent on availability. Classic Tuscan dishes are given the personal touch by skillfully incorporating fresh vegetables.

CELLAR	●	●		
COMFORT	●	●		
TRADITION	●	●	●	
Q/P	●	●	●	

MASSA MARITTIMA (GR)

Bracali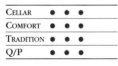

località Ghirlanda
📞 0566 902318
🔴 Tues; Mon evening (except August).
€€€€€

This family-run restaurant offers creative cooking that is inspired by the regional tradition of light, well balanced meat and fish dishes. The menu includes a masterly, innovative Tuscan lamb recipe consisting of two dishes: one dish is cold, the other, made from leg and ribs of lamb, is served hot. The pastries are also extremely good and well worth sampling.

CELLAR	●	●	●	●	●
COMFORT	●	●	●	●	
TRADITION	●	●			
Q/P	●	●	●		

MONTEMERANO (GR)

Da Caino

via Canonica, 3
📞 0564 602817
🔴 Wed, Thu midday.
€€€€€

This is one of the most important, up-and-coming restaurants in Italy, renowned for quality. Although it is off the beaten track and the prices are high, this is one not to miss. It serves a cuisine that mirrors the territory to a small number of patrons each night. The salumi *and extra-virgin olive oil are from the restaurant's own estate. The desserts, liquors, and selection of coffees are very good.*

CELLAR	●	●	●	●	●
COMFORT	●	●	●	●	●
TRADITION	●	●	●	●	
Q/P	●	●	●		

SEGGIANO (GR)

Silene

località La Pescina Est
📞 0564 950805
🔴 Mon.
€

Set in the mountains, this restaurant offers Tuscan home cooking with the emphasis on woodland produce – mushrooms and truffles in season, and wild boar and venison. The meat is mostly grilled over charcoal. The pasta is homemade. There are some rooms available.

CELLAR	●	●	●		
COMFORT	●	●	●		
TRADITION	●	●	●	●	●
Q/P	●	●	●		

Accommodation

Tuscany is probably the region of Italy with the most charming inns and small country hotels offering wonderful hospitality and comfort in settings of great natural beauty. The guide below takes into account, as far as possible, the price quality ratio, so this means it excludes some of the world's finest and most luxurious hotels – such as Villa San Michele at Fiesole, for example – because the average price of a room goes well beyond the limits set for this guide.

Most of the inns listed here are situated deep in the hills, surrounded by breathtaking countryside. The rooms are furnished with typical Tuscan country furniture, and the food offered is the traditional local cuisine.

Bagni di Lucca (LU)

Locanda Maiola

località Maiola di Sotto
0583 86296.
Jan 15–30 , Nov 1–20 .
€

This is a 17th-century Tuscan house, set in the green hills near Lucca, that has been converted to a welcoming family inn. In the kitchen, Signora Simonetta makes exquisite dishes reflecting the cuisine of Lucca and Garfagnana, such as her zuppa di farro with vegetables, or the homemade pasta with chickpeas or beans. The five tastefully renovated rooms are furnished with dark wood furniture. The panoramic view is magnificent.

Balbano (LU)

Villa Casanova

via di Casanova, 1600
0583 548429
FAX 0583 368955
Annexe ● Nov–Mar.
€€

Nestling in the green hills between Lucca and Pisa, this 18th-century villa offers good value for money. The rooms, some very spacious, have terra-cotta floors, some fine period furniture, and a splendid view over the Valle del Serchio. Next to the villa the Antica Foresteria (annexe), dating back to the 15th century, accommodates guests in smaller rooms, some of

them extremely pleasant. The restaurant, which is open from April to November, serves wholesome home cooking. There is a good swimming pool, which is open to guests from June to September.

Borgo San Lorenzo (FI)

Casa Palmira

località Feriolo, Statale, 302 via Faentina
FAX 055 8409749
Jan–Feb. €€

A small rural building has been converted into this delightful hotel deep in the green hills between the Mugello and Florence. It has six rooms, each one different, but all furnished in good taste and with objects belonging to the family to give a personal touch. Eat at the nearby restaurant "Il Feriolo," set in a 15th-century monastery, which specializes in good home cooking based on mushrooms and game.

Bucine (AR)

Le Antiche Sere

località Sogna
& FAX 055 998149
Nov.
€€

A medieval village called Sogna ("dream") is the setting for this fascinating

inn. The owners' idea is to let guests isolate themselves from the outside world and lose themselves in the relaxing atmosphere. The old stables have been converted into the restaurant, which serves an imaginative cuisine with lots of interesting dishes made with fresh produce. The menu changes two or three times a week and there is a good selection of wines. There are four suites with country-style furniture, fireplaces, and, above all, no telephone. The hotel has a park, a swimming pool and tennis courts.

Castellina in Chianti (SI)

Belvedere di San Leonino

località San Leonino
0577 740887
FAX 0577 740924
Nov 15–Mar 15.
€€€

Set in a tiny rural village, this is a cluster of adjoining houses providing accommodation in 28 rooms, all spacious and pleasantly furnished. There is a lovely garden with a lawn and swimming pool with a great view over the valley. The restaurant serves good, imaginative Tuscan cuisine.

Il Colombaio

via Chiantigiana, 29
& FAX 0577 740444
all year. €€

You come across this hotel with its inviting name set in a 16th-century farmhouse at the entrance to the village. The rooms, all with 19th-century furniture, have wooden beams and terra-cotta floors. There is a lovely garden with a swimming pool and a view over the village and valley. Eat at the nearby restaurant "Le Tre Porte," run by the hotelier's son, where real Tuscan food, such as crostini, pasta, and ribollita is served.

CASTIGLIONE D'ORCIA (SI)

Cantina Il Borgo

località Rocca d'Orcia
& FAX 0577 887280
Jan, Feb.
€€

In this little medieval village overlooking the Val d'Orcia, these are three delightful rooms set in one of the fine houses of light-colored brick. The walls are whitewashed, there are wrought-iron bedsteads, and typical Tuscan country furniture. The restaurant offers real local cooking, with exquisite pecorino from Pienza. Do not miss the excursion to the splendid spa, the Bagno Vignoni, which can be visited in the evening when the hot bath in the middle of the piazza exhales vapors reminiscent of a scene from Dante's Inferno.

CERTALDO (FI)

Osteria del Vicario

via Rivellino, 3
& FAX 0571 668228
Jan. €€

In the Middle Ages this inn was the residence of the vicar of Certaldo Alto. Set in the depths of the Val

d'Elsa, between Siena and Florence, it has 11 rooms, each very different, very romantic, and with fine Tuscan furnishings. The skilled restaurant chef presents a creative cuisine based on beautifully fresh produce – meat, poultry, mushrooms, and truffles.

CORTONA (AR)

Relais Il Falconiere

località San Martino
0575 612616
FAX 0575 612927
all year.
€€€€€

This splendid 17th-century country house, now converted into a hotel, part of the Relais & Châteaux group, has a stunning hill-top location amid vines and olives facing Cortona. There are 10 rooms, all spacious and filled with period furniture and attractive wall hangings. As well as wooden beams and parquet floors, some rooms have a fireplace. The two suites overlook the garden and swimming pool. The restaurant is renowned for its very fine cuisine, based on genuine local produce.

Locanda del Molino

località Montanare
0575 614192
FAX 0575 614054
Nov 15–Mar 15.
€€

Situated a few miles from Cortona, this pleasant, small inn, deep in the countryside, is famed for its authentic cuisine and courteous hospitality. The ground floor restaurant's specialties, like the torte al testo (griddle cakes), reflect Umbrian influence. The rooms on the first floor are all furnished with fine local antiques. There are antique toilets in some of the rooms.

FIESOLE (FI)

Pensione Bencistà

via Benedetto da Maiano, 4
FAX 055 59163
all year.
€€€€ with half board

This calls itself a modest pensione but is actually a pleasant villa situated in the hills of Fiesole and, in fact, looks more like a small inn. The living areas are very attractive – there are intimate lounges with fireplaces, and there is a small library. The comfortable bedrooms are furnished with period furniture. The restaurant offers good Tuscan cuisine, and there is a pleasant garden and terrace with a view over Florence.

FLORENCE

Villa Montartino

via suor Maria Celeste, 19/21
055 223520
FAX 055 223495
all year. €€€€€

You can find this corner of paradise just a few miles from Florence on the road from Certosa to Impruneta. Montartino was originally an 11th-century watchtower guarding the valley of the Ema, where goods were brought from Chianti to Florence. The tower was later converted into a charming and graceful mansion. The enormous rooms with four-poster beds and the original terra-cotta floors contain elegant Tuscan craft furniture. Some rooms have a terrace with splendid views over the surrounding hills. Guests can use the lovely swimming pool. The food is refined but wholesome, using all local produce, including the excellent extra-virgin olive oil and

the local red wine –
Chianti. The favorite
Tuscan beef steak dish,
bistecca alla fiorentina,
which a small butcher in
Impruneta supplies to the
villa, is truly wonderful.

GAIOLE IN CHIANTI
(SI)

Relais San Sano

località San Sano
🚹 0577 746130.
📠 0577 746156.
⬤ Nov 15–Mar 15.
€€€

This cluster of stone
farmhouses overlooking
the Chianti hills nestles in
an ancient hamlet. Each
of the rooms has a name
suggesting its character:
for instance, "Il nido" (The
nest) is isolated and
romantic, while "Camera
con vista" (Room with a
view) has a view over the
gently rolling Tuscan hills.
The food served each
evening in the restaurant is
the local cuisine.

LUCCA

Locanda L'Elisa

via Nuova to Pisa
at 3 miles (5 km)
🚹 0583 379737
📠 0583 379019
◻ all year.
€€€€€

This beautiful mauve-
colored villa was restored
in the early 19th century
by a steward of Princess
Elisa Baiocchi. It has two
rooms and eight suites,
all of them graciously
furnished with 19th-
century mahogany
furniture, four-poster beds,
and fine damask fabrics.
The spectacular park has a
swimming pool in it and
a myriad of geraniums,
trees, and water plants.
The veranda-gazebo
housing the restaurant
overlooks the park.

MANCIANO
(GR)

Il Poderino

strada statale Maremmana
at 19 miles (30 km)
🚹 & 📠 0564 625031
⬤ 2 weeks in Jan.
€€

This ancient converted
farmhouse at the gates of
Manciano has 11 spacious,
well-furnished rooms. This
is a very friendly, well-run
hotel with a splendid
panoramic view across to
Monte Argentario. The
restaurant serves Maremma
cuisine with the addition of
some interesting new dishes.

PIENZA
(SI)

Dal Falco

piazza Dante Alighieri, 3
🚹 & 📠 0578 748551
◻ all year. €€

Visitors to this attractive
Tuscan town can find
inexpensive family
accommodation at this
small inn situated in the
center. The restaurant's
cuisine is good; specialties
include excellent pici
all'aglione, handmade
ravioli, ribollita, and meat
grilled over charcoal. The
simple, comfortable rooms
all have TV and bathrooms
with furnishings in "arte
povera" style.

ORBETELLO
(GR)

Locanda d'Ansedonia

via Aurelia toward
Ansedonia
🚹 0564 881317
📠 0564 881727
⬤ Feb. €€

This strategically placed
inn has a wonderful view
overlooking the fascinating
lagoon of Orbetello, a few
miles from Argentario and

the Etruscan citadel of
Ansedonia. The 12 rooms
are whitewashed and
furnished in Maremma
style with fine wrought-iron
bedsteads. The restaurant
cuisine is typical of the
area, with Maremma
dishes and seafood – try the
famous acquacotta as well
as excellent Orbetello eel.

PITECCIO
(PT)

Villa Vannini

Villa di Piteccio
🚹 0573 42031
📠 0573 26331
◻ all year.
€€

Surrounded by a pleasant,
quiet garden, this lovely
villa is set just above
Pistoia. Friendly, family
hospitality is extended by
Signora Vannini who
oversees every detail, from
furnishing the rooms to the
homemade produce served
at breakfast and dinner.

RADDA IN CHIANTI
(SI)

Podere Terreno

road to Volpaia,
🚹 & 📠 0577 738312
◻ all year.
€€ with half board.

This farm is on the road
to the village of Volpaia,
famous for its Chianti
Classico and olive oil. The
owners, Sylvie Heniez
(who is French) and her
husband Roberto Melosi,
see to every last detail from
furnishing the farmhouse
with genuine rustic
furniture to organizing the
kitchen. The seven rooms
are full of charm and very
relaxing. At mealtimes
everyone eats together
around a single large table
and it is common to hear
two or three languages
spoken by diners from
different continents.

La Locanda

località Montanino
C & **FAX** 0577 738833
● Jan and Feb.
€€€€

This fascinating inn in the splendid Chianti hills was a 17th-century farmhouse. The seven rooms, all very different, are furnished with handsome country furniture and each has a different color scheme. They have chests and wardrobes in dark wood, and bedsteads with Viennese woven rush headboards. Particularly interesting is the arched bedroom and a suite with a loggia and a magnificent view. In good weather you can lounge by the pool and nibble pecorino *cheese or* finocchiona (salame).

RADICOFANI (SI)

La Palazzina

località Le Vigne
C & **FAX** 0578 55771
● Nov–Mar.
€€

This vacation farm in the hills of the Alta Valle d'Orcia is in an area rich in spas. The 18th-century Medici villa has bright, spacious rooms, all very tastefully furnished. There is a swimming pool on the grounds. The cuisine is based on the revival of ancient Medici recipes and uses the same fresh local produce as in the past. The villa is a good starting point for various sightseeing excursions.

SATURNIA (GR)

La Stellata

località Pian del Bagno
C 0564 602978
FAX 0564 602934
□ all year.
€€€

Surrounded by luxuriant vegetation in the Etruscan spa zone, this hotel is the younger brother of the Grand Hotel delle Terme. The beauty of the stone building, the garden, and the peace and quiet are incomparable. The pretty rooms are simply furnished. Sample the specialties of the outdoor grill and restaurant, the "Osteria del Bagno."

SIENA

Certosa di Maggiano

strada di Certosa, 82
C 0577 288180.
FAX 0577 288189.
□ all year.
€€€€€

This splendid 16th-century Charterhouse is just outside the center of Siena. The building is laid out around a courtyard and comprises six rooms and 11 suites, luxuriously and tastefully furnished in a choice of fabrics and colors. In the inner rooms are prized Sienese paintings and antique furniture. The restaurant's cuisine is of a high level, using plenty of fresh ingredients. In summer the tables are laid in the cloister portico. There is a park with a swimming pool and tennis courts.

SINALUNGA (SI)

Locanda della Bandita

località Bettolle
via Bandita, 72
C & **FAX** 0577 624649
● two weeks in Dec.
€€

This small farmhouse in Val di Chiana has just seven rooms, all furnished with wrought-iron beds, country furniture, and curtains in shades of blue. The restaurant cuisine is outstanding: it offers local salumi *and specialty meats, Tuscan crostini, homemade pasta and excellent Chianina beef steaks. There is a good choice of Tuscan wines.*

SOVANA (GR)

Taverna Etrusca

piazza del Pretorio, 16
C 0564 616183
FAX 0564 614193
● Jan. €

This charming inn is housed in a 13th-century building in this Etruscan village in the Maremma. It has eight air-conditioned rooms with fine dark wooden furnishings and parquet floors. The restaurant, which has a mezzanine and a ceiling with wooden beams, offers typical Maremman dishes like acquacotta, *nettle soup, and* pici all'agliata, *as well as modern ideas, such as tomato with marjoram and ravioli with* caciotta.

VOLTERRA (PI)

Villa Nencini

borgo Santo Stefano, 55
C 0588 86571
FAX 0588 80601
□ all year.
€€

You can find this small rustic-style hotel – a real oasis of peace and quiet – just below Volterra's medieval quarter. The rooms are simple and tastefully furnished; some face the fine swimming pool. Surrounding the hotel is a private park, with trees providing shady spots, and lots of nooks and crannies where you can relax or read a book in peace. The genuine Tuscan cuisine is very reasonably priced and the hotel staff are obliging.

Practical Information

Traveling to Tuscany is most easily done by air, but although planes arrive from European airports, there are no direct intercontinental flights, and visitors from outside Europe have to transfer. The nearest intercontinental airports are Milan and Rome. Tuscany's main airport is in Pisa; it receives both domestic and European flights as well as most charter traffic. Florence's airport is smaller and is located slightly north of the city, a short bus ride away from the center. Almost exclusively, it deals with scheduled flights. Florence is also the main arrival point for the far-reaching European train and bus network, and Pisa has good international rail connections. Once in Tuscany, travel around the region is straightforward by train, bus, or car. In the cities, it is best to visit the sights on foot wherever possible.

TRAVELLING BY AIR

Useful Numbers

Alitalia
National Flights
📞 1478 656 41
International Flights
📞 1478 656 42
Information
📞 1478 656 43
🌐 www.alitalia.it

British Airways
📞 1478 122 66
🌐 www.britishairways.com

Meridiana
📞 055 230 23 14
🌐 www.meridiana.it

TWA
📞 055 28 46 91
🌐 www.twa.com

CIT Viaggi
Florence 📞 055 28 41 45
London 📞 020 8686 0677
Sydney 📞 (2) 267 12 55

American Express
Via Dante Alighieri, 22r
Florence 📞 055 509 81

Airport Information
Florence 📞 055 306 15
🌐 www.safnet.it
Pisa 📞 050 50 07 07
🌐 www.pisa-airport.com

Direct flights connect Pisa and Florence to London, Paris, and Frankfurt all year round. There are also flights to Florence from Barcelona and Brussels. During the summer months, Pisa can be reached directly from Madrid, Manchester, and Glasgow.

There are no direct inter-continental flights to Pisa or Florence, but you can transfer in Rome or Milan. Alitalia also runs a fast (though expensive) train link between Rome's Fiumicino airport and Florence. You may find it cheaper to get a budget flight to London, Paris, or Frankfurt and transfer to another carrier.

Daily scheduled flights to Pisa are operated by British Airways, Ryanair, Alitalia, Air France, and Lufthansa from London, Paris, Munich, and Frankfurt. During the summer, Viva Air flies from Madrid.

Meridiana operates a daily scheduled flight to Florence from London Gatwick. Sabena flies from Brussels. Austrian Airlines offers flights from London to Florence via Lugano. Excursion fares generally offer the best deal in scheduled flights, but they must be purchased well in advance; at least 14 days in the UK and 21 days in the US.

Pisa Airport

Trains run directly from Pisa's Galileo Galilei airport to Florence's Santa Maria Novella station. To reach the trains, turn left as you leave the airport arrivals hall. Train tickets can be bought from the information kiosk at the airport. The journey to Florence takes an hour and the service runs once an hour, but is less regular or frequent in the early morning and late evening. There is also an infrequent train serving Lucca and Montecatini. The through train to Florence stops at Pisa Centrale, and Empoli, where you can change on to the local line for Siena.

The No. 7 bus runs from Pisa airport to the town center. Buy tickets before you get on the bus from the airport information kiosk. There is also a taxi stand at the front of the airport. Buy some euros before landing, as there are no facilities for changing money in the baggage claim hall.

Florence Airport

Florence's Amerigo Vespucci airport, often known as Peretola, is very small. The local SITA bus to the city center leaves from the front of the airport building. The bus goes to and from the airport every 30 minutes. The bus to the airport leaves from the SITA station at Via di Santa Caterina di Siena, 15r.

Only take a taxi from the official stand. They will charge a supplement for coming from the airport plus another for luggage. There is also an extra charge on Sundays and holidays. Most drivers are honest, but check that the meter is switched on and showing the minimum fare before setting off.

Car Rental

All the major car rental firms have offices at both Florence and Pisa airports. However, it is wise to make a booking well in advance, because it will be cheaper than renting after you arrive in Italy.

Leaving Pisa airport by car it is easy to get on to the divided highway linking Pisa and Florence.

At Florence airport, it might be easier to take public transportation into the city center and pick up your rental car there.

Airport Car Rental Companies

Avis
Florence Airport 🄲 055 31 55 88
Pisa Airport 🄲 050 420 28
🅆 www.avis.com

Hertz
Florence Airport 🄲 055 30 73 70
Pisa Airport 🄲 050 432 20
🅆 www.hertz.com

Maggiore
Florence Airport 🄲 055 31 12 56
Pisa Airport 🄲 050 425 74

TRAVELING BY TRAIN

Traveling across country by train can be a very pleasurable way of getting to and traveling around Tuscany. Italy's state railway (Ferrovie dello Stato, or FS) has a train for every type of journey, from the quaintly, maddeningly slow locali *(stopping trains) through various levels of rapid intercity service, to the luxurious, superfast Eurostar, which rushes between Italian cities at a speed to match its ticket price. The train network between large cities is very good, but journeys to towns on branch lines may be quicker by bus.*

Arriving by Train

Florence and Pisa are the main arrival points for trains from Europe. The Galilei from Paris and the Italia Express from Frankfurt travel direct to Florence. Passengers from London have to change in Paris or Lille.

From Florence, there is also a direct Alitalia train

link with Pisa's Galileo Galilei airport, which can be very useful.

Europe-wide train passes, such as EurRail (US) or InterRail for those under 26 (Europe), are accepted on the FS network. You may have to pay a supplement to travel on fast trains. Always check first before using any private rail lines.

Train Travel in Italy

Trains from all over Italy arrive at and depart from Pisa Centrale and Florence's Santa Maria Novella station, while the Eurostar uses Florence's Rifredi station. If you are planning to travel around, there are passes which allow unlimited travel on the FS network for a determined period of time, such as the Italy Rail Card and the Italy Flexi Rail Card. Available only to nonresidents, the cards can be purchased from the station. There is a biglietto chilometrico *which allows 20 trips totaling no more than 1,865 miles (3,000 km) for up to five people. This is available from international and Italian CIT offices, and from any travel agent selling train tickets. There are facilities for disabled travelers on some intercity services.*

Booking and Reservations

Booking is obligatory on the Eurostar and on some other intercity services, indicated on the timetable by a black R on a white background. The booking office is at the front of Florence station.

Alternatively, you can book on the FS website (www.fs-on-line.com). Users must first register on the site, then follow the instructions on how to book and pay for seats. Tickets booked online can be delivered by courier for an additional charge, or

picked up for free at a self-service ticket machine in stations offering this service, but bring the booking code (PNR) you receive via email after completing the transaction online. Travel agents can book tickets free of charge.

Booking is advisable if you wish to travel at busy times: during the high season or on weekends. Buying your intercity ticket at least five hours before traveling entitles you to a free seat reservation. For a small fee, you can reserve a seat on any train, except local trains.

Booking Agents

CIT Viaggi
Piazza della Stazione, 51r, Florence
🄲 055 28 41 45

Palio Viaggi
Piazza Gramsci, Siena
🄲 0577 28 08 28

Train Tickets

Always buy a ticket before you travel: if you purchase your ticket on the train, you will be surcharged a percentage of the ticket price. You can upgrade to first class or sleeper by paying the conductor.

*If the ticket office is busy, try one of the self-service ticket machines found at most stations. They accept coins, notes, and credit cards. The instructions are easy to follow and come in six European languages. If you are traveling no more than 124 miles (200 km), you can buy a short-range ticket (*biglietto a fasce chilometriche*) from a station newsstand. The name of your station of departure will usually be stamped on the ticket, but if it is not, write it on the back. You must then validate the ticket by stamping it in one of the gold-colored machines situated at the entrance to most platforms. These machines must also be*

used to time stamp the return portion of a ticket.

Both the outward and return portions of a return ticket must be used within three days of purchase. Singles are issued in 124-mile (200-km) bands and are valid according to band: for example, a ticket for 124 miles (200 km) lasts for a day, a ticket for 248 miles (400 km) lasts for two days, and so on.

On all intercity trains you will be charged a supplementary fee (supplemento) *even if you have an InterRail card.* This includes the Eurostar and Eurocity services. The cost depends on how far you are traveling.

TRAVELING BY BUS

Florence is linked by bus to most major European cities and local companies operate an extensive network of services within Tuscany. Buses are quicker where there is no direct train link, especially in the countryside. The train is faster for long journeys, but the bus may be cheaper. To plan trips around Tuscany by bus, maps and timetables are available from all the bus companies' offices, which are usually situated near city railway stations.

Arriving by Bus

Santa Maria Novella railway station in Florence is Tuscany's main arrival and departure point for all long-distance coach journeys, and the hub of the extensive local coach network. The Lazzi company runs coach links with major European cities from Florence and sells tickets for Eurolines coaches. Book tickets at their office by Santa Maria Novella station. Express services to Rome are run by Lazzi from Florence and TRA-IN from Siena.

Florence

Florence has four main bus companies. Lazzi serves the region north and west of Florence and SITA the southern and eastern region. The COPIT bus company connects the city with the Abetone/Pistoia region and CAP links Florence to the Mugello area north of the city. All these companies have ticket and information offices a stone's throw from Santa Maria Novella railway station.

Lazzi
Piazza della Stazione
📞 055 21 51 55 (all services)
🌐 www.lazzi.it

SITA
Via di Santa Caterina da Siena, 15r
📞 800 373760 (Tuscany);
055 29 49 55 (national)

COPIT of Pistoia
Piazza San Francesco
📞 0573 211 70

CAP
Largo Fratelli Alinari 9
📞 055 21 46 37
🌐 www.capautolinee.it

Siena

Siena's main bus company is TRA-IN, which runs urban, local, and regional services. Local services leave from Piazza Antonio Gramsci and regional buses from Piazza San Domenico. There is an information/ticket office in both squares. TRA-IN operates buses to most parts of Tuscany, as well as a direct bus to Rome twice daily.

TRA-IN
Piazza Antonio Gramsci
📞 0577 20 42 46 (local)
Piazza San Domenico
📞 0577 20 42 45 (regional).

Pisa

The city bus company CPT also serves the surrounding area, including the towns of Volterra, Livorno, San Miniato, and Pontedera. Buses leave from Piazza Sant'Antonio. Lazzi runs a service to Viareggio, Lucca, and Florence from Pisa, departing from Piazza Vittorio Emanuele II, which has a Lazzi ticket office.

CPT
Piazza Sant'Antonio, 1
📞 050 50 55 11

Lazzi
Piazza Vittorio Emanuele II
📞 050 462 88 🌐 www.lazzi.it

GETTING AROUND ON FOOT AND BY BUS

Tuscan cities are compact enough to get around reasonably comfortably on foot, and the city buses are relatively cheap, regular and wide-ranging. A single ticket will take you up to 10 miles (15 km) out of town, making the bus ideal for trips from the city center to outlying areas of Florence, Pisa, or Siena. The buses get very hot in the summer and are popular with pickpockets (especially the No. 7 bus), so take care when they're crowded.

Walking

Sightseeing on foot in Tuscan cities is made all the more pleasurable by the fact that there are plenty of squares in which to rest and watch the world go by, or cool churches to pop into when the heat gets too much. Moreover, there are limited-traffic zones in the center of most towns, which make life slightly easier for pedestrians.

Signs for sights and landmarks are usually quite clear, especially those in Siena. In Florence it is easy to pick out the Duomo and the river and orientate yourself in relation to them. A gentle stroll around the main sights of Florence can take just a couple of hours. The Duomo, Santa Maria

Novella, Ponte Vecchio, and the Accademia are all within 10 minutes' walk of each other. The main sights in Pisa are all in the same square. Siena is also compact but hilly, so wear comfortable shoes.

The cities can, however, be unbearably hot in the summer. Plan your day so that you are inside for the hottest part. Recuperate Italian-style with a leisurely lunch followed by a siesta. Shopping is more pleasant in the early evening when it is cooler and the streets start to come alive.

Crossing Roads

Use the sottopassaggio (underpass) wherever possible. The busiest roads also have signals to help you cross: the green avanti sign gives you right of way, in theory, but never expect drivers to recognize this as a matter of course. Seize your opportunity and walk out slowly and confidently, glaring at the traffic and maintaining a determined pace: the traffic should stop, or at least swerve. Take extra care at night: traffic lights are switched to flashing amber and the road crossings become free-for-alls.

City Buses

Florence's city bus company is called ATAF, Pisa's is CPT, and Siena's TRA-IN. All the buses are bright orange. Most lines run until at least 9:30pm, with the most popular running until midnight or 1am in Florence.

In Pisa and Florence, buses run near the main sights. Useful Florentine routes for visitors are the No. 12 and the No. 13 (they make hour-long clockwise/counterclockwise circuits of the city), the No. 7 to Fiesole, and the new "eco-routes" A, B, C, and D which are electric or eco-diesel-fueled minibuses.

Using Local Services

Florence does not have a main terminus, but most buses can be picked up alongside Santa Maria Novella station. In Pisa, most buses stop at the railway station and Piazza Vittorio Emanuele II; in Siena, at Piazza Antonio Gramsci, and Piazza San Domenico. There are bus information kiosks at all these points, but they are not always open. Tourist information offices can usually help.

Enter the bus at the front or back and get off through the middle doors. However, when the bus is full, you have to struggle on and off wherever you can.

The four low seats at the front of the bus are meant for the elderly, the disabled, and people with children.

Fare dodging is common, but so are inspectors. The fine is at least 50 times the cost of a ticket.

Bus Tickets

Tickets for city buses must be bought before you travel. Buy them from newsstands, bars displaying the bus company sign (ATAF, APT, TRA-IN), tobacconists, or at the bus terminal. If you are likely to make a few trips, buy several tickets at once; they become valid when you time stamp them in the machine in the bus. There are also ticket vending machines in the streets, which take any coins and low-value notes.

Ticket prices and validity vary from town to town. You can usually buy a ticket valid for one, two, or sometimes four hours' unlimited travel. The time limit starts when you stamp your ticket on the first bus. You can also buy daily passes, or a tesserino consisting of one or four tickets, each valid for a number of rides. A tesserino is slightly cheaper than the same number of single tickets. You just

stamp it as and when needed until you have made the permitted number of trips.

Long-Term Passes

If staying for a long time in one town, a monthly pass for unlimited travel is a good idea. You will need an identity card with your photograph. These are available for a small charge from the ATAF Ufficio Abbonamenti located in Piazza della Stazione. In Siena, photocards are available from the TRA-IN office in Piazza San Domenico. Monthly passes can be bought wherever bus tickets are on sale.

In Florence, the best bus ticket for visitors is the plurigiornale, from the ATAF office, newsstands, bars, and tobacconists. These are valid for two, three, or seven days. The ATAF also sells a ticket called an abbonamento plurigiornaliero, valid for between 2–25 days. These are nontransferable.

You can also buy a carta arancio, valid for seven days on trains and bus lines within the province of Florence. You can buy it from any train or bus company ticket office.

Useful Addresses

ATAF
Ufficio Informazioni & Abbonamenti, Piazza della Stazione, Florence
w www.ataf.net

CPT
Ufficio Informazioni, Piazza Sant'Antonio, 1, Pisa
C 050 505 511 w www.cpt.pisa.it

EUROLINES
UK C 01582 404511
w www.eurolines.co.uk

Taxis in Tuscany

Official taxis are white in Tuscan cities, with a "Taxi" sign on the roof. Only take

taxis at official stands, not offers from freelancers at the stations. There are supplements for baggage, for rides between 10pm and 7am, on Sundays and on public holidays, and for journeys to and from the airport. If you phone for a taxi, the meter starts to run from the moment you book the taxi; by the time it arrives there could already be several euros clocked up. Generally, taxis are costly. Taxi drivers are usually honest, but make sure you know what any supplements are for. Italians give very small tips or nothing at all, but 10 percent is expected from visitors.

In Florence, there are ranks at Via Pellicceria, Piazza di Santa Maria Novella, and Piazza di San Marco. In Siena, taxis can be found in Piazza Matteotti and Piazza della Stazione. In Pisa, they can be found at the Piazza del Duomo, Piazza Garibaldi, and Piazza della Stazione.

Booking Numbers

Florence Radiotaxi
📞 055 47 98 or 055 42 42 or 055 43 90

Siena Radiotaxi
📞 0577 492 22

Pisa Radiotaxi
📞 050 54 16 00

DRIVING IN TUSCANY

A driving tour of Tuscan vineyards makes a memorable vacation, if you are prepared for high fuel costs and erratic Italian driving. If you are staying in Siena or Florence, with no plans to travel around, there is little point in having a car: both are small enough to walk around and parking is difficult and expensive. If you are staying in the countryside and visiting towns by car, it is best to park on the outskirts and walk or take a bus into the center.

Arriving by Car

Drivers from Britain need a Green Card for insurance purposes and the vehicle's registration document. EU nationals who intend to stay for more than six months and do not have the standard pink license will need an Italian translation of their licence, available from most automobile organizations and Italian tourist offices.

The ACI (Automobile Club d'Italia) provides excellent maps and invaluable help. It will tow anyone free, and offers free repairs to members of affiliated associations, such as the AA or RAC in Britain, ADAC in Germany, the AIT in France, the RACE in Spain, and ANWB in Holland. SOS columns on highways allow instant access to the emergency services.

Car Rental

Car rental in Italy is expensive and, ideally, should be organized through a travel agent before leaving for Tuscany. Cars can be prebooked through any rental firm with branches in Italy. If you rent a car when in Tuscany, a local firm such as Maggiore may be cheaper. Book well in advance, especially for weekend outings.

To rent a car you must be over 21, and have held a license for at least a year. Visitors from outside the EU need an international license. Make sure the rental includes collision damage waiver, breakdown service, and insurance against theft.

Bike and Moped Rental

A day spent cycling out in the countryside can be a healthy and relaxing pastime, and a moped or scooter makes lighter and swifter work of the Tuscan hills. Bicycles can be rented

for around 3 euros per hour; moped prices start at about 25 euros per day. Helmets are mandatory on mopeds. Bicycles can also be rented from the main paying parking areas of Florence for a cheaper price.

Rules of the Road

Drive on the right and, generally, give way to the right. Seat belts are compulsory in the front and the back, and children should be properly restrained. You must carry a warning triangle in case of breakdown.

In town centers, the speed limit is 30 mph (50 km/h); on ordinary roads 55 mph (90 km/h); and on highways 70 mph (110 km/h) for cars up to 1099cc, and 80 mph (130 km/h) for more powerful cars. Penalties for speeding include fines on the spot and license points, and there are strict drunk-driving laws as elsewhere in the EU.

Driving in Town

City centers are usually fraught with one-way systems, limited-traffic zones, and erratic drivers, and are only recommended to the confident driver. In Lucca, Siena, and San Gimignano, only residents and taxis may drive inside the city walls. Visitors may go in to unload at their hotel but must then park outside the walls.

Pisa has limited-traffic zones around the Arno, and the rule for tourists unloading also applies in Florence, with its zona traffico limitato or zona blu, which covers most of the center. There is a pedestrian zone around the Duomo, although pedestrians here should be prepared to step aside for taxis, mopeds, and bicycles. The latter two often do not comply with the traffic-light instructions.

Parking

Official parking areas are marked by blue lines, usually with meters or an attendant nearby. There are two large underground parking lots in Florence: at Santa Maria Novella station, open daily 6:30am until 1am; and on the northeast side of Piazza della Libertà. The disco orario system allows free parking for a fixed period, mainly outside city centers. Set the disc to your time of arrival and you then usually have one or two hours (un'ora or due ore). Rental cars have discs, and gas stations sell them.

If you park illegally, your car could be towed away. In Tuscany, one day a week is set aside for street cleaning, when parking is forbidden. This is indicated by signs saying zona rimozione with the day and time. Beware of residents-only parking areas, marked riservato ai residenti.

If your car is towed away, phone the Vigili, the municipal police, to find out where it has been taken.

Driving in the Countryside

Driving on the quiet Tuscan country roads can be a pleasure. Distances can be deceptive. What may look like a short trip on the map could actually take much longer because of winding roads. Some back roads may not be paved, so beware of flat tires. You may also find driving at night disorientating as roads and signs are generally poorly lit.

Tolls and Gasoline

Tolls operate on highways, but there are some free divided highways. Toll-booths take cash or prepaid magnetic "swipe" cards called Viacards, available from tobacconists and ACI. Highway service stations occur at irregular intervals, and there are fewer gas stations in the countryside than the cities. Hardly any outside the cities take credit cards. Many close at noon and reopen about 3:30pm until 7:30pm; few open on Sundays. Many in the countryside close in August.

At gas stations with self-service pumps, put notes or credit cards in the machine. Lead-free gas is senza piombo.

City Car Rental

Avis
Borgo Ognissanti, 128r, Florence
[055 21 36 29
c/o de Martino Autonoleggi, Via Simone Martini, 36, Siena
[0577 27 03 05
[w] www.avis.com

Hertz
Via Maso Finiguerra, 33r, Florence
[055 239 82 05
[w] www.hertz.com

Maggiore
Via Maso Finiguerra, 31r, Florence
[055 21 02 38

Cycle and Moped Hire

Ciclo Posse
Pienza
[0578 71 63 92
[w] www.cicloposse.com

Motorent
Via San Zanobi, 9r, Florence

DF Bike
Via Massetani, 54, Siena
[0577 27 19 05

DF Moto
Via dei Gazzani, 16, Siena
[0577 28 83 87

Breakdown

Automobile Club d'Italia
Viale G. Amendola, 36, Florence
Via Cisanello, 168, Pisa
[050 95 01 11
Viale Vittorio Veneto, 47, Siena
[0577 490 01

Emergencies [116

Towing Away

Vigili (Municipal Police)
Florence [055 30 82 49

Pisa [050 91 03 78
Siena [0577 29 25 58

24-Hour Gas Stations, Florence

AGIP
Viale dei Mille [055 58 70 91.
Via Senese [055 204 97 85

FOOD AND DRINK IN TUSCANY

A Typical Tuscan Meal

The traditional Tuscan meal begins with antipasti, such as crostini or bruschetta and a plate of cured meats (salumi), followed by the first course (primo) which is often pasta with a meat sauce, or a hearty soup. The secondo, the main course, is usually a meat dish such as bistecca fiorentina, poultry, or fish. Many restaurants serve a "tasting menu" (degustazione guidata) serving three or four smaller portions together. Tuscan desserts (dolce) include the traditional biscotti or cantucci (see p34) and many homemade (fatti a casa) cakelike desserts. (Note: at the time this guide was published there was a temporary ban on bistecca fiorentina and all beef on the bone in Italy.)

Visiting Estates

Wine-makers welcome visitors, and it is usually quite easy to arrange a visit to an estate. They vary considerably, but many offer tours and wine tastings and sell produce. They are commercial enterprises: estate owners cannot spend all day chatting to visitors, so it is best to telephone to make an appointment. Agriturismo (farm and vineyard estate vacations) are becoming increasing popular and there is a wide choice of farm houses, apartments and rooms in villas to rent, but many of them need booking well in advance.

General Index

Acknowledgments

DORLING KINDERSLEY would like to thank the following associations and people whose contributions and assistance have made the preparation of this book possible.

Donatella Cinelli Colombini, president of Movimento Turismo del Vino; Sylvie Heiniz, agriturismo Podere Terreno alla Volpaia; Flavio Zaramella, president of Oil Masters Corporation; journalists Stefano Tesi (Firenze) and Marzia Tempestini (Prato); Sauro Brunicardi, Ristorante La Mora; Romano Franceschini, Ristorante Romano; Fulvio Pierangelini, Ristorante Gambero Rosso; Lorenzo Totò, Osteria Da Totò, Lucignano; Ristorante La Torre del Mangia, Milano; Loris Bocconi, fishmarket wholesaler in Milan; Sandro Carelli, SAMA, Milan; Azienda agricola Belsedere, Trequanda; Hubert Ciacci, Montalcino; Pa.Ri.V., Sinalunga; Silvana Cugusi, Montepulciano; butchers shops: Franco Scarpelli in Lucignano, Cecchini in Panzano in Chianti, Falorni in Greve in Chianti, Porciatti in Radda in Chianti, Chini in Gaiole in Chianti, Pollo San Marco in Arezzo; Moris Farms, Massa Marittima; Fattoria di Celaja di Crespina; Aziende agricole Danei (Giglio), Acquabona and La Chiusa (Elba).

PICTURE CREDITS
Guido Stecchi (mushrooms, herbs and fruits, typical products, farms), Paolo Liverani (herbs and fruits), Giuseppe Masciadri (pp 71, 85, 169); many pictures come from Image Bank, APT of Versilia, Livorno and Arcipelago toscano, and from Comune di Montespertoli (Florence).

Phrase Book

IN EMERGENCY

Help!	Aiuto!	eye-**yoo**-toh
Stop!	Fermate!	fair-**mah**-teh
Call a doctor.	Chiama un medico.	kee-**ah**-mah oon **meb**-dee-koh
Call an ambulance.	Chiama un' ambulanza.	kee-**ah**-mah oon am-boo-**lan**-tsa
Call the police.	Chiama la polizia.	kee-**ah**-mah lah pol-ee-**tsee**-ah
Call the fire department.	Chiama i pompieri.	kee-**ah**-mah ee pom-pee-**air**-ee
Where is the telephone?	Dov'è il telefono?	dov-**eh** eel teb-**leb**-foh-noh?
The nearest hospital?	L'ospedale più vicino?	loss-peh-**dab**-leb pee-oovee-**chee**-noh?

COMMUNICATION ESSENTIALS

Yes/No	Sì/No	see/**nob**
Please	Per favore	pair fah-**vor**-eh
Thank you	Grazie	**grab**-tsee-eh
Excuse me	Mi scusi	mee **skoo**-zee
Hello	Buon giorno	bwon **jor**-nob
Good-bye	Arrivederci	ah-ree-veb-**dair**-chee
Good evening	Buona sera	**bwon**-ah **sair**-ah
morning	la mattina	lah mat-**tee**-nah
afternoon	il pomeriggio	eel poh-meh-**ree**-joh
evening	la sera	lah **sair**-ah
yesterday	ieri	ee-**air**-ee
today	oggi	**ob**-jee
tomorrow	domani	doh-**mab**-nee
here	qui	kwee
there	la	lah
What?	Quale?	**kwab**-leb?
When?	Quando?	**kwan**-doh?
Why?	Perchè?	pair-**keb**?
Where?	Dove?	**dob**-veb?

USEFUL PHRASES

How are you?	Come sta?	**kob**-meb stah?
Very well, thank you.	Molto bene, grazie.	**moll**-toh **beb**-neh **grab**-tsee-eb
Pleased to meet you.	Piacere di conoscerla.	pee-ah-**chair**-eb dee cob-**nob**-sbair-lah
See you soon.	A più tardi.	ah pee-**oo** tar-dee
That's fine.	Va bene.	va **beb**-neb
Where is/are ...?	Dov'è/Dove sono ...?	dov-**eb**/doveb **sob**-nob?
How long does it take to get to ...?	Quanto tempo ci vuole per andare a ...?	**kwan**-tob **tem**-poh chee voo-**ob**-leb pair an-**dar**-eb ab...?
How do I get to ...?	Come faccio per arrivare a ...?	**kob**-meb **fab**-chob pair arri-**var**-eb ab..?
Do you speak English?	Parla inglese?	**par**-lah een-**gleb**-zeb?
I don't understand.	Non capisco.	non ka-**pee**-skob
Could you speak more slowly, please?	Può parlare più lentamente, per favore?	pwoh par-**lab**-reh pee-**oo** len-ta-**men**-teb pair fah-**vor**-eb?
I'm sorry.	Mi dispiace.	mee dee-spee-**ab**-cheb

USEFUL WORDS

big	grande	**gran**-deb
small	piccolo	**pee**-kob-lob
hot	caldo	**kal**-dob
cold	freddo	**fred**-dob
good	buono	**bwob**-nob
bad	cattivo	kat-**tee**-vob
enough	basta	**bas**-tab
well	bene	**beb**-neb
open	aperto	ab-**pair**-tob
closed	chiuso	kee-**oo**-zob
left	a sinistra	ab see-**nee**-strab
right	a destra	ab **dess**-trab
straight ahead	sempre dritto	**sem**-preb **dree**-tob
near	vicino	vee-**cbee**-nob
far	lontano	lon-**tab**-nob
up	su	soo
down	giù	joo
early	presto	**press**-tob
late	tardi	**tar**-dee
entrance	entrata	en-**trab**-tab
exit	uscita	oo-**sbee**-ta
lavatory	il gabinetto	eel gab-bee-**net**-tob
free, unoccupied	libero	**lee**-bair-ob
free, no charge	gratuito	grab-**too**-ee-tob

MAKING A TELEPHONE CALL

I'd like to place a long-distance call.	Vorrei fare una interurbana.	vor-**ray far**-eb oona in-tair-oor-**bab**-nab
I'd like to make a collect call.	Vorrei fare una telefonata a carico del destinatario.	vor-**ray far**-eb oona teb-leb-fon-**ab**-tab ab **kar**-ee-koh dell dess-tee-nah-**tar**-ree-ob
I'll try again later.	Ritelefono più tardi.	ree-teb-**leb**-foh-nob pee-oo tar-dee
Can I leave a message?	Posso lasciare un messaggio?	**poss**-oh lash-**ab**-reb oon mess-**sab**-job?
Hold on.	Un attimo, per favore	oon **ab**-tee-mob, pair fah-vor-eb
Could you speak up a little please?	Può parlare più forte, per favore?	pwoh par-**lab**-reb pee-**oo for**-teb, pair fah-vor-eb?
local call	la telefonata locale	lah teb-leb-fon-**ab**-ta lob-**kab**-leb

SHOPPING

How much does this cost?	Quant'è, per favore?	kwan-**teb** pair fah-**vor**-eb?
I would like ...	Vorrei ...	vor-**ray**
Do you have ...?	Avete ...?	ab-**veb**-teb.. ?
I'm just looking.	Sto soltanto guardando.	stob sol-**tan**-tob gwar-**dan**-dob
Do you take credit cards?	Accettate carte di credito?	ab-cbet-**tab**-teb **kar**-teb dee **creb**-dee-tob?
What time do you open/close?	A che ora apre/ chiude?	ah keb **or**-ab **ab**-preb/kee-**oo**-deb?
this one	questo	**kweb**-stoh
that one	quello	**kwell**-ob
expensive	caro	**kar**-ob
cheap	a buon prezzo	ab bwon **pret**-soh
size, clothes	la taglia	lah **tab**-lee-ab
size, shoes	il numero	eel **noo**-mair-ob
white	bianco	bee-**ang**-kob
black	nero	**neb**-rob
red	rosso	**ross**-ob
yellow	giallo	**jal**-lob
green	verde	**vair**-deb
blue	blu	bloo
brown	marrone	mar-**rob**-neb

TYPES OF STORES

antique dealer	l'antiquario	lan-tee-**kwab**-ree-ab
bakery	la panetteria	lah pab-net-tair-**ree**-ab
bank	la banca	lah **bang**-kab
bookstore	la libreria	lah lee-breb-**ree**-ab
butcher's	la macelleria	lah mah-cbell-eb-**ree**-ab
cake store	la pasticceria	lah pas-tee-cbair-**ee**-ab
pharmacy	la farmacia	lah far-mab-**cbee**-ab
delicatessen	la salumeria	lah sab-loo-meb-**ree**-ab
department store	il grande magazzino	eel **gran**-deb mag-gad-**zee**-nob
fish store	la pescheria	lah pess-keb-**ree**-ab
florist	il fioraio	eel fee-or-**eye**-ob
vegetable stand	il fruttivendolo	eel froo-tee-**ven**-dob-lob
grocery	alimentari	ab-lee-men-**tab**-ree
hairdresser	il parrucchiere	eel par-oo-kee-**air**-eb
ice cream parlor	la gelateria	lah jel-lab-tair-**ree**-ab
market	il mercato	eel mair-**kab**-tob
news-stand	l'edicola	leb-**dee**-koh-lab
post office	l'ufficio postale	loo-**fee**-cbob pos-**tab**-leb
shoe store	il negozio di scarpe	eel neb-**gob**-tsiob dee **skar**-peb
supermarket	il supermercato	su-pair-mair-**kab**-tob
tobacco store	il tabaccaio	eel tab-bak-**eye**-ob
travel agent	l'agenzia di viaggi	lah-jen-**tsee**-ab dee vee-**ad**-jee

SIGHTSEEING

art gallery	la pinacoteca	lah peena-koh-**teb**-kab
bus stop	la fermata dell'autobus	lah fair-**mab**-tab dell **ow**-tob-booss
church	la chiesa	lah kee-**eb**-zah
	la basilica	lah bab-**seel**-i-kab
closed for the public holiday	chiuso per la festa	kee-**oo**-zob pair lah **fess**-tab
garden	il giardino	eel jar-**dee**-no
library	la biblioteca	lah beeb-lee-ob-**teb**-kab
museum	il museo	eel moo-**zeb**-ob
railroad station	la stazione	lah stab-tsee-**ob**-neb
tourist information	l'ufficio turistico	loo-**fee**-cbob too-**ree**-stee-kob

STAYING IN A HOTEL

Do you have any vacant rooms?	**Avete camere libere?**	ah-veh-teh **kah**-mair-eh **lee**-bair-eh?
double room	**una camera doppia**	oona **kah**-mair-ah **dob**-pee-ah
with double bed	**con letto matrimoniale**	kon **let**-toh mah-tree-moh-nee-**ah**-leh
twin room	**una camera con due letti**	oona **kah**-mair-ah kon **doo**-eh **let**-tee
single room	**una camera singola**	oona **kah**-mair-ah **sing**-goh-lah
room with a bath, shower	**una camera con bagno, con doccia**	oona **kah**-mair-ah kon **ban**-yoh, kon **dot**-chah
porter	**il facchino**	eel fah-**kee**-noh
key	**la chiave**	lah kee-**ah**-veh
I have a reservation.	**Ho fatto una prenotazione.**	oh **fat**-toh oona preh-noh-tah-tsee-**oh**-neh

EATING OUT

Have you got a table for ...?	**Avete una tavola per ... ?**	ah-veh-teh oona **tah**-voh-lah pair ...?
I'd like to reserve a table.	**Vorrei riservare una tavola.**	vor-**ray** ree-sair-**vah**-reh oona **tah**-voh-lah
breakfast	**colazione**	koh-lah-tsee-**oh**-neh
lunch	**pranzo**	**pran**-tsoh
dinner	**cena**	**cheh**-nah
Enjoy your meal.	**Buon appetito.**	bwon ah-peh-**tee**-toh
The bill, please.	**Il conto, per favore.**	eel **kon**-toh pair fah-**vor**-eh
I am a vegetarian.	**Sono vegetariano/a.**	**soh**-noh veh-jeh-tar-ee-**ah**-noh/nah
waitress	**cameriera**	kah-mair-ee-**air**-ah
waiter	**cameriere**	kah-mair-ee-**air**-eh
fixed price	**il menù a prezzo fisso**	eel meh-**noo** ah **pret**-soh **fee**-soh
menu	**il menù a prezzo fisso**	
dish of the day	**piatto del giorno**	pee-**ah**-toh dell **jor**-no
appetizer	**antipasto**	an-tee-**pass**-toh
first course	**il primo**	eel **pree**-moh
main course	**il secondo**	eel seh-**kon**-doh
vegetables	**il contorno**	eel kon-**tor**-noh
dessert	**il dolce**	eel **doll**-cheh
cover charge	**il coperto**	eel koh-**pair**-toh
wine list	**la lista dei vini**	lah **lee**-stah day **vee**-nee
rare	**al sangue**	al **sang**-gweh
medium	**al puntino**	al poon-**tee**-noh
well done	**ben cotto**	ben **kot**-toh
glass	**il bicchiere**	eel bee-kee-**air**-eh
bottle	**la bottiglia**	lah bot-**teel**-yah
knife	**il coltello**	eel kol-**tell**-oh
fork	**la forchetta**	lah for-**ket**-tah
spoon	**il cucchiaio**	eel koo-kee-**eye**-oh

MENU DECODER

l'abbacchio	lah-**back**-kee-oh	lamb
l'aceto	lah-**cheh**-toh	vinegar
l'acqua	**lah**-kwah	water
l'acqua minerale gasata/naturale	**lah**-kwah mee-nair-**ah**-leh gah-**zah**-tah/ nah-too-**rah**-leh	mineral water carbonated/still
l'aglio	**labl**-yoh	garlic
al forno	al **for**-noh	baked
alla griglia	ah-lah **greel**-yah	grilled
l'anatra	**lah**-nah-trah	duck
l'aragosta	lah-rah-**goss**-tah	lobster
l'arancia	lah-**ran**-chah	orange
arrosto	ar-**ross**-toh	roast
la birra	lah **beer**-rah	beer
la bistecca	lah bee-**stek**-kah	steak
il brodo	eel **broh**-doh	broth, soup
il burro	eel **boor**-oh	butter
il caffè	eel kah-**feh**	coffee
il carciofo	eel kar-**choff**-oh	artichoke
la carne	la **kar**-neh	meat
carne di maiale	**kar**-neh dee mah-**yah**-leh	pork
la cipolla	lah chee-**poll**-ah	onion
i fagioli	ee fah-**joh**-lee	beans
il formaggio	eel for-**mad**-joh	cheese
le fragole	leh **frah**-goh-leh	strawberries
frutta fresca	**froo**-tah **fress**-kah	fresh fruit
frutti di mare	**froo**-tee dee **mah**-reh	seafood
i funghi	ee **foon**-gee	mushrooms
i gamberi	ee **gam**-bair-ee	shrimp
il gelato	eel jel-**lah**-toh	ice cream
l'insalata	leen-sah-**lah**-tah	salad
il latte	eel **laht**-teh	milk
i legumi	ee leh-**goo**-mee	vegetables

lesso	**less**-oh	boiled
il manzo	eel **man**-tsoh	beef
la mela	lah **meb**-lah	apple
la melanzana	lah meb-lan-**tsah**-nah	eggplant
la minestra	lah mee-**ness**-trah	soup
l'olio	**loll**-yoh	oil
l'oliva	loh-**lee**-vah	olive
il pane	eel **pah**-neh	bread
il panino	eel pah-**nee**-noh	roll
le patate	leh pah-**tah**-teh	potatoes
patatine fritte	pah-tah-**tee**-neh **free**-teh	french fries
il pepe	eel **peb**-peh	pepper
la pesca	lah **pess**-kah	peach
il pesce	eel **pesb**-eh	fish
il pollo	eel **poll**-oh	chicken
il pomodoro	eel poh-moh-**dor**-oh	tomato
il prosciutto cotto/crudo	eel pro-**shoo**-toh **kot**-toh/**kroo**-doh	ham cooked/cured
il riso	eel **ree**-zoh	rice
il sale	eel **sah**-leh	salt
la salsiccia	lah sal-**see**-chah	sausage
secco	**sek**-koh	dry
succo d'arancia/ di limone	**soo**-koh dah-**ran**-chah/ dee lee-**moh**-neh	orange/lemon juice
il tè	eel **teb**	tea
la tisana	lah tee-**zah**-nah	herb tea
il tonno	**ton**-noh	tuna
la torta	lah **tor**-tah	cake
l'uovo	loo-**oh**-voh	egg
l'uva	**loo**-vah	grapes
vino bianco	**vee**-noh bee-**ang**-koh	white wine
vino rosso	**vee**-noh **ross**-oh	red wine
il vitello	eel vee-**tell**-oh	veal
le vongole	leh **von**-goh-leh	baby clams
lo zucchero	loh **zoo**-kair-oh	sugar
gli zucchini	lyee dzo-**kee**-nee	zucchini
la zuppa	lah **tsoo**-pah	soup

NUMBERS

1	**uno**	**oo**-noh
2	**due**	**doo**-eh
3	**tre**	treh
4	**quattro**	**kwat**-roh
5	**cinque**	**ching**-kweh
6	**sei**	**say**-ee
7	**sette**	**set**-teh
8	**otto**	**ot**-toh
9	**nove**	**nob**-veh
10	**dieci**	dee-**eh**-chee
11	**undici**	**oon**-dee-chee
12	**dodici**	**dob**-dee-chee
13	**tredici**	**tray**-dee-chee
14	**quattordici**	kwat-**tor**-dee-chee
15	**quindici**	**kwin**-dee-chee
16	**sedici**	**say**-dee-chee
17	**diciassette**	dee-chah-**set**-teh
18	**diciotto**	dee-**chot**-toh
19	**diciannove**	dee-chah-**nob**-veh
20	**venti**	**ven**-tee
30	**trenta**	**tren**-tah
40	**quaranta**	kwah-**ran**-tah
50	**cinquanta**	ching-**kwan**-tah
60	**sessanta**	sess-**an**-tah
70	**settanta**	set-**tan**-tah
80	**ottanta**	ot-**tan**-tah
90	**novanta**	nob-**van**-tah
100	**cento**	**chen**-toh
1,000	**mille**	**mee**-leh
2,000	**duemila**	**doo**-eh **mee**-lah
5,000	**cinquemila**	**ching**-kweh **mee**-lah
1,000,000	**un milione**	oon meel-**yob**-neh

TIME

one minute	**un minuto**	oon mee-**noo**-toh
one hour	**un'ora**	oon **or**-ah
half an hour	**mezz'ora**	medz-**or**-ah
a day	**un giorno**	oon **jor**-noh
a week	**una settimana**	oona set-tee-**mah**-nah
Monday	**lunedì**	loo-neb-**dee**
Tuesday	**martedì**	mar-teh-**dee**
Wednesday	**mercoledì**	mair-koh-leb-**dee**
Thursday	**giovedì**	joh-veh-**dee**
Friday	**venerdì**	ven-air-**dee**
Saturday	**sabato**	**sab**-bah-toh
Sunday	**domenica**	dob-**meb**-nee-kah

EYEWITNESS *TRAVEL GUIDES*

COUNTRY GUIDES

AUSTRALIA • CANADA • CRUISE GUIDE TO EUROPE AND THE
MEDITERRANEAN • EGYPT • FRANCE • GERMANY • GREAT BRITAIN
GREECE: ATHENS & THE MAINLAND • THE GREEK ISLANDS
IRELAND • ITALY • JAPAN • MEXICO • POLAND
PORTUGAL • SCOTLAND • SINGAPORE
SOUTH AFRICA • SPAIN • THAILAND
GREAT PLACES TO STAY IN EUROPE
A TASTE OF SCOTLAND

REGIONAL GUIDES

BALI & LOMBOK • BARCELONA & CATALONIA • CALIFORNIA
EUROPE • FLORENCE & TUSCANY • FLORIDA • HAWAII
JERUSALEM & THE HOLY LAND • LOIRE VALLEY
MILAN & THE LAKES • NAPLES WITH POMPEII & THE AMALFI
COAST • NEW ENGLAND • NEW ZEALAND
PROVENCE & THE COTE D'AZUR • SARDINIA
SEVILLE & ANDALUSIA • SICILY • SOUTHWEST USA & LAS VEGAS
A TASTE OF TUSCANY • VENICE & THE VENETO

CITY GUIDES

AMSTERDAM • BERLIN • BOSTON • BRUSSELS • BUDAPEST
CHICAGO • CRACOW • DELHI, AGRA & JAIPUR • DUBLIN
ISTANBUL • LISBON • LONDON • MADRID
MOSCOW • NEW YORK • PARIS • PRAGUE • ROME
SAN FRANCISCO • STOCKHOLM • ST PETERSBURG
SYDNEY • VIENNA • WARSAW • WASHINGTON, DC

NEW FOR SPRING 2002

CUBA • INDIA • MUNICH & THE BAVARIAN ALPS
NEW ORLEANS • TURKEY

DES , AND INFORMATION ON
S, CITY MAPS, &
S TRAVEL GUIDES
EBOOKS

US AT
ravel.dk.com

Tuscany Road Map

3 1221 06722 4811

KEY

- Area covered by this guide
- Motorway
- Main road
- Secondary road
- Railway line
- Regional boundary
- ✈ Airport
- 🚉 Railway station
- ⛴ Ferry service

0 kilometres 25

0 miles 25